CAN'T BE SATISFIED

This is the earliest known photograph of Muddy Waters, probably taken in Memphis in 1942. He is holding his Fisk–Library of Congress 78 rpm record. Courtesy of the Estate of McKinley Morganfield

CAN'T BE SATISFIED

The Life and Times of

MUDDY WATERS

ROBERT GORDON

foreword by KEITH RICHARDS

LITTLE, BROWN AND COMPANY
Boston   New York   London

FIRST EDITION

The author is grateful for permission to reprint the following: "I Be's Troubled," aka "I Can't Be Satisfied" copyright © 1959, 1987; "Country Blues," aka "Feel Like Going Home" copyright © 1964, 1992; "Train Fare Home," aka "Train Fare Blues" copyright © 1967, 1995; "Rollin' & Tumblin'" copyright © 1960, 1988; "Rollin' Stone," aka "Catfish Blues" copyright © 1959, 1987. All written by McKinley Morganfield, pka Muddy Waters. WATERTOONS MUSIC (BMI) / Administered by BUG. All rights reserved. Used by permission. "Mannish Boy" written by McKinley Morganfield, pka Muddy Waters, E. McDaniel, and Melvin London. Copyright © 1955, 1983 WATERTOONS MUSIC (BMI) / Administered by BUG / ARC MUSIC. All rights reserved. Used by permission. "Hoochie Coochie Man" written by Willie Dixon. Copyright © 1957, 1964 (renewed) HOOCHIE COOCHIE MUSIC (BMI) / Administered by BUG. All rights reserved. Used by permission. "Mannish Boy" (Elias McDaniel, Mel London, McKinley Morganfield) copyright © 1955 (renewed) by Arc Music Corporation, Lonmel Publishing, and Watertoons Music. All rights reserved. Used by permission. International copyright secured. "Cotton Crop Blues" (James Cotton) copyright © 1954 (renewed) 1982 by Hi-Lo Music, BMI. All rights reserved. Used by permission. International copyright secured.

Library of Congress Cataloging-in-Publication Data

Gordon, Robert.
Can't be satisfied : the life and times of Muddy Waters / Robert Gordon.
p. cm.
Includes bibliographical references (p.) and index.
ISBN 0-316-32849-9
1. Muddy Waters, 1915–1983. 2. Blues musicians — United States — Biography.
3. Rhythm and blues music — History and criticism. I. Title.

ML420.M748 G67 2002
782.421643'092 — dc21
[B]   2001050473
10 9 8 7 6 5 4 3 2 1
Q-Mart

Book design by Fearn Cutler de Vicq
Printed in the United States of America

For my children
Lila Miriam and Esther Rose

For my parents
Alvin and Elaine

For my old friend
Peter Guralnick

For my new friend
Amelia Cooper

They said it was no accident of circumstance that a man be born in a
certain country and not some other
and they said that the weathers and
seasons that form a land form also
the inner fortunes of men. . . .
— Cormac McCarthy
All the Pretty Horses

Contents

APPENDICES

FOREWORD

BY KEITH RICHARDS

There's a demon in me. I think there's a demon in everyone, a dark piece in us all. And the blues is a recognition of that and the ability to express it and make fun out of it, have joy out of that dark stuff. When you listen to Muddy Waters, you can hear all of the angst and all of the power and all of the hardship that made that man. But Muddy let it out through music, set the feelings loose in the air. The blues makes me feel better.

I heard Muddy through Mick Jagger. We were childhood friends, hadn't seen each other for a few years, and I met him on a train around 1961. He had a Chuck Berry record and *The Best of Muddy Waters*. I was going to mug the guy for the Chuck Berry because I wasn't familiar with Muddy. We started talking, went 'round to his house, and he played me Muddy and I said, "Wow. Again." And about ten hours later, I was still going, "Okay, again." When I got to Muddy and heard "Still a Fool" and "Hoochie Coochie Man" — that is the most powerful music I've ever heard. The most expressive.

He named us in a way, and we basically wanted to turn the world on to Muddy and his like. This little band of ours had finally found a gig, and we put our last few pennies in for this ad in a magazine. We called to tell them where we were playing at and they said, "Well what's your name?" And on the floor was *The Best of Muddy Waters* and on the first side was "Rollin' Stone." So we named ourselves the Rolling Stones. I always felt that Muddy ran the band, that there was a real connection.

What Muddy was doing at Chess in the late forties and in the fifties was transforming the blues to meet the needs of the society. It had been acoustic blues before World War II; after that, they started shouting it out in Chicago. The whole city was louder, and the music became city blues. They were inventing it as they went along because nobody knew anything about the electric guitar or how to record it. It was just beautiful experimentation.

Muddy was like a map, he was really the key to all of the other stuff. I found out Muddy and Chuck were working out of the same studio and on the same Chess label, and there was the Willie Dixon connection too. Then I had to find everything of Muddy's that I could and at the same time find where Muddy got it from. So I sat and listened to Robert Lockwood Jr. and to cousins and relations. Via Muddy, I found Robert Johnson, and then it all started to make sense.

Twentieth-century music is based on the blues. You wouldn't have jazz or any other modern music without the blues. And therefore every pop song, no matter how trite or crass, has got a bit of the blues somewhere in it — even without them knowing, even though they've washed most of it out. This music got called the blues about a hundred years ago, but the music is about a feeling and feelings didn't just start a hundred years ago. Feelings start in the person and I think that's why the blues is universal, because it's part of everybody. Muddy is like a very comforting arm around the shoulder. You need that, you know? It can be dark down there, man.

INTRODUCTION

Muddy Waters was barefoot when he got word a white man was looking for him. It was Sunday, the last day of August, 1941. The cotton had bloomed and was set, the crop as it would be until picked in about a month. Muddy, like the other blacks who farmed a piece of someone else's land in Mississippi, was enjoying his lay-by. Soon, he'd be working that cotton from sun to sun.

Word reached Muddy before the white man did. "Uh-oh! This is it," Muddy remembered thinking. "They done found out I'm sellin' whiskey."

He went to neutral ground, the plantation commissary, away from his home where his hooch was hid. The white man found him there. "I went there, I said, 'Yassuh?' He said, 'Hey, hey, don't *yassuh* me. Say no and yes to me.' He said, 'I been looking for you.' I said, 'For what?' 'I want you to play something for me. Where's your guitar at?' I say, 'It's down in my house.' 'Come on, get it. I want you to play for me.'"

The white man's name was Alan Lomax. He was twenty-six years old. Muddy was twenty-eight. "I couldn't figure it out when he first got there," Muddy said. "I didn't know whether he was one of them smart police coming after me, or what the heck was goin' on. I couldn't handle this white man going to put me in *his* car and drive me around, going into my house. I say, 'Uh-huh, revenue man trying to get into me.'" But it was hard to peg this Lomax character. His accent was strange — Texas, but watered down by Washington. And he had a strange manner. He asked Muddy for some water and then astonished the Mississippian by sharing. "Same cup I drink out of, he drinks out of that too. I said, 'Not a white man doing this!' No no, this was too much, he going too far. But my mind still thinking, 'Oh, he'd do anything to see can he bust you.'"

Hovering in the background, accompanying Lomax but kept at arm's length, was the man who initiated the historic expedition, John Work III, a black man. Work mostly stayed quiet. In the deep South, he would be perceived as nothing more than Lomax's flunky. And Lomax did little to counter such a perception. Work's presence intensified Muddy's suspicions, as did the absence of Captain Holt, the Stovall Plantation overseer. Plantations did not take kindly to "agitators" of any sort coming on their land, and anyone not a resident and not known was an agitator until his presence was explained. The same grapevine that warned Muddy he was wanted would have first reached Captain Holt. Muddy was well liked on Stovall, both by the tenant farmers and by the Stovall family. Whenever revenue agents had previously come around, Colonel Stovall himself had come to warn Muddy. If he were carted off, the hands would be losing not only one of their bootleggers, but also their most popular musician. But Holt's absence meant this revenuer's visit was approved, and Muddy realized the farm was sacrificing him to the government, a pawn between two kings.

He was a peculiar revenue agent, this white man. Instead of extracting a badge, Lomax went to his car, pulled out a Martin guitar, and began to pick some blues. Muddy could now see what he'd only glimpsed before: the entire backseat and most of the trunk were occupied by a recording machine, a disc cutter, and a generator that converted the automobile's DC current to AC. The recording device also had a playback arm, allowing Lomax to share what he'd been given before taking it away.

"He brought his machine," said Muddy, "[and] he got his old guitar and he started playing, and he said, '. . . I heard Robert Johnson's dead and I heard you's just as good and I want you to do something for me. Will you let me record some of your songs, and I'll play them back and let you listen to them? I want to take it to the Library of Congress.' I didn't know what did he mean by the Library of Congress."

But enough was adding up: this stranger's interest *was* music and not whiskey stills. Word about the turn of events quickly reached Son Sims, Muddy's musical partner, and instead of keeping far from there, he now hurried to Muddy's house, guitar in hand. "We got his stuff out of the trunk of his car," said Muddy, "and all his long batteries and set 'em up on my front porch, and I was in my front room with my guitar, my little microphone, and he ground his wire down through the window and he went to work."

The discs were thick slabs of glass (metals were conserved for military use during World War II) sprayed with a black acetate coating, into which a lathe cut grooves that captured the sound transmitted through the microphones. These discs were sixteen inches across; the standard LP is twelve inches and a 78 is ten inches, so these were unlike anything Muddy had seen on a jukebox or in a store. Their imposing size underscored the importance of the event.

The fellowship was christened, and the distrust dismissed, with a toast. The whiskey warm in everyone's belly, Muddy's first recording session began. "So I just went along and made that 'Country Blues,'" said Muddy. "When he played back the first song, I sounded just like anybody's records. Man, you don't know how I felt that afternoon when I heard that voice and it was my own voice. I thought, 'Man, I can sing.' Later on he sent me two copies of the pressing and a check for twenty bucks, and I carried that record up the corner and put it on the jukebox. Just played it and played it and said, 'I can do it, I can do it.'"

◇　◇　◇

More than half a century has passed since that encounter, and geography is losing its importance. Cultures are increasingly the same everywhere. Where once the Mississippi Delta was a unique place — poverty made it a quarantined culture long after television and other mass media had penetrated similar outposts — now a person can live anywhere and grow up with the blues.

Muddy's boyhood home, where Lomax recorded him, still stands — though not in the same place. It used to be on the county road that runs along the edge of Stovall Farms (as the former plantation is today known); I was raised in Memphis, the capital of the Mis-

sissippi Delta, and I remember more than once detouring to drive by
Muddy's cabin. In the 1980s, a tornado blew off its roof, and the
Stovalls, for safety reasons, removed the rooms that had been added
over the years, leaving just the single-room cypress-planked structure
that had been built by trappers around the time of the Civil War.
Tourists began to remove splinters and hunks of those planks as me-
mentos. Between the treasure hunters, the insects, and the natural elements, the cabin began to disintegrate. In the late 1990s, the House
of Blues, a chain of nightclubs, leased the structure from the Stovalls,
dismantled it, transported it, cleaned and treated the wood, created a
museum display within it, and sent it on a tour; it became itinerant,
like the blues musician it sheltered, though collecting more money
than he did. In the course of his life, Muddy became emblematic for
so much — not just the blues generally, but also the twentieth-century
migration from a southern rural culture to a northern urban one, the
evolution from acoustic music to electric music, and the acceptance of
African American culture into American society. And now his cabin
assumed its own meaning: the commodification of the blues.

The blues, a music and culture once denigrated and dismissed by
white society, has become big business. Some of the world's largest
corporations have used blues stars or their music to help sell their
products. Musicians, painters, and artists of all sorts cite the music's
influence. The art is exquisite, but the conditions that created it
were heartbreaking. One truth about the blues today remains little
changed over the decades: it is still considered a music rooted in impoverishment.

Perhaps that's one reason why the cabin has been given mythic
meaning, while Muddy's home in Chicago, the place he lived when
he made his most famous and memorable records, and made his
money, has been virtually ignored. When we think of the blues, we
often think of cotton fields and summer heat. But the reason the blues
has affected so many different kinds of people in so many different
cultures, the reason the music still speaks to us, is that the blues isn't
about place so much as circumstance. House of Blues may prefer the
imagery of Mississippi Delta shacks, but the truth is that America is

full of dead ends. The first time I saw Muddy's Chicago home, it stood vacant and dilapidated. A group of local men, ranging in age from fifteen to a hundred and fifteen, sat on the abandoned house's stoop and in pieces of chairs scattered around the front yard. Each of their faces told a million stories.

One of the men was Muddy's stepson Charles Williams, who was raised in the house. Charles, known through most of his life as Bang Bang — "Bang Bang," he explained, "he might do anythang" — still lived there. There was no electricity, no running water, and the windows and doors were boarded up. But, when it was not too cold outside, this was where Charles called home. I traipsed behind him through the vacant lot next to Muddy's, stepping over broken glass and the detritus of a decaying neighborhood, into Muddy's backyard. "This is the carport," he said, standing beneath a low-roofed structure that would, by the time of my next visit, have blown over in the wind and been swept away as if it never existed.

Like the front, the back was all boarded up. The four or so stairs that should have led to the landing outside the back door were gone. Charles scrambled smoothly up. I followed, with less grace and practice, using the space between bricks as a foothold; Charles pulled me up by the shoulder, even though I didn't think I needed the extra help. We were backdoor men. "Step back," he said, though there was little room for me to do so. He pulled at a corner of the board that covered the rear entrance, stooped, and like insects between floorboards, we crawled inside the shell of the home of Muddy Waters.

Our eyes adjusted to the dim light that seeped in. The cupboards were in place over the kitchen counters, bare. The pantry was open. There was a hole in the middle of the kitchen floor wide enough for a large person to fall through. We moved across the room, stepping carefully. A hallway extended in front of us, sunlight breaking through rooms on the left, falling onto the right wall. The building felt charged with emptiness, a powerful vacancy. Dust stirred in the air, as if someone had just passed through.

He took me to the room where Muddy slept, where Muddy lay in bed and watched the White Sox on TV. The wallpaper farthest from the window was still a pretty yellow. There was a pattern on it, something like a diner's Formica countertop. It wasn't hard to imagine a lamp in the corner, a night table, a bed — the feeling of life and activity was nearly palpable. We moved into the front room, where Memphis Slim and B. B. King and Leonard Chess and James Cotton sat and visited and sipped whiskey and gin and beer. Where the photograph of Little Walter graced the mantelpiece for nearly two decades. Where music and singles and albums were discussed and debated and breathed and created. Now this house, like Charles, like so many people in Muddy's life, was on the verge of crumbling to dust.

It would be easy to look at the irony of what is embraced and what is discarded in assembling the myth of Muddy Waters and say, "That's the blues." It *is* easy to put Muddy in that cabin, easy to relocate him and his rural beginnings around the world, a neat stitch in the American quilt — picturesque and just the right colors. But easy doesn't make it so. The purity and simplicity of the blues — its primitiveness — is myth. The blues, like an emotion, is complex. Blues is the singing to relieve woefulness, feeling good about feeling bad. It's a music born of pain, but it inspires pleasure, a vehicle that takes us from grief to relief. Muddy and his fans were aware of the conflict inherent in his later life, of being enriched by the poor man's music. He was a longtime success in Chicago when, in 1970, he was asked if he'd like to go back to Mississippi. His response was emphatic: "I wanted to get out of Mississippi in the worst way. Go back? What I want to go back for?" Yet in his music, every time he played he went back, every note recalled the poverty and suffering of the Mississippi Delta. Musician after musician whom I interviewed talked about the way Muddy's music changed so little; he stuck to the old, slow blues that he'd learned in Mississippi, and which evoked the life and the land there. "That Mississippi sound, that Delta sound is in them old records," Muddy said, referring to his music. "You can hear it all the way through."

In 1958 the Mississippi bluesman was in London. He had already cut his career-defining hits; he was on the cusp of assuming his role as patriarch of rock and roll. After this trip, the Rolling Stones, named for one of his songs, would form; their first number-one hit in America would be a thematic reworking of Muddy's first hit — his "I Can't Be Satisfied" would evolve into their "(I Can't Get No) Satisfaction."

Muddy was over the shock of these Brits speaking English and sounding nothing like him. He was over the shock of them driving on the wrong side of the road. He was over the biggest shock of all — that these people knew something about him, a farmer from the Mississippi Delta. He was sitting in a nice hotel room and speaking with a British journalist who had followed much of the tour. They'd become friendly and the writer knew Muddy's history, knew his music, had heard him play live. But there was one thing that really perplexed him, and that he knew perplexed so many other blues fans and listeners. So how, this writer asked, how? How do you still have the blues?

The question snapped Muddy like a broken guitar string. He reached into his pocket and pulled out a wad of money, the foreign funny money mixed in with some real American bills, and he waved the boodle over his head, around and around, showing it off as he answered. "There's no way in the world I can feel the same blues the way I used to," Muddy said. "When I play in Chicago I'm playing up-to-date, not the blues I was born with. People should hear the pure blues — the blues we used to have when we had no money."

Woe to the successful bluesman or blueswoman — or those who live to enjoy their success. He gets a little money in the bank, his authenticity is questioned. The fan demands, "Show me the poverty." And yet, sometimes looking at a scar brings back memories of the wound. Perhaps the great artists are not always those still wounded, but those who remember. "I been in the blues all of my life," Muddy said another time. "I'm still delivering 'cause I got a long memory."

Muddy Waters, for whom there was so little paperwork for so much of his life, was born into a culture that white society did not believe worthy of documentation. Some papers exist, but the panoply of racism, sexism, classism, and various other prejudices generally overshadowed the historical impulse. By the time the media began to document him extensively, his first career in music was over (as was his farming career), and he was enjoying renewed popularity with a new audience, a white audience. His relationship to whites had been formed in Mississippi; he was a grown man — thirty years old — when he left. He'd been trained to "yassuh" and "nossuh" on demand, to tell the white man what he believed the white man wanted to hear. (In addition to being an illiterate man from an oral culture, Muddy was generally quiet; one of his oft-expressed aphorisms was, "If you got something you don't want other people to know, keep it in your pocket.") Lomax's field trips, predating World War II, were encumbered with all the paternalism inherent in those times. In some ways, that paternalism always exists. Cultures collide, and in that collision, nothing is unchanged. The explorer becomes a factor, the culture being viewed bears the taint of another's eyes. A different writer interviewing the same musicians, lovers, family members, and business associates of Muddy's would likely have left each interview with different results.

Biography is the process of securing what is mutable. Undertaking the creation of one requires embracing the paradoxical: the writer is asked to create the skin and soul of a person, but not to inhabit it. Standing inside Muddy's crumbling Chicago home with his stepson, I listened for the man who occupied it, saw where ghosts thrive, felt a pulse of the past still beating. On my most recent visit, the house had been stripped by rehabbers, the walls removed to the slats, the vestiges of the former occupant smashed, trashed, and hauled away. The renovation was being done for Muddy's great-granddaughter, who recently purchased the property. His spirit will live on in the stories she tells.

Muddy Waters shaped our culture: his song "Rollin' Stone" inspired a band name and a magazine. When Bob Dylan went from acoustic folk music to rock and roll, he hired white musicians who'd learned from Muddy in Chicago. Songs that Muddy wrote or made famous have become mainstream hits when performed by Led Zeppelin, Jimi Hendrix, Eric Clapton, and plenty of others. These musicians find in Muddy's songs — and convey to others — an honesty about pain. And that is something to which everyone can relate. Everybody hurts, sometime.

CAN'T BE SATISFIED

CHAPTER I

MANNISH BOY
1913–1925

M uddy Waters usually told people he was born in Rolling Fork,
Mississippi. That's in Sharkey County, the lower quarter of
the Mississippi Delta. Rolling Fork was where the train stopped,
where Muddy's family would get their mail and do their shopping.
Rolling Fork was on the map. But Muddy's actual birthplace is to the
west and north of there, in the next county over — Issaquena, pronounced "Essaquena," the initial "e" the only thing soft in this hard
land.

Berta Grant, Muddy's mother, lived next to the Cottonwood
Plantation, at a bend in the road known as Jug's Corner. It was a tiny
settlement in the shadow of the Mississippi's levee, a cluster of shacks
and cabins undistinguished from most others in the Mississippi
Delta. Among locals, however, Jug's Corner was well known: they
had the fish fries on Saturday nights.

At Jug's Corner, and throughout the Delta, farmhands partied on
the weekend because they'd survived another week, because the land
didn't swallow them, the river didn't drink them, the boss man didn't
kill them, and the mud, a half step from the dust and ashes from
whence they came, did not engulf them.

Muddy's father, Ollie Morganfield, used to attend those Jug's
Corner frolics. Ollie was from the Magnolia Plantation on Steele
Bayou, two miles between Jug's Corner and Rolling Fork. Big boned
and handsome, he could entertain with a guitar. "Ollie could play
good blues," said one long-lived resident of Issaquena County. "He'd
go around, folks would get him to play at a party. Dark, tall, real
friendly. Full faced. Sing? He used to holler. Played old-timey blues."

"I've heard them say that a party didn't brighten up until Ollie appeared," recalled his son Robert Morganfield, Muddy's half brother. "He would sing, blow a jug, play guitar, beat a washboard." Ollie was five-feet, eight-inches tall, with brown eyes and black hair. Born October 20, 1890, he was twenty-one the summer of 1912, already the father of one child though separated from his wife.

Berta — probably Alberta or Roberta, but called Berta by everyone — lived with her younger brother Joe and their mother, Della Grant. Berta was a young girl the summer she conceived her only child. There is no record of Berta's birth or death, no one left alive who knew her. If she was counted in any census, she has eluded researchers. Like Jug's Corner, she was off the map, a cipher around which scant information is collected: Berta was born between 1893 and 1901. Her mother, Della — Muddy's grandmother, a plump, light-skinned woman — was born in 1881, so Muddy's grandmother was all of thirty-two years old when Muddy was born in 1913. (Generations came quick in Muddy's family: his own granddaughter was thirteen when she first conceived; Muddy's response was, "Young girls make strong babies.")

Ollie brightened Berta's party that summer's eve (probably the July 4 weekend), and the next spring, on April 4, 1913, Berta — at least twelve years old, but less than twenty — gave birth to a boy. (It was, despite what would later be sung, neither the seventh hour nor the seventh day; it was not the seventh month and there were not seven doctors. But like the lyrics to "Hoochie Coochie Man" suggest, Muddy did seem born for good luck, he did make pretty women jump and shout, and everybody knew that blues and sex were what Muddy Waters was all about.) Though his parents never married, the child was given his father's last name: McKinley A. Morganfield.

In years to come, after he moved to Chicago, Muddy usually told people he was born in 1915, oddly shaving only two years off his age (if his goal was to appear younger for the entertainment field). He thus became a man born in a year he wasn't born in, from a town where he wasn't born, carrying a name he wasn't born with.

◇   ◇   ◇

John Work's 1941 field notes. Note the birth year of 1913.
Courtesy of Fisk University Library, Special Collections

The Morganfield name was relatively new to the Jug's Corner area. The Delta had been a swampy jungle of wildcats and bears when David Morganfield, Muddy's grandfather, arrived from Birmingham, Alabama at the turn of the twentieth century. His wife had died and he carried with him three sons, Ollie, Eddie, and Lewis. Birmingham must have offered very little, for the family left the city and moved to the poorest region in the nation's poorest state.

David Morganfield was a man of some heft, and he found work in Issaquena County as an ox driver. "I've heard people say he was the only man they ever saw turn a team of oxen away from water when they get hot," said Robert Morganfield. "They say up here from [the town of] Glen Allan, he was hauling some logs and those oxen was hot and saw Lake Washington and started for it, and he demanded them to go a different way. When they didn't, he was good with a whip — they tell me he could put one to the ground with the whip — and he turned them around."

Ollie, the eldest son, found work as a mule skinner, hauling logs from cleared land to a groundhog sawmill in the woods and sometimes more than forty miles to the large mill in Vicksburg. As it was cleared, the richness of the Delta's alluvial soil revealed itself. The Mississippi Delta is a large bowl that runs from Memphis south to Vicksburg, bounded by the Yazoo River to the east and the Mississippi River to the west. It is North America's mulch basin, the dumping ground for the mighty Mississippi River's deposit of fish and animal bones, decomposing trees, and topsoil from mountaintops in the north central states — the erosion of a continent. It is sixty-five hundred square miles of mellow, black, loamy soil, centuries in the making and much of it more than a hundred feet deep. A flood plain, the Delta is everywhere flat, except where the Chickasaw Indians built burial mounds — sites on which the earliest white settlers established their homes. Once the levee system was finished in the early twentieth century, landowners became rich. Vast plantations were established, many of which are still maintained by the original families, thousands and thousands of acres spread over dirt so blessed and smooth that locals refer to it as ice cream soil.

In the Mississippi Delta, cotton determined the rich and the poor, the poor and the poorest. It determined who had butter with their bread, when school was in session, and what weeks men would stay up late and get up early. Break the land, plow, plant, cultivate, pick, gin; the plant dictated how a man spent his day, his season, his life. King Cotton.

The cotton plant is a perennial, and it would grow forever — become a tree — but for the frost, the freeze, and the floods. (Before plant control through chemicals, cotton grew over six feet tall.) Mississippi cotton is planted in mid-April, after the danger of freeze and when the river waters have settled. When the plants begin to sprout, the cotton is chopped; row by cold steel row, the Johnson grass and morning glory vine that can choke the plant are hoed from around it and the plants are thinned. Come midsummer, the cotton plants flower, and the farmer knows the harvest will begin in fifty days. The next weeks are less labor intensive, the lay-by, when churches hold mass baptisms, doctors tend to the sick, and the healthy tend to the farm errands and the business of partying.

Cotton is green when it opens, and weighty. The longer it sits, the drier it becomes, and less weight equals less pay. The bolls nearest the ground open first, and field hands would pick every opened boll of cotton, then come back and pick again. Cotton sacks were seven to nine feet long and held about a hundred pounds. They strapped over the shoulder, the mouth hanging open, so in one fluid motion the boll was picked and sacked. Most adults filled two sacks a day. Some could fill five. Harvesters worked from sun to sun; they didn't need hands on a watch. Like all of them — his father, his mother (about whom so little else is known), his brothers, sisters, cousins, and friends — Muddy Waters picked cotton. On someone else's land.

The sharecropper. Also called the tenant farmer. When sharecropping was conceived during Reconstruction, the noble idea was to empower the poor laborer with the responsibility of land, for which he would pay the landowner with a portion of what he raised. But landowners had other designs, indenturing their help through crafty accounting and debt. Working as a sharecropper was like being knocked to the ground every time you started to stand up.

According to the office manager at Stovall Farms, the plantation where Muddy was raised, "The fairness of what the sharecropper got was strictly based on the moral fiber of that particular plantation owner. No two landowners did it the same way."

"What the sharecropper got" was called "the furnish." That included a cut of land (ten or so acres) and a tenant house on that land; field hands stepped out the back door and went to work, wasting no time with travel. The furnish included seed, tools, mules, and credit at the plantation store.

The sharecropper, in return, gave the landowner half of his harvest and then had his expenses deducted from what remained. Prices at the plantation store were often set arbitrarily high. Fees were assessed over which the 'cropper had no control. Most did not have the mathematical or literacy skills to challenge the accounting. Settlement came at Christmas, and Delta farmers still tell of one landowner who invited each 'cropper individually into his office, served bonded whiskey from his good glassware, then asked the farmer whether he wanted to take home a thin check or run his hands through a tub of silver dollars and carry home an armload.

A plantation was a privately owned small town, and its owners generally ignored what few laws or protection its citizenry might have been entitled to. Many farms minted their own tin scrip — "brozine" — good only at their store. Some provided regular visits from a doctor. Each had its own moonshiner. The Stovall Plantation built a juke joint for its workers — right next to the commissary, which supplied it; the farm got its cut of everything. The nearby Dockery Plantation maintained a brothel for its men. The furnish meant you wouldn't die; a good boss meant comfort, a chance at solvency, possibly progress. Families too far in debt fled a plantation in the cover of night. Those caught bought a trip to the company store, the site of plantation justice: a farmer wearing a big hat, meting out beatings.

Don't cross the boss. That was the guiding principle for the sharecropper. Stay in your place, laugh at his jokes, and you could reap the benefits — a warning of an imminent moonshine bust, a better handout from the kitchen when making a delivery at the big house. Sharecropping put the field hand on a treadmill, robbing him of his self-worth; debt was so arbitrary and constant, it didn't matter if he got ahead.

Sharecropping — getting less than half of what you've got coming to you — was good training for a life in the music business.

The tenuousness of the sharecropper's life was reflected in the geography itself. Flooding often and suddenly, bringing death or crop ruin — a slower death — the Mississippi River inflicted punishment with its discharge. But it also brought life, the rich topsoil, the loam, the minerals and decay that replenished the strength that man sapped through cotton farming. Like everyone that lived so closely to and so closely off of the land, Della Grant knew these truths as well as she knew the layout of her small home. She lost her daughter, McKinley's mother, soon after he was born. No one knows what killed Berta — childbed fever, a neglected cut, or an incautious walk through the night woods. Some sort of waters rose, then receded, and she was gone. It was left to Della to take McKinley as her own and to raise him with her son Joe, three years Muddy's senior.

When her beloved grandson, now her son, took to playing in the dangerous waters that were everywhere around Jug's Corner, Della tried to stop him. (The Mississippi Delta drains south and east, making the Issaquena and Sharkey counties the marshiest.) Knowing that something could carry him off as quickly and as surely as her own Berta was carried off, Della assumed what little power she could. She put the danger and dankness and mystery and life of those shallow brumal fluids into a name the boy would carry through his life. She renamed him Muddy, as if by claiming the Mississippi's cruel and divine identity for this child she would somehow neuter its power.

(It would be years later, when he was establishing himself as a performer, that his friends would add "Water" to his name, and the final "s" would come in Chicago when McKinley's transformation was complete.)

Della struggled at the Cottonwood Plantation. "My grandmother," Muddy told the authors of *Beale Black and Blue* in the mid-1970s, "she furnished for me and my uncle. She was a woman, she didn't know how to git out there and hustle as good as some men. I know I got up one Christmas morning and we didn't have nothing to eat. We didn't have a apple, we didn't have a orange, we didn't have a cake, we didn't have nothing."

Eventually Della Grant moved with her son and grandson eighty miles north to Stovall, in Coahoma County, a six-mile walk northwest of Clarksdale. Exactly when Della moved to Stovall is not known (probably when Muddy was between the ages of six months and three years), but by March 6, 1920, she was there to answer the census taker's questions. A large plantation — four thousand acres — with a kindly reputation, Stovall was home to Della's cousins, the Dan "Duke" Jones family; Ollie Morganfield's two brothers were also there. After Muddy moved, Ollie did not pursue contact, devoting himself to his next wife and their ten children. "I never did see my dad when I was living [on Stovall]," said Muddy. "I didn't see him at all."

Tenant homes throughout the Delta followed a standard boxy design. And plantation owners treated the dwellings like the dwellers: as a group, units for a prosperous whole. They painted them all at once, and all one color — usually green or brown, trimmed in white. Most were two big rooms. Della's cabin (Route 1, Box 84) had begun as a single room built from hand-hewn cypress planks by a hunter before the Civil War. By the time she occupied it, a kitchen and two more small rooms had been added. Tenant houses had neither running water nor electricity. Mattresses were ticks — fabric stuffed with cotton bolls and cotton shuck that had to be fluffed before sleeping and smoothed after waking. Water was hand pumped, and pumps had to be primed, which took an eternity on cold mornings; light came from kerosene ("coal oil") lamps. Women sometimes mopped the wooden floors with lye and hot water to make them white. At Christmas or other occasions, they'd get newspaper from a trash can in Clarksdale, make a paste with flour, and plaster the walls, which both brightened and insulated the rooms. (Bits of newspaper are still evident on the walls of Muddy's cabin.)

People grew what they ate, buying flour and sugar, and the Stovalls made sure the vegetable gardens were prepared before the cotton, so there would always be food. Fruits and vegetables, grown in gardens behind or beside the house, were preserved in jars for the winter. There was no refrigeration, no freezers. When there was ice, it was put in croaker sacks (the burlap shipping bags for grain and corn), then insulated with sawdust to make it last. Sharecroppers had to be practical and efficient; even waste was not wasted, with the animal dung used as fertilizer. Bootlegging, gambling, and parties were protected, even encouraged, by Colonel Howard Stovall III, the boss man. "Mr. Stovall wouldn't let his folks go hungry," said longtime resident Manuel Jackson. "If you didn't have enough money, he'd let you get it from the store. 'Tell 'em not just half either,' he'd say, 'all of it. Now get what you want.' He was fine like that. He'd been in the service and he cussed all the time. You'd hear him cussing and think he was going to eat you up, but he wasn't fighting nobody."

According to Stovall's current farm manager, Pete Hunter, "Stovall supplied the sharecropper his house, his food, lard, medical care, many times hogs and chickens, milk cows. Stovall had a dairy. It was not unusual, around Christmas, to furnish people with hogs and beef. The furnish also included their plows and harnesses, their mules, the fertilizer, their seed, and insecticide — which was powdered arsenic put in croaker sacks on the backs of mules, and a guy would ride that mule down the rows beating the sack with a stick, breathing arsenic all day long. You probably can dig him up and he'll look like he did the day he died. All that was furnished and charged." Overall, Stovall was a relatively friendly place, though the region was much less so. One of Muddy's girlfriends had a friend from Stovall who was promptly lynched after he allegedly flirted with a white woman. (Often this was the trumped-up charge for a lynching, when the real reason may have been "attitude," prosperousness, or a form of manhood interpreted as a threat to white womanhood.)

Stovall was bustling with kids. Children were an asset to sharecroppers; more hands picking more cotton meant more pay. Duke Jones had a son, Dan Jr., who was five years older than Muddy. Eddie Boyd, who would become a recording artist in Chicago, lived up the road and visited often; his cousin married Muddy's uncle. Joe Willie Wilkins, who would gain repute as a guitarist, was often around. And Andrew Bolton, known always as "Bo," who was like a brother to Muddy throughout their lives, was from Stovall. He followed Muddy to Chicago and worked for him as a driver and bodyguard. Even as a child he was physically threatening; lifelong, his running joke was intimidating people.

Life was slow: two mules to a wagon, four mules to a plow. That slow and steady turning of the wheels set the rhythm for the music, the pace for the life. Kids on the farm didn't have much but each other to play with. A barrel hoop and a stick, a piece of a bicycle; on Christmas they'd have firecrackers. Muddy's cousin remembers when his family got a radio. "There was just so much you could get on it." Most of that was country-inflected white music; the Grand Ole Opry was popular among all cultures.

Life was fast: sexual explorations began at a young age. Teenage pregnancies were common. A generation was often less than twenty years. Treatable diseases regularly received no attention, and many children died preventable deaths.

A day on Stovall began early. Colonel Stovall's daughter Marie Stovall Webster remembered, "They used to ring the bell at four o'clock in the morning to wake all the hands on the place." The lifetime of labor began before the age of reason, five or six years old. Children too small to hold a cotton sack were sent to the fields with a cart, a keg of water, and a dipper. "Waterboy!" was the holler they answered to, slaking the picker's thirst. "There were some things we couldn't do because we weren't old enough," said the Reverend Willie Morganfield, the seventh son of Muddy's uncle Lewis. "But as we grew, we learned to do whatever had to be done."

"I started early on, burning corn stumps, carrying water to the people that was working." Muddy laughed. "Oh I started out young. They handed me a cotton sack when I was about eight years old. Give me a little small one, tell me to fill it up. Really that never was my speed, I never did like the farm but I was out there with my grandmother, didn't want to get away from around her too far. Them older people like my grandmother, they didn't think you could make it in no kind of city. They think if you get in the city — starvation. But they were living in starvation on the plantation."

Education was a consideration far enough behind work that many things could get in the way of it. While white children enjoyed a standard nine-month term, blacks began school after the cotton had been picked, around Christmas. Black schools were usually one room — often the church — and convened only during the coldest months. Because the spring planting was less labor-intensive than the fall harvest and could be handled by the men, the young girls were afforded an extra month of education.

"I went to school," said Muddy, who quit after his third year, "but they didn't give you too much schooling because just as soon as you was big enough, you get to working in the fields. I guess I was a big boy for my age, but I was just a boy and they put me to working right alongside the men. I handled the plow, chopped cotton, did all of them things." In the course of his life, though he could articulate complex emotions, Muddy learned only how to sound out words on a page, but could not simultaneously comprehend them.

"We'd get up early in the morning, we'd work all day, and the only sound I recall from nights were crickets hollering," said the Reverend Willie Morganfield. "You really didn't get much of a chance to hear anything because when you'd go to sleep, you'd just sleep."

"It was really dark out there," said Muddy's cousin Elve Morganfield. "But when you've been in the dark so long, you get used to it, you learn to see your way."

◇   ◇   ◇

Had Muddy been born half a century earlier into slavery, or half a century later, his living conditions would not have been much different. The Delta land itself rebels against change; when the seasons move from cold to warm, tornados wreak havoc, one wind battling for change, the other for the status quo. But the music would have been different. Muddy Waters was raised on a musical cusp, coming of age at the time the blues was crystalizing as a genre. The catalyst was the Reconstruction period following the Civil War, when a large population of blacks were unmoored, searching for their place in a society which had previously defined them as chattel. Like a kiln, this integration fired the mix of Anglo-Scottish ballad traditions and jigs (which had cascaded down the mountains and into the Delta like water into a basin) with the existing dominant form in black music — string bands, led by violins and banjos, with mandolins and guitars playing two-chord breakdowns. The blues, born of the frustration of freedom, began taking shape.

Blues came from hardship and became nothing less than a tool for survival. Like gospel music, blues offered release, relief. It commands the present moment, demanding that you forget the toil of your past, forget the woes ahead, that you get into this song and this feeling right now and give yourself over entirely to it. Though the blues draws from a large pool of preexisting lyrics, couplets, game songs, and sayings, it is a deeply personal sort of music. Its generic lines always combine with the singer's own thoughts and expressions. (In "I Feel Like Going Home," Muddy follows "Brooks run into the ocean / the ocean runs into the sea" with "If I don't find my baby, somebody's sure going to bury me.") Over the years, the form has become somewhat standardized, with many blues fitting a twelve-bar pattern and taking the lyrical shape of AAB — the first line (often a generic truth) repeated twice, and then resolved in the more intimate third. But many of the masters disregard convention and create their blues in the way that suits them best. At that moment. At that time. Do it again? It'll be different. Songs are *feel* over *form,* eleven bars or thirteen or thirty bars. The singer changes chords when he's ready and not according to formalistic demands. If he's getting down with one particular verse and wants to drag it on, he does. This is especially easy when performing solo, but any accomplished blues accompanist knows to change when the leader changes and not to count measures. Muddy called himself a "delay singer" because people — the audience and the band — "have to hang around and wait and see what's going to happen next."

One of the earliest descriptions of blues comes from a 1903 article in the *Journal of American Folklore,* written by Charles Peabody, an archaeologist who was excavating Indian mounds near Stovall. He noted "the distichs and improvisations in rhythm more or less phrased sung to an intoning more or less approaching melody. These ditties and distichs were either of a general application referring to manners, customs, and events of Negro life or of special appositeness improvised on the spur of the moment on a topic then interesting." He cites several refrains that remain common in blues songs a century later ("They had me arrested for murder / And I never harmed a man" and "Some folks say a preacher won't steal / But I found two in my cornfield"). Peabody even found himself — his idleness — a subject of their work songs ("I'm so tired I'm most dead / [He's] sittin' up there playing mumblely-peg").

Also in 1903, W. C. Handy, who would be the first to write sheet music for the blues, had been playing waltzes and other formal styles with his Knights of Pythias Band and Orchestra when he heard a guitarist sliding the neck of a bottle along his strings at a Delta train station. The sound, he wrote in his autobiography, was "the weirdest music I had ever heard." That same year, in Cleveland, Mississippi, he encountered his first blues band, a trio featuring "a battered guitar, a mandolin, and a worn-out bass." Handy described the trio's music as "disturbing . . . agonizing . . . haunting," and continued, "I commenced to wonder if anybody besides small-town rounders and their running mates would go for it. The answer was not long in coming. A rain of silver dollars began to fall. . . . There before the boys lay more money than my nine musicians were being paid for the entire engagement. Then I saw the beauty of primitive music."

The introduction of the bottleneck style was essential in moving the guitar from the rhythm section of a group to the fore. Sliding a bottleneck across the strings produces a metallic, keening sound that was refined to high art in the Mississippi Delta. The bottleneck — sometimes a butter knife or penknife — could be applied to one or several of the strings, creating a whining sound that complemented the natural ambiguities of the human voice. The slide could also be pounded like a smooth fist along the guitar's neck to add impact and intent to the singer's plaint. When coaxed by an accomplished player, the slide guitar became an extension of the voice, a responsive chorus, an animate entity, called forth and evoked like a spirit, with a character of its own. It also created volume enough to be heard over the din of a raucous good time. The hand's movement when playing slide is like a beckoning, taking in the listener: "C'mon with me, don't you want to go? I'm going up the country, where the water tastes like cherry wine."

Muddy's introduction to the blues came early, in the dark seclusion of the rural countryside. "Our little house was way back in the country," Muddy said. "We had one house close to us, and hell the next one would've been a mile. If you got sick, you could holler and wouldn't nobody hear you. . . . The lady that lived across the field from us had a phonograph when I was a little bitty boy. She used to let us go over there all the time, and I played it night and day." These were the earliest "race" records, recordings made after the Okeh label had taken a chance in 1921 and released Mamie Smith's "The Crazy Blues"; it sold seventy-five thousand copies in a month and announced the presence of the African American record-buying audience. Many existing popular-music companies formed subsidiary labels with their established names nowhere evident, afraid of the association with black music.

Muddy also listened to his preacher — to an extent. His childhood friend Myles Long, who himself became a preacher, remembered, "On Stovall, there's a church and on up the road to Farrell, there was another church. You look up the road, there's another church on another plantation, and there's another church on up the road. Churches in walking distance of the houses." The Fisk University sociologist Lewis Jones, who did fieldwork around Stovall, wrote in late 1941, "There are perhaps more churches than stores and schools combined." In the world of the field hand, the church was a dominant force.

Church folks did not appreciate blues. "My grandmother told me when I first picked that harmonica up," said Muddy, "she said, 'Son, you're sinning. You're playing for the devil. Devil's gonna get you.'"

But in fact church spirituals and the rhythms of preaching were quickly incorporated into the blues, and within decades were supplanted by this new style. By the middle of the twentieth century, the power of the church was losing influence to the power of the blues. The essential difference between the blues and spirituals was summed up in 1943 by John Work, the pioneering black musicologist from Nashville: "The spirituals are choral and communal, the blues are solo and individual. The spirituals are intensely religious, and the blues are just as intensely worldly. The spirituals sing of heaven, and of the fervent hope that after death the singer may enjoy the celestial views to be found there. The blues singer has no interest in heaven, and not much hope in earth." And yet without the church, there could have been no blues. Perhaps it goes back to what Muddy's cousin Elve said about plantation life: "But when you've been in the dark so long, you get used to it, you learn to see your way." The blues and gospel music were two different lanterns, but the path that they illuminated, if forking ahead, had a single origin.

Under the care of his grandmother, Muddy attended church every Sunday. Services were lively, and they built to an emotional frenzy. "You get a heck of a sound from the church," said Muddy. "Can't you hear it in my voice?"

Soon people would.

CHAPTER 2

Man, I Can Sing

1926–1940

In these communities without electricity, acoustic instruments, makeshift and manufactured, were a chief source of entertainment: a guitar, harmonica, paper on a comb. The smaller instruments could be carried in a pocket, retrieved during a work break to help transport the soul to a kinder place. Initially, Muddy beat on a kerosene can, then squeezed an old accordion around his grandmother's house ("It was old, I sort of ramshacked it on out"), then fooled with the limited sounds of a Jew's harp. "All the kids made they own git-tars," Muddy remembered. "Made mine out of a box and bit of stick for a neck. Couldn't do much with it, but that's how you learn."

It took Muddy six years to master the harmonica. "I was messing around with the harmonica ever since I got large enough to say, 'Santy Claus, bring me a harp,'" said Muddy. "But I was thirteen before I got a real good note out of it." When he made too much racket in the house, his grandmother told him to take it outside, where he blew it some more, picking up quick lessons from more accomplished players as well as a penny or two from a passing, sympathetic ear.

At Stovall, Della had purchased her own phonograph, powered by a hand crank. "My grandmother didn't buy hardly anything but church songs," Muddy said. "But I got hold of some records with my little nickels, and borrowed some, listened to them very, very carefully. Texas Alexander and Barbecue Bob and Blind Lemon Jefferson and Blind Blake — they was my thing to listen to. And to get down to the heavy thing, you go into Son House, Charlie Patton. Roosevelt

Sykes been playing at 'Forty-Four Blues' on the piano, I thought that's the best I ever heard. And then here come Little Brother Montgomery with 'Vicksburg Blues,' and I say, 'Goodgodamighty, these cats going wild.'"

He was "a kid," he said, when he knew he wanted to be famous. "I wanted to definitely be a musician or a good preacher or a heck of a baseball player. I couldn't play ball too good — I hurt my finger and I stopped that. I couldn't preach, and well, all I had left was getting into the music thing."

It was Blind Lemon Jefferson who, in 1926, made record companies aware of the country blues market, the style of blues pervasive in the Mississippi Delta. Earlier in the decade, blues songs usually featured female singers, such as Ma Rainey and Bessie Smith, backed by jazzy, orchestra-influenced ensembles. Soon after Blind Lemon, Charlie Patton recorded, then Son House, Skip James, Tommy McLennan, and many more. There were other types of music available, but Muddy had no interest. His emotions did not resonate to Bing Crosby, Rudy Vallee, or Arturo Toscanini. Paul Whiteman was not in his universe, nor Fanny Brice, Maurice Chevalier. The Harry James Orchestra was not playing in any of the towns nearby. A little country or gospel sometimes on a stray radio, but when it came to records and Muddy, it was basically all blues, Mississippi Delta blues.

"Every man would be hollering but you didn't pay that no mind," Muddy told author Paul Oliver. "Yeah, of course I'd holler too. You might call them blues but they was just made-up things. Like a feller be working or most likely some gal be working near and you want to say something to 'em. So you holler it. Sing it. Or maybe to your mule or something, or it's getting late and you wanna go home. I was always singing just the way I felt, and maybe I didn't exactly know it, but I just didn't like the way things were down there — in Mississippi."

Myles Long, who took a job cooking and driving for Mrs. Stovall instead of moving up north, said of his friend, "In the fields, Muddy would always be humming something." Muddy later recalled, "When I was comin' up, of course I had no ideas as to playin' music for a livin'. I just sing the blues 'cause I had to — it was just somethin' I had to do."

"Muddy wasn't a fellow that hung around people too much, but he had his associates in music," said Elve Morganfield. Muddy palled around with a guy named Ed Moore, who could thump on the guitar and liked to be with musicians. Buddy Bo Bolton liked to mess around at the fish fries and honky-tonks. And there was a tall guy, slightly older, named Scott Bohaner (often misidentified as "Bowhandle"), who owned a guitar, was a bit heavyset, and favored overalls. "We learnt together," Muddy said. "I was playin' harp then. I used to watch him makin' chords and try to copy them. After I learned guitar, he just played second guitar, but he played lead when I was blowing harmonica."

Before too long, Muddy went a bit more public with his passion. "Cotton farming, you don't have too many 'cabaret nights,'" Muddy said. "Saturday night is your big night. Everybody used to fry up fish and have one hell of a time. Find me playing till sunrise for fifty cents and a sandwich. And be glad of it. And they really liked the lowdown blues." At their first gig, Muddy and Bohaner were given a dollar and half a pint of moonshine between them; they each got their own fish sandwich.

Stovall had a baseball team and Muddy played second base, but there were other diamonds that glittered brighter. Merchants in Clarksdale, the Delta's shipping center, would send trucks on circuits through the country, picking up rural customers on Saturdays. So many blacks would fill the Clarksdale streets, cars couldn't get through. Whites would sometimes park at the edge of the activity and watch. A barber would set up his chair, the beautician would lay out her supplies. You could get your clothes pressed, your shoes shined. There were sharp suits and hats, there were revellers and dandies. Musicians shacking up in the vicinity played in front of the furniture store, where furniture-sized phonographs were sold, as were the records to play on them.

Clarksdale had pool halls and beer joints for African Americans. Many of the clubs hired musicians, though the newfangled jukebox was steadily taking many of those gigs. But Clarksdale also had something that the country juke joints didn't — a curfew. "Twelve o'clock you'd better be out of there," said Muddy. "You had to git off the streets. That great big police come down Sunflower with that big cap on, man, just waving that stick. You had to go in the country." Bootleggers and others who ran juke joints would come into town by afternoon and see who was drawing crowds. They'd hire the entertainer — and thereby his crowd — to bring it on down to the bootlegger's place.

The country was wide open with gambling and music. This was a land where "juke joint" rhymed with "half-pint," and where the heating liquid Sterno was consumed for kicks; it was known as "canned heat" but pronounced "can-dy." "They would have the parties just where they lived at," said Muddy. "They would put the beds outside and have the whole little room to do their little dancing in. They'd pull up a cotton house [a covered trailer used during harvest] and that's their little gambling shed. And they made lamps with coal oil. Take the plow line that they plows the mule with, stick it in a bottle, put a little wet on top and light it, had lamps hanging all around like that."

"You'd find that house by the lights shining in the trees," said bluesman Honeyboy Edwards, a contemporary of Muddy's. "You'd get about a quarter mile from that house and you hear the piano and the guitar thumping; you start to running then."

"When you were playing in a place like that, you sit there on the floor in a cane-bottomed chair, just rear back and cut loose. There were no microphones or PA setups, you just loud as you can," said Johnny Shines, a bluesman who traveled with Robert Johnson. "The thing was to get the womens there to get the mens there so they'd gamble. And [the man throwing the party], he'd cut the game, get his money that way. Sell whiskey too. . . . Beer was served in cups, whiskey you had to drink out of the bottle. They couldn't use mugs in there because the people would commit mayhem, tear people's head up with those mugs. Rough places they were."

"At that time," Muddy said, "seem like everybody could play

some kind of instrument and there were so many fellers playing in the jukes 'round Clarksdale I can't remember them all. But the best we had to my ideas was Sonny House. He used to have a neck of a bottle over his little finger, touch the strings with that and make them sing. That's where I got the idea from."

Muddy was fourteen years old when he first saw Son House perform. Son House was a powerful guitar player and a formidable presence. He could be as even as the rows he furrowed as a tractor driver, or as fiery as the harsh white whiskey he liked to drink. Tall, angular, and bony, he had a deep, gravelly voice, coarse as a leveeman's holler, that carried easily over a packed juke house. A hammer of a man, a lanky, hard-hitting slide player, House favored a steel guitar, a Dobro-like instrument with a more metallic sound than the wooden guitar. His style was very percussive; he struck the strings with vehemence. His upstroke was as powerful as his down and, in combination with the slide over his finger, he sounded like a lineman driving steel. Listening to Son House was as bracing as a coldcock punch.

"I stone got crazy when I seen somebody run down them strings with a bottleneck," Muddy said. "My eyes lit up like a Christmas tree and I said that I had to learn. I used to say to Son House, 'Would you play so and so and so?' because I was trying to get that touch on that thing he did." Muddy was awed by this lanky wizard. He'd been previously getting pointers from an older boy on Stovall named James Smith. "When I heard Son House, I should have broke my bottlenecks because this other cat hadn't learned me nothing. Once, [Son House] played a month in a row every Saturday night. I was there every night, close to him. You couldn't get me out of that corner, listening to him. I watched that man's fingers and look like to me he was so good he was unlimited."

Three years after seeing Son House for the first time, Muddy bought his first guitar. "I sold the last horse we had, made about fifteen dollars for him, gave my grandmother seven dollars and fifty cents, I kept seven-fifty and paid about two-fifty for that guitar. It was a Stella, a second-handed one." He purchased the instrument from a player in the area, Ed Moore. "The first time I played on it

I made fifty cents at one of those all-night places, and then the man that run it raised me to two-fifty a night, and I knew I was doing right." When he'd socked away fourteen dollars in gig money, he ordered a guitar from the Sears Roebuck catalog. "I had a beautiful box then."

The first guitar piece Muddy learned was Leroy Carr's "How Long Blues." Carr was a piano player; the guitar was just coming into its own as a lead instrument, and many signature guitar riffs were transposed from the pounding piano. But Carr was unlike the barrel-house players around Muddy. He played a smoother, more urban style, with a light edge to it. His playing, often accompanied by guitarist Scrapper Blackwell, captured a carefree, lackadaisical feel. Before Carr died at the age of thirty in 1935, he had achieved substantial popularity through his recordings. His style was antithetical to Son House's, the two of them defining the range of influence on Muddy.

There were other influences too, among them Robert Johnson and the songster Charlie Patton, who added syncopation to material that had been relatively staid. Born in 1891, Patton was raised on the Dockery Plantation in the county adjoining Stovall's. By 1910 — three years before Muddy was born — he had so developed his style that he was already attracting imitators. He sang in a heavy, bold voice, and his repertoire included spirituals, ballads, breakdowns, and Anglo songs familiar and pleasing to white plantation owners. His innovations with the slide and with the structure of songs — breaking from their Victorian roots to a more hook-oriented form — made him a cornerstone of modern blues.

"I saw Patton in my younger life days," said Muddy. "What got to me about Patton was that he was such a good clown man with the guitar. Pattin' it and beatin' on it and puttin' it behind his neck and turnin' it over. . . . I loved that, but I loved Son House because he used the bottleneck so beautiful."

◇　◇　◇

As Muddy progressed, music became more than a hobby. "I worked for fifty cents a day from sun to sun. That means fifteen, sixteen hours a day. But on the sideline I loved my guitar. I would get out at night and do that guitar. The blacks have their parties, hustle a little liquor, get some things together, and I used to play for those peoples. They'd come get me on time but they wouldn't bring me back on time. And lot of mornings I get home and change my little ironed blue jeans and put on my cotton-picking clothes and go to the field and work. Done picked cotton all day, play all night long, then pick cotton all day the next day before I could get a chance to sleep."

Muddy also picked up extra money trapping furs. That again meant working after a long day in the field, setting and checking traps at night, but game was plentiful: possum, raccoons, rabbits, and mink. Mink hides paid the best; raccoons also sold, but possum and rabbit were thin-skinned and the hair came off too easily. All of the meat was fit to eat, or to sell as food. He'd stretch and dry the skins, then sell them in batches.

And all his life he'd made extra money assisting bootleggers. As a kid, Muddy would scout empty bottles and sell them back to the moonshiner. Homemade whiskey came in half-pints — called shorts — and also six-ounce bottles. He learned to make whiskey, though mostly he worked as a middleman. "We made the whiskey in canal ditches in the woods, hid off the highways. We'd get some of them fifty-gallon oil drums, that's what you cook it in. You got to know how to burn it so ain't no oil in there no more. You got to get the copper pipe, make a coil, get one of them big wooden barrels, that's your cooling barrel. Get that flour dough and cinch up where your pipe go through so no steam come out. You start the fire. And you set there. You can't rush the fire. It's a baby, you got to nurse it. It start to doing its thing and you can hear the pipe start making a little funny noise. *Pop. Pop. Pop. Pop-pop-pop.* There it is. All of the South was dry then, the people so thirsty for it.... You make it, you sell it. No aging, no nothing. Sell."

Whiskey, wild game, and music — the world over, that spelled *party,* and Muddy soon began hosting his own. "I'd have my own Saturday-night dances. I got hip and started making and selling my own whiskey, playing for myself. I had my little crap table going in the back. I'd put coal oil in bottles, take a rope and hang 'em up there on the porch to let people know my dance was going on, and I had a lot of them lights for people to gamble by. It's pretty hard to see the dice sometimes in that lamplight. They had some fast boys with the dice down there, you had to have good eyes.

"At night in the country, you'd be surprised how that music carries. The sound be empty out there. You could hear my guitar way before you get to the house, and you could hear the peoples hollerin' and screamin'."

Money flowed around musicians and whiskey sellers, and Muddy, embracing technology, put a down payment on a used 1934 V8 Ford. "I was so wild and crazy and dumb in my car," said Muddy. "My grandmother said I'm going to kill myself. It didn't run but thirty miles an hour, how you going to kill yourself? You could take a good fast horse and keep up with them." The gravel road was hell on wheels then, and one local trick for beating flats was to fill the tubes with cotton seeds, then soak them until they'd swell up. You made do.

The car wasn't just for fun. "He'd go back and forth to town to buy groceries and carry people," said Magnolia Hunter, a neighbor. "He'd get him a carload, make a couple dollars." Always hustling.

◇　◇　◇

When cotton was not in season, farmers still kept their fields active. Muddy learned early he could pick up extra money following the crops, running from berry harvest to sugar-beet harvest to pea and bean harvest. Hopping rails made moving about easy, though the police plucked free labor for county penal farms by arresting hobos. "I rambled all the time," Muddy remembered, "and that's why I made that song 'Rollin' Stone.' I was just like that, like a rollin' stone. But I didn't ramble that far. I was in love with my grandmother. She was gettin' old, and I didn't want to push out and leave her."

Like a pollinating bee, Muddy made journeys that put him in contact with other musicians and playing styles not common around Stovall. "I knew Robert Nighthawk before I could pick nary a note on the guitar," Muddy recalled. "That was in Clarksdale. We had one round circle — we all swam in that circle. Now he definitely knew

Robert Johnson, because they all grew up around Friar's Point way, from Friar's Point over to Helena, and I stayed from Clarksdale down to Rosedale, and Duncan, and Hillhouse, Rena Lara, and all them places. We had a circle we was going in."

Other musicians in their ring included Tommy Johnson, Houston Stackhouse, Robert Lockwood Jr., Joe Willie Wilkins, Rice Miller (Sonny Boy Williamson II), and Big Joe Williams. Big Joe was a peripatetic guitarist who encountered nearly all the Delta bluesmen in his rambles (and who invented his own nine-string guitar). "I played with Big Joe Williams when I was a kid," said Muddy. "Used to blow harmonica with Big Joe." Big Joe has claimed to be the first to take Muddy on the road, though that depends on how one defines *the road*. "I used to sorta pal around with him, but he do add a little bit to it," Muddy said. "Really, I wasn't travelin' that much with him like he tell everybody. We went right around to a few places in Mississippi, we didn't even get to Memphis."

But Big Joe's influence extended beyond just playing. He was proof that music could earn a man his living and that it had other payoffs as well. "Big Joe made Muddy quit coming around with him," said Blewett Thomas, who was friends with Big Joe. "Joe said, 'One morning I got up and left Muddy 'cause he was taking all my women away. All these women coming up going, "Oh, your little son's so nice and attractive."'"

Muddy was tall and strong, "a big-sized man, good-conditioned fella" said Magnolia Hunter, who worked beside him on Stovall, but his manner was more bashful than imposing. His skin was a deep, dark black, with hints of red and brown. His face was distinct: round and flat, with high cheekbones and heavy-lidded eyes that hinted of Asian descent. Oh, those eyes. Almond shaped, the deep pools of blackness sharply demarcated by the extraordinary whiteness around his eyeballs. These eyes were seductive and alluring, and people drowned in them. Muddy wore a pained expression, not unlike a grimace, and spoke with a stutter; he charmed with his vulnerability and warmed with his virility. And he rarely said no. He liked to get his johnny pepper picked, his natural-born ashes hauled. "You got to keep your head when it comes to women and whiskey," said

Reverend Myles Long. "Muddy, he wasn't so bad at whiskey, it was the women. The women messed him up."

"Every girl I met mistreated me," said Muddy. "I'm tellin' you — every girl. Come into my teenage years, every girl I met mistreated me. I says, 'Do I have a curse on me? Why everybody got something but me?'"

But if the girls burned him when he was young, Muddy spent his life spitting back fire. He went through several wives, and always had women on the side, and women on the other side too. "Cotton-field women" was what the men called an easy lay in that land; you didn't even need to make a pallet on the floor.

The first of Muddy's wives was a girl on Stovall named Mabel Berry. Her brother played guitar in a string band popular in the area, the Son Sims Four. "Mabel was a tall, skinny, dark lady, nice looking," said Elve Morganfield. "She worked on the farm. Very soft-spoken, very easygoing, didn't hardly raise no sand about nothing. She got along with people, but she'd get you up off her." On November 17, 1932, Muddy traveled to the Coahoma County clerk's office and bought a license to marry Berry. Three days later, on the twentieth, the wedding took place. Muddy returned to Clarksdale on the twenty-fourth to file the marriage certificate. They lived with his grandmother. He was nineteen years old.

"Robert Nighthawk played at my first wedding," Muddy said. "Him and Percy, his brother. Supposed to been his brother — I don't think they was brothers though. Robert was popular all over Mississippi." The wedding party got so wild that Muddy's floor fell in. But the joy didn't stay in the marriage. "He had a lot of trouble with his first wife, Mabel," remembered Myles. "He was running around on her. He'd make a lot of money at the juke house, then spend it. Easy come, easy go."

"Muddy was a good guy," said Elve, "but he was a man. He said that in his song. Muddy loved women. Just like any other man, you supposed to love a woman. But you ain't supposed to try to have all of 'em."

◇   ◇   ◇

A guitar player could get a break in a string band. The fiddle, because it was louder, usually played lead, but occasionally the guitarist could step out and solo. The most popular string band of the era was a local group, the Mississippi Sheiks. They'd been playing most of Muddy's life, but became stars in 1930 with "Sitting on Top of the World." "They was high-time through there, makin' them good records, man," said Muddy. "Anytime they's in my vicinity, I was there. Walk, catch a ride on a wagon, steal a mule out of her lot — I was there."

The Son Sims Four were in the Sheiks' mold. Henry "Son" Sims played fiddle; he'd been associated with Charlie Patton since 1910 and recorded with him in Wisconsin in 1930. Born on August 22, 1890, near Rolling Fork in Anguilla, Mississippi, he was the grandson of a slave who also played fiddle. Sims was not the most accomplished musician, but he was versatile — he played the piano, bass, viola, mandolin, and guitar. "Kinda like a saw" was how Sims's sister described his fiddling. "He didn't put any resin on. I didn't take time to ask him about the roughness, I'd be enjoying the music."

Sims formed the band in 1922. Guitarist Percy Thomas, who played a black Stella guitar and the kazoo, set a foundation for Sims's fiddling, and he also sang. They recruited an older mandolin player (and occasional vocalist) from Farrell named Lewis Ford, and rounded out the lineup with a rotund man on bass known to history only as Pittypat (for the percussive sound he made with his bare feet), who also entertained the crowds with dancing. They played a white square dance for a Clarksdale social club on the first Friday of each month at the Riverside Hotel.

In 1933, Percy Thomas recalled, Muddy got into Sims's group as a singer. Before long, the Son Sims Four started to call on Muddy's other skills. His harmonica playing was a nice complement to their sound, and his guitar work — well, he had his own guitar and he was learning fast. "We played juke joints, frolics, Saturday-night suppers, we was even playing white folks' parties three or four times a year," said Muddy. "My boss really liked that kinda carrying on. He'd give a party and he'd get me to come do his things for him. Sometimes the fish fries didn't have enough money to pay the four or five of us — just two of us had to go. Me and Son Sims, we'd play there sometimes by ourselves. Or somebody'd sit in with us, maybe me and Lewis Ford. Some harp player come by and we let him jam. We really just have a good time."

◊ ◊ ◊

On May 1, 1935, twenty-two-year-old Muddy had his first child, Azelene. Her mother was Leola Spain. "She was a little brown-skinned country girl," said Magnolia Hunter. "Kinda smallish, wasn't heavy."

"She was a young little girl," remembered cousin Elve. "Nice figure, about five foot three, nice grade of hair. She wasn't over sixteen. Muddy went for beautiful women, young women. That's all I ever knew him to like. Leola was married to a man named Steve, and she was going with a guy named Tucker. Her husband caught them together. It gets complicated." And Muddy was in the middle. Mabel, tired of being on the outside, left Muddy, not even bothering with divorce papers, and moved to Chicago.

Though he ultimately established a household and kept a home for twenty years with a wife in Chicago (and several outside women), he never lost touch with Leola. She followed him to Chicago, and there from the West Side to the South Side. "They always had a special bond with each other," said Amelia "Cookie" Cooper, the couple's grandchild, "all through his life until his death. He kept a very good tie with my grandmother because of the child that they had and then once the grandchildren came it made the bond even closer." Throughout all the women Muddy picked up and discarded, Leola was the only one with whom he maintained a lifelong friendship.

◊ ◊ ◊

As Muddy was becoming more accomplished and more confident, he saw many of his friends and acquaintances releasing records. Tommy Johnson began recording in 1928. Robert Nighthawk's first recordings featured backing from Big Joe Williams. The Chatmon Brothers, Skip James — his running buddies, his moonshine pals — were now recording artists. Muddy sought the popularity of Leroy Carr and the force of Son House, but insisted on an identity of his own. He knew it was possible to take the influence of others and create something unique. He'd seen one of his neighbors do just that: Robert Johnson.

Robert Johnson's two recording sessions, before he was murdered in 1938, have made him the most popular of the early blues artists. He was born, raised, and he died in the Mississippi Delta. His legend, even during his lifetime, grew around the sudden facility of his playing; reportedly he'd made a deal with the devil. But what has kept his name at the fore is his command of the form, his artistry with the three-minute song. Each of the twenty-nine songs in his legacy is carefully crafted — the musical hook, the lyrical image, the totality of the piece — a conscious recognition of the recording process, its limitations, its possibilities. He recycled melodies and words, sometimes nearly the whole of a song, but he reshaped them into creations of his own, singularly passionate manifestations that have reached across generations.

Johnson recorded and was killed before Muddy faced a microphone, but they were of the same musical generation, each descended directly from Charlie Patton through Son House. "I loved [Robert Johnson's] music," Muddy said. "I first heard him when he came out with 'Terraplane,' and I believe 'Walkin' Blues' was on the other side. I always followed his records right down the line." Muddy had only seen him once, on the street in Friar's Point, and the experience had been overwhelming. "People were crowdin' 'round him, and I stopped and peeked over. I got back into the car and left, because he was a dangerous man . . . and he really was using the git-tar. . . . I crawled away and pulled out, because it was too heavy for me."

Little commercial recording was done in the Delta; musicians were taken to Chicago, or the East Coast, or Grafton, Wisconsin. Sometimes labels would hold sessions in hotels — in Memphis, in Jackson, in Dallas. Muddy, like most Delta residents, would make occasional trips to Memphis, the largest city in the region. There, on the Delta side of town, was Beale Street — Harlem of the South — where black lawyers and dentists offered their services alongside bookies and hookers. And in the center of Beale Street was a park.

Music and card games were plentiful. On weekends it was an open-air market where you could find anything fresh: fruit, corn liquor, women, dope. On weekdays, it was harder to find fruit.

"Memphis," said Muddy, a pause afterward indicating the enormity of the city. "M-E-M-P-H-I-S, only thing I can spell yet. I can't even spell Clarksdale. Memphis was up north. Beale Street was the black man's street. Memphis was like you was going almost to California. Get in a car going to Memphis, you'd change drivers: 'You drive some, I'm tired.' That road wasn't very good and your tires wasn't very good. Me and Son Sims, sometime we'd go up to Memphis just to come back for the big word: 'We's in *Memphis* last night.'"

But as big and wild and slick as Memphis may have been, Chicago was of a different order. "Robert Nighthawk came to see me and said he was going to Chicago and get a record," Muddy said. "He says, 'You go along and you might get on with me.' I thought, 'Oh man, this cat is just jiving, he ain't going to Chicago.' I thought going to Chicago was like going out of the world. Finally he split, and the next time I heard [1937], he had a record out."

By 1938, when he was twenty-five, Muddy's reputation had spread more widely; he was known for playing "Bluebird Blues," which he learned from the recent Sonny Boy Williamson record, featuring Big Joe Williams on guitar. He played in Friar's Point for a man who'd taught him to fix cars. He played the Trump Club in Clarksdale, where tamales and watermelon slices were sold on the street. "I got big enough to start playing for the white things," said Muddy. "I used to play Howard Stovall's store for these [county agricultural] agents. A white dance, you could play a waltz all night long. And then you'd play them something a little jumpy, end up with 'Sittin' on Top of the World' and they would get down."

By then, much like when her boy played in the mud, Muddy's grandmother had to reconcile herself to her grandson's ways. "My grandmother, she say I shouldn't be playing, I should go to church. Finally, I say I'm going do this, I'm going do it. And she got where she didn't bother me about it."

Yet, despite the occasional urban foray, Muddy's world remained the backwoods. "Muddy stayed in the country a long time," said Honeyboy Edwards, who'd been rambling far and wide. "When he come to Clarksdale, that's the brightest place he was."

In the late 1930s, when the Silas Green traveling tent show set up in Farrell, three miles south of Stovall, Muddy attended. A traveling show was a major attraction, an alien culture bringing new ideas. Unlike the medicine shows, where the music was a vehicle for drawing crowds to whom elixirs with high alcohol contents could be sold, the Silas Green show was professional, a show built around music. These performers didn't just count on tips, they had regular wages (or the promise thereof). And the show was on wheels — it was a way out of town, a way off the plantation. But Muddy's brush with Silas Green was limited to Farrell. "I didn't follow the show. I played with them right there for a night or two. We had five or six of us, we made a lot of noise out there."

Even if he had had the desire to move on, Muddy wasn't sure where he should go. "I started asking some of my friends that had went to Chicago, 'Can I make it with my guitar?'

"'Naww, they don't listen to that kind of old blues you're doing now, don't nobody listen to that, not in Chicago.'"

Indeed, Chicago was still a jazz town, accustomed to sophisticated arrangements. RCA's Bluebird label, a Chicago-based subsidiary that targeted the black audience, had begun recording some of the rawer blues artists in 1933, but its focus (and its successes) was sweeter, ragtimey numbers, blues with the dust shaken off. Artists such as Tampa Red, the first Sonny Boy Williamson, and Big Maceo Merriweather were playing a more up-tempo, danceable sound; Robert Johnson's records had found an audience, but the buyers were not so much popular music fans as dedicated blues heavies. The growth of jazz reflected the penetration of African American culture into broader American society.

Then there was St. Louis, where, it was said, blues changed its stride. The saying fits, referring not only to the stride piano stylings popular there, but also to the city's location. During the Great Migration, when southern people used all available resources to strike out for a new life up north, passing St. Louis meant getting over the hump. Located halfway between Memphis and Chicago, St. Louis was a city of size — more industrial than Memphis, not as overwhelming as Chicago — and it had its own black city within a city: East St. Louis. St. Louis was both familiar and daunting, and it invigorated the travelers with a thrill and new excitement; it put a little more bounce in their step, a little more pep in their stride.

Muddy knew of many great blues artists who called St. Louis home, including Lonnie Johnson, Big Joe Williams, Roosevelt Sykes, Peetie Wheatstraw (the devil's son-in-law), and Charley Jordan. Pianist Walter Davis lived there, and Muddy had many of his records. If "going to Chicago was like going out of the world," then St. Louis was the last stop within Muddy's stratosphere. It was conceivable, reachable, possible. And so Muddy set out for an exploratory trip away from home but not out of this world.

"In 1940 I went to St. Louis for a little while," Muddy said, "and didn't like it." In his first taste of life outside the Mississippi Delta, he heard people speaking in mild midwestern accents and he encountered a town with more progressive ideas about race relations, though many of the faux-slavery attitudes of Mississippi were certainly still present. But perhaps most frustrating to Muddy was that his reputation did not precede him and that, musically, he would have to prove himself all over again.

"He said he met Henry Townsend there, and some other musicians," Jimmy Rogers, an early Chicago friend, remembered Muddy saying. "He was just up there scouting around, fooling around, trying to get hooked up with some people."

"I was trying to be a musician there," Muddy said. "I stayed maybe a couple months or so. I wasn't gettin' enough work with my guitar, went back to Clarksdale."

Clarksdale was familiar, but it couldn't help but seem even smaller and more isolated after St. Louis. Traveling shows beckoned and Muddy passed. St. Louis opened her arms and he just shrugged. Muddy Waters, it seems, could not be satisfied.

CHAPTER 3

AUGUST 31, 1941

1941

B y the early 1940s, Muddy was famous in his "circle we was going in," the skinny strip of Delta that fanned out from Clarksdale to the Mississippi River along Number One Highway. There
were plenty of little back-road juke houses along there — he'd never
want for a job — but it wasn't exactly international fame.

Muddy Waters's first real break into the outside world came in
the summer of 1941, during a field recording trip under the combined auspices of Nashville's Fisk University and the Library of Congress in Washington, D.C. He made his first recordings that summer
and then several more the following summer when the group returned; a year after that, with the courage of a recording veteran, he
would leave the Delta for Chicago. These encounters were perhaps
the most crucial to his future career.

The idea for the 1941 and 1942 expeditions — in which the
recorded subjects would also include Son House, Honeyboy Edwards, Willie Brown, Fiddling Joe Martin, and Son Sims — began
with Professor John Wesley Work III, a member of the music department at Fisk University, a prestigious black school in Nashville. For
several generations, John Work's family had been in Nashville's community of black professionals. His father, also something of a folklorist, had been responsible for resurrecting the Fisk Jubilee Singers
in the mid-1890s, presenting to America an African American alter-
native to minstrelsy and blackface.

Work was skilled at operating Fisk's Presto (Model D) portable
disc recorder and had already made field recordings around Nashville. His philosophy, he explained in a speech at Fisk, was "that in

each of your communities there is an abundance of significant folklore of which you have been generally unaware but which can easily be discovered and usually made available for the community's appreciation and education." In May of 1940, he realized the importance of a recording trip to Natchez, Mississippi, where a fire the previous month had killed two hundred black patrons of the Rhythm Night Club. "I would like very much to have the opportunity of collecting songs in that area next spring," he proposed to Fisk's president. "At that time, the anniversary of that fire, there undoubted will be many folk expressions and memorials.... To the abundance of folklore natural to the community, a new body of lore is due to be added. It is the ballads and music arising out of the holocaust of last April."

Searching for funds to finance the trip, Fisk contacted the Library of Congress. Their Archive of American Folk Song, in the person of folklorist Alan Lomax, recognized the strength of the project and agreed to collaborate. Lomax was himself the son of a folklorist, John Lomax — a ranging collector for the Archive, with which he'd been associated since soon after its founding in 1928. Alan became the Archive's first full-time employee in 1937. Work's study jibed with the Lomax family's perception of "folklore," a more malleable notion than the reigning tradition in which the oldest songs — dating prior to the Industrial Revolution (indeed prior to the printing press) and unchanged by time — were considered purest; Alan and his father believed that the living folk and their input were as vital as the original source of the material.

The Lomax family hailed from Austin, Texas, where a young Alan had witnessed subcultures of cowboys, Indians, and Hispanic people existing along with, but separate from, the affluent white society. In 1921, at the age of six, Alan started traveling with his father and in 1933 began assisting him with Library of Congress field expeditions. They used a portable disc recorder, documenting Texas cowboys, Louisiana Cajuns, Kentucky hillbillies, and Mississippi chain-gang singers. (The relative meaning of "portable" was evident in the machine's weight of several hundred pounds.)

By the time Fisk and the Library of Congress worked out their partnership, they'd shifted the site to Clarksdale, Mississippi — all of Coahoma County — the nation's densest concentration of African Americans and the largest town in the Mississippi Delta. The goals of the joint field trip were summarized by Alan Lomax in a 1941 Library of Congress report: "The agreed-upon study was to explore objectively and exhaustively the musical habits of a single Negro community in the Delta, to find out and describe the function of music in the community, to ascertain the history of music in the community, and to document adequately the cultural and social backgrounds for music in the community."

Lomax and Work arrived in Coahoma County late in the evening on Thursday, August 28, 1941. "Everywhere we went," Alan Lomax wrote to a friend, "we were asked point-blank, were we or were we not union organizers." With World War II looming and the North's factory work heating up, and with the threat of mechanized farming ever greater in the South, the Great Migration was achieving epic proportions. Farmers were afraid of losing their help before they could afford the technology that would replace them. And the prospect of their workforce organizing induced panic and resentment.

Since churches were easier to find than blues singers — they were less mobile and more sober — Lomax and Work began recording services, and inquired after blues singers in the style of Robert Johnson. One name kept coming up.

On Sunday the thirty-first, Lomax and Work arrived early and unannounced on the Stovall Plantation. They sought Captain Holt, the friendly, pipe-smoking overseer, and gained permission to mix with the black population, especially one "Muddy Water." The singer, suspicious of being busted by a conniving moonshiner, came to the commissary before this stranger could find him at home. The trust between them was established by Lomax's guitar, sealed with a whiskey, and then Lomax began setting up the equipment that Muddy had helped bring in. Lomax did not like for Work to handle the equipment. Son Sims had appeared by the time the bottle was being uncorked, and he accompanied Muddy on their original song

"Burr Clover Blues" so recording levels could be set. While Lomax made final adjustments with the knobs, John Work conducted a brief interview with the two musicians. Asked to state their names, Muddy identified himself as "Name McKinley Morganfield, nickname Muddy Water," then added, "Stovall's famous guitar picker."

And so, on August 31, 1941, after lunch and before supper, Muddy Waters recorded one of the songs for which he was known in his neck of the Delta and for which he would later become known throughout the world. "Country Blues" was the name Lomax appended to it; "I Feel Like Going Home" was the title in John Work's notes and the title when it took Chicago by storm a few years later. These first recordings were quite different from the electric versions Muddy would later record. They were about the marriage of acoustic space created by the human voice and a wooden guitar. "You get more pure thing out of an acoustic," Muddy later reflected. "I prefer an acoustic." The power in Muddy's playing is comparable to the way a blade cuts rows into a field; his music is informed and defined by the immediacy of touching a string and the knowledge of how it affects the air around it.

It's a great performance, Muddy alone, singing and playing guitar. Unlike the emotional desperation of Robert Johnson, Muddy conveys power, the physicality of a human being worked by the system. In the voice of Robert Johnson, we hear the man who played hooky from fieldwork. In Muddy's voice, we hear — we feel — the field, the plow, the dirt. "Country Blues" begins with high notes and tumbles low, inviting us in. The melody is instantly familiar; it was the basis of Son House's "My Black Mama," the same song that inspired Robert Johnson's "Walkin' Blues." By picking some notes and simultaneously sliding along the neck with the bottleneck over his pinky, Muddy sounds like two people. He gives the song a rhythmic bounce, pinging a high note at the end of a line for emphasis. It's not a boogie, it's a slow number, but we can hear someone's hip cocked north at a juke house, and the sound that hip makes when it swings south, riding the sharp *ping* like an undulating whip about to crack.

The song evokes both the beauty and futility of the field hand's struggle to survive. Comfort is found in the warmth of a lover's body ("I feel like blowing my horn"), and her absence leaves a loneliness as big as the rural sky:

It gets late on in the evening
I feel like blowing my horn
I woke up this morning
and find my little baby gone. . . .
Some folks say the worried blues ain't bad,
That's the miserablest feeling child I most ever had. . . .
Minutes seem like hours
And hours seem like days
Seem like my baby
Would stop her low-down ways. . . .
I been mistreated
And I don't mind dying

After Muddy completed "Country Blues," the recording captured him leaning back in his chair, a creaking, and then a bassy rumbling that becomes recognizable: footsteps crossing a wooden floor. It was Lomax, not stopping until he was right next to Muddy; he was speaking into the microphone when he said, "I wonder if you can tell me, if you can remember, when it was that you made that blues, Muddy Water?"

Muddy answered straight away, a bit anxious and almost stepping on Lomax's question. "I made that blues up in thirty-eight."

"Do you remember the time of the year?"

"I made it up about the eighth of October in thirty-eight." Muddy clustered his words together, with a halting nervousness between them.

Lomax inquired in a comfortable, almost intimate voice. By this point, he, Work, and Muddy had been together several hours, during which Muddy had seen this untold dream unfold and assemble itself in his very living room. Lomax, realizing he could capture Muddy while this mood still hung, got close and casual.

"I remember thinking how low-key Morganfield was, grave even to the point of shyness," Lomax wrote in his field notes. "But I was bowled over by his artistry. There was nothing uncertain about his performances. He sang and played with such finesse, with such a mercurial and sensitive relation between voice and guitar and he expressed so much tenderness in the way he handled his lyrics that he went right beyond all his predecessors — Blind Lemon, [Charlie] Patton, Robert Johnson, Son House, and Willie Brown. His own pieces were more than blues, they were love songs of the Deep South, gently erotic and deeply sentimental."

Lomax's questions continued: "Do you remember where you were when you were doing your singing, how it happened —"

"— No I —"

"No I mean, where you were sitting, what you were thinking about?"

"I was fixing the punction [puncture] on a car, and I had been mistreated by a girl and it looked like that run in my mind to sing that song."

"Tell me a little of the story of it if you don't mind, if it's not too personal. I want to know the facts, and how you felt and why you felt the way you did. It's a very beautiful song."

This white man complimented the field hand, and he answered like an artist: "Well I just felt blue, and the song fell into my mind, come to me just like that song and I started to sing and went on with it."

Muddy may not have been in the boisterous voice he'd have when frying Saturday fish sandwiches and laughing with friends, but he was loosening up. Things were working out.

Well, when you, do you know, is that tune the tune for any other blues that you know?

Well yassir, it's been some blues played like that.

What tunes, other blues, do you remember that went to that same tune?

Well this song comes from the cotton field and the boy went and put the record out, Robert Johnson, he put it out, "Walkin' Blues."

What was the title he put it out under?
He put it out, the name of "Walkin' Blues."

Did you know the tune —
Yassir —

— before you heard it on the record?

Muddy interrupted to answer, a bold action. But he'd been complimented, appreciated. And he may have been aware that the lathe was still cutting — cutting his very words into the acetate posterity of forever, and he probably wanted this white man from far away to know this music was important to him. Muddy appreciated the value, the impact, of recording. These two men, one comfortable in New York museums and the other among animal traps in muddy fields, were the objects of each other's desires; each was helping the other achieve his goal.

"Yassir," Muddy continued, "I knew the tune before I heard it on the record." Then he told Lomax a little about Son House.

How did it come to you first that you wanted to play the guitar? Why did you decide?
I just loved the music. I saw Son Sims and them playing. I just wanted to do it and I took after them.

. . . Do you remember what the first piece that you ever tried to learn was?
The first piece I ever tried to learn was "How Long Blues," Leroy Carr.

Did you learn that from a record or from seeing him?
I learned that from the record.

How would you do that? How would you learn that song?
*We just heard the song, you know, it was put out, Leroy Carr
done put it out.*

Would you sit down with the record and play a little of it and
then try to do it?
I just got the song in my ear and then went on and tried to play it.

What a field day for Work and Lomax. At this, their first interview, they found a man who could not only take them back to Charlie Patton's world when the blues were an unformed, swirling mass
about to come together like a tornado across the flat Delta jungle, but
also could play in a style that indicated the music's future. If they'd
found Son House first, they'd have gotten a sense of the past and present, but his style was fully evolved and would remain the same for
life. In Muddy Waters they found the perfect crux, the living breathing Mississippi Delta musical zeitgeist.

And how did you learn to play with this bottle?
Picked that up from Son House.

And what do you call that?
Bottleneck. I calls it a slide.

You call it a slide.
Yassir.

You wear it on your little finger.
Yassir.

And how do you have that guitar tuned, what's the name of
that tuning?
Spanish. [And Muddy strums D G D G B D — low to high,
a musician in the know.]

. . . Well can you play that other country blues you played in there a while ago, that fast one? Is it in the same tuning here?
Yessir.

I'll tell you when I'm ready.

Lomax returned to his seat on the porch. The tension, documented in Lomax's field notes, was high between the field recordists — whose trip was this? — and John Work stepped to the doorway where he could watch Muddy perform. The signal was given, and we hear the bouncing, rollicking notes of "I Be's Troubled" (titled "I've Never Been Satisfied" in John Work's notes, titled "I Can't Be Satisfied" when cut in Chicago), slide and strum working together to ride us like a tractor seat through the instrumental introduction, making the listener want to move, have to move.

If I feel tomorrow
Like I feel today
I'm gonna pack my suitcase
Make my getaway
I'm troubled, I'm all worried in mind
I never been satisfied
I just can't keep from crying

This song has been perfected at Saturday-night fish fries and is a sure party pleaser. Muddy's playing is smooth, and his performance of it must have been something for tired dancers to watch: the right hand accenting the beat like a drummer, the left hand careening up and down the neck, sometimes sliding and sometimes fretting, always in the right place, always percolating.

The first verse leaves the song's subject open, but the story unfolds; it ain't farm trouble what's bothering him:

I know somebody
Sure been talking to you

I don't need no telling girl
I can watch the way you do

"I Be's Troubled" had barely ended when John Work immediately began speaking from nearby.

How did you come to develop that one, where did you first hear it?
I made it up my own self. That's a song I made up.

How did you come to make it up? Tell us the story.
The reason I come to make that record up once, I was just walking along the road, I heard a church song, kind of mind of that, I just dealed off a little song from that. And I started playing it.

Do you make up verses and sing often like that, just sitting around —
Yassir, I make up verses pretty often, and I deal 'em up.

Then how do you get the music, the tune?
After I get my verses made up, then I come get my guitar and try it, two, three different tunes and see which one take the best with it, which is better to play it in, then I start.

Are there many of these country blues around in this neighborhood?
Yassir, ain't so many around in here. Good little deal or two.

Most people around here like 'em?
Yeah, they crazy about them.

Work's interview was cut short by Lomax, perhaps because the recording disc was running out. Lomax retrieved a second one (leaving an entire side unused) and Muddy played another original, "Number One Highway Blues," about the road that ran right by his

These transcriptions by John Work III are from lost recordings by Muddy Waters.
Courtesy of Fisk University Library, Special Collections

front door, the backbone of his universe. Then another interview, this one including Son Sims, followed by the duo playing their treatment of "The Worried Blues," popularized in the area by the Mississippi Sheiks. Following that, Muddy sang "Corn Song" a cappella and then a version of Charlie Patton's "Pea Vine Blues." The recording session now over, Lomax and Work converted the contraption to something like a jukebox, playing back what they'd just recorded, with Muddy in both the audience and the spotlight. He heard himself sing.

Afterward, as the equipment was loaded back into the car, Muddy told Lomax that he couldn't see a big city in his future. As this field trip was preparatory to a more extensive one scheduled for October, Muddy was likely told to expect their return within a couple months. Discussion about recording his entire band may have ensued. The whole encounter took about seven hours, from the commissary meeting to Lomax's brake lights reflecting red on Muddy's eyes. But in that time, Muddy's life had irrevocably changed.

◇ ◇ ◇

Two days after Lomax and Work departed, Muddy dictated the first of several letters he'd send over the course of a year. These letters were spoken to a semiliterate field hand who picked up spare coin as a letter writer and reader. They are all written on five-by-eight-inch rag paper carefully pulled from a tablet; there is no fraying across the top. The pencil had each time been freshly sharpened — the heading of "Stovall" was in crisp and thin lead. The handwriting doesn't quite stay on the lines; the periods that follow so many of the words may simply be where the writer is pausing.

At the time of the first writing, Lomax was still in the region. The morning after recording Muddy, he and Work went to Money, Mississippi, fifty miles to the southeast, recorded a Baptist church service, then doubled all the way back and more to catch an 8:30 Church of God in Christ service on the Moorhead Plantation near Lula. All this driving was not good for those precious discs with their glass base; Muddy's second disc broke in transit and has not been played since Muddy heard it in 1941.

On the day Muddy wrote his first letter, Work and Lomax were interviewing a man who'd been indentured to Jefferson Davis; the following day, the researchers traveled to Lake Cormorant and met Son House.

> Stovall. Miss.
> Sept 2, 1941
>
> Alan Lomard
>
> dear Co.
> this is the boy. that put
> out Bur Clover Blues. and
> number one high Way Blues.
> and several. more. blues.
> Want to know did they
> take. Please sir if they did
> please send some to Clarksdale. Missposie. sir
> answer soon to.
>
> M.C.
> Morganfield

"Did they take?" Muddy Waters asked, using the language he knew — his songs were like a seed taking to the ground.

◇   ◇   ◇

Half a year later, on March 17, 1942, Lomax wrote to Muddy, asking him to sign a form allowing the Library of Congress to reproduce copies of "Country Blues" and "I Be's Troubled" for use in an album. In return, he would be paid twenty dollars. Lomax also wrote, "I think the release of this record will serve to make you known in quarters where greater use might be found for your talent."

Muddy would see Lomax again before he would see his money or his records.

Stovall Miss
April 29 1942

Alan Lomax

My dear trusty,
definitely a
I have answer your letter
and haven got any.
answer. from. you what
is the trouble. I thought
I. would. write you again
see have you got it
or not. it is all. right
to go. on. and do. what
you. want. to do with
the Records. Write me
and tell. me. what you
have doing. Be. sure
to send. me to of the
Records. please sir.
I. look for. answer. all
the time from. you.
I will close. from.

M.C.Kinley Morganfield
Stovall. Miss.
answer soon.

Lomax advised him to be patient and forwarded a government
form for his signature.

Stovall Miss
June 25 1942

dear Alan. Lomax

I. thought I. wood write
you all about my check

Stovall, Miss.
June 25 1942

Dear Alan Lomax
I thought I would write
you all about my check
I am still waiting on it
but I haven't got any
answer from you all.
Did you get the blank
that I fill out and
let me hear from you
all. So answer soon.
... from your
Truly.
M. G. McKinney Morgan

Stovall, Miss.

One of four letters sent by Muddy to Alan Lomax between
September 1941 and June 1942.
Courtesy of the Library of Congress, American Folklife Center

I. am. still wating on it
but I haven got any
answer from. you all.
did you get the blank
that I. fill Write and
let me here from you
all. so answer soon.
to me from. your.
truly,

M.C.Kinney Morganfield
Stovall Miss

◆   ◆   ◆

Months passed without an answer. It is hard to know why Lomax ignored these letters; his own account of this time is somewhat self-serving. In 1993, fifty years after his two summers in the Delta and a quarter century after John Work III's death, Alan Lomax wrote a book about his experiences. *The Land Where the Blues Began* won a National Book Critics Circle award, among other plaudits. In the book, Lomax relegates John Work to a single mention, an aside in the preface. (He also makes no mention of his 1941 trip, setting it all in 1942.)

In *The Land Where the Blues Began,* Lomax writes, "Gradually, I began to see Delta culture as the product of the reaction of a powerful African tradition to a new and often harsher social environment. . . . [B]lack African nonverbal performance traditions had survived virtually intact in African America, and had shaped all its distinctive rhythmic arts, during both the colonial and the postcolonial periods. It was this unwritten but rich African tradition that empowered the creativity we had encountered in the lower depths of the Mississippi Delta. The error in African American studies had been to look to print and to language for evidence of African survivals. For instance, musicologists discovered that American blacks performed many European-like melodies, but failed to notice that the whole performance context — voicing, rhythmic organization, orchestration — remained essentially African."

Fifty-three years before Alan Lomax wrote the above, and one year before the first Delta expedition, John Work III wrote in the introduction to his book, *American Negro Songs:* "The fatal error made by many writers in this field is that in their analysis of these songs they relate altogether upon the verse, rather than upon the music. The Negro slave was too handicapped by inadequate vocabulary and too absorbed in the music to give much attention to the words. In many instances his verse was magnificent, yet throughout his songs we definitely sense the importance of music over words."

Pioneers in any field create the context in which they can be criticized by those who follow in the privileged position cultivated for them. Lomax played an essential role in raising the public's awareness of the beauty, importance, and significance of African American culture. Without his participation in the project, the "discovery" of Muddy Waters might have languished in the vaults of Fisk University. But in a world where authorship is authority, Lomax virtually erased the scholarship of John Work. Far more troubling than his blending of dates is Lomax's refusal to acknowledge the contribution of others, especially of an African American whose ideas, research, and knowledge were pivotal to his own achievements. Bluesmen were much more generous and fluid in the exchange of inspiration and artistry. Lomax recorded the blues culture, but did not absorb the spirit of cooperation that made that culture thrive.

CHAPTER 4

COUNTRY BLUES
1941–1943

Three months after the initial visit by John Work and Alan Lomax, an event occurred in the Mississippi Delta that would
have a profound effect on Muddy, on blues artists, and on blues fans.
When it went on the air, radio station KFFA was a tiny place, but its
impact was enormous. KFFA reached farther than the loudest juke
joint and into every home, regardless of race, economics, or social station. The station broadcast right from the Mississippi Delta — the
banks of Helena, Arkansas — and for the first time, the Delta heard
itself. Man, it could sing.

KFFA was established by three businessmen. Sam Anderson
teamed with John Franklin, of the Franklin Ice Company, and Quin
Floyd, a truck-line owner; their surnames form the call letters. The
studios were established in an office upstairs over Floyd Truck Lines,
a block from the Mississippi River levee. The owners were businessmen, not radio engineers, and were more interested in paying rent to
themselves than in the proximity of microphones to the din of roaring trucks. Broadcasting began in November of 1941.

Harmonica player Sonny Boy Williamson and guitarist Robert
Lockwood Jr. — two prominent musicians in the area — approached
owner Sam Anderson with the hopes of getting a regular broadcast
slot. Anderson knew a grocer around the corner interested in spon-
soring a show. Max Moore's Interstate Grocer Company had been
packaging the King Biscuit brand of flour since 1931, and radio
seemed like a great way to reach new customers. Dubbed King Biscuit Time, the program broadcast weekdays from noon to 12:15, and
for half an hour on Saturday, coinciding with the field hands' lunch

break. "We did the very first show and it took off like a house on fire," said "Sunshine" Sonny Payne, an early KFFA disc jockey. "The blues was something we heard every day on the street, and we took the blues for granted. I said, 'These people aren't going to go for [blues radio],' but it was the best thing that ever hit this part of the country."

Born Aleck Miller (or perhaps Aleck Ford) on December 5, 1899 (or perhaps 1897 or 1909), Sonny Boy Williamson was known to musicians by many names — among them Willie Williams, Willie Miller, Alex Miller, and Little Boy Blue. Those who knew him best called him Rice, despite his blatantly co-opting "Sonny Boy Williamson," a name still in use by a popular harmonica player who'd been releasing blues hits on the Bluebird label since 1937.

Sonny Boy II, as Miller became known, was in his forties when his radio career started. A tall and lanky man, he made up in physical energy what he lacked in meat on his bones. According to Hank Harvey, who delivered laundry in Helena, "Sonny Boy in action was worth the trip. Even with the old Coca-Cola thermometer on the side of the grocery store pushing 100, he stood there in knee boots with slits cut in the sides. He wore a thick belt with loops for his harmonicas. When he played, he flapped his arms sometimes and did a dance step. He could make the harmonica cry or yell, or make it moan like a steamboat whistle if he wanted to. He got right up next to the microphone and played, then sang, and sometimes seemed to play and sing at the same time. He sometimes put the harmonica completely inside his mouth and played it that way."

Although fifteen years Sonny's junior, Robert Lockwood had been sharing gigs with him for five years. Lockwood, with an ear for accompaniment, had fleshed out the pair's sound with melodies and contrast. It helped that the innovative guitarist had received guidance around 1927 from his mother's husband — Robert Johnson.

Lockwood and Williamson — the King Biscuit Boys — were paid a few dollars for each week's six shows. The real money came through announcing their forthcoming gigs, directing an audience of thirsty patrons to the joint where they'd next be throwing down. Proprietors got packed houses and the band often took home more than their weekly wage in a single night. Muddy hired Sonny Boy and his band to play on Stovall. "He'd [announce] every spot they're playin' at," Muddy explained. "You could hear it all over the country down there. Drew them peoples from all in the back of them cotton fields, everywhere." Sonny Boy was the first harp player and Lockwood the first guitarist that Muddy heard playing through an amplifier. "Every time there wasn't a radio around," said Muddy, "I'd run to the next house where one was at to hear them play."

If white cotton had made slaves of African Americans, white flour now made them paid musicians. And flour companies and blues seemed to get along, perhaps because so many black women worked in white kitchens. By reaching the black audience, the companies were in effect reaching white dinner tables as well.

"There was not much interference for KFFA's two hundred fifty watts of power," recalled Sonny Payne. "We would go anywhere from seventy-five to one hundred miles in four directions." The King Biscuit Boys found themselves in demand at increasingly distant juke joints across the river, but they were not alone. An appearance on the show could be a huge career boost — something Muddy soon realized.

"I met [Sonny Boy] over in Helena," Muddy remembered, his initial foray into the city only twenty miles from his house inspired by the radio program. "I went up, and he let me did a couple of numbers on one Saturday. We drove up to Friar's Point — leave the car on this side — cross on the ferry to Helena. We went over one Friday and they had a show come on in the days. He let me and my buddy play a couple a numbers along with the band, Son Sims."

His King Biscuit appearance upped Muddy's star quotient. "If we got a chance to set in and do a couple of songs, man, when we got back on Stovall, that was the whole talk. Everybody that's heard it on the radio was running, telling all the people all on the plantation, 'I hear them, man, I hear them, they on it!'" Indeed KFFA's impact on Muddy was so forceful that fulfilling the dream of having his own show there would draw him back for an extended stay even after he had achieved success in Chicago.

King Biscuit Time pioneered black radio programming, and its success did not go unnoticed. Black programming spread from Greenville, Mississippi, to West Memphis, Arkansas. By 1948, in the big city of Memphis, WDIA became the nation's first radio station to format black voices on the air, programming for black listeners — full-time. Technology was presenting new types of mobility to Muddy and his peers. Most of the great Delta artists performed on King Biscuit Time or its competitors. Reputations were built on the show. With blues radio, the modern blues star was born.

❖ ❖ ❖

In mid-April, 1942, after the chance of freeze had passed, Muddy mounted Colonel Stovall's tractor to harrow the ground. In mid-June, with the plants a foot high, he manned a hoe to chop cotton. When his plants were set with blossoms, Muddy enjoyed his lay-by. With time on his hands, he might have reflected on St. Louis, time and distance making what had seemed cold and foreign less daunting, the thrill and excitement of a fast-paced city now taking on a dreamy glimmer. And he might have looked forward, wondering about the white man from Washington, D.C., and his black university associate. Would they come back? Had Muddy been forgotten?

He had not. After several delays, Alan Lomax arrived in Nashville on the evening of July 12, 1942, driving his new green Hudson Super Six. Air-conditioning was not yet standard in automobiles, and he arrived hot and bothered, writing in his field notebook, "Violently hot all day in this filthy and ugly old town." One day down, fourteen to go.

Lomax had assumed authority over the study and arranged for John Work to be excluded from this return trip: proprietary tensions, personality conflicts, operation of the recording machine — they didn't get along. As a replacement, Lomax enlisted a member of the Fisk sociology department, Lewis Jones, with whom he'd struck a friendship on his previous visits to the university.

Friday, Lomax and "Sr. Eduardo from Sao Paulo" (a sociology student of Jones's) stopped in Tunica County, where Lomax reunited with Son House. This time, he pushed further for information on Robert Johnson. Interest in Johnson's blues and his life had continued to build since his murder in 1938.

"How it come about that [Robert Johnson] played Lemon's style is this," Lomax reported House saying. "Little Robert learnt from me, and I learnt from an old fellow they call Lemon down in Clarksdale, and he was called Lemon because he had learnt all Blind Lemon's pieces off the phonograph."

With his luck running high, Lomax forged on, his previous year's discovery affirmed: "But isn't there anybody alive who plays this style?"

House replied, "An old boy called Muddy Waters 'round Clarksdale, he learnt from me and Little Robert, and they say he gettin' to be a pretty fair player — that's one. And they's me, but I about done quit. I'm getting to be an old man." (Son House was all of thirty-nine; he would live another forty-six years and enjoy a second career.)

A week later, Lomax reunited with Muddy. "Spent a fine day with my old cronies — Muddy Waters, Son Simms [sic], and their friends on the Stovall Place — five miles east [from the King and Anderson Plantation, where Lomax was staying and where the Fiskites were studying farm life]. Planned another session for Monday [July 27]. They really like me." The previous month, Muddy had written Lomax about the check and records he'd been promised; he'd not yet been paid, and Lomax made no note of Muddy inquiring in person.

There was, however, an entire evening devoted to interview. On July 29, Lomax visited Muddy's home. With the family gathered — Della, Uncle Joe, Muddy and his live-in girlfriend Sallie Ann Adams — Lomax took out his pen and the four mimeographed sheets of paper that he'd titled the Tentative Family Schedule, a questionnaire developed for the Fisk–Library of Congress Coahoma County Study. In addition to information on education, labor, and travel experience, the final page was entitled "General Musical Questionnaire," reflecting the emphasis of their study. On this page, Muddy cited the kind of music he liked best: *Blues.* Why? "I can play it a little bit." He added, "I don't hardly ever have the blues, but just

2.

Woman done quit 'em.

I don't hardly ever have the blues, but just plays 'em... I don't have the blues when I play 'em.

<u>General Musical Questionnaire</u>

(To be filled out, if possible, on all persons with whom you discuss music in
the community.)

I can play it a little bit.

What kind of music do you like best? **Blues.** Why?

What kind of instrument or instruments do you like the best? **(1) Guitar (2) Piano
(3) Harp –**

What are your favorite songs?

1.	6.
2.	7.
3.	8.
4.	9.
5.	10.

What kinds of songs do you know? (Spirituals, jazz songs, blues, singing games,
sentimental songs, work songs.)

Do you play a musical instrument? **Yes** What? **Guitar**

Did you ever take music lessons? **No** What kind?

If you once played, but don't play now, what was the instrument? _____
_____ Why did you stop? _____

Do you like to dance? **~~yes~~ no** Why or why not? *I can't dance – quit tryin'. Just*

If you once danced, but do not do so now, why did you stop? *wasn't in... need to dance – some time you be dancin' wid a girl & people would... her an' go on & I just never did try to learn.*

What are your favorite dance pieces? |—|—|—|—|—|

1.
2.
3.
4.
5.

What songs did you know when you were a child? *I Don't Want No Black Woman to
Charley Ham Jug Bones –*

What songs do you want sung at your funeral? *Hain't thought.*

What songs do you think are wrong to sing? *None*

Do you listen to symphonic music and opera on the radio? *no*

What bands do you listen to on the radio? *Fats Waller*

Who is your favorite musician? *Walter Davis (on Bluebird records)*

Do you like singing in a group? *not much* What kinds of singing? (Choir singing,
Jazz Orchestra, quartets, hill billy songs, "Old Black Joe," and "Swanee River,"
Long meter hymns, Rally spirituals.)

Which do you prefer, Negro or white music and why? *Negro – got more harmony –
in the blues line – white people can't play 'em.*

For the 1942 Fisk–Library of Congress Coahoma County visit, Alan Lomax
created a four-page questionnaire, with one page devoted to music.
This is Muddy's questionnaire.
Courtesy of the Alan Lomax Archives

plays 'em. I don't have the blues when I play 'em." He does go on to say, should his qualifications be questioned, that "women done quit 'im."

What songs did you know when you were a child?
"I Don't Want No Black Woman to Charley Ham My Bones."

What bands do you listen to on the radio?
Fats Waller.

Who is your favorite musician?
Walter Davis (on Bluebird records).

Which do you prefer, Negro or white music and why?
Negro — got more harmony — in the blues line — white people can't play 'em.

In his field notes, Lomax wrote that Muddy "plays at country balls two or three times to seven times a week. Fall the biggest time — plays mostly in the country and immediate neighborhood. Private houses give the parties — two of us get $6 — the whole band gets $16 for a picnic or something like that." (He also noted that Muddy "Just wasn't a hand to dance — sometimes you be dancing with a girl and people snatch her and go on so I just never did try to learn.")

The evening concluded with an extensive listing of Muddy's repertoire. Its range reflected his disparate audience — gutbucket blues ("I Be's Troubled"), smoother black pop songs ("St. Louis Blues"), white country-and-western numbers ("Deep in the Heart of Texas," Bill Monroe's "Be Honest with Me"), waltzes ("Missouri Waltz"), and the occasional pop pap ("Red Sails in the Sunset").

The researchers devoted two full days between July 24 and 26 to recording Muddy and the band, and returned again on July 30. The sessions yielded five solo takes of Muddy, ten others that featured him and some combination of the Son Sims Four, and one brief recorded Muddy interview. These sessions were recorded with high-grade ribbon microphones. They are quality field recordings that stand at a crossroads: Muddy is the intersection, old enough to have inherited the preblues, young enough to be involved in the creation of something new. Son Sims was a graduate of square dances, where the band played standards such as "Turkey in the Straw," "Leather Britches," and "Arkansas Traveler." Muddy's music, on the other hand, was imbued with passion and personality; in Muddy, the voice of individual expression was emerging.

❖ ❖ ❖

Exactly one week before Christmas of 1942, on a Friday, McKinley Morganfield returned to the county clerk's office in Clarksdale and bought another marriage license. The signature line on his "Affidavit of Applicant" is distinguished by his X, around which Clerk J. N. Smith has written "his mark" and then spelled out "McKinley Morganfield."

After celebrating the engagement that weekend, Muddy, in a small ceremony on December 23, married Sallie Ann Adams, twenty-seven, formerly of Farrell (where she attended school through the sixth grade) and recently of Stovall, Mississippi. A light-skinned woman, "she wasn't small and wasn't large, just twixt and between," said Magnolia Hunter, who worked on Stovall with Muddy. Sallie worked the field alongside Muddy and sometimes cooked hamburgers at the Stovall juke house while he played. He was twenty-nine years old, married again.

❖ ❖ ❖

"I Be's Troubled" and "Country Blues" were included in a six-album package issued by the Library of Congress in January of 1943. His songs were in the album *Afro-American Blues and Game Songs,* alongside albums devoted to Anglo-American traditions, Bahamian songs, and recordings made of the Iroquois Indians. "This was the first time that a government had ever published its sort of unwashed authentic folksingers on records," Lomax wrote in *The Land Where the Blues Began.* Indeed, this collection, issued when record companies still hid their participation in "race" music, was a harbinger of the societal de-segregation to come.

While Lomax was releasing these timeless songs rooted in tradi-tion, pop radio was focusing on the issue of the day: World War II. America had entered the fray on December 8, 1941, and the home front rallied to hits such as Kay Kyser's "Praise the Lord and Pass the Ammunition" and Johnny Mercer's "GI Jive." Colonel Stovall, who'd become a flying ace in the first war, reenlisted. His sons served in the Air Force too: William Howard Stovall IV was killed in action at the Battle of the Bulge. Plantations and farms, because they served the country with their crops, were able to protect some of their work-ers from the draft; Muddy, already in his late twenties and thus not prime pickings, had yet to be called up.

On January 23, 1943, Muddy had someone sign his name to an-other form sent by Alan Lomax acknowledging receipt of two copies of "Record 18 in Album IV of *Folk Music of the United States from Records in the Archive of American Folk Song* (1942)." There was no mention of the payment, but Muddy remembered receiving a twenty-dollar check. "It would have taken me, well, how long to make twenty dollars if I worked five days for three dollars, seventy-five cents? That's good money, twenty dollars. I was a big recording star." He had no pictures made with either of his wives, but when his record arrived, he put on his best suit and carried it to a photogra-pher's studio, where he was photographed holding the love of his life. He put the other copy on the jukebox at Will McComb's cafe, located nearby on Highway Number One between his house and Farrell. "I carried that record up the corner and put it on the jukebox. Just played it and played it and said, 'I can do it, I can do it.'"

Before the jukebox and way before blues radio, the way a person played a particular song could reveal the town or plantation where they'd learned it. Musical styles — indeed whole cultures — had been quarantined. Itinerant musicians, like birds dropping seeds, carried songs and styles; music was a communal experience shared through live performance, and techniques were exchanged through personal interaction. The popularization of recordings as a medium broadened the listener's horizon of experience; standing before a jukebox, one could be exposed to twenty different artists and styles, and a week later, twenty more. (Recordings also etched a permanence to lyrics that had previously been mutable, introducing sticky issues of authorship.) Regionalistic traits began a slow melt into the national pool. As always, technology proved a mixed blessing. This was true when it came to music and when it came to the fields. The recent roar of the tractor had already killed off the field holler. Researching his doctoral thesis in Coahoma County in 1941, Fisk graduate student Samuel Adams found that

On one occasion when an old cotton picker was asked whether or not the people sang as they worked, he laughed as he repeated the question to others. In fact he yelled it out across the field. They all seemed to be amused by the question. "Ain't got no time for no singing," he ended. Moreover, the influence of mechanization is to make man "not want to sing." A young informant emphatically states: "There ain't nothing about a tractor that makes a man want to sing. The thing keeps so much noise, and you so far away from the other folks. There ain't a thing to do but sit up there and drive."

Muddy, too, was keenly aware of the machines. The mechanical cotton picker, long rumored in development, was being publicly tested for the first time just down the road from Stovall on the Hopson Plantation. The machine was ready to take the jobs of men and would be much more tolerant of the long hours and verbal abuse. Three years had passed since Muddy saw St. Louis. The billowing factories strong in his memory, he couldn't help but see the tufts of smoke blown by the Delta's newest device as evermore threatening.

People went north not only because work was available, but also because work at home was diminishing. Northern industrial employment opportunities had increased with foreign munitions orders, and the employment pool had been drained by the demand for soldiers. The big city's gravitational pull was strengthening. Robert

Nighthawk had already left the Delta for Chicago, and his "Prowling Night-Hawk" had come out in 1937. Robert Lockwood's "Black Spider Blues" came out in 1941. Tommy McClennan had been recording since 1939 and had a hit with "Bluebird Blues" in 1942. Muddy started 1943 with a twenty-dollar boost. He had records on a jukebox. Letters from his uncle Joe and cousin Dan spoke of the opportunities in Chicago. His first wife was making it up there.

But the draw at Stovall remained powerful. When John Work returned in June of 1943 for further research, he heard Muddy perform at the Colonel's home; perhaps one of the military men was home on a visit. "I remember them setting up the Japanese lanterns," said Colonel Stovall's son Bobby, "and the band setting up on the porch." According to Bobby's sister Marie Stovall Webster, "We used to hear the music from the honky-tonk in our house across from the gin on Saturday nights. And my grandmother played lots of Negro spirituals on the Victrola. My mother and father had grown up with Handy's music, and my father [the Colonel] loved Mahalia Jackson. He did not look down on black music at all."

John Work spent much time with Muddy in 1943: "Muddy Water ... explains that it is necessary to use two different repertoires to accommodate the demands of white and Negro dancers. The white dancers prefer tunes more akin to the old reels than to the blues, although the 'St. Louis Blues' is a great favorite among them.... For the colored dancers, Morganfield must play blues and music which stem from them, such as 'Number Thirteen Highway' and 'I'm Goin' Down Slow' — his current favorite pieces. Muddy Water would like to join the church but to do so would mean to abandon his guitar — a sacrifice too dear to make."

But sacrifices were in Muddy's future.

In the absence of the Stovalls from their farm, the feel and conditions had changed. It was, anyway, a period of turmoil: the mules, which had driven the plantation since its inception, were being sold off and replaced by tractors; Captain Holt, the longtime overseer, quit or was fired by the recently hired plantation general manager, the trim, brown-haired Mr. T. O. Fulton. The man Fulton hired as a replacement, Ellis Rhett, "was kind of mean," Stovall resident Manuel Jackson remembered, citing an instance where Rhett had whipped another field hand with a bridle. According to Bobby Stovall, "Mr. Rhett was the kind of guy that gave the South a bad name. There was a lot of old school about him. He was not user-friendly for black people." (When Colonel Stovall returned in the summer of 1945 to an upset farm and unhappy tenants, he fired Fulton and Rhett immediately.)

Muddy was making twenty-two and a half cents an hour for driving the tractor. "I was doing the same thing," Muddy said, "his top men was doing for twenty-seven cents an hour." One summer day in 1943, Muddy asked Rhett to raise him to a quarter. "[Rhett] says I'm the only man ever ask him for a raise," Muddy said, "and if I don't want to work for what I'm working for, get down off his tractor — leave it setting on the road, don't take it to the barn, don't take it to the shop. He came on like that three times, and when he was coming on, my mind was making up like this: Ain't but one thing to do — he'd never like me no more and I'd never like him no more — kiss him good-bye."

According to the Reverend Myles Long, who was baling alfalfa hay with Muddy that day, "Muddy wasn't too hard to get along with. We worked in the field together. That particular evening, we pulled under a shade tree to rest. I didn't know what he [and Rhett] was fighting about, but I saw Muddy start to walking."

"Muddy got off," said Jackson, "walked away from there, and I didn't see him until he come back with his band from Chicago."

"His grandmother told him it was time to go," Muddy's last wife, Marva, remembered Muddy explaining. She knew how hard an overseer could make it on a field hand, and she worried for her grandson's safety. Muddy's friend Bo, who had recently been drafted, had one pair of good clothes that he wouldn't need in the army; he gave them to Muddy for Chicago. Two days after the confrontation, Muddy caught an afternoon train carrying a suit of clothes and an acoustic Sears Silvertone guitar. He left Sallie Ann behind, again not bothering, apparently, with a divorce; she moved back to Farrell.

Myles Long remembers Muddy reaching for a nail and scratching the hay baler before disappearing. He went to see what Muddy had done, and though it contradicts what is known about Muddy's literacy, he is sure that he found scrawled there, whether addressed to his friend, or his former employer, or perhaps to the land all around him — the mother's dust from whence he came — "God bless you."

Muddy Waters was gone.

CHAPTER 5

CITY BLUES
1943–1946

I was thinking to myself that I could do better in a big city," Muddy recollected to writer and friend Pete Welding in 1970. "I thought I could make more money, and then I would have more opportunities to get into the big record field."

The only big city on Muddy's mind was Chicago. Its presence in the Delta was long established. That which did not come from the ground or the furnish came from Chicago, usually through the catalogs of Sears and Montgomery Ward. Since 1916, the city's black newspaper, the *Chicago Defender,* had been promoting what it called "The Great Northern Drive": "Every black man for the sake of his wife and daughter should leave even at a financial sacrifice every spot in the South where his worth is not appreciated enough to give him the standing of a man and a citizen in the community. We know full well that this would almost mean a depopulation of that section and if it were possible we would glory in its accomplishment." By 1930, the largest population of Mississippians outside the state was in Chicago. And as America's entrance into World War II rekindled the industrial fires of the northern factories, the need for soldiers created a manpower crisis. Of the African Americans who went north in the first half of the century, nearly half migrated between 1940 and 1947. By the end of the forties, the median annual wage for blacks in Chicago was $1,919, while in the Magnolia state of Mississippi it was $439. Field hands took work on the assembly line at the Caterpillar factory in Peoria, Illinois, making money by making the machines that had taken their work.

"I went straight to Chicago, didn't travel around at all," said

Muddy. "I went by train from Clarksdale to Memphis, changed in Memphis, and came up on the train they call Chicago Nine." In 1940, Memphis to Chicago on the Illinois Central was a sixteen-hour trip costing eleven dollars and ten cents. If Muddy's recording payment was socked away, he could have traveled north on it, with money left to spend.

Small towns dotted the line between Memphis and Chicago, the view from the train window mostly of farmland. The continuity of the landscape would reassure apprehensive travelers, the familiar to-pography soothing the first and most violent pangs of homesickness in people who were both nurtured and disciplined by the land.

But somewhere north of St. Louis, the look and feel of the towns changed, the churches becoming taller and narrower in design, with Germanic steeples and turrets. There was more money in these northern communities, and the wealth was reflected in the architec-ture. North of Cairo, Illinois, blacks would have moved forward on the train, exercising — many for the first time — their civil rights be-yond Jim Crow's grasp. A rolling plain feels different from a cleared jungle. And then over the earth's curve, unfolding like a wide high-way, was the capital of this new kingdom, the tall, storied buildings of Chicago. Chicago was a prairie town, spreading like pancake bat-ter, widening along Lake Michigan, deepening in an endless absorp-tion of farmland and ethnic settlements (reflected in the diversity of its modern urban checkerboard).

A porter at the Illinois Central Station in Chicago remembered the befuddlement he regularly witnessed: "If there was no one to meet [the arriving passengers], the newcomers seldom knew where to go. They might ask a Red Cap to direct them to the home of a friend — unaware that without an address the porter could be of lit-tle help in a city as large as Chicago. Or they might employ one of the professional guides who, for a fee, would help them find lodging. Some of the guides were honest, others were little more than confi-dence men. Travelers Aid and the railroad police tried to help the mi-grants and prevent exploitation; but for the newcomer without friends or relatives the first few days were often a terrifying experience."

Greeted by the red glow of steel mills and the billowy, black, gritty smoke of factories working overtime, Muddy had moved from the world of the born to the world of the made.

"I had some people there [relatives]," Muddy recalled, "but I didn't know where they was. I didn't know nothing." Leaving Stovall was the fulfillment of a dream so large he'd been almost unable to face it; he'd barely prepared. From the train station, he took a taxi, showing the driver the South Side address that had been burning a hole in his pocket, 3652 Calumet. He paid the driver to wait while he rang the bell. "I looked up a address of some boys that we's raised up together and I came to their house and I stayed there. I got here on a Saturday, got a job working at [the Joanna Western Mills] paper factory, making containers. I was working Monday. Swing shift, three to eleven in the evening. Man, that's the heaviest jive you ever saw in your life." An arresting statement from a man long yoked to a cotton sack.

"Work there eight hours a day — I never did that before. My paycheck was forty-something bucks or fifty-something bucks a week. You got to be kiddin', you know. Soon I put in some overtime, worked twelve hours a day and I brought a hundred and something bring-home pay. I said, 'Goodgodamighty, look at the money I got.' I have picked that cotton all the year, chop cotton all year, and I didn't draw a hundred dollars."

The heady times distracted him from the racial tensions underlying his bustling new home. Racism in Chicago was exacerbated by the competition for jobs between blacks and whites. Living conditions were cramped, Chicago's South and West Sides bursting with southern black immigrants, many of whom were unprepared and ill-equipped to adapt to city life. Race riots were breaking out in other parts of the country, and Chicago's Mayor "Big Ed" Kelly established a Committee on Race Relations. "During the last war we made a study after the riot," commented one local African American politician. "This time let's make the study before."

The easy money eased Muddy's transition, but music remained his focus. "I never did go get good jobs," said Muddy. "I'd get them little old cheap jobs because I didn't ever keep one too long. I got a job at the paper mill [loading] those forklift trucks, and then I got a little job workin' for a firm that made parts for radios." He also worked at a glass factory and as a truck driver, in addition to working the music scene at night. The clubs were active, but the recording studios were quiet. Muddy's arrival coincided with a ban on all new recordings (August 1942 through November 1944) decreed by the president of the American Federation of Musicians, James Petrillo; Petrillo was trying to protect musicians who were losing live gigs to recordings.

Of course there was also the war to worry about and, still steamed, Stovall's T. O. Fulton made sure that war caught up with Muddy quick. "Before I left," Muddy recalled, "I go by Coahoma, tell this man at the [draft] board I got to go to Chicago to take care of a little business. You know they's calling 'em into the army fast then. I say, 'If you should need me in a couple of weeks, send the papers to Chicago.' He gets on the phone, calls the manager at Stovall, and the manager says, 'We done had this falling out,' and *bam,* the papers was there. I don't know what to do now. So this boy take me over to this little branch board up here and I told 'em my story and the man there say, 'Don't worry, you got a job?'

"'Yeah, I'm working now,' I tell him.

"'Go on to your work,' he says. 'Don't do nothing till you hear from us. Forget these papers.'"

✧   ✧   ✧

Blues sounds in the early 1940s were still dominated by the Bluebird label, which had been releasing budget-priced 78s since 1933. Their roster had originally included such country blues artists as Sleepy John Estes, Big Joe Williams, and Blind Willie McTell, but the sounds had become increasingly diluted.

"The blues Waters found on his arrival in Chicago was as well-turned and sophisticated as it often was empty of genuine emotion, and without the latter its guts were gone," Pete Welding wrote. Welding was a music critic who founded Testament Records and, while living in Chicago in the 1960s and recording some of Muddy's finest music, became a personal friend. "The vigorous, country-based blues that Chicago had refined, polished, and institutionalized since the 1920s, when the city had been established as the most influential blues recording center, had been progressively emasculated. . . . The once forceful, highly individualized blues had been diluted by large record firms to glossy, mechanistic self-parody and tasteless double entendre." Muddy called it sweet jazz; the style has since come to be called hokum.

Bluebird was, at any rate, a marginal label. When Muddy arrived in 1943, Chicago was a jazz town. Nat "King" Cole's "Straighten Up and Fly Right" was big; also Johnny Moore and the Three Blazers, and Billy Eckstine. "When Chicago was invaded [by southerners], there was nothing but swing music," recalled Dave Myers, a pioneering electric bassist who came up from Mississippi in the 1930s. "Glenn Miller, Tommy Dorsey, Count Basie, Duke Ellington, the big bands. Swing was on the radio all the time, then [you hear] somebody playing records across the way and it's all swing. My daddy played that old shoe stump, Mississippi stuff, and wasn't nothing here relating to that at all."

"People were going at that time for, I think you call it bebop," said Muddy. "My blues still was the sad, old-time blues. You'd go in and tell [the club owners] you played blues, and a lot of them, they'd shake their head and say, 'Sorry, can't use you.'"

Some jazz clubs had a blues night — gigs that usually went to high-profile names familiar to Muddy through 78s and jukeboxes. Even those gigs weren't great: according to union contracts, the pay for established names such as Big Bill Broonzy and Memphis Slim was around ten dollars per person on a weekend night, or six dollars on a weeknight.

Without the clubs, the only venue open to Muddy was the house party, a get-together in someone's home where the drinks were cheaper, the food more plentiful, the audience nearer the band, and where the musicians could establish their reputations. He was on unfamiliar turf, but it was a hustle he knew. "I played mostly on weekends, but I have played seven nights a week, worked five days, sometimes six days. Plenty of food, whiskey, fried chicken, and they had bootleg whiskey. I was making five dollars a night playing. That was good side money for me." He purchased a suit of new clothes. It was one thing to look country in Memphis; in Chicago, even the cheap clothes were fine.

After flopping with his friends, Muddy sought out his relatives. Chicago blacks were largely segregated into two sprawling ghettos: the West Side and, a half-rung up the social ladder, the South Side. Within these tight communities were organizations, such as the Clarksdale Citizens Association, that were built around the tight communities left behind. Through their network, Muddy may have located his cousin Dan Jones, to whose West Side apartment he moved within several weeks of his arrival. Muddy's daughter Azelene and her mother, Leola Spain, lived nearby.

Not long after, he got his own place. Dan Jones Sr., whom he'd known on Stovall, had a large truck, which he hired out to landlords who needed apartments and houses cleaned out or moved. One of the job's perks was scavenging appliances and furniture left behind. Another perk was the advance notice on upcoming vacancies, and when a real estate company had him clean out an apartment near his own, he slid Muddy right in. Four doors down from Jones, at 1851 West Thirteenth Street, second floor, Muddy faced north, enjoying a comfortable morning light and temperate afternoons. His rent was cheap; while his cousin paid thirty-five dollars a month, Muddy paid twelve, plus utilities, for four rooms. "Old Man Jones fixed Muddy up," Jimmy Rogers said of Muddy's cousin. "Muddy had furniture all through that house, bed and dressers, end tables, stove, refrigerator, a little radio, and a record player."

By 1944, Muddy was meeting the established musicians, including Big Bill Broonzy. "I call my style country style," said Muddy. "Big Bill was the daddy of country-style blues singers. When I got here, he was the top man."

In a photograph from the 1940s, a proud young Muddy is shaking hands with Big Bill. Bill's left arm is around Muddy's shoulders, which slump as if unable to support the notion of Broonzy's embrace. Muddy's serious expression cannot hide his pleasure — it may be disbelief — at where he finds himself, and with whom. The folks back home, he seems to be thinking, will never believe it.

For decades, Big Bill's character resonated with Muddy. "You done made hits, you got a big name, the little fellow ain't nothing," Muddy said in the 1970s about the star attitude. "But Big Bill, he don't care where you from. He didn't look over you 'cause he been on records a long time. 'Do your thing, stay with it, man. If you stay with it, you going to make it.' That's what Big Bill told me. Mostly I try to be like him."

◇   ◇   ◇

One of the earliest, most important, and longest-lasting friendships Muddy Waters made when he came to Chicago was with fellow guitarist Jimmy Rogers. Rogers worked at Sonora Radio and Cabinet Company, where he had been befriended by Jesse Jones, Muddy's cousin. Jesse and his brother Dan Jr. didn't play music, but they liked to be around those who did. They admired Jimmy's skill — his relaxed and smooth vocal style, his uncomplicated yet intricate guitar chording and strumming. Their friendship solidified when Jesse got Jimmy transferred to a less dangerous department of the factory. "He got me into that part where my hands wouldn't get cut off."

Both Muddy and Jimmy were from the Delta, each raised by his grandmother. Rogers, however, had a more nomadic youth. He was born James A. Lane in Ruleville, Mississippi, on June 3, 1924. Shortly after moving the family to his home state of Georgia, Jimmy's father was killed in a scuffle among coworkers at a sawmill. Jimmy's mother moved them back to the Delta, and Jimmy was taken in by his grandmother. They moved often, living in several towns in several states: Tennessee, Arkansas, and Mississippi.

His first guitar was a diddley bow, common in the country — broom wire nailed to the side of a house and plucked. More portable than a wall, harmonicas were inexpensive and accessible, and Rogers switched to one, learning music basics on that before practicing on other people's guitars. "My grandmother, she was a Christian-type woman, and man, they's really against music, blues, period," said

Rogers. "After I got of age, my grandmother seen where she wasn't gonna be able to stop me from trying to play, so she just give me up, said, 'Well, okay, you can do what you want to as far as that's concerned.'"

He was soon exposed to live musicians: Houston Stackhouse, Tommy McLennan, Robert Petway, Bukka White. "They was men then," he said. "I was a youngster." He too had grown up listening to Sonny Boy Williamson II. "I would rush home every day around twelve o'clock to hear him. I'd be digging every inch of his sounds."

Rogers began to earn a reputation, appearing at house parties and playing for "small change, all the whiskey that I could drink, and maybe a dollar and a half cash money." In Memphis, he befriended Robert Lockwood Jr. and Joe Willie Wilkins ("My favorite men, I played with them quite a bit, picked up some chords from them too.") When his grandmother moved to St. Louis, Jimmy encountered Roosevelt Sykes and Walter Davis.

As he matured, Rogers felt the pull to move north. "I could feel [racism] at the age of ten," he remembered. "I could see it going through my grandmother and my uncles and other people that were older. I could see what they were going through, and I understood what they be talking about. I didn't like the South. I always said, 'As soon as I get big, I'm gone.'"

Rogers had family in Chicago and had been there several times before settling permanently in the mid-1940s. Initially, he lived with his great-uncle, but soon found an apartment of his own on the Near West Side, next to the Maxwell Street Market, which is where he was living when his cousin Jesse brought Muddy by.

"We started talking and he said he played guitar," said Rogers. "So one weekend, we got together and started jamming over at his house. I knew what I was listening for on guitar, and Muddy felt the same way. . . . I was playing with different musicians. They didn't really know what I wanted. I would hum it to them, and I would phrase it on the guitar, run the notes on the harmonica — they still couldn't get it. Then Muddy Waters, I listened to him and I said, 'I know what he need.' I'd just add sound — what he was singing, that's the way I would play, and give him a feeling to it that he could really open up and come on out with it. It rang a bell." Rogers didn't play with a slide and didn't need to. "I let Muddy do all that and I just harmonize it and play along, fill in for him and make a turnaround. He liked it that way."

Rogers had amplified his acoustic guitar with a DeArmond pickup, which fit beneath the strings in the sound hole. "Muddy had a hollow S curve [model] like the Gene Autry guitar," said Rogers, who played a Gibson L-5, "and I took him to Eighteenth and Halsted [The Chicago Music Company] and got him a DeArmond pickup put on his guitar, got him a little amplifier, and then you could get sound out of it." The pure acoustic guitar was fine in rural Mississippi because there were no sounds at night but the shallow breathing of God at rest, and the steady percussion of crickets and cicadas. Not so in a Chicago of clanging streetcars, trains, and automobiles out late on a party. Muddy also began using a thumbpick, which further intensified his volume.

The two men continued to meet at Muddy's apartment, about a ten-minute walk for Jimmy. "Wouldn't be nobody home but us musicians," Rogers said. "We come in, plug up the amp, get us one of these half-pint or pint bottles and get some ideas. We'd run through a few verses and move on to something else and keep on. Finally, after maybe three or four days fooling around, you'd be done built a number. On weekends, we'd buy a few drinks and play guitar. So we decided then we'd start this house-party deal over again here in Chicago."

◇   ◇   ◇

Another important and early friendship, though not as long-lasting, was between Muddy and a guitarist named Claude Smith, better known as Blue Smitty. Smitty was born in Arkansas the same year as Jimmy Rogers, but began visiting Chicago when he was only four.

As he told it, Smitty's guitar skills came "as a gift." "One night it was raining," he recalled. "It was summertime. A guy lived down the road from us and I got up at about one o'clock at night — everybody was asleep — and I walked down and asked him to let me use his guitar. He said, 'What are you gonna do with the guitar this time of night?' I said, 'I'm gonna play it.' And he let me have it, we wrapped it up to keep it from getting wet, and I went home and sat on the porch and started playing them six strings. And my mother get up and come to the door, she hear me out there: 'When did you learn how to play the guitar?' I said, 'Tonight.' And we sat up all night and listened to me play that guitar. I was about fourteen."

In the mid-1940s, Smitty, about twenty, found work in Chicago as an electrician. Muddy met him through the gregarious Jesse Jones. At the time, his music was a mix of southern gutbucket blues and fancier finger work, blending the likes of Arthur "Big Boy" Crudup and jazz master Charlie Christian.

"I went down in Jewtown to buy some guitar strings," said Smitty, referring, like Greektown, to the colloquial name of the immigrant market neighborhood on the Near West Side. "It started raining and we were standing under the canopy. This one guy was going in the music store and he asked me if I would hold his guitar. He had five strings on the guitar and I just started playing it. This fellow was standing next to me, he said, 'Do you play?' I said, 'Sure I can play.' He said, 'I got somebody I'd like for you to meet. Then maybe you can teach him something.' I said, 'Who is that?' He said, 'His name is McKinley Morganfield, he's my cousin, but they call him Muddy Waters.'"

Smitty went to Muddy's apartment. "Muddy was sitting down in the middle of the floor and he had the pickup out of his guitar, and he was trying to fix it," Smitty recalled. "The ground wire had come a-loose, it needed soldering. So I soldered the wire in his pickup and put it back in the guitar. Muddy played first. He had a cheap little amplifier there, but it sounded pretty good. He said, 'Do you play?' I said, 'Yeah, I can play.'" They were like an eager couple on a first date. Muddy handed Smitty his guitar, and Smitty retuned it from the Spanish to standard tuning. Smitty remembered Muddy saying, "I don't know anything about that other tuning, I play with slide all the time."

Motivated by Muddy, Smitty found steady work, buying a Gibson amplifier and then his own DeArmond pickup. "So Muddy and I started practicing together. I tried getting him away from that slide, 'cause I could play single-note picking. And I would teach him how to play the bass to what I was playing. He always had a good sense of timing. And from then on, every week, sometimes four or five times a week, in the evenings, we'd get together."

Himself inspired, Muddy began taking two guitars to house parties, one tuned to standard for picking, and one tuned to Spanish (open G) for sliding. "He really learnt me some things on the guitar, too," confirmed Muddy. "I played mostly bottleneck until I met Smitty. It was a very, very good improvement he did for me, because I didn't have to try to do everything with the slide by itself."

⬥   ⬥   ⬥

The world of South Side blues was small. Smitty and Jimmy Rogers had already been performing together — with Jimmy on harmonica, a piano player called King, and a drummer known as Pork Chop. "I was playing with Smitty and I got a few ideas from him," said Rogers. "When Muddy came to Chicago, we started hanging around together, him and Smitty and myself."

Smitty was cursed, however, with a good day job. Unlike Muddy and Jimmy, he wasn't stone committed to music, and though he was a natural talent, he often wouldn't show up. "If Blue Smitty wasn't there," said Rogers. "I'd have to play the guitar. If he was, I'd play harmonica." Drummers were scarce. The country blues had never demanded one — a guitarist stomping the wood floor resonated well enough. In Chicago, the paying gigs were jazz, and no blues drummers had developed. So the second guitarist would loosen his strings to play bass parts and keep rhythm.

Calvin Jones, who later joined Muddy's band as a bassist, stumbled onto the newcomer at a small nightspot a few blocks from Muddy's apartment. "I went to a skin game [cards], gambling in someone's apartment, and I heard this guitar, he had his slide going. So I went to the window and he was right across the street. I left the game and went down there. He had a harmonica player with him. It was an acoustic guitar what Muddy had. It was a weeknight, they didn't even have a bandstand, they were just sitting in their chairs playing. Wasn't nobody in the joint, three peoples maybe. I asked him what his name was. 'Muddy Waters.' He said it real cool."

"We'd call it scabbing," said Rogers. "You hit here, you set up with asking this guy that owns the club if he wouldn't mind you playing a few numbers — quite naturally it was good for his business, he would say okay. You'd play a number or two, they'd like it, you'd pick up a buck here, a buck there."

Before long Blue Smitty managed to land the band a proper club gig. "So one day I was going to get a haircut" — Smitty's career-changing stories have the most prosaic of beginnings — "and while I was in this barber shop at the corner of Ogden and Twelfth, this one guy said to me, 'While you're waiting, play us a piece or two.'" Smitty did, and the guy told him, "I'd like to have some guys that can play as good as you, Friday, Saturday, and Sunday. What are you gonna charge me for playing?" Smitty reported back to Muddy and the trio was hired for five dollars apiece per night. The response was good; they added Thursdays.

As his fan base grew, Muddy must have heard time and again, "Hey, you're pretty good, you ever record for anybody?" That none of his peers had heard of the Library of Congress probably slowed him not at all from pulling out a copy of his record, maybe wrapped in cloth so it wouldn't break, his name typed on the label, visible if you squinted because he'd worn it out playing and showing it off. Hell yes he'd recorded.

And while his fellow rural city dwellers had found little kinship in the jaunty, unemotional, ragtimey sounds that predominated, they loved music that evoked the sawdust on a juke-joint floor, the dust that the mule plow kicked up, the emptiness of a lonely country road. Muddy had never aspired to play with urban flash, basking instead in the slow country blues feel, keeping it as his foundation even as he modernized it. It was Muddy's own deal with the devil: he left his native community but gained a larger one, a wealthier one that could purchase the nostalgia and authenticity of his music.

◇   ◇   ◇

Much of that modernization came via a new instrument. The electric guitar was the Delta bluesman's answer to the mechanical cotton picker. "We were playing our little clubs and a 'cue-stick' [acoustic] guitar wouldn't answer there, not in a liquor club," recalled Muddy. "My uncle Joe [Grant] had been in Chicago a long time and everybody played those electric guitars. He told me I ought to play one, and he bought me one. It wasn't no name-brand electric guitar, but it was a built-in electric guitar, not a pickup just stuck on. It gave me so much trouble that that's probably why I forgot the name. Every time I looked around I had to have it fixed. Finally it got stoled from me in one of them little neighborhood clubs, and the next one I got me was a Gretsch, and that's the one I used on all my early hits." The DeArmond had allowed for a longer sustain in the notes, but the electric guitar was a whole new beast. It affected the approach to singing and the role of the other instruments. With it — and in particular with Muddy taking it on — the Chicago blues, the urban blues, the modern blues, were nascent.

"It was a very different sound, not just louder," said Muddy. "I thought that I'd come to like it — if I could ever learn to play it." The difference was not in the music Muddy created, but in how he created it — how his fingers attacked the string, how his slide worked the neck. "That loud sound would tell everything you were doing," he explained. "On acoustic you could mess up a lot of stuff and no one would know that you'd ever missed."

The sound was heavy, especially when all three guitars played together, intertwined and forceful — Muddy sliding, Jimmy laying patterns under him, and Smitty punching up the bass parts. Each could trade off roles (except for the slide), and their vocal styles were varied. And strangely, wonderfully, behind the closed walls of a club in the later hours of the evening, at the end of a long day, a heartless day, an exhilarating day, a calm resembling quiet could settle on the city and the electrified sound could evoke a downright backcountry night.

Eddie Boyd, kin to Muddy and raised near Stovall, had come to

Chicago in 1941, and he played a sleek, smoother style. "He wanted me to play like Johnny Moore," said Muddy, "which I wasn't able to play the guitar like. He wanted it to be a kind of sweet blues." With Eddie's guidance, Muddy and Smitty joined Local 208, the "Negro" chapter of the American Federation of Musicians, and fell into a good gig. "Jimmy Rogers, he was having girl trouble during that time, so some way or the other he got out of the band," remembered Smitty. He and Muddy began playing with Boyd. A sign went up at the Flame Club: BLUES, BLUES, AND MORE BLUES. When Boyd took another gig in nearby Gary, Indiana, Muddy and Smitty got Sunnyland Slim, another popular pianist, to replace him. That trio left the Flame and went to the Purple Cat on Madison.

Jimmy Rogers got his act together about the time Blue Smitty was losing his, so Muddy never lacked accompaniment for house parties and small clubs. Nor did he lack accompaniment in his apartment. In the mid-1940s, Muddy was shacking up with Annie Mae Anderson, whom he'd known at Stovall. "Nice-looking girl," said Elve Morganfield. "At Stovall, she was married to Sam Anderson. Like I said, Muddy was a Casanova, he was happy-go-lucky. He had 'em all. He loved them young women, oh yeah."

In Chicago, Muddy was becoming his own man. His grandmother died in 1946, and home may never have seemed more distant. He was a beneficiary on her insurance, quickly spending the money on a luxury he'd grown accustomed to in Mississippi. "He got his paycheck and with that other little money he inherited he paid the down payment on the car," Jimmy Rogers remembered. "It was a rust-colored Chevy, nineteen forty two-door. Musicians, blues players, didn't have cars too much then, and that's what really started him into going around." John Lee "Sonny Boy" Williamson began hiring Muddy for gigs in Gary, Indiana, and other distant places.

Sonny Boy's skills on the harmonica thrust the instrument from back pockets to center stage. He had a good-time *bomp bomp abomp bomp* sound. "If you liked blues, you liked his," said Muddy. "He had that particular little twinkle in the voice that got to people." One name for the harmonica is "mouth organ," and his mastery on the twenty-five-cent novelty item brought it to a level of respect shared by the piano. When notes were held, the harmonica could lay a foundation not unlike a keyboard, but the instrument really shined when riffs punctuated or bolstered lyrics. "Mississippi saxophone" was another name, and blues bands made it the poor man's horn section. Sonny Boy developed a choking style, not squeezing the life out of the harmonica, but bellowing his life's breath into it. The bends and slurs — making the instrument say "wah wah" — gave it personality. A song such as "Good Morning Little Schoolgirl" could have both a sense of humor and an undercurrent of terror, all built around a hook that made it wildly popular.

Sonny Boy drank on his gigs and couldn't keep a band together. "Eddie Boyd and myself and Sonny Boy was playing together," Muddy said. "Sonny Boy was mostly doing all the singing and they wanted to keep me in the background. But Sonny Boy'd keep a-gettin' high, we got to try to carry it on. So one night Eddie done got tired of singing all night, and Sonny Boy got drunk — Eddie know I could sing 'cause we raised together — Eddie said, 'Why don't you sing one?' I could see he was sung out. I pulled the mike to me, opened this big mouth up, boy, and the house went crazy, man. I sang one of [Lowell] Fulsom's songs, 'Trouble.' 'Trouble, trouble, trouble, all in this world I see.' And I was talkin' quietly to the people, quietly, and they went nuts. And Sonny Boy heard that noise goin' on, he jumped up, grabbed that harp and taken that mike. 'My baby left me, left me a mule to ride.'" Muddy laughed. "He seen how I brought down the house. We worked around quite a little bit together, till Sonny Boy got drunk and got us fired. Sonny Boy wouldn't do right. He had that big name too, all them big records out, but he loved whiskey better than he did his work, man."

They stayed friendly until June 1, 1948. While walking home from a gig, Sonny Boy was robbed. His assailant, never identified, took his wallet, his watch, three harmonicas, and most of his life. Despite intercranial hemorrhaging, Sonny Boy crawled the last block home to his doorstep, where his wife found him — and presumed him drunk. Three hours later he was dead.

◇   ◇   ◇

By now, the Petrillo ban on recording had been lifted, and the recording industry had awakened to a new and different scene. Talent scouts once again scurried from club to club, but instead of the smooth, sappy music from between the wars, they found another new sound had taken root in the raucous clubs. New artists had reinvigorated old ideas, and new record labels were springing up to give them a shot. After three years of trying, Muddy's devotion to music, to the late nights playing to spilled beer, the next day's ache at his day job — paid off in 1946 with his first two commercial sessions. Muddy's first session was for an independent producer; the second had him in the ranks of the major labels.

From the first, only one track was issued. "Mean Red Spider," produced by J. Mayo Williams, the pioneering African American independent producer, was more representative of the existing Chicago sound than of the new developments Muddy was forging. He sings lead, but his guitar is buried beneath a squealing clarinet, a busy saxophone, and a ragtimey piano. The presence of these reed instruments reflects the influence of the big-band sound; the fact that there's only two and not a whole section indicates the style's diminishing sway.

"I remember that session," said Muddy. "Somewhere here in Chicago we did it. We got half sideman [half the union-scale sideman's rates]. We didn't get forty-one twenty-five. Forty-one twenty-five was sidemen's then, eighty-two fifty was the leader. I musta got twenty-something dollars out of it."

Muddy's name isn't even on the record. "Mean Red Spider" was attributed to James "Sweet Lucy" Carter and His Orchestra. Mr. Carter may be featured on the A-side ("Let Me Be Your Coal Man"), but he's nowhere on Muddy's track. "James Carter, I don't know," said Muddy, looking at the label copy brought to him in the 1970s by blues researcher Jim O'Neal, who was confirming what sounded like Muddy's presence. "But that is me. I got a little guitar in there somewhere, I hear it every once in a while. I thought that record was drownded in the river."

Through acquaintances made at that session, Muddy was introduced to "Baby Face" Leroy Foster, a skinny, smiling guy who'd hit Chicago from the South earlier that year. Foster was a skilled guitarist who also had a knack for drumming, and unlike the jazz players, he shared the juke-house aggressiveness that Muddy and Jimmy were putting into electric blues. With drums, the group landed a gig on Roosevelt Road and their following continued to build. Baby Face switched between guitar and drums, Jimmy could pull out his harmonica, or all three could play guitars and sing. "When we discovered what was going down," Muddy remembered, "then I said, 'Wow, man! We got something here!'"

This boost in popularity brought him to the attention of producer Lester Melrose, who was responsible for "the Bluebird sound," the chiffon blues — what Muddy called sweet jazz — that was waning in popularity. Melrose, a white Illinoisian in his fifties when Muddy arrived, had been the dominating force on the blues recording scene for the past decade and a half. He was responsible for much of the roster at both major blues labels, RCA (which controlled Bluebird) and Columbia.

On Friday, September 27, 1946, Muddy cut eight tracks for Columbia Records under Melrose's supervision. Muddy was leader on three tracks, backed vocalist Homer Harris on three, and backed pianist Jimmy Clark on two. There are no horns on any tracks. The arrangements, with piano, drums, and bass, might have seemed crowded in a Mississippi juke joint, but they were positively spare for Chicago. Booking three heavy-throated, unknown vocalists, Melrose was clearly looking for the next big thing. Stylistically, he was on target — Muddy's vocals would be imitated by a generation — but Melrose's roots in sweet blues bog these tracks in the past. In his introductions, Muddy almost pushes the sound into the future: his guitar is prominent and hitting heavy, but when a second guitar should kick in, it's instead the piano, sounding like yesterday and miked to play lead.

Muddy exhibits great confidence in his playing. His amplifier is turned up and, when appropriate, he lets the distortion rip. On Harris's topical "Atomic Bomb Blues," Muddy and pianist James Clark trade the hammered triplets that would become a feature of Muddy's later band. Cognizant of Melrose's sophisticated tastes, Muddy kept his slide in his pocket. "That country stuff might sound funny to 'em," he later remembered thinking. His phrasing, nonetheless, is imbued with a Delta feel; Muddy has Mississippi at his core. He also has Chicago at his fingertips; his comfort with the piano indicates that, through regular scabbing, he and his cronies had become accustomed to larger lineups.

As fall turned to winter and 1946 became history, Muddy watched these sessions sit neglected on Lester Melrose's shelf. The Jimmy Clark tracks came out ("Blues singer with piano, string bass, drums, and guitar," with no names given on the label), but Muddy's, along with those of Homer Harris, remained vaulted for almost a quarter century.

"You gotta have something that the record company wants," said Muddy. "And sometimes they are afraid to take a chance. They got a good blues seller, don't have to make another blues singer. People interested in people selling. You runs a store and you carrying brand-new merchandise, you don't know whether it'll sell or not. And they wasn't takin' a chance on mine."

CHAPTER 6

Rollin' and Tumblin'

1947–1950

Music was always in the air at the Maxwell Street Market on the Near West Side. The Market, the heart of Jewtown, ran about eight blocks and at least a block deep on either side. Behind the narrow doors and large display windows were stores of all types — dry goods, fresh produce, meats and fish, textiles and garments, jewelers and barbers, pharmacies, pawn shops. The back rooms of many shops were devoted to card games or dice, some for the entertainment of the proprietors and others for the bamboozlement of the patrons. Outside there were shambling carts selling secondhand goods and junk, the useless items commingled with the useful. The scene was similar at Handy Park on Memphis's Beale Street, but, like everything in Chicago, it was on a much larger scale.

Musicians would set up all along the stretch, some competing on corners, some seeking quiet on a midblock stoop, a hat or a carton or a lousy paper bag laid before them, banging a box and singing hambone for change. "Jewtown, on Saturdays and Sundays from around eleven o'clock to about five in the evening," said Jimmy Rogers, who lived just off Maxwell, "you could make more money with three or four guys than you could make in a club in the whole week. Man, there'd be hundreds of people around."

And hundreds of sounds. "I heard this harmonica one Sunday morning — woke me up!" Jimmy Rogers remembered. "I put my clothes on, went down in the crowd on Maxwell Street.

"I was familiar with Little Walter's sound, I had met him in Helena, Arkansas, when he was just a kid. I went on down to the street and there he was! Little squirrel-faced boy." Walter's sound had an acrobatic litheness to it, a humor to its swing. He listened to Louis Jordan's small combo, jump and jive records. "It was amazing," recalled Rogers, "this youngster was blowing harp and that was my instrument. He had a bass player, a guitar, and a drum playing with him, but the only thing that was really standing out to me was the harmonica. I sat in with them and we had a wonderful time. That's the way we really met, communicating."

Walter was a cat what liked a hat. Crisp suits, snappy shirts, he dressed like cash money, or the lack thereof: one day chicken, the next day feathers. A slight, attractive young man, Walter Jacobs had a sharp face and red-complected skin, a hint of Native American blood. He kept his wavy hair short and combed off his face. His eyes were dark and penetrating. "Walter was wild," said Rogers. "Walter was likely to kill you or anybody that crossed him. A young buck with a lot of temper. He had more nerve than brains. He'd fuck up — and we'd have to get him out of jail, me and Muddy."

Under the tutelage of Muddy and Jimmy, Little Walter would develop into a harmonica player whose influence would rank alongside the two Sonny Boys. Born Marion Walter Jacobs in Alexandria, Louisiana, May 1, 1930 (or perhaps Marksville, Louisiana, May 2, 1931), he heard the cry of a lonesome harmonica in the big open sky, and at the age of eight (or twelve), set out to answer its calling. "What really made me choose [harmonica] was that most of the kids, my mother too, tried to dissuade me from playin' it. Of course that made me more int'rested and the more they tried to disgust me with it, the more I caught on. If you give up, you lose the fight." He hopped trains, followed harvests and parties. In Monroe, Louisiana, he was a regular at the Liberty Night Club in 1943, eventually working his way to Helena, where — when not hounding Sonny Boy Williamson II for technique — he was sleeping on pool tables. In Helena, he also spent time with the influential guitarists Houston Stackhouse and Robert Lockwood Jr., picking up guitar basics. Then it was New Orleans, Memphis, and St. Louis — "playing," he said, "around a few shoeshine stands, pool rooms, you know."

When he got to Chicago, the teenaged Walter took a room at

Newberry and Fourteenth, about two blocks from Jimmy Rogers. "I told Muddy I met a boy down in Jewtown that could really blow," said Rogers. He walked Walter the mile west to Muddy's house. "We had our guitars and started banging away and we could see he'd fit in. Muddy and I could hear a different type harmony on guitar, but we couldn't find anyone else who could play that way. So I just give Walter the privilege to play harmonica and I turned completely to guitar."

"When I met him he wasn't drinking nothing but Pepsi-Cola," said Muddy. "Just a kid. And I'll tell you, I had the best harmonica player in the business, man. He didn't have very good time, but me and Jimmy teached him that. Plus we taught him how to settle down. He was wild, he had to play fast! He was always a jump boy, had that up 'n go power. His mind was so fast he could think twice to your once, that's how he learned to harp so good."

Rogers added about Walter, "Really the big problem was getting him to settle down enough to play. He'd get executing and go on. He was worse than the Bird, Charlie Parker. I would say, 'Look, I don't care how far you range on the wall, just meet me at the corner.'" So, the past met the future and enjoyed the company. Muddy: stolid, composed, authoritative — rooted in the dust of Mississippi. Walter: half his age and galloping on Louisiana swamp funk and Kansas City swing. There to mediate the distance: Jimmy Rogers.

The three were further propelled by Baby Face Leroy's Saturday-night frolic drumming. "There were four of us," Muddy said, "and that's when we began hitting heavy." Jimmy Rogers stated flatly, "Me and Muddy and Walter with a drum, we could sell just about anything."

The group continued to meet at Muddy's house for rehearsal. "There wouldn't be nobody there to give you no problem," said Rogers. "So we would suck on these little half-pints, and Muddy would cook some rice and chicken gizzards. We'd have a pot on in the kitchen and we'd get us a bowl, get us some water and get a little drink, then we'd sit back down and do it some more."

Muddy would bring in a song idea, lyrics that suggested a rhythm. Many songs were variations on established ones that each player would have learned differently — in different counties in the Delta. "We'd find a pattern that fit what he's saying," said Jimmy, "and then I'd build and Walter would fall in, find him a pocket. Then we'd run them patterns. It's like pushing a car — once you get it started rolling, you can't stop."

The car found a garage when the Zanzibar club opened in 1946 at the corner of Ashland and Thirteenth, half a block from Muddy's apartment. Muddy began stopping there for half-pints, and he befriended the proprietor, Hy Marzen. "Muddy lived in the neighborhood where our store was at," Marzen said. "He was almost like a bum off the street, just getting started." The Zanzibar was nicer than a hole-in-the-wall, but not much larger. The bandstand was in the back, a semicircular bar was in the middle, and at the front was a counter for delicatessen and liquor. "We sold corned-beef sandwiches by the ton, hard-boiled eggs, hot dogs, pigs feet, cole slaw. And I had two jeeps running up and down the street making deliveries," Marzen continued. The club became a home base for Muddy's band until it closed, eight years later, in 1954. "I used to make out the checks to McKinley Morganfield. I paid him a hundred dollars weekly, plus drinks, and he paid the others."

At the Zanzibar, the band gelled, and it was as exciting for them as for the audience. Marzen had to post an off-duty cop near the bandstand "to make sure people behaved themselves." The band played sitting down, and the audience, especially as the night progressed, liked to stand up. "The clubs were very violent," said Rogers. "After we got into bigger clubs they'd fight, or some guy would get mad with his old lady and they'd fight. Somebody would get cut or get shot. Clubs had two o'clock regular license, and if you wanted to stay open till three, you would pay extra, a patrol buy. That was a little gimmick the gangsters had going."

"I'd go up there with him to the Zanzibar," said bluesman R. L. Burnside, Muddy's girlfriend's cousin. "The sound was great. Electric. Big sound, good sound. It was unusual to see someone on electric then. I learned a lot of stuff just watching him."

Others were studying the band too, and even before they established their reknown at the Zanzibar, people began to know Muddy, Jimmy, and Walter by name, by sound, and by reputation. "We used to go around calling ourselves the Headhunters," said Muddy. "We'd go from club to club looking for bands that are playing and cut their heads [engage in a musical duel]. 'Here come them boys,' they'd say."

"We used to just do it for kicks," said Jimmy Rogers, "to keep from sitting around at home. As soon as we would get in a place, somebody would want us to play. We would go to the car and maybe get an amp and quick bring it in there and set up and jam a few numbers. We could take the gig if we wanted it, but it wasn't paying nothing, so we just drink and have some fun. That would mean a bigger crowd for us on the places that we were playing on weekends, because we'd announce where we were. Free publicity. By the time the taverns closed at two, we maybe done hit four or five, maybe six different taverns, and we had a pocket of money, maybe fifteen, twenty dollars apiece. And other bands, they would be glad for us to come around, because they were trying to get into the beat that we had." Muddy, Jimmy, and Walter plugged in, and musicians threw down their instruments, not to flee but as an invitation, anxious to witness the sound of the future up close, to feel the jolt of their industrial power. Muddy Waters was creating the blues anew.

❖   ❖   ❖

The Chess Brothers, Leonard and Phil, were not African American and were not from the South. But they were, like Muddy, like Jimmy Rogers, and like many of the artists they would make stars on their record label, immigrants to Chicago, angling for a foothold in this urban new world.

Jewish and from Poland, the brothers arrived with their mother in New York on Columbus Day, 1928. They quickly boarded a train to join their father, Joseph, who had settled in Chicago several years earlier and was beginning to realize the better life for which he'd crossed an ocean. At first, booze was their business. They bought increasingly larger liquor stores, graduating to a nightclub.

Chicago, liquor, and nightclubs have a long history together, and if the Chess brothers were no Al Capones, they shared his instinct for creating a large organization from a small business. "Their club, the Macomba, was small," said drummer Freddie Crutchfield, who occasionally performed there with Tom Archia's house band. "It had the booths on one side and the bar on the other. It was narrow and long, but it was a beautiful joint." It was in a musical neighborhood, near places such as the Green Gable Hotel, where Lionel Hampton might visit.

The brothers soon deduced that the Macomba's patrons might want to take the nightclub music home with them. Through a friend who owned Universal Recording Studios, the Chesses learned of a fledgling label that was seeking investors. They bought in. "Aristocrat [Records] was doing all white stuff then," recalled Phil Chess, the younger brother, "'Get On the Ball, Paul' kind of stuff, by a bunch of groups I never heard of. But they were selling a little bit around Chicago. And we had the black bands playing at our club, and we thought we'd take a shot and record one of those groups. That's how we got into the business." The business was nascent at the time, and Leonard's intimate familiarity with the South Side was essential to his success. He was entering the business, he later recalled, when "every porter, Pullman conductor, beauty and barbershop was selling records."

One afternoon at the musician's union hall, Aristocrat's recently hired African American talent scout, Sammy Goldberg, ran into Muddy and asked to hear him play. "[Leonard] had Goldstein [*sic*], a black guy, scouting for him," said Muddy, "and he wanted to hear me play a piece. I didn't have no guitar with me, and Lonnie Johnson was there with his. Lonnie said, 'No, man, I don't loan my guitar to nobody.' The man said, 'Let the man play one piece on the guitar. What he gonna do to it? He can't eat it.'" What Goldberg heard confirmed the rumors of Muddy's talent.

◇ ◇ ◇

Muddy was not home the autumn day of 1947 to receive the call that changed his career. He was at his day job, in his delivery truck, as unaware of the encounter ahead as he had been of Alan Lomax's arrival. Muddy was driving for the Westerngrade Venetian Blinds Company. "He'd deliver them, then he'd go home, play around, then go back to the factory," said Jimmy Rogers. "You'd see that doggone truck sitting in front of Muddy's place a lot of the time. He'd be in there eating or something. He had a good gig like that." Annie Mae had by then found her own place, and Muddy's childhood friend Bo, back from serving Uncle Sam, moved into the second bedroom, helping Muddy with the rent.

The invitation to record for Leonard Chess came from piano player Sunnyland Slim, who had talked himself onto an Aristocrat session in the last quarter of 1947. Sunnyland, never one to miss a gig and a catalyst for many artists of Muddy's generation, knew that Leonard was trying to get the label going, and rumors of another musician's union ban on recording were forcing label owners to stockpile material. Leonard, having cut a full band, was interested in trying a smaller group, where the complications were fewer, the studio time more cost-efficient, and the results — two songs on a ten-inch 78 RPM record — about the same. Lightnin' Hopkins was hot at the time, John Lee Hooker. Sunnyland, who'd been gigging with Muddy, told Leonard he had just the man for this new sound. Goldberg, Leonard's scout, was at the studio and verified this new artist's talent. Sunny phoned Muddy, who was out on the truck. Leonard told Sunny, "Hell man, go get him," and Goldberg told Sunny, "Find him today, find him today."

Sunny again called Muddy's house and, with Muddy's roommate Bo, devised a scheme. Bo phoned the Westerngrade office and left a message for McKinley Morganfield — "Mac" to his coworkers — that his mother was sick, please come home. His mother being long dead, Muddy knew something was up. Sunnyland, in the meantime, hopped a bus over to the West Side. When Muddy got home, Sunny was there, jumpy most likely, as valuable session time was ticking by, which is what he explained to Muddy. "Bang!" said Jimmy Rogers. "That was right up Muddy's alley." They drove Muddy's car back to the session.

As for money, the job at Westerngrade Venetian Blinds would have paid better. As for records, Muddy would soon make better. But for historic moments, this session was mighty, inaugurating a twenty-eight-year relationship between Muddy Waters and the Chess brothers.

"Two or three days after the session, Muddy told me he done made a tape for Chess," said Jimmy Rogers. "Muddy said, 'Man, I don't know how it's gonna sound but I got my foot in the door, I think.' Finally we got a hold of a disc of it, and we played it." Rogers was surprised by the emptiness of what he heard. All their work at building a band sound had been dismissed in favor of Leonard's misguided attempt to recreate country blues. The session had not involved Muddy's regular band; Ernest "Big" Crawford, a bassist, was there to record with Andrew Tibbs, and Sunnyland had grabbed him and a drummer to back up Muddy. But it was more than that. Leonard wanted a country blues hit, but he didn't understand country blues. Piano players were what taverns hired; Leonard simply couldn't grasp the guitar as a lead instrument. So when Muddy's "Little Anna Mae" should rip into a guitar solo, the piano takes the lead. Muddy's talents were again thwarted.

Sunnyland's sides were released ("Sunny Land Slim with Muddy Water"), but Leonard shelved Muddy's for several agonizing months. When "Gypsy Woman" and "Little Anna Mae" were finally released in February of 1948, they didn't set Chicago afire, but there was interest.

Muddy had to wait until April of 1948 for his next invitation to the studio. Despite yet another ban called by James Petrillo, the independent labels continued to work, staking a claim to the blues market. Still Leonard continued moving in the wrong direction, resisting Muddy's efforts to bring in his band. Clinging to his own partialities, Leonard introduced a saxophone to the lineup. As a result, "Good Lookin' Woman" and "Mean Disposition" also ended up on a shelf, unreleased during Muddy's lifetime.

After Muddy, Sunnyland cut two with the same combo. When the session was finished — Leonard's way — Muddy could contain himself no longer. "I said, let me do one," recounted Muddy, "by myself." And Muddy started in on his material, playing his Delta blues on an electric guitar. His choice was a sure thing, a song with an undeniable bounce that had worked on Alan Lomax, was working in the Chicago clubs, and like eyesight to the blind, should have worked on Leonard Chess: "I Can't Be Satisfied."

The sound was not the full urban blues of Muddy's band, but the amplifier did sustain longer than an acoustic guitar — the notes hung in the air like Delta humidity, and there was a ferociousness to the full chord. Big Crawford thumped out a doghouse sound on his upright bass, bolstering the rhythm. "He was laughing at me," remembered Muddy. "Said, 'This is my type of stuff.'" The bottleneck slide sang of the South, the electric instrument rang of the North. Leonard asked aloud, "What the hell is he singing?"

He still couldn't hear it.

"Leonard Chess, he didn't know what it was," said Muddy of his boldly amplified country blues. "He didn't like my style of singing. The woman that was his partner, Evelyn Aron, she dug me." Muddy, ever the ladies' man.

Aristocrat 1305 — Muddy Waters with Rythm (*sic*) Accompaniment, "I Can't Be Satisfied" / "I Feel Like Going Home" — was released early on an April weekend in 1948. These are the same two songs he recorded for the 1941 Fisk–Library of Congress Coahoma County Study. Perhaps not surprisingly, though the notes are nearly the same (yet so much richer), the feel — and the lyrics — are different. He's no longer singing behind a mule or beneath an open sky; he's a factory worker whose vision of God behind the stars is narrowed by a maze of buildings. He picks notes, but with the strength of one fighting an unyielding metal machine, and when he strikes chords, it's with force enough to fell a streetcar. "Country Blues" has become "I Feel Like Going Home," a mishearing of the double entendre "feel like blowing my horn," though similar in its yearning for comfort and companionship. The verse about "leaving this morning if I have to ride the blinds" has been dropped; Muddy and his audience have ridden those blinds.

Released on a Friday, the first pressing was nearly gone by Saturday night. The first Petrillo ban was like a flood that swept that insincere chiffon world clean, and Muddy, a blues Noah, cultivated a music devoted to emotion, feeling, truth. "You couldn't get one in Chicago nowhere," said Muddy. "The people were buyin' two or three at a time. They started a limit, one to a customer." Stores jacked up the prices, the seventy-nine-cent record soon selling for more than a dollar. At the Maxwell Street Radio Company, Muddy exclaimed, "But I'm the man who made it." He left with a single copy.

The record caught the ear of *Billboard,* the music industry's leading trade paper. Though their reviewer didn't care for it ("Poor recording distorts vocal and steel guitar backing"), it rose to number eleven on their Most-Played Jukebox Race Records chart. And though Muddy found the music "empty" without his band, the popularity of the record made it easy to like. "Muddy was playing when I was plowing," B. B. King remembered, "mules that is. When I first heard of Muddy Waters, I had never left Mississippi. Then finally we started to get records on him — 'I Feel Like Going Home.' He had something that no one else had, and I loved to hear him play."

Others loved to hear Muddy too. "Then Chess began to come close to me, because Andrew Tibbs [Chess's bet] had done failed," said Muddy. "'Come down and let's have coffee together.' 'I don't drink coffee.' 'We'll get a sandwich. Come on down to the office.' Yeah, he was my buddy, but I was glad, man. Hey, I had worked all my life to get my name up there. He did a lot for me, putting out the first record and everything. I didn't even sign no contract with him, no nothing. It was just 'I belongs to the Chess family.'"

Belonging to a family was an arrangement comfortable for Muddy in its familiarity. In Mississippi, Muddy had "belonged" to a family, knew how to get by — and get ahead — through a personal relationship with a boss man. The Chicago factories, on the other hand, were huge impersonal places. And through their work together, Leonard and Muddy developed a real friendship, a lasting friendship, two outsiders who captured the zeitgeist of not just an era but also a people and a place. When Muddy had his first promotional photo made, he was beaming.

The record's success paid in bigger crowds and better gigs — the Zanzibar and the nearby Boogie Woogie Inn on Roosevelt. Then it was the Chicken Shack, the Purple Cat, Lowell King's club down from the White Sox ballpark. On Sundays, they played afternoon gigs at Silvio's, breaking down around eight to set up elsewhere for a night gig, nine till two. Docie's Lounge on the South Side, Romeo's Place, the Squeeze Club, Brown's Village, the 708 Club (a fancier place despite the exposed plumbing pipes that ran throughout), the Ebony Lounge. At the Du Drop Lounge, 3609 Wentworth, they shared the bill with Big Bill Broonzy and Memphis Minnie, a capsule history of recent musical changes presented in one evening.

Prophetically, the printed label of this record put an "s" on Muddy's last name. The transformation of backwater McKinley Morganfield was complete. About a month after his hit record's release, Muddy rode home from a gig. "I could hear that record all up in people's houses. I'd stop my car and look up and listen a little while. Ooooh, once I got a little scared. I used to wonder if I had died! All of a sudden I became Muddy Waters. Just overnight." He'd become a blues star.

◇   ◇   ◇

In the two and a half years he was with Aristocrat, Muddy recorded thirty-five sides, twenty-five of them as bandleader. If Evelyn Aron, Leonard's partner, dug Muddy's music, Leonard quickly dug the way he sold.

Muddy knew that his band was forging an exciting sound and he never stopped pressing Leonard to record them together. Leonard finally paid a visit to the Zanzibar. White faces there were uncommon, but Leonard was accustomed to that. "Muddy said, 'Leonard's here,'" Rogers remembered. "'He wants to hear us play some of the stuff that we do.' Leonard sat there and listened, looked around to see what the people thought about it. It was moving them. Leonard's saying, 'Yeah, that sounds good.'" Sounds good then, sounds good now. Sounds eternally good. But the idea of wrangling that sound in the studio was beyond Leonard's accomplishments. He'd recorded combos, but no groups as aggressive as this, and based on Muddy's sales, he didn't need to learn.

While sales were good, royalties were not forthcoming. "Muddy couldn't pay his car note," said Jimmy Rogers. "We used to hide his old car to keep the finance company from takin' it. He'd stay in it, send somebody in the store to get what he wanted. Then he'd come back over to my house and hide it in my garage. Chess would dodge him, say he's not in or something, 'cause Chess was scufflin' himself. But Muddy had to pay rent. He'd say, 'Damn! It's a wild-goose chase there with Chess.'"

To keep a roof over their heads, they began picking up outside sessions. Sunnyland Slim gathered Muddy, Little Walter, Baby Face Leroy Foster, and a few others on a session for the small label Tempo Tone. Poorly recorded, it's mostly piano with Walter singing. Jimmy Rogers, through backing Memphis Minnie in clubs, landed a session in 1949 for Regal Records. Everyone — Muddy, Walter, Big Crawford, the omnipresent Sunnyland Slim, and a drummer — pushed through the door with him. Walter grabbed the piano's mike, relegating Sunnyland to the background and letting his harp assume a lead sound, diving like a duck between the guitars. The whole band cut just one song, "Ludella," and the audio was again impaired by equipment limitations; it doesn't capture the band's full power, but it's an exciting early sketch.

By Muddy's two Aristocrat sessions in the summer of 1949, he was showing off remarkable slide prowess. His solo on "Canary Bird" opens with a frenetic, crazed wallop on the strings, then unwinds like a madness over several bars. With "Little Geneva," he introduced fans to his new girlfriend, Geneva Wade, who became Geneva Morganfield over the course of their nearly quarter of a century together, though never in the eyes of the county registrar. Born September 3, 1915, she was from Lexington, Mississippi, not too far from Rolling Fork. "I'd come across many, many women, but it seems like you know immediately when you find the one who's exactly fit for you," Muddy stated in a later as-told-to feature article syndicated to black newspapers. "When I met her, even though I was a recording success, there were still people who scorned my music. Geneva encouraged me to ignore them and fight for what I wanted to accomplish. I'll never be able to put in words the way I feel about her." She had two children when they met, Dennis and Charles, and Muddy raised them as his own. Muddy's granddaughter Cookie, reared by the couple, remembers hushed conversations about a baby girl who died in childbirth. "It was never discussed," she said. "But Geneva couldn't have children after that."

The power in the spare sound of the Aristocrat singles was reinforced by Muddy's songwriting. His third release, "Train Fare Home," cut to the homesickness that resided at the new urbanite's emotional core. Opening with plaintive slide notes, the electric guitar has a rich and intimate tone, softer on the strings than the keening sound of his first hit. Crawford's bass, inconspicuous, lends an appropriate heaviness to the rhythm. Muddy sings:

> *Blues and trouble just keep on worrying me*
> *Blues and trouble just keep on worrying me*
> *They bother me so bad, I just can't stay here, no peace.*
> *If I could get lucky and win my train fare home*
> *If I could get lucky and win my train fare home*
> *I believe I'll go back down in Clarksdale, little girl that's where I*
>   *belong.*
> *It seems so sad, child I wonder just how can it be*
> *It seems so sad, child I wonder just how can it be*
> *Everybody seems welcome in this old place but me.*

◇   ◇   ◇

Muddy had been on a couple trips out of town with Leonard to visit disc jockeys, and he knew their records were reaching beyond Chicago. Now Muddy called Mr. Anderson at KFFA in Helena, Arkansas, and arranged for a radio slot. In late September of 1949, before harvest time, he took Jimmy Rogers, Little Walter, and Baby Face Leroy for a long month in the Delta. They arranged time off their day jobs or quit them to fulfill an old fantasy — becoming the disembodied voice they had so admired when Sonny Boy began broadcasting. On KFFA, their sponsor was a Helena store, Katz Clothing. The hour, however, came as something of a surprise: six in the morning, every morning.

While Leonard may have been upset about temporarily losing his new main man, he appreciated the market Muddy's southern stint would build. "All the time that we were on that radio station, we were touring through the South," said Jimmy Rogers. "We played gigs till maybe one in the morning, then leave out of Mississippi and take the ferry over to Helena and go to bed. At five, you gotta be up getting ready to go to the studio. We were on from six till seven. It was rough.

"One morning there, Little Walter and myself, we overslept. We were staying one place and Muddy Waters was staying another. When he gets to the studio, he had Leroy Foster playing the drums, and they went in and was beating away with the guitar, his slide, and his drums. We had the radio on in the hotel we were staying in, and that's what woke me up. After they played this number the radio announcer said, 'Well Jimmy Rogers and Little Walter is somewhere sleeping it off. If they hear us, come on in.' Then I had to wake Walter up, we get dressed and go down to the studio. They had played about three or four tunes. And I was gonna sneak me a peek and Muddy was looking right in my face, man. So he beckoned for us to come on in, so between the commercial and the song we came in and he had set up all the equipment. We just jumped in and started working out. Yeah, it was a lot of fun."

"We did a couple of little gigs in Helena," said Muddy. "But as far as the radio would reach, people was callin' me, like over in Mississippi and in some parts of Arkansas. We were playing all them little towns — Clarksdale, Shelby, Cleveland, Boyle, all the little towns. People would call up the station and get a date on me. I got a lot of bookings like that."

The band played juke joints run by friends from Muddy's old days and gigs for strangers who heard them on the radio. They were featured at the grand opening of Clarksdale's New Roxy movie theater. Electric instruments were spreading in the South, but Muddy's ensemble sound was new. Even when they played acoustic in the unwired backwoods, the sensibility they brought to the old music was something to behold. Blues *bands,* four players creating one big sound, were not yet common.

Robert Morganfield, Muddy's half brother, saw him play at a little joint in Glen Allan, not far from Jug's Corner. "It was an eating place during the day, had a Piccolo [jukebox], and on the Piccolo was some of Muddy's songs, which was a favorite of the people. His band was two guitars, a drum, and harmonica. He had an electric guitar, stores had electricity. They had a huge crowd, bigger than the building."

And there was a command performance at Colonel Stovall's home. "When he came back through in 1949, he had him a van and a band. And they was having a party — Colonel Stovall — and Muddy came up to the house where the party was in the van with the band," said Myles Long. "And Muddy played there till late. Was about thirty people, everybody there knew him. Muddy had cut a lot of records. It was day when he left, around five the next morning. Muddy had a woman in there with him. Every time he'd come, he'd have a different woman with him."

"I couldn't leave until I got over there to play for [Colonel Stovall]," said Muddy. "I'm on my way to Helena, he said, 'You don't go nowhere.' He give us, oh, seven or eight dollars apiece and a whole good sip of whiskey. When I was there living, you couldn't make but a dollar and a half."

The band was back in Chicago by November 6 to participate in a promotion at the 708 Club. It had been exciting to get out of town, gratifying to return south a success, and invigorating to hear the old sounds played the old way. But now the band — the musical unit *as* a unit, working as one to convey the emotion and feeling of a solo blues artist — was wired, fired, and inspired, and totally fed up with being shut out of the Chess studio. In January of 1950, they fell into a warehouse for the tiny Parkway label to cut "Rollin' and Tumblin'," a victory whoop, a collision between the thrill of visiting a former life and the rush of resuming a contemporary one. Jimmy Rogers arrived late and is on only two of the eight tracks; these Parkway sessions were the first time that Muddy's club band was in the studio together. "Boll Weevil" includes the full band and is truly an ensemble piece, with no one person or instrument taking the lead. The lyrics are a variation on a field holler about the boll weevil's quick proliferation, but musically the statement is about eradication, if not of the farmer's pest then of the old-style Bluebird blues.

The standout track was recorded with just Muddy, Walter, and Baby Face Leroy. This "Rollin' and Tumblin'" (issued variously under Little Walter's and Baby Face Leroy's names) could easily have disintegrated into an overenthused party record. The song is little more than a harmonica, a bass drum in overdrive, an occasionally ferocious slide guitar, and the orgiastic humming of several grown men. The sounds are pugilistic and sexual. Someone yelps. Someone else responds. The randomness of the interjections is frightening, the rapid-fire drumming disorienting. Muddy's slide rings like loose spokes on an iron wheel, haywire. The harp is hypnotic. Chant and hum, chant and hum. Violence hangs everywhere, the sex heated and raw.

The lyric's tale of excitement and aftermath — "I roll and I tumble / I cry the whole night long / I woke up this morning baby / all I had was gone" — induces the musicians to lose themselves in the performance. The humming that was interspersed at the song's start dominates the latter half; words are too confining. People are sweating to make this music, submerged in their being, transcendent in their passion, gone. The sonic quality is awful, the song more powerful as a result, as if this wouldn't be allowed in a proper studio, needing a dark and surreptitious place to germinate.

Muddy's prominent presence, even if his name was not on the release, got Leonard Chess's attention — and ire. Not pleased at having his star artist help a rival, he promptly marched Muddy to Universal Studios and, with only Big Crawford, made him record another version of "Rollin' and Tumblin'." The Aristocrat version is exciting — Muddy's guitar playing is prominent and clear — but it does not approach the transcendence of Parkway's. Yet Aristocrat's dominance in the marketplace assured that theirs would kill the shelf life of Parkway's, and it did.

Two more songs were cut at Muddy's Aristocrat session, but not released for several months. These would be in the first batch of issues on a new label, formed when Leonard and Phil Chess bought out their partner. The B-side of Chess 1426 — the label took the owners' names — looked backward to Muddy's Mississippi roots, a version of the song Robert Johnson cut as "Walkin' Blues."

The A-side also had one eye back, but the other was looking at the future. Like farmers who experimented to improve their crops, Muddy dug up his roots, cupping the treasured dirt that clung, and set them in a new field. He hadn't hurried them. They acclimated. Over seven years he had become a Chicagoan. And now this would be the song to capture the young men overseas a decade later and, in the emerging days of rock and roll, it would name a magazine. They'd been singing "Catfish Blues" for years in the Delta, but it never sounded like "Rollin' Stone."

CHAPTER 7

ALL-STARS

1951–1952

M uddy Waters was nearly thirty-eight years old and entering the best years of his recording career. There in Chicago — which had become the Delta's second home, which had given new breath to the spirit of Harlem's Renaissance, which had factories burning 'round the clock — Muddy was about to help shape modern music.

Words were becoming a major Chicago export: the *Chicago Defender* had become the most influential black publication in the country. Elijah Muhammad, whose Muslim theology was changing the way many African Americans thought about their place in the world, moved his headquarters there. Novelist Richard Wright, after living there for a decade, wrote the classic *Black Boy*. But Muddy, in less than three minutes, struck in the gut, no eyeglasses or education required.

Lyrically, most of Muddy's songs were about sex — sex with someone else's wife, sex with someone else's girlfriend, sex and trouble. But it was always a trouble he survived, a scrape he escaped. Sex was sex, but sex also became an analogy for a kind of freedom, a freedom to serve himself, to damn the torpedoes, the shift supervisor, and the overseer's big gun. The sound of the songs reflected the newfound ebullience: Muddy, near the bottom of the socioeconomic ladder, corralled the sense of postwar possibility and excitement. The have-nots were finally having — not having much, but even a little was a lot. The muscle of his electric guitar and the force of his ensemble sound and the fierce assertiveness of his voice unleashed the exuberance of a people. There was cause for celebration, and Muddy was the vehicle.

Billboard, July 1950: "Leonard Chess busts right into the disk field with his first two records on his very own 'Chess' label. Real clickeroos. 'My Foolish Heart' by Gene Ammons in the number-one spot among the jazz and blues locations here [Chicago], and 'Rollin' Stone' by Muddy Waters getting gobs of orders from the Southland."

"Rollin' Stone" is a song about power, about rootless — and ruthless — independence. Muddy plays the electric guitar with all the force he's been brandishing in the noisy clubs, though completely unaccompanied, laying bare every flick of his thumb and pull of his forefinger. A quick couple bass notes establish the rhythm, then a loping third note. A few more to catch your balance, then the whole angular riff again. Its jaggedness draws all attention to his right hand, his long fingers, the creases on the skin, the shadows from his cotton picking, guitar picking calluses. The distortion is bone rattling: the sound of teeth chattering, or being smashed. It's the sound of industrialized, amplified, sex drive, overdrive power. He begins to sing: "I weesh," enunciating to rhyme with the next line, "I was a catfish." The sound is animalistic — predatory, after whatever comes his way:

> *Swimming in the ho-oh, deep blue sea.*
> *I would have all you good looking women feeshing*
> *Feeshing after me.*
> *Sure enough after me.*

Then the guitar says it one time, leaving us a moment to contemplate this bottom-feeder.

> *I went to my baby's house*
> *And I set down, o-oh, on her step.*
> *She said, "Come on in now, Muddy.*
> *You know my husband just now left."*
> *Sure enough he just now left.*

The guitar says it a couple times this verse, symmetry giving way to feeling. The riff saunters and scoots, a dog caught eating from another's bowl, caught sleeping in his master's bed, under his covers and all up in his sheets, sure enough where he's not supposed to be.

Well my mother told my father
Just before I was born
"I got a boy-child coming, gonna be
He's gonna be a rolling stone."
Sure enough, he's a rolling stone.

The guitar break is lightly picked, his bass notes punctuating this little dance on the high notes. It's not gleeful, but it's impudent, buying the husband a shot at the bar while still tasting his wife's lips.

Well I feel
Yes I feel
Baby like that low-down time ain't long.
I'm going to catch the first thing smoking
Back down to Rolling Fork.

And a parting ping from the high notes, dust settling where once was a man, escaped. The stealth is reflected in the menacing distortion, the craggy amplified sustain; Muddy is a thin snake that cuts a wide swath. There is much empty space in this performance, imbued with the power of a pause, of letting a note hang in the air, the anticipation of the next one. Muddy doesn't tell all. His pause asks us to fill the emptiness; it draws out our emotions, feelings, fears, compelling us to add meaning.

This monument to time and rhythm, this anthem to mobility, is a remarkable appreciation of the divisions and subdivisions of space, of patterns and how they change. And it was an auspicious announcement by a new label, especially when paired with Gene Ammons's solid but derivative interpretation of the standard "My Foolish Heart," which was released simultaneously. "Rollin' Stone" sold well and Muddy left his day job. Jimmy Rogers soon followed suit. Walter never needed what he couldn't get on Maxwell Street; he had no job to quit.

❖ ❖ ❖

In the summer of 1950, Leonard finally began expanding Muddy's sound. He wouldn't listen to reason or to the musical possibilities, but he'd heard the response to the renegade "Rollin' and Tumblin'." First he added Walter, and then finally Jimmy, who brought his first hit, "That's All Right," to his first Chess session. Over the coming year and a half, Jimmy recorded all his material at the end of Muddy's sessions, sometimes with Muddy and members of the band, but also with a group he put together for his own gigs. "Muddy was never a binding man or a selfish man," said Jimmy. "So when I would be playing with Muddy, naturally the audience would know my records and ask for me to play them, so I would step forward, within the show Muddy was doing, and take my numbers." Just as Big Bill and Sonny Boy had spawned his career, Muddy helped others, even if it ultimately meant losing their help. "I know when you make 'em a star they're gonna leave. But I can't hold the whole world by myself, they should get out there and do something."

After playing, Muddy, Jimmy, and Walter cruised the streets of Chicago's night, free from the day shift, a few little bottles along for the ride. The musicians analyzed the night's work, considered new musical possibilities, the Chicago competition, the Mississippi competition. In the driver's seat was Muddy's childhood friend Bo — Andrew Bolton, the backstage member of the band.

"Bo was from Stovall," said the Reverend Willie Morganfield, Muddy's cousin. "He was a fine person, he just didn't take anything. He was like a bodyguard for Muddy. And you just didn't bother Muddy if he was around. He was that kind of guy." When fans got too excited around Muddy, Bo would institute calm; when jealous women came at Muddy, Bo was a wall they couldn't bust through. "Bo was a nice boy, just couldn't read and write," said one of Muddy's later bandmates. "Wouldn't know his name in boxcar letters. He got his learning from just looking and looking."

Muddy and Bo shared responsibility for each other. Bo ran errands for Geneva, cooked pancakes for Geneva's sons at the kitchen stove, would later teach Cookie to drive. In the meantime, he kept his regular job. "I always remember Bo telling me that he got paid every week," said Muddy's granddaughter Cookie, "and therefore, if Muddy had a gig on Friday or Saturday, they were set because Bo would have money so Muddy could get his hair did."

"Seven nights a week, that's how my schedule ran," said Muddy. "And then Sunday afternoon we would do a matinee somewhere. I played out of town, but we could stay in the city and work seven nights a week." Weekends in Gary or as far away as Memphis were common. Muddy handled many of his own gigs, though Leonard helped, and so did Big Bill Hill, a disc jockey with his own Colt Management Company.

Days, Muddy stayed at home. He relaxed, recovering from the previous night, preparing to expend it all again that evening. Geneva would make him ice packs, which he'd wear across his forehead, lying in his bed or watching a baseball game on TV. The White Sox were his team, though he admired Brooklyn's Jackie Robinson, who had recently integrated Major League Baseball. He looked after Geneva's two boys. "My first memory of Muddy?" Charles, Muddy's younger stepson, said. "I was coming home from school, living on the West Side, and he was listening to his record with a fella that lived across the street. And when he would play down to different clubs, he would slick his hair back, have bangs the way black people used to wear their hair. When I got out of order, he'd put me over his lap and whip me with a belt, a big heavy thick belt. But I really didn't get that much out of order."

Muddy's classic lineup solidified with two new members, first in 1950, then in 1951. Drummer Elga Edmonds — that's his rarely used correct name; friends usually called him Elgin, like both the dependable clock company and the nearby city in Illinois (though other variations for his last name included Edwards, Edmonton, and Evans) — was born in the land of Lincoln and had a musical mind-set different from the Delta. "Elgin" was steady playing jazz gigs and was known throughout town for the book he kept; if you needed a drummer or any other musician, Elgin could help.

Muddy needed a drummer who knew to follow his singing and not to force turnarounds and changes just because standard convention called for it every eight or twelve bars. Elgin's timing was good, he liked brushes so he wasn't too loud, and if he lacked flair, flair was not short in Muddy's group. As a jazzman, Elgin was not thrilled about taking a blues gig, but they paid and jazz bookings were increasingly losing out; the blues was drawing better audiences in Chicago, building on the excitement of the new sound.

Despite their differing musical backgrounds, Elgin quickly found common ground with Muddy: cards, drinking, and food. "Elgin could eat," drummer Freddie Crutchfield recalled. "He was a pork eater, wouldn't eat no beef, nothing but pork. Ten dollars worth of pork chops, ten dollars worth of pork loin, nothing but pork. Pork, pork, pork, and all these sauces. He was a short guy but short and fat. He had a big round face, nice-looking guy, smiled a lot. He could talk and play cards. Him and Muddy and all of them, they'd be playing." A dependable drummer who played Casino was just right for this band.

When the fifth card player joined the band on piano in 1951, the template for the modern pop group was set. Otis Spann, a solid man who boxed in his youth and competed in semipro football, played the eighty-eights with fluidity, his left-hand rumble as agile as his right-hand tinkle. He could amble on the bottom and crash on the top — without getting in the way of the vocalist. Born on March 21, 1930, Spann was the child of musicians. His mother, Josephine Erby Spann, played guitar and recorded once with Memphis Minnie. His father, Frank Houston Spann, played piano and preached. Spann's mother died in the mid-1940s, and her teenaged son went to Chicago, where his father and an aunt resided. He plastered walls by day and got plastered by night, hanging in bars and sidling up to pianos. He befriended the smoky-voiced Big Maceo Merriweather, listening to his swinging bass hand entwine with Tampa Red's guitar; he keenly observed the rough-and-tumble piano style of Little Brother Montgomery and Sunnyland Slim. His boozy voice was early earned. Gin. Or anything alcoholic. It had little discernible effect on his behavior, and his playing was always superb, intricate, and relevant.

Spann had lost a gig and Jimmy knew he was "scufflin', sleepin' in cars. So I told him Muddy needed a piano player. He said, 'Yeah, man.' As long as he get him a few nickels and get him some whiskey and get a girl to look at him — that was Spann." Muddy was not eager for a piano, but Spann hounded him. They soon became such close friends that they called themselves brothers. Though they were not related by blood, their musical kinship, like their friendship, was of the closest kind.

"It made a big difference to bring him in because we had a full-bodied music. That piano really fill up things," said Muddy. "See, my blues is not as easy to play as most people think they are. I makes my blues in different numbers, sometimes thirteen, fifteen, fourteen, just the way I feel. Spann, that's the way he was. He don't care what kind of time you break, he can break it with you." And Otis Spann was happy to serve as the preeminent blues sideman; he fully appreciated the possibilities of playing backup, and leading a band would have interfered with his drinking.

Muddy, Jimmy, Walter, Elgin, and Spann were a solid unit for a year and a half. Muddy's classic group was not only powerful, they were also a good show; Spann, Jimmy, and Walter could step in to sing backup and also take the lead on their own songs, and Walter and Jimmy could double on the other's instrument. There was always something to watch. The piano had previously restrained Muddy's contemporary edge, but that was before he heard Otis Spann; the band would revolve around both men for the next two decades, fully two-thirds of Muddy's career. But while club patrons heard the sound of the future, Leonard (his sales indicating no need to change Muddy's sound) didn't, and it would be two years before Otis Spann appeared on a Muddy Waters recording.

Powered by the band's club success, Muddy cut several of his deepest amplified Delta blues over the next eight months: "Long Distance Call," "Honey Bee," "She Moves Me," "Still a Fool," and, first, "Louisiana Blues."

"All that stuff came to me real good," said Muddy. "I can remember that a lot of the records I have made, I first made those songs up during my workdays out on the farm." Muddy's wiry electric slide and Walter's acoustic harmonica entwine in this backwoods shuffle like Spanish moss on an oak. The rhythm evokes the banging of a tattered suitcase being pulled down a bumpy road. "Louisiana Blues," a slowed variation on the "Rollin' and Tumblin'" melody, secured

Muddy's introduction to a national audience by becoming his first top-ten blues hit.

With a hit, times got real good for the new blues stars. They picked up a regular night at Ada's Lounge and Chicken Shack, and three gigs weekly at Joe's Rendezvous Lounge. They played regular Sunday afternoon matinees at Silvio's, rushing over to Sam Evans's Ebony Lounge for a night gig, Sam hawking Muddy's talent on his daily radio show. (Muddy dedicated the flip side of "Louisiana Blues" to his patron, naming the instrumental the "Evans Shuffle.") Previous ads had announced him as "Young Muddy Waters," but with the release of "Louisiana Blues," they began trumpeting: "Blues Guitar King."

Muddy did not forget those he'd displaced. He gave his intermission spots to Big Bill Broonzy and tried to assist Tampa Red. "I was playing at the 708 Club on the South Side," said Muddy. "I tried to give Tampa a few dollars. He say, 'No, I don't need no charity.' That kinda embarrassed me. I thought I was doing something great."

"Long Distance Call" and "Honey Bee," from the same session, followed "Louisiana Blues" onto the charts — three top-ten hits within six months. "Long Distance Call" was a cheating song, but the perspective was Geneva's. Outside his home, even just blocks away, Muddy made no pretense of hiding his extramarital affairs. He openly courted young women, even while his young mistress *du jour* was in the club. Soul star Bobby Rush remembered he and Willie Mabon playing and three women getting in a fight over Muddy. "I instigated it just to get them fighting," said Rush. "Willie Mabon was playing the piano, his hands never stopped, he said, 'Let 'em fight, me and you will fuck 'em all.'"

The session on July 11, 1951, was one of the most amazing of Muddy's career. Walter, barely twenty-one and still dismissive of the world's slow turning, was at a creative peak this day, what Jimmy Rogers called "popping." This session, which produced "She Moves Me" and "Still a Fool," was later called Independence Day for the harmonica, but really it was Independence Day for Walter. Previously, he played his harp into a microphone that, like a vocal, went directly to the tape recorder. On this session, he plugged into an amplifier and had the engineer mike that instead. He could manipulate the amp and have that mediating sound recorded instead of his harp directly. The difference is night and day, akin to the change Muddy achieved on electric guitar. The harmonica was about to move from the country to the city. It was a revolution.

(The new route for Walter's microphone caused some complications. The studio amplifier — there was only one — had two inputs, and with Walter joining Muddy, he displaced Jimmy. Jimmy had very little but contempt for Leonard, so he may not have felt like giving his blood and guts that day; he sat out. But Walter was on a tear. He was heaving blood and guts.)

Leonard was on edge. Not one for changes, he was already made tense by the vocal echo chamber he'd just jury-rigged from a sewer pipe. Now Walter was seriously fucking with the sound. Something had to give, and it did after the first tune, when they were cutting "She Moves Me." "My drummer couldn't get that beat on 'She Moves Me,'" said Muddy. "My drummer wasn't doin' nothing, just *dum-chick dum,* but he couldn't hold it there to save his damn life, and Leonard Chess knew where it was, so Leonard told him, 'Get the fuck out of the way. I'll do that.'" Leonard liked the beat emphasized, appealing to the dance floor. ("You sure worked for your money," said Odie Payne, another Chess drummer. "[Leonard] had you playing so hard, I just didn't believe it. The drummer would be the loudest thing in there.") When Elgin could not deliver, Leonard burst from the studio glass and, as if on a dare, took the drumsticks from him.

Psychology has as much to do with record producing as does musical knowledge. If artists are trying too hard and have lost their natural feel, the producer deflects their attention, unleashing their innate artistry. A producer will set an artist on edge — if that discomfort will create great art. "Blues is nothing but the truth, truth that at one time or another in his lifetime the singer has felt," said Phil Chess. "Our job was to try to bring out points in his mind that he might have forgotten, to give him ideas, to get him to think about some things that were happening down in Rolling Fork, Mississippi, or wherever. It's actually like psychiatry, you try to talk to him for him to bring out the things himself."

Leonard was known as a particularly aggressive shrink. "Leonard calling people a motherfucker," said Jimmy Rogers, "that was just his way of saying good morning to blues musicians. At Chess if you didn't curse you wasn't recognized!" (Muddy was immediately comfortable with that; Colonel Stovall had been the same way.)

On "She Moves Me," Leonard pounded the bass drum to make the dead jump up and run. It reverberates through the years right to the listener's gut, like a heart that pounds when your crush enters the room. In response, Walter shapes his notes like a sculptor — elongating, eliding, quivering, and shaking. You can almost hear him figuring out how to play by listening to the sounds he's just made emanate from the amp. His notes float like crimson leaves that skip in the wind. "Oh man, I wished you could have seen Little Walter," Muddy said. "While you're recording, he be dashing all around you everywhere, changing harps, running all around the studio, but he never get in your way. He had ideas, put a lot of trick things in there, getting all different sounds. Aww, he was the greatest. He always had ideas." "She Moves Me" again put Muddy on *Billboard*'s top ten.

But they weren't done yet. Next, Walter put down his harp and plugged in Jimmy's guitar. The creative juices were spilling off him and Jimmy didn't want to slip in the puddle. Walter couldn't play a lot of guitar, but the bit he learned he mastered, and he throws his whole physical self into this song. "Still a Fool" is played with all the heaviness of Muddy's full band in the clubs, but with the band stripped away. No concessions are made, no accommodations for the pared-down instrumentation. Two guitars and a drum in 1951 can't get more electric than this; in Glen Allan, Mississippi, or broadcast live on the Delta's KFFA, this sound would have caused riots.

"Still a Fool," a paean to the outside woman, is a song as important for what it suggests as what it says. The guitar's burning distortion evokes an over-the-top madness, an uncontrollable desire beyond all reason, of fucking a woman between rows of cotton, then stepping one row over and having her sister. "They say she's no good," he sings, "but she's all right by me." Women were a matter of quantity over quality to Muddy, and "Still a Fool" is his best attempt to explain himself. Musically, the song revisits the "Rollin' Stone" riff. Leonard is still on the studio floor, banging the bass drum; the sweat has got to be soaking his shirt, pouring from his brow. Walter's bass notes are like a pulse: you can feel the beat as it approaches, as it rides through you, as it passes. Muddy picks the six strings, raw and visceral, a deep world of hard blues, ominous, horrific, his guitar in unison with his vocal, Walter attuned to Muddy's spatial and aural insights, dirty dancing around him. Moaning and humming reach for what words fail to say. There are four verses with no guitar break, nothing to diminish the onslaught; and slaughter is ultimately this music's subject.

"Still a Fool" hit the national top-ten charts in late November of 1951, and advertisements announced "King of Blues Muddy Waters and His Blues Boys." Playing a Chicago jazz club during an off night, they were drawing bigger crowds than the main attraction. "They even named it the Muddy Waters Blues," said Freddie Crutchfield. "When they were going to play the blues, most of the guys said, 'We're going to play the Muddy Waters Blues.'" He was becoming his own genre.

❖   ❖   ❖

Down in Memphis, meanwhile, just before "She Moves Me" was recorded, a middle-aged man named Chester Burnett walked through the doors of the Memphis Recording Service and recorded his first single for producer Sam Phillips, who had yet to start his Sun Records label and was instead selling and leasing his tracks. Leonard Chess bought Burnett's first recording and would later acquire the man's contract; Burnett recorded under a pseudonym, and his "Moaning at Midnight" was about to make Howlin' Wolf a star.

Like Muddy, Wolf embraced the Delta feel. His parents lived in Drew, Mississippi, which was near Charlie Patton's home, and Wolf learned directly from the seminal Delta artist. He roamed the Delta juke joints, picking up gigs and earning a reputation. He later got a radio show in West Memphis, where his trademark howl, a variation on the falsetto favored by Robert Johnson, Tommy Johnson, Muddy, and others, was broadcast far and wide. The burst in popularity of Muddy's electric blues band sound — "Long Distance Call" was on the charts just before Wolf made his first recordings and "Honey Bee" was rising — informed Wolf's music, whetted Sam Phillips's appetite, and answered Leonard's supplications for another star artist.

"When I heard him," said producer Sam Phillips, "I said, 'This is for me. This is where the soul of man never dies.' Then the Wolf came to the studio and he was about six foot six, with the biggest feet I've ever seen on a human being. Big Foot Chester is one name they used to call him. He would sit there with those feet planted wide apart, playing nothing but the French harp, and I tell you, the greatest sight you could see today would be Chester Burnett doing one of those sessions in my studio. God, what it would be worth to see the veins on his neck and, buddy, there was *nothing* on his mind but that song. He sang with his damn soul."

Also in May of 1951, at the same studio, B. B. King made his second recordings (his first had been three years earlier at a radio station). He'd left the Delta and become a prominent disc jockey in Memphis, where, seeking pointers, he met Muddy. "One of the things he told me then that I tell all the young musicians today: practice. He told me to be yourself, not to play for these people one way and these people another way, be they black or white. As great as I thought he was, he was very modest. I call him the godfather of the blues. He did more for the blues than most of us."

Change was in the air. Jackie Brenston had released "Rocket 88" in May of 1951, its beat presaging rock and roll. Alan Freed went on the radio in July of the same year, calling himself Moondog and featuring artists such as Muddy, Wolf, and Brenston; he popularized the term "rock and roll," and developed a white audience that liked the name. In Memphis, Dewey Phillips had, for three years, been playing these black artists back-to-back with whites, mixing bluegrass and blues, divining the feel beneath the rhythm and ignoring the industry's categorizations. One of his most dedicated fans was a young listener by the name of Elvis Presley.

When "Still a Fool" left the national charts, "She Moves Me" ascended in its place. The other big sellers were Howlin' Wolf's "How Many More Years," B. B. King's "Three O'Clock Blues," John Lee Hooker's "I'm in the Mood," and Lightnin' Hopkins's "Give Me Central 209." "At one time there was a wide gulf between the sophisticated big-city blues and rocking novelties waxed for the northern market, and the country or Delta blues that were popular in the southern regions," *Billboard* wrote in March of 1952. "Gradually the two forms intermingled and the country blues tune [is] now dressed up in arrangements palatable to both northern and southern tastes." Mainstream acceptance was first confirmed when major labels began jockeying for position. But it was the independents who better understood the business, and Chess Records, which had forged this new sound, was the leading independent. Establishing itself on Muddy's back and using the demand for his records to shoehorn more of its releases into the marketplace, Chess had the industry in check.

◇   ◇   ◇

The idea at the May 1952 session was to create an all-star band. Muddy had a marquee name, Jimmy had developed one, and if Little Walter could get a hit, they'd have a three-man front line. There'd been one session between "Still a Fool" and this one, at which Walter had failed to arrange for his own amp and had to play acoustically. This time, amps abounded, everyone was juiced. "We were sitting down [in the studio]," said Jimmy Rogers. "They would put a mike on the amp and a mike to the vocal. Sitting in a chair, we could see each other, and we'd play off each other in the studio, like we were on the stage. We would build it and then we would give a listen to the tape. Then we'd keep it running till we get the right sound we like." Warming up with their theme song, they caught Leonard's ear.

"At the time we called it the jam," said Jimmy. "We'd do it coming on stage and during intermission we'd do a couple of verses and take a break." Muddy or the others could address the audience, introduce band members or guests, make announcements, or generally clown around over a beat that would pique interest in the coming set, or make anyone think twice before hitting the door. ("If you couldn't play that song, you couldn't play harmonica," said Jimmy Rogers. "They'd sit there all night to hear it, and we'd have harps singing up there on the street all the next day trying to do it.") The jam that would become Little Walter's classic "Juke" had no name. The give and take of the groove let everyone stretch out, and they'd pass the solo around like a pint bottle among friends. Jimmy and Walter could push their progressive ideas, while Muddy rooted the song with his slide. It brought out the best in all of them, especially Walter, curling his notes through the amplifier — and gradually the band let him take command of the tune.

Feeding his trademark quiver through the amplifier took Walter to another realm. "All my best records, I made them with the amplifier," said Walter. "You can fill that harp with air. If you don't, it'll kill you. I can keep a whole lot of wind in that harp, I don't have to do nothing but navigate with it then."

Leonard leapt to the song. "He said, 'What's that?'" recalled Rogers. "He said, 'Play that again.'" It struck Leonard the way it struck Muddy's fans. "I could've had the song or Muddy, either one of us could have taken it," Rogers recalled. "But we wanted Walter on record as well. We were trying to make an all-star unit out of the deal. And Leonard went for it."

The harmonica kicks off the song with a short running riff, punctuated by a jazzy guitar strum; Jimmy's influence is strong. In the middle section, Walter blows the riff big and fat, *skronking* like a horn, then retracts, changing the harp's tone to the simpler country feel; he's making taffy of the instrument. "Juke" shuffles and glides, it rolls and cajoles, brings a smile to listeners' cake holes.

Among those who would end up smiling were the Three Deuces, a trio of kids still in their teens. Louis and Dave Myers had come to Chicago in the early 1930s, still kids and musically inclined. Playing a house party, they were introduced by some girls to a harmonica player their own age. "This kid was so small," said Dave Myers. "He sit in with us, he could play all that Muddy Waters kind of stuff, and we clicked real good." The kid's name was Junior Wells, and he and Little Walter would soon switch places.

While readying Muddy's next release, Leonard played an acetate of the instrumental in the Chess offices. The day was warm and he opened the door for a breeze. At the bus stop, a woman danced to the song. He played it again and she stayed, stamping her feet and doing the shimmy. There's no higher test market than the street, and the song was rushed to release on August 6, 1952. On tour in the South, the band was between sets in a Shreveport, Louisiana, club when the song came on. Walter, recognizing his own harp — no one else played like that — rushed to the jukebox, saw the call number being played, traced it on the menu, and found his song, now titled "Juke," by the band Little Walter and His Night Cats. The patrons played it several times in the course of the night, always dancing. Walter watched, listened, and set to ruminating. He phoned Chicago and spoke to his girlfriend, who told him the song was getting a big push on the radio from the major disc jockeys. *Billboard* also took immediate notice: "Little Walter flashes some nice harmonica work in fronting a fast instrumental. The Night Cats back him solidly."

Still in Shreveport, the band went to get new outfits. They'd left Chicago's cool summer unprepared for the swamps of Louisiana. "It was so hot down there that we got little stuff you could wear and rinse out, it'd be ready to go the next morning," said Jimmy. They bought seersucker suits, short-sleeved eggshell-colored shirts, and beige pants. The tailor told them everything would be ready that afternoon. "When we got back to the hotel, oh man, the girl up at the desk said, 'The little guy with the checkered hat on' — that was Walter — 'he said for you to take care of his amplifier. He had a terrific nosebleed, he's goin' back to Chicago.'"

It was true that Walter suffered nosebleeds, and the band worried for him. For the moment, however, there was nothing to do but book a saxophone player to finish the tour — no other harmonica player could command Walter's big sounds. "We made out with him," Rogers continued. "Picked stuff you could kind of handle pretty good to make the nights."

Back in Chicago, Walter immediately powwowed with the Myers

brothers. He was ready to walk away from Muddy's old-fashioned slow stuff, jumping to bring in the new. When Muddy's band returned, they found their harmonica player in good health, if a little bigheaded (he tried to get his share of the pay for the gigs he'd missed), and they resumed playing — for about a week. When Walter jumped from Muddy, Junior Wells jumped toward him. Muddy never missed a beat, and Walter gained one: the East Coast–based Shaw Artists Corporation, booking and promotion, opened a Chicago office and signed Little Walter to a five-year contract; the Aces became the Jukes. Walter's debut single spent twenty weeks on the R&B charts, where it hit number one.

◇ ◇ ◇

Junior Wells was grounded in the country and the city, traveling between his father in Arkansas and his mother in Chicago. As a child, he remembered visiting a place where he saw the people dancing wildly, heard the hollering, and told his mother he liked that blues joint. "She said, 'You wasn't at no blues joint, you was at a sanctified church.'"

Born December 9, 1934, he was raised in Marion, Arkansas, near West Memphis — a barefoot kid getting dusty with another future blues star, Junior Parker, the two jamming on twenty-five-cent Marine Band harmonicas they bought at the Rexall drugstore. Junior and guitarist Earl Hooker learned to please crowds on the Chicago streetcar, riding "from one end of the line to the other, takin' up a little change from it. We had a guy played the tub with that rope broom for a bass."

As a teenager, Junior tried to buy a harmonica at a Chicago pawn shop, but didn't have enough money. He took the instrument anyway and tried to raise the difference by playing for spare change outside the store. The salesman had him arrested and Wells was taken to court. Muddy signed papers as his guardian. "The judge asked me to play the harp," Wells said, "and when I did, the judge gave the salesman the fifty cents and hollered, 'Case dismissed.'" Then Muddy took him outside and popped him on the forehead.

"I raised Junior Wells from about a kid," said Muddy. "He was in my band. He was too young to be in the clubs. I had to be his guardian. I had to keep him down because first thing you know he'd wanna fight!" Spann worked Junior into the band, as he would for each successive member, harpist or otherwise, teaching the songs and Muddy's way of toying with the beat. But harmonica players were especially close to Spann's heart. "I figure the harmonica is the mother of the band," he said. "Once you get a good harp lead off, you in business." Junior was young and quick. Within a month of joining, he was in the studio. He was seventeen and played amplified harmonica like he'd been playing it for all his seventeen years. His screaming harp on "Standing Around Crying" is every bit as exciting as Walter's playing. Junior pushes the amplified harmonica till it wails in pain, then pulls it softly to make it purr. There was soon an irony to the title. Out one weekend with the band, Junior scored a girl and took her back to the hotel after the gig. Muddy's date had fallen through, and not long after Junior entered his room, Muddy knocked on his door. When Junior opened it, Muddy barged in, threw Junior out, and locked the door. Junior was left standing around crying.

Still, ladies would come and go, and Junior had no reason to leave the band. When the army drafted him on his eighteenth birthday, he ignored the notice and was carted off by military police. He went AWOL and had to be hauled back once again. "Every time we'd look around," said Muddy, "two of them big mens there looking for him, and he used to run 'tween their legs."

About three months after Little Walter's defection, Jimmy signed his own deal with the Shaw agency. His singles weren't as popular as Walter's or Muddy's, but as bandleader he was better paid. Steadfastly holding to his formula, Leonard tried to keep the core band together in the studio. "We was running in and out of town," said Jimmy Rogers, "and sometimes we'd meet up in Chicago and get a chance to cut a session." He continued to make club appearances with Muddy; when his own gigs conflicted, guitarist Eddie Taylor filled his role.

Muddy's selflessness made his sidemen more satisfied while in his band, but it encouraged their solo aspirations, creating an instability in his lineup: someone was always thinking about going out on his own. Those who wanted independence would want it anyway, and Muddy, despite the repercussions and the personal pain, remained undeterred in sharing the spotlight with his band members. "If somebody can shine, put the light on them, let them shine. It makes a better feeling in the band. [But] it goes hard when you get used to one sound and you have to go and get into another one," said Muddy. "See, we knew one another's thing, and we had no trouble out of that. When it fell apart, it went hard."

CHAPTER 8

HOOCHIE COOCHIE MAN

1953–1955

S ong publishing is a complex and slippery aspect of the music business, but it is where most of the money is made. Artists recording songs written by others must pay a copyright fee — for the right to copy the song — to the publishing company, and the publisher pays the writer. (So, when rock bands began covering songs Muddy wrote, there was money for Muddy and his publisher — though the publisher kept it until a lawsuit in the late 1970s. When the Rolling Stones would record a Muddy Waters hit written by Willie Dixon, however, no matter how much they copied Muddy's arrangement, the publishing payment would go only to Dixon, as writer, and his publisher — not to the original performer.)

Muddy's phenomenal success caught the attention of Gene Goodman in New York, brother of Benny Goodman and a wealthy song publisher. He approached the Chess brothers and was surprised — and no doubt pleased — to learn that they had not been publishing their music. "They came to my father," said Leonard's son Marshall, "asking, 'Who is handling your stuff internationally? Who is hustling your stuff with cover records? What about performance fees?' We didn't know about any of this, and my father thought it was better to have half of something than all of nothing." The Chesses and Gene Goodman incorporated the publishing company Arc Music (an acronym for Aristocrat Record Corporation) on August 1, 1953. Leonard bought his first Cadillac soon after.

For Muddy and his band, not much changed immediately. When a session was completed, the artists lined up to sign or make their mark on union forms and receive their forty-one dollars in session money (double for the bandleader). Songwriters signed a publishing form, a penny per sale — to be paid later. The band's money, their living money, still came from gigs, which paid better when records sold better.

Songwriting styles were changing. Jimmy's solo success and Walter's popularity indicated the record-buying audience was developing a taste for a more urban sound. Sensing that his star artist was on the verge of becoming the new "shoe stump" music, Leonard finally acceded to Otis Spann's presence in the studio. In late 1953, they cut the two-sided classic "Mad Love (I Want You to Love Me)," which featured a stop-time rhythm (several unified beats followed by a pause for the vocalist), and "Blow Wind Blow." On a club's jukebox, either side of this one would have filled the dance floor. Walter howls like a tornado siren. Spann's playing is perfect — nearly invisible. He rolls under lyrics, anticipates the guitar riff, hides beneath it, bolsters the harp: he is generally all over the place without seeming to be much of anywhere. "People were wondering at first because I have short fingers," Spann once said. "They figured I couldn't physically play that much piano. But you can make a piano do what you want it to do. The piano is made for both hands." (James Cotton, who would join Muddy's band the following year, remembers Spann having the webbing between the base of his fingers surgically opened.)

The piano's percussiveness created a need for more complex time-keeping; the fills were no longer so obvious. Walter's drummer, Fred Below, came up with the Myers brothers, and both Muddy and Leonard had watched him. Like Elgin, he came from a jazz background, but his youth lent an innovation to his style. "I put a little swing into [the blues] to fill out the rest of the measure. I was dropping bombs in there to make phrases, sort of punctuating the end of the sentence. Sometimes I have to phrase to pick up the harp player and then push him into another phrase, because he's breathing in and breathing out." Below, who'd met the Aces through Elgin, began replacing him on Muddy's recordings.

"Mad Love" proved a test run for Muddy's biggest hit. "Hoochie Coochie Man" was brought to Muddy by Willie Dixon, a bassist and songwriter who would, within a year, bring Muddy other songs that solidified his hoochie coochie image: "Just Make Love to Me," "I'm Ready," and "Natural Born Lover." Dixon untied, sorted, and repackaged songs, lyrics, toasts, children's games, and an array of quips and boasts, putting his name on them and creating a catalog of his own, which other, more dynamic singers made into hits. He drew heavily from traditional sources, the era of recording and mass distribution codifying what had been a loose and communal pool of melodies and lyrics. "There was quite a few people around singing the blues," he said. "But most of 'em was singing all sad blues. Muddy was giving his blues a little pep, and I began trying to think of things in a peppier form." And of course a hit benefited its author as much as its performer (sometimes more so).

One night Dixon came to Muddy's Zanzibar gig. The band was drinking and working up the audience, until the heat and sweat was too much, the cigarette smoke too thick, and they needed a break. Women and fans always surrounded Muddy after each set, and he greeted them politely, though his eye was on making his way to the bathroom. Dixon saw him enter and followed him in. "I was in the men's house when Willie Dixon came in and said he had a song he wanted me to look at," recalled Muddy. Dixon's reputation was established among Chicago's blues musicians, and Muddy knew he'd recently got tight with the Chess brothers. Dixon ran down the song's lyrics; if he had them on paper, they did Muddy no good. Muddy liked what he heard. (One commercial aspect of the song was that it had a chorus; many of Muddy's tunes, even hits such as "Long Distance Call," were built on a feeling and did not even have a refrain.) "He got his guitar," said Dixon, "we was standing up in there playing and practicing." Willie Dixon was a behemoth of a man, over six feet tall and topping three hundred pounds. It was hard to find a space he didn't crowd, the cramped quarters of the Zanzibar men's room no exception. One imagines Muddy leaning against the hand sink, his feet beneath Dixon's girth, his head back against the mirror; Dixon, for whom this moment is initially more important — he's doing the pitching — with his head at an odd angle around the hand towel dispenser, pressing back his weight to give Muddy's guitar room. He told Muddy, "Well, just get a little rhythm pattern y' know. You can do the same thing over again, and keep the words in your mind." Muddy reached back to "Mad Love" (still selling rapidly) and reworked the stop-time rhythm. It fit.

Suddenly the noise in the Zanzibar seemed to die away, the stench of old beer and gin-soaked floorboards dissipated, the smoke dispersed. Muddy's only concern was to gather the band and hit the stage before he forgot the lyrics. He told Dixon he was going to open the set with it. Muddy gave the band the key, played them the pattern. *Repeat it, here's where it changes, listen at me* — they knew how to back him. After several rounds of exchange, they fell in together. "Oh man, the people went crazy," said Muddy. Dixon remembered, "He done it two or three times that night." Like his grandaddy with an ox and whip, Muddy could bring a song down.

Lyrically, "Hoochie Coochie Man" was perfectly suited to the stop-time rhythm. The first pause follows quickly on the song's opening notes, a tease for the listener — what was that? And when it happens again, it's like a game, the band messing with the audience. Walter's playing may be his most saxophone-like ever. Muddy Waters sings sex and seduction, boasting and braying, preening like a peacock, voodoo imagery enhancing his masculine power:

I got a black cat bone
I got a mojo too
I got a John the Conquerer root
I got to mess with you
I'm gonna make you girls
Lead me by my hand
Then the world'll know
I'm the Hoochie Coochie Man

The club's reaction was only the first indication of the song's potential. *Billboard* couldn't keep quiet about it: "We're so happy with Muddy Waters on Chess 1560 doing 'Hoochy Coochy [*sic*] Man' that we can't help mention it again for a top spot. Action gets better every week." Leonard went south to bolster sales, and Phil told the magazine that the record had sold an astounding four thousand copies in a single week. It became Muddy's top-selling single and spent three months in the national charts, where it rose to number three.

The success of "Hoochie Coochie Man" affirmed what each previous single had hinted at and what the steady gigging was trying to make plain: Muddy's music had become his career. He was ready to buy a house and went to Leonard for advice. Marshall Chess, Leonard's son, remembers the meeting. "I was out in the yard and this big car pulled up. The guy walks out and he had on this chartreuse green, bright, bright green suit. I looked down and his shoes were made of cow skin, the fur was on them, black and white and brown. And I looked up and he had one of those five-inch hat brims. I was young enough that I didn't know this was a blues artist, it could have been a spaceship landed. He got out, totally secure, walked over to me, looked down, and said, 'You must be Chess's son. Is your daddy home?' They sat at the kitchen table talking, drinking coffee. Muddy would come to him for advice, but we didn't have many artists come to the house. My father was never there. He was a workaholic. He took me on the road with him when I was ten because he wanted to be with me, but the only way was to go to work."

After the discussion, Leonard sent Mud to his personal lawyer. With Geneva and her two kids, Muddy moved up the social ladder from the West Side to the South Side, settling in for a twenty-year stay at 4339 South Lake Park. Little Walter, Jimmy Rogers, and Otis Spann helped them move furniture. ("I represented Muddy when he bought his home on the South Side," said attorney Nate Notkin. "I said, 'Muddy, you want this to be in joint tenancy with your wife?' I explained what that meant, and he said, 'You might as well put her on but you know, she's my common law wife.' Well, there hasn't been common law in Illinois since 1920.")

The West Side, according to one Chicago aphorism, is the South Side's basement. The West Side was managed by absentee aldermen;

those who had the power to bring improvements were not around to even know what was needed. The South Side was controlled by its own. The South Side was the headquarters for Congressman William Dawson, the New Deal Democrat who'd been serving in Washington since 1942, at one time the sole black face in Congress. He controlled three of Chicago's fifty wards, accumulating two more as the city's black population expanded; his machine made blacks an essential cog in Chicago's political machine. He arranged a line of credit for the *Chicago Defender,* controlled the NAACP, evicted white organized crime from the South Side so blacks could run it, and then represented these policy kings in his legal practice. He was tight with Chicago's leading black ministers. He walked the South Side on a wooden leg, and what he surveyed was his.

Across town, another power was rising: six years after becoming the Cook County clerk, Richard Daley would, in 1956, become mayor of Chicago. Daley envisioned a political machine embraced by a cross section of Chicago's constituents, and he addressed the black population's housing squeeze early on, establishing tens of thousands of low-income housing opportunities, each with a majestic beginning — the Henry Horner Homes, Stateway Gardens, Cabrini-Green, the Robert Taylor Homes — but deteriorating quickly, as control was wrested from the city by local gangs. In addition to the resulting territorial fights, black expansion south was still being fought by whites who, despite the Supreme Court's mandating integration in February of 1954, could not imagine an integrated neighborhood; the National Guard had recently been called to quell a riot over housing. Nonetheless, this was a move toward possibilities, toward promise and enterprise.

"On the West Side," said Muddy's stepson Charles, "we was living in a two-bedroom apartment. We had a commode, and we had to wash our face and hands in a little small pan. But after 'Hoochie Coochie Man' we accumulated enough money and paid down on this building here. Hell yeah, hell yeah, Leonard Chess would come to this house and eat!"

Muddy's house on South Lake Park was built at the turn of the century, when the flourish and detail of the Victorian era had passed, but the era of cookie-cutter homes was yet to come. A large picture window filled the spacious, paneled living room with afternoon light — and heat; the blinds stayed drawn till evening, when the air cooled and a light breeze cracked the heaviness. He had a sizable dining room, separate bedrooms for stepsons Charles and Dennis, and a big kitchen where he and Geneva could cook. Muddy, accustomed to a sideline, quickly installed tenants upstairs and in the basement, adding three more kitchen areas. Otis Spann claimed the basement's front room, Bo took the middle room, and Muddy put his uncle from Stovall, Joe Grant, in the back of the basement. The band rehearsed in the basement's common room. Band members and a valet rented the upstairs apartments.

Several people could comfortably gather on the front stoop, and with a crowd spilling down the steps, maybe a chair or two at the bottom, there was room enough for two poker tables of people to gather, jive, and talk trash. A wino in the neighborhood went up and down the streets with a cat on a leash and a recorder in his pocket, stepping around the tamale, watermelon, and Sno-Kone vendors. He'd have a trail of kids behind him, Muddy would see him, say, "Hit it," and he'd blow a work song that sent the kids dancing. There was a patio in the backyard, and Muddy put two wrought-iron flamingoes on his front door, his name inverted beneath: Waters Muddy. He was confirmed middle class.

His new home was just blocks from where the new Chess offices were about to be established, South Cottage Grove at Forty-seventh. Muddy could easily stop in to see Leonard, shake hands with him — and shake him down for some of his own money. "My old man would go there almost every day to talk to Leonard," said Charles, "and I used to come with him. He'd drive here, he wasn't the walking type, hell no." He'd done his walking in Mississippi.

Muddy asked Geneva to quit her factory job. As Charles told it, "My old man said, 'I don't want you to work no more.' She was a damn good cook. He used to tell people that if it wasn't for her, he wouldn't have been the same man, because he was real young and wild. That old saying, it takes a good woman behind a successful man." Even Muddy's stepson reaped the benefits. "A lot of kids knew who my father was, singing blues," said Charles, "and they kind of put me on a pedestal." Not coincidentally, Muddy's move brought Leola Spain south; her child with Muddy, Azelene, was almost twenty. "He really, really respected my grandmother," Cookie said. "He often would ask her her opinion, and as he got financially stable, he would buy her groceries or send money, do extra things for the grandkids."

One of Muddy's first guests in the home was Howlin' Wolf, who had continued to have hits with Chess and finally left the Memphis area for Chicago in early 1954. Proud, he drove his own car north. He'd intended to stay in a hotel until he found his way around, but Muddy, happy to help a friend of Leonard's, insisted he stay with him. Staying with Muddy would have impressed Wolf, even if Muddy weren't in his new home. Wolf hadn't begun to record until he was forty, in 1951, well after Muddy was established in the blues world. One of the early tracks he'd cut was a version of Muddy's "Streamline Woman." Muddy brought Wolf to the Zanzibar, to Silvio's, the 708 Club; Leonard was family, so introducing Wolf was a family favor. Soon, wherever Muddy had a night (which was almost every night), Wolf had another one. He was quickly as popular in Chicago as established local stars such as Willie Mabon and Elmore James.

"I had Chicago sewed up in my hand, it didn't bother me," said Muddy. But Wolf was the jealous type, not sharing his spotlight with his sidemen, not letting his sidemen associate with Muddy's band. Though Muddy and Wolf sometimes downplayed it — Muddy more often than Wolf — genuine dissension existed between them. Wolf soon made his home on the West Side, and their conflict somewhat mirrored the undercurrent of jealousy between the two neighborhoods. The jealousy fueled a rivalry; one time, each proving his fame, Muddy and Wolf began burning money, seeing who would stop lighting bills first. "I know the peoples thought we hated one another," Muddy recalled, "but we didn't. But Wolf wanted to be the best and I wasn't gonna let him come up here and take over the best."

Evidence of their conflict, perhaps even its source, was found in the minutes of a meeting from Chicago's African American branch of the American Federation of Musicians. Howlin' Wolf filed a grievance against Muddy in early 1955, claiming Muddy, who was booked regularly at Silvio's, had subcontracted Wolf to cover for him while he went on the road in April. Having accepted, Wolf turned down two offers for gigs. When he found that Silvio's had someone else booked for April, Wolf went to the union claiming Muddy should pay him for the gigs he was going to miss. Muddy told the union board that his contract with Silvio had expired so he'd have had no reason to subcontract. Mr. Silvio Corroza was called to testify, and he supported Muddy's account; the board found in Muddy's favor.

Tension between the stars stayed high, and Willie Dixon found himself caught between the two of them, each suspecting that Dixon was giving his better material to the other. To entice them, he would sometimes introduce a song to one by saying he'd written it for the other. "I'd say this is a song for Muddy if I wanted Wolf to do it. He would be glad to get in on it by him thinking it was somebody else's, especially Muddy's."

❖ ❖ ❖

In March, both "Hoochie Coochie Man" and Little Walter's "You're So Fine" were national top sellers. While the success was on them, Muddy and the crew stepped up the pace of recording. On a Tuesday in April, Muddy and the recording band — Jimmy, Walter, Spann, Below, and Dixon — cut "Just Make Love to Me" (also known by its refrain, "I Just Want to Make Love to You"), which entered the top five on the national charts. It was his third record on the charts in half a year, the ninth of his career.

Muddy was at the height of his powers. His music harnessed the potency, the virility, in the blues. His lyrics did not flinch in their openness about sex. His braggadocio was salacious and uninhibited. This was not the image of America that Eisenhower's White House nor television's *I Love Lucy* suggested. The boldness of his delivery and the lyrics to his songs disquieted the establishment, frightened them. The blues were considered obscene, making Muddy the boogie-man incarnate.

Rolling with success, Leonard moved the Chess offices a block and a half north, into a former automobile garage behind a stationery store at 4750 South Cottage Grove. There was space enough for administrative offices, warehousing and shipping, and a recording studio that doubled as rehearsal space. The sonic fidelity at the new place, however, was not as high as at Universal; the early sides recorded there are thinner, with less bottom. Sales, however, were unaffected. As a gesture of his appreciation to Muddy, Leonard presented him with a new car, a 1954 Oldsmobile 98. It was yellow and green, to match his outfits.

Like his furnish on the plantation, Muddy's labor actually paid for this car and for all the future "gifts" and cars. At the time, he was probably unaware he'd bought the car himself, but in later years he'd know. And even then he didn't stop taking them. "Chess would get him a car every two years," said Jimmy. "Chess would take it off his royalties. Wolf wouldn't do that. Wolf would get his own car." Wolf wanted to see the money, but Muddy embraced the sense of mutual dependence engendered by the gift, even if it was false; it felt like he had some kind of power or protection at the company.

Muddy promptly had opportunity to test his new ride. He was booked that month in Newark, New Jersey, for Alan Freed's first big East Coast Moondog Coronation Ball. Muddy shared the bill with, among others, the Clovers, a vocal group, and Sam Butera's jumping swing combo. *Billboard* stated, "Most of the attendees at the Newark clambake were youngsters from fifteen to twenty, and about twenty percent of the crowd was made up of white youngsters." The mixed audience was Muddy's first hint that he could reach a whole new record-buying public.

In June of 1954, Muddy was the subject of a two-page spread in the national glossy magazine *Hue*. Directed at an African American audience, the short article emphasized Muddy's sex appeal, creating the nickname "Dreamy Eyes" for him. He was a star.

◇ ◇ ◇

The night before "I Just Want to Make Love to You" debuted on the national charts — where it would stay all summer and into the fall — Muddy was playing the Zanzibar. About to leave for another tour, including a show before 30,000 people at another Alan Freed concert in Cleveland, Muddy was breaking in harmonica player Henry Strong, known to everyone as "Pot" because of his fondness for reefer. The band's music was locking together in intimate and complex ways. Muddy played the bottleneck slide less frequently; often, he'd set his guitar aside and just sing, working the stage like a star, growling into the mike, shaking and rolling his head to create different vocal sounds, breaking into a nimble dance or thrusting his hips with the beat, evoking squeals of delight from the ladies in the house.

As if to commemorate their success, the band paused during the evening to pose for a photograph. Jimmy and Muddy bookend the group, supporting it since its start. Muddy is playing a Les Paul Standard, a solid body guitar he'd recently purchased. Its tone is dense, prototypically electric. Jimmy is playing a Gibson L-5, a hollow body with a woodier, more natural sound. Spann is seated in the center, the new foundation; he plays an upright piano. Pot is on harmonica, twenty-five years old, seated in front, greeting his burgeoning career. A sign painter, Henry Armstrong, who helped the band make posters in return for being allowed to sit in at gigs, was there on maracas, trolling for the band's leftover women. Elgin, still playing on gigs even if he'd lost his studio spot, stands at the rear, a distance between him and the group. They're all wearing suits, long neckties, with neatly combed, close-cropped hair. The world may not be theirs, but this club is, this one and every one on the big road that lies open before them.

After the gig, Jimmy gave Pot a ride home. Pot lived in an apartment building about two blocks from Muddy's house, at 4554 South Greenwood, run by Leonard's father. Leonard could arrange digs there, and he'd helped Pot get a place, like he'd helped Wolf get a transitional place there, and Wolf's guitarists Jody Williams and Hubert Sumlin, and a girlfriend of Muddy's whom Muddy was visiting after that night's gig. "So I got him home," said Jimmy Rogers. "Muddy was in the building. He wasn't living there but he was there. Muddy say he heard the rumbling going on. He heard somebody call, 'Muddy!' He went to the door, looked out, Pot was in the lobby on the marble floor. He was bleeding like hell, didn't have no shirt on. Muddy got a quilt and wrapped him up in it and carried him out there and put him in his car. Didn't have time to wait for no ambulance to come and get him." Juanita, Pot's wife, had been in the club that night, mad too, because she'd seen Pot speaking with his other woman. Muddy wheeled to the hospital, but Pot was graveyard dead before they arrived. Juanita's knife had penetrated his lungs. He was still wearing his gig pants.

The band was booked solid and needed a harp. Walter had made the instrument essential to any popular band. "Saxophone players were starving, piano players weren't working at all," said Billy Boy Arnold, then a rising harp player. "At that time you couldn't get a job without a harmonica player." Jimmy Rogers contacted Little George Smith, six foot two and lanky, who had been sitting in at various clubs, jamming with the Aces and Otis Rush. Rogers was recruiting personnel rather than Muddy, because Jimmy continued to hang out in clubs, visit Maxwell Street, and jam with musicians. Muddy, with women coming at him, preferred to diddle rather than fiddle. "Muddy, man he didn't hardly know what Maxwell Street was at that time," said Jimmy. "He didn't know nothing about no musicians and places that we would go to. He'd go out to some woman's house or take one to a hotel or something. That's where Muddy was."

The band returned in August, resuming their club gigs without missing a beat. It would be their final stint at the Zanzibar, which closed after eight years in 1954. On the first of September, they cut their first session at the new Chess studios, yielding their next hit, "I'm Ready." Harmonica player Willie Foster, who occasionally accompanied Muddy on the road in 1954, went to Muddy's house one Friday at the start of a weekend jaunt. Willie Dixon answered the door while Muddy was in the bathroom shaving. Foster recounts Muddy sticking his lathered face out the door, asking: "'Are you ready?' and I said, 'Ready as anybody can be.' Muddy went back in the bathroom to wipe the shaving cream off his face. Then he came back out and said [to Dixon], 'Willie, are you thinking about what I'm thinking about? Let's make a song out of it.' We sat up there, I don't know how long, trying to figure out what to put on it, you know. It took [Dixon] three days, I think, to finish it out."

"Willie Dixon got credit for being a writer on a lot of songs he just played a part in," said Jimmy Rogers. "But he made him some money that way. I had enough edge on him there not to let him hook me up that way, but Muddy went for it."

The drums on "I'm Ready" pound with a furor, one of Fred Below's finest moments. Walter plays a wondrous chromatic harp solo, holding notes twice the duration expected, then jiggling on down while Jimmy's guitar supports him with a fancy dance. (The standard harp is like the white keys on a piano, but the chromatic includes the black; there's a valve, activated with the thumb, that makes the chromatic notes an inherent part of the instrument. It can be played in any key at any time. It puts more color, an extra flex, in Walter's wailing; the tone is different, more robust in a way.) Muddy sings with the force of a boxer; he's not standing still enough to play guitar. "Muddy swings out. Lyrics are pretty potent and Waters's delivery is Grade A," wrote *Cash Box,* an industry trade journal, reserving their heaviest jive for the band. "Beat is solid and ork-ing is torrid." That autumn, while the band was out on tour (at three months, their longest yet, including sixteen one-nighters with Little Walter, tearing up Texas like a tornado), "I'm Ready" hit *Billboard*'s charts, rising to number four over a nine-week stay.

The popularity of blues was crossing over to white audiences, opening up an incomparably large market. "It is becoming increasingly apparent these days that rhythm and blues is no longer restricted wholly to a Negro audience," stated *Billboard* in an article titled "Pop Music Rides R&B Tidal Wave." The story tells of a jukebox operator who "does a terrific business selling used jukebox records to [white] neighborhood kids. [He] claims the first items they ask for are numbers by such artists as Muddy Waters, Willie Mabon, and Ruth Brown." Muddy was ready as anybody could be, but even that wasn't enough for what was coming over the hill.

◇ ◇ ◇

Harmonica player James Cotton was in West Memphis, Arkansas, finishing a Friday's work hauling gravel when a man approached, said, "I'm Muddy Waters." Cotton, who'd recently released a single called "Cotton Crop Blues," had never seen a picture of Muddy Waters and had no expectations of meeting him. He looked at the stranger, tapped the vanishing half-pint of Echo Springs in his back pocket, and said, "That's nice. I'm Jesus Christ."

Then Muddy's driver came forward. It was James Triplett, who had grown up with Cotton. Years had passed, and Triplett told of his move north, hanging out on the South Side of Chicago, and his recent employment with Muddy Waters.

Jesus Christ, it was Muddy Waters.

Muddy had been heading north from Florida when the harp position opened. "I had done got Junior back in the band, but he was running from the Army. We had a date in Memphis and James Triplett, he say he knowed a boy could play real good over to West Memphis." "Cotton Crop Blues" spoke directly to Muddy Waters when Sun Records released it six months earlier, Cotton's lyrics resonating deep within his being: "Raising a good cotton crop is just like a lucky man shooting dice / Work all the summer to make your cotton, fall comes it still ain't no price." Pat Hare's ultradistorted guitar played low-down blues that swung like striptease accompaniment. Hare, who'd known Cotton more than half his life, would soon follow Cotton into Muddy's band.

Cotton remembered, "We worked the Hippodrome on Beale Street Saturday night, that Sunday we played the state line of Arkansas and Missouri, and that Monday we was in Chicago. I moved in on the second floor."

Elgin and his wife lived in the upstairs rear, Triplett was in front with his girlfriend and her two children. He was driver, bodyguard, woman wrangler, and general factotum. He was tall and slight, dressed like the knives he carried — sharp; he kept his fingernails polished and left the fisticuffs to others. The ladies called him "Killer" and so did the men.

Cotton paid Muddy twelve dollars and fifty cents a week for a room. "Paid it whether we was in town or on the road. No food with it, but by me knowing Triplett good as I did, I could cook in his kitchen anytime I wanted." He was sent to the fabric shop at the corner of Halsted and Maxwell Street and fitted for two uniforms from the same bolts of cloth as the band. "Muddy paid for it and I started paying him back." Cotton was in the music business and back on a furnish.

Cotton was a car man (he wrote one verse of "Rocket 88"), and Muddy liked that. While Bo was off chasing tail in Flint, Michigan, Cotton took to driving Muddy around Chicago at night. They'd talk about Sonny Boy II — Cotton (born near Tunica, Mississippi, July 1, 1935) was nine when he became Sonny Boy's protege, covering the door while Sonny Boy played, covering the stage when Sonny Boy drank. They'd talk about Wolf — Cotton had recorded with Wolf at Sun. And they talked about the record biz — the Sun label was Memphis's version of Chess and had released some heavy blues records. "It started because I was a pretty good driver," said Cotton. "When Muddy would drink, I didn't have anybody to go home to and if he wanted to stay out two days, I'd hang right with him. We'd just ride and drink gin. Muddy would never buy no more than a half-pint at a time. The guy at Forty-third and Drexel knowed him. Was a drugstore, hotel, whiskey store all in one. The store part was open all night, selling cookies and cold drinks. Muddy would come in, signal the guy with one finger, and the guy would slip him one. We also knowed a bootlegger right up the street from Muddy's house. He didn't make his own, but you could go after hours and get it. Muddy would go on these drinking sprees and he'd do a couple days — a half a pint at a time."

As if filling Walter's shoes was not intimidating enough, Cotton was promptly put on his toes. Jimmy Rogers picked up Cotton's harp, said, "Let me show you something," and dazzled him with his own playing. "Muddy sitting there," said Cotton, "he [Muddy] grabbed it, played 'Baby Please Don't Go.'" Cotton played like Sonny Boy — straight notes — where Walter made the harp swing. When Cotton asked Walter how he did it, Walter turned his back and demonstrated. "It hurt me so bad I never asked him again. Spann was sitting there and Spann said, 'Come on, Bro Cotton, I'll show you.' He played triplets on the piano and I started playing them on the harmonica. Spann learnt me how to play with Muddy. We were so close on him, we knew what he could and couldn't say. Like, Muddy lisped and couldn't say 'trouble.' Spann would say, 'Watch him on the third verse, he's gonna jump time.' We knew how to catch the man."

Spann coached Cotton during the day, and they caroused at night. "Me and Spann used to go all over Chicago together. Muddy'd get off the gig and go his way, we'd go our way to other clubs. Chicago never closes if you know the right places. Spann had been there for years, and he knew all the places. We drank so much Seagram's gin till I sat in the theater one Sunday evening on Forty-third Street, and I could smell it coming through my skin, Seagram's gin and grapefruit juice."

Gigs were still plentiful. A night would have three or four sets, sometimes six. The band would play the first one themselves, warming up the house, passing the spotlight, each member singing and soloing on his favorite songs of the day — some blues, but also their treatments of popular songs, from ballads such as "Misty" to the more rocking Lloyd Price numbers. When it was star time, Jimmy Rogers would hype the audience; if he wasn't on the show, Spann would take it; if Spann was too drunk, Cotton emceed. The audience would put their hands together, *all the way from Chicago's South Side, Chess Records's most famous recording artist, do you feel like going home? Are you ready? The Hoochie Coochie Man himself, Muddy Mississippi Waters.* The band would launch into "I'm Ready," their rhythm as crisp as the creases in Muddy's tailored suit. Heading toward the microphone, he acknowledged the audience with a nod of his head, acknowledged the band with the rhythmic tapping of his foot. As he'd lean into the mike, he'd bend his right arm at the elbow — your maître d' for the evening, fine blues our specialty — and snap his fingers. The night's special: nourishment for the soul.

Top pay on the road was around five hundred dollars, though usually closer to three hundred — from which the whole band had to be paid, plus drivers, gas, and wear on the tires. Band members earned between twenty-five and thirty-five dollars each working night; they paid their own travel expenses and food. (The penurious sax player Bob Hadley carried a hot plate and often finished other people's meals.) They stayed in all-black hotels, costing between ten and fifteen dollars a night, sometimes less. "Rooms was cheap," Cotton said, "and girls was plentiful."

Cotton usually drove the station wagon. "In our car, Spann's sitting in the front seat with me, snoring," said Cotton. "Bob Hadley, sax player, would be sitting behind me, asleep most of the time, and Elgin would be sitting on the other side, eating carrots all night, like a rabbit, so he could stay awake. He was a good company keeper." The station wagon carried the gear — the suitcases filled Muddy's capacious trunk.

Muddy was a friend to his band members, but he was also their boss. After a show, he'd have a drink, maybe a bite to eat, discuss what needed discussing, and then return to his hotel room, where the door closed on him and his road wife. Jimmy Rogers, as bandleader and disciplinarian, also distanced himself. Reefer was not allowed; tardiness to the bandstand or to the departing vehicles was not tolerated. Uniforms had to match. "One night," Cotton recalled, "the dry cleaner had took the handkerchief out of my pocket and forgot to put it back. Jimmy Rogers fined me. They were that strict. They wanted a band and they had one." How great the distance traveled from Stovall. Posing for John Work's camera, Muddy did not ask Son Sims to pull up his right sock to match his left. Now he had an assistant to observe such matters.

Though Spann served many of the duties of bandleader, he had no interest in officially assuming such a position. "Spann didn't care nothing about being the bandleader," said Cotton. "He didn't want to have to stay sober."

Harvest time was always wild in the South. Money was flowing, and a loose audience pushed the band. There might be long drives between gigs; there might be difficulty finding a hotel that would accept cash from black patrons; there might be a bar owner who didn't want to pay, or who wanted to flip a coin for double or nothing; or there might be a particularly good party after the show, where there was a piano, and whores, and whiskey, and Spann got to drive the eighty-eight keys like a Cadillac on the open road.

In Tuscaloosa, on a tour without a road wife, the whole band got thrown into jail. The trouble started, Cotton recounted, when "this guy bought us all this corn whiskey." Everyone went on a bender. At some point, Muddy hid his money, then shacked up with the hotel maid. When he awoke, he accused her of stealing and went at her with one of her buckets. The cops came. A frantic call to Leonard Chess resulted in the appearance of a Tuscaloosa lawyer, who finally wrangled Muddy's release. "I seen Muddy slap his girlfriend or something like that, but that was very very uncommon," Cotton said. "To go out and grab the hotel maid like that, that was uncommon too."

The South was where racism held strongest, but the South was also home. After a gig in Georgia, the band hit the highway. "I was driving the station wagon, following Muddy," said Cotton. "We pulled into Rolling Fork. I thought, 'This is Muddy's hometown.' He just went right through the little town, took us about five seconds, on out to his father's house. He was driving a big white Cadillac. We got in about five or six o'clock in the morning, old man Morganfield came out there and looked" — Cotton furrowed his face in imitation of Ollie's look — "looked again, then said, 'That's my son.' Him and Muddy hugged one another. I enjoyed seeing them do that.

"Muddy's daddy was a bit taller than he was, but you could see that Morganfield resemblance, and I guess from him working the field, he looked a little bit harder than Muddy did. They lived in a farmhouse, Muddy's father and his sister [Luella McNeil], and if it rained, it rained right in on you. Muddy went in and went to bed. There wasn't no entertainment but a big ole persimmon tree in the front yard. I cut some wood, I got Muddy's car and wanted to go into town, the old man went with me. He showed me little stores and stuff, which there wasn't much to show. We got some ribs, started a barbecue in the yard. I asked him could he play the guitar, I'll never forget that, and he pointed to Muddy, said, 'No, that boy!' He was proud."

❖ ❖ ❖

At home, the South Side house stayed rocking. Phones ringing, meats frying, and greens boiling, the TV broadcasting a baseball game with the volume high or no volume at all, sometimes a shoot-'em-up ("Somebody with a gun shootin' at one another," Muddy said, "I can watch that all day"). Muddy, if he wasn't going anywhere, stayed in cotton pajamas or a black T-shirt and black boxers. And always there was music. Spann, when he wasn't seated at the Lake Park Liquors bar, was playing the day away, making up songs in the basement, Cotton always ready to jam, Elgin nearby, Jimmy Rogers stopping in.

The basement was Muddy's musical epicenter, though he was rarely down there. He kept musical instruments leaning against the wall, some album covers tacked above them. Whenever a song didn't go right on a gig, the band would regroup in the basement the next day and Spann would go over it with them. The rehearsal room was long and hexagonal, with light from the one small window blocked by the large gas meter. The informality provided a comfortable place to let ideas germinate, though Muddy's participation lent a new meaning to "sleeping on it." He usually stayed upstairs, and if he heard something he liked, he'd holler down. When Muddy would actually come down, according to Cotton, "We knew that the next day or the day after we'd go into the recording studio. He'd be done learnt the songs because me and Spann would sing them. Spann was the master, but Muddy would take the credit. Spann didn't care. Spann was a whiskey-drinking piano player. His interest was playing."

Geneva made the place a home. She liked flowers and plants and painted the house with light, bright colors. She appreciated the step up the ladder, and as she could afford it, she purchased new furniture, French provincial for the living room. The bedroom she shared with Muddy was wallpapered with a calm yellow, a small pattern repeated on it. A clean house, a pretty house, was important to her; to battle the detritus from the constant flow of people, she covered the new chairs and sofas in firm, bubbled plastic. Drunk guests and rambunctious kids could spill what they would.

"I went to Muddy's house to take a record to Spann," Billy Boy Arnold remembered. "Muddy's house was well furnished and real comfortable. He was wearing a nice beautiful robe and pajamas and they were looking at the ball game. Muddy's wife had some steaks big as your forearm, and gravy. Cotton came in the back door and went in the skillet or pot and got one out of there, started eating it."

"You could always go raid her pots," remembered Jimmy Lee Morris, a Delta guitarist who joined Muddy's band as a bass player. "She'd see Mud going in the kitchen. 'Don't eat up all my goddamn food.'"

"The house was beautiful," said James Cotton. "Being around Geneva was a pleasure. She was a good cook, a very nice lady. I used to bring her home some Old Grandaddy. We all used to bring her a bottle." Either because of her preference for bourbon brands, or because of the way she mothered Muddy's band, Geneva came to be called — by most everyone, including Muddy — "Grandma." (Muddy, at the time, was referring to himself as the "Old Man," and that name also stuck.)

When Muddy wasn't working, and between dates, he was a homebody. He liked to fix a big bowl of black walnut ice cream, pour a grape Nehi over it, and make a soup. "He'd lay in the bed all day and look at TV," said Cookie, Muddy's granddaughter who moved into the house before she was three years old. "And he'd eat ice cream. Sometimes he'd go on the front porch, but usually he'd be cooking or just be cooling out in his bedroom. When he was there."

The phone rang all the time, and Geneva, who took care of the business around the house, knew not all those soft, cooing voices could be calling her husband about booking clubs. "They got along okay but it was a lot of friction because of outside women," said Cookie. "He might be home five days and three days were good and then someone might call or he'd stay out all night."

"I defended him in a number of paternity cases, probably four or five," attorney Nate Notkin remembers, "and I never lost one. We always proved that the woman had other contacts." In the mid-1950s, "the woman" — Muddy's outside wife — was named Mildred.

Muddy was around forty, she was about twenty. She had the nickname "Bubba" and was unable to get enough of her man. Around
long enough to have a child with Muddy — nicknamed Poppa because he looked like Mud — Bubba's spot was eventually taken by
Dorothy.

Dorothy was a dancer, good looking and young, worked as a
waitress on the West Side. "Kind of drove the old man crazy," Cotton
said. "She was attractive, it wasn't hard for her to get a man. Muddy
was kind of jealous." To keep better tabs on her, Muddy got her a
South Side apartment around the corner from his house. Cotton
drove Muddy there after work one night, and she wasn't in. They sat
inside drinking gin. When their bottles were empty, they went back
for new ones. And still no Dorothy. "Muddy's pissed off now," said
Cotton. "Just as we walked out the door, there was someone who
drove past in a Studebaker, and the lady in the passenger seat ducked
down. Muddy said, 'There they go.' Muddy had a brand-new Chevro-
let station wagon, red and white. Had about ten miles on it. We took
off behind the car, Muddy driving. I don't think the other guy knew
the neighborhood, and we were so close up on him, the guy hit a post.
Muddy run into the back of him. The guy jumped out running,
Muddy told me to catch him. I knocked him down, brought him
back. Muddy said, 'Hey, this is the wrong people.' The woman in the
car wasn't Dorothy. The guy was white, must have been scared out of
his mind. Antifreeze and stuff was running out of Muddy's brand-
new car. Muddy said, 'Let's get away from here.' We jumped in the
car, left them there." Ah, home sweet home.

⋄   ⋄   ⋄

"Only a few artists," *Billboard* wrote in 1955, "such as Muddy Waters,
Dinah Washington, Memphis Slim, and B. B. King have what is
known in pop stores as a standby market — that group which will
buy an artist rather than the tune." Muddy was also the focus of a
feature article syndicated to black newspapers around the country;
it told the story of his career in his own words. In May of that
year, Muddy cut his tenth top-ten hit. "Mannish Boy" was a slightly

modified version of a tune he'd heard a new Chess artist named Bo
Diddley performing for Leonard at an audition. "We were playing
and Little Walter came in and Muddy came in," said Billy Boy
Arnold, Bo Diddley's harmonica player. "Muddy was always coming
to Leonard for one thing or another. Muddy wanted to take 'I'm a
Man.' He heard it and he figured, 'This guy is nothing, give me that
song.'"

"Bo Diddley, he was tracking me down with my beat when he
made 'I'm a Man,'" said Muddy. "That's from 'Hoochie Coochie
Man.' Then I got on it with 'Mannish Boy' and just drove him out of
my way."

"Mannish Boy," like "Hoochie Coochie Man," was built on Muddy's
sexual persona, the song's growling tone perfectly suited to Muddy's
declamatory delivery. "No matter what you do, some things come out
all different, just your own. It's like singing. Your face, and what
you're doing on your face, will change the tone of your voice. That's
where my tone is." "Mannish Boy" is a facial workout. Pulling his
cheeks so tight his eyes squint, rocking from his knees to give his
throat an extra vibrato, wagging his head side to side like a dog shaking off the wet — against the stop-time accompaniment — Muddy
sounds like a man possessed, a dog that meows, a cat that barks. He
quivers and shivers, all sex; he grunts and swaggers, all school-yard
boast; he moans and hums, cocky in his triumph. As he sings, girls
squeal with delight, a party he can handle:

> *Sittin' on the outside, just me and my mate*
> *I made the moon come up two hours late.*
> *Isn't that a man?*
> *I spell "M," "A" child, "N."*
> *That represent man.*
> *No "B," "O" child, "Y."*
> *That spell mannish boy.*
> *I'm a man.*
> *I'm a full-grown man.*
> *I'm a man.*

I'm a rolling stone.
I'm a man.
I'm a full-grown man.

But even a full-grown man was going to have trouble standing up
to the force about to be unleashed.

CHAPTER 9

THE BLUES HAD A BABY

1955–1958

In Chicago after a gig at the Palladium, a large room, in the spring of 1955, Muddy was greeting the after-show lingerers and late-night drinkers. One wiry kid wormed his way to the crowd's front. He'd come up from St. Louis, where his band played all Muddy's tunes. And with good reason: "He was my favorite singer," Chuck Berry later acknowledged.

"Chuck wanted to get onto Chess," Jimmy Rogers remembered. "Chess was the big thing for blues at that time. I told him to check with Muddy, that he could probably work out something." Not only did Muddy Waters establish Chess as the label that young black artists aspired to, he also helped them get there. "Yeah, see Leonard Chess. Yeah, Chess Records over on Forty-seventh and Cottage," Muddy told the young fan.

At Chess, Chuck Berry auditioned his homemade demo of a song called "Ida Red," soon to be recast as "Maybellene." "Maybellene" was a white country song performed with black musical accents. Inverting Elvis Presley, whose regional success would explode into national prominence the following year, Chuck was a black man playing white-inflected music with black accents. Leonard was skeptical. "Chess didn't like no rock and roll for himself," said Jimmy Rogers. "He was hung up on blues, because that was his meal ticket at the time."

"When I came down there the next morning," said Muddy, "Leonard didn't understand what 'Maybellene' was. [I said] 'You better record that, that's something new here.'" Leonard listened to Muddy.

Chuck Berry recorded "Maybellene" at his first session for Chess in May of 1955, three days before Muddy cut "Mannish Boy." Muddy's early Aristocrat singles had been released over Leonard Chess's objections, and they became his bread and butter. But still, after a decade immersed in the business, his ears highly tuned, Leonard Chess listened to Chuck Berry, silver on a silver platter, and the big record man could not hear it. But by now he trusted those around him, and he took a chance.

It would prove to be a brilliant gamble. Blues fans had grown up with Muddy Waters, coalesced around his music, and now their younger siblings and children wanted a say, a voice of their own. In 1940, there had been three million farms in the South; over the next three decades, that number plummeted by nearly two-thirds. Share-croppers, which had numbered more than half a million, vanished — were no longer even a category in *Historical Statistics of the United States* by the end of the 1950s. The Illinois Central Railroad would soon cease its passenger service between Mississippi and Chicago. In 1955, when the new sound was breaking out, Rosa Parks refused to move to the back of the bus. Art and society reflected each other, inspired each other. A bridge had been crossed, and it was now time to cross another. The blues — Muddy's electric blues — had become a new music, a rebel music, until it became the established sound from which a new one could be born. The blues had a baby, and they named it rock and roll.

The blues remained Leonard's bread and butter, though not his gravy. He knew his average blues single would sell twenty to fifty thousand pieces, enough to assure business as usual, enough to finance risks with new material. "Fuck the hits," Leonard often said. "Give me thirty thousand on every record." But with Chuck Berry, it was hard not to lose all restraint. "The big beat, cars, and young love," said Leonard Chess. "It was a trend and we jumped on it." Chuck Berry was awarded *Billboard*'s Triple Crown for "Maybellene," "his towering hit," number one on all three of their R&B charts: retail, jukebox, and disc jockey play. "Roll Over Beethoven" and "Brown-Eyed Handsome Man" came out in 1956, followed by regular chart appearances over the next two years, usually in the top twenty.

Flush, in the fall of 1956, Chess again moved its offices and studios, this time to Record Row, 2120 South Michigan Avenue. This studio was built from scratch, using the latest technology — a new studio for a new sound. But even with Berry's profits, business was a struggle. Rock and roll was a risk and foreign to Leonard's ears; he was not long from his first heart attack.

"The stuff that really started him," Jimmy Rogers said of Leonard Chess, "he pushed it aside. And that happened to be Muddy Waters, myself, and Sunnyland Slim, Wolf, Eddie Boyd, Willie Mabon, Bobby Lester and the Moonglows, and a bunch of fellows. Chess, he got away from the blues."

"Rock and roll kind of took over there for a while," said James Cotton. "There was weekends that we couldn't get jobs." The music left them, literally, out in the cold. "Me and Muddy would get in the station wagon and drive around and listen to rock and roll. We wouldn't go in the clubs, just listen to what's going on. Lloyd Price was happening, 'Ain't It a Shame,' 'Heartbreak Hotel' by Elvis Presley." Sensing desperate times as the road gigs dwindled, Muddy left the local booking agencies and in August of 1955 signed with New York–based Shaw Artists, which had been booking Walter for three years. They kept him busy as "Trouble No More" and "Sugar Sweet" climbed the national charts, but it was definitely feeling like the party was over.

⬥　⬥　⬥

Sometimes they're called hits for a reason: Chuck's struck Muddy hard. Like Muddy's blues had done to swing a decade earlier, the new sound was antiquating him, intimidating Muddy so much that in 1956 he simply stopped playing guitar. He'd stroll onto the stage and sing — the star — and didn't resume playing until his first trip overseas, nearly two years later. Along with the guitar, Muddy also gave up much of his stage time. Around Chicago, instead of coming out after the first couple songs of each set, he came out only for the last few. While the band played, Muddy entertained from a table, granting audiences to his fans, shilling drinks for the clubs.

His first replacement was Cotton's guitarist, Auburn "Pat" Hare, who, for almost a decade (until his temper led him to a life sentence in jail), remained a steady component in the band. Hare had the manic volatility of a street prophet, and favored a dirty, grungy sound. Playing with Wolf as a teen, he took potshots at him with live bullets, sending the huge man scurrying over a log pile. Wolf advised Hare's parents to beat the lad, but he didn't consider letting go of the kid's guitar sound. Hare was in Houston with Junior Parker and Bobby "Blue" Bland when Muddy found him. Leonard welcomed him into the studio. At his first session, Hare shared guitar parts with Jimmy Rogers, and in addition to the classic "All Aboard," they cut "Forty Days and Forty Nights," which broke the top ten during its six weeks on the charts. Hare's crunching power chords rippled with distortion that was well suited for blues in the rock and roll explosion.

But still rock ruled. The blues gigs weren't paying anything like they had, and in 1956 Jimmy Rogers finally quit Muddy, no hard feelings, it just wasn't happening for him anymore. He'd stick it out a couple more years with Leonard, then join Wolf for sessions and some gigs, but by 1961 the new sounds got the better of him and he retired from music for a civilian career. The way that fashions change, that's the way music changes. Jimmy Rogers, despite so many hits so recently, was unable to make the transition.

Looking to replace Rogers, Muddy's ears stopped at Wolf's band. Wolf could be a volcano and word was out that his guitarist, Hubert Sumlin, was recently lava burned. Muddy bedecked Bo in diamonds and jewelry, loaded his pockets with cash, and sent him to the Zanzibar, enticing Hubert by tripling his pay. It was diamonds over coals any day, and Hubert went. "Man," said Hubert without the slightest sarcasm, "I cried a-a-a-all the way over there." Taking Hubert Sumlin was like taking Wolf's gizzards.

Hubert played on his first session shortly after joining, cutting "Don't Go No Further," Muddy's last top-ten hit for two years. With Hare and Sumlin replacing Muddy and Jimmy, the sound was quite different: no slide guitar, not much Mississippi Delta, and a huge bed of distortion. Replacing the Mississippi night, which had lingered in the shadows of even Muddy's most urban work, was the blue glow of television's cathode rays, the teen beats emanating from variety shows such as Ed Sullivan's and Milton Berle's.

Sumlin stayed with Muddy about seven months. "What got to me was being on the road," he said. In November of 1956, when harvest money was flowing in the South, Muddy set out for an extended tour. Hubert showed up with his guitar, amp, and a little hanging bag. "Mud asked me, 'Is that all you got, just that one suit? You know we gonna be away about forty days?' I'm going, 'What the . . . This man ain't told me nothing about forty days.' . . . We did so much driving, I got the hemorrhoids so bad I couldn't sit down. They brought me feather pillows that I had to sit on!"

For half of this southern tour, they were billed with a singer named Ann Cole, who also had a following throughout the South. Muddy's band backed her, learning her songs as the tour progressed. There was one that particularly impressed Muddy, and upon returning to Chicago, on the first of December, he promptly hit the studio. Cole's version of "Got My Mojo Working" comes out of doo-wop, but Muddy turns around the rhythm to give it more driving force. And though he changed only a few of the words, Muddy's version credits himself as songwriter. Cole also recorded her version after the tour; it is credited to Preston Foster, the original author. A lawsuit between Foster and Chess was settled out of court, with the stipulation that Foster receive future credit; he sometimes does.

From the "Mojo" session, the band went to play the 708 Club. Muddy mingled with the audience, sipped from a fifth of Old Grand Dad, sat with a young girl. He didn't get on the stage until the last two numbers before intermission. Sumlin was tired, dejected, and angry. He steadied himself on the bandstand's electric fan and, either because he was full of fire or because of a faulty circuit, he got jolted by a mighty shock. "So I told Muddy I couldn't play out the night. He got mad at me, called me all kinds of things, and raised his foot to kick me. I grabbed him. Here come Spann with a chain, gonna whip me about Muddy. I had a hold of Muddy, and every time Spann tried to get me with that chain, he hit Muddy. I said, 'Man, when you get right, I'll turn him loose.'"

Sumlin phoned Wolf from the club. "I said, 'Hey man, that's it.

Whoever you got in there, they got to go. I'm coming back.' He said, 'No problem.' After the gig, Wolf met us at Muddy's house. He told Muddy, 'Next time you do that, man, I'll kill you over him.' Muddy didn't speak to me for a year, but we finally come back to being friends. Things were never right between him and Wolf, though. Those two were just like the McCoys, man!"

❖ ❖ ❖

To keep up with rock and roll's rhythms, the drums had to change. Elgin Edmonds had managed moving from jazz to blues, but when Chuck Berry changed blues, Elgin couldn't keep up. Muddy fired him many times, but he never found a replacement and always hired Elgin back.

In 1957, drummer Francis Clay was living in New York and touring with Gene Ammons. Ammons got busted for heroin in Chicago that winter and Clay was stranded. Muddy was booked for a week in Cleveland, nearly halfway home, and Clay caught a ride. They arrived without time to rehearse. "I found out playing down-home blues was not as simple as I thought," said Clay. He had performed in church and at circuses, behind vaudeville and with country and western groups, could do bird and animal imitations, but he couldn't get a handle when it came to Muddy's stuff. "You need four separate minds to play the drums anyway, but this was so simple, I couldn't get it." Muddy took Clay's sticks and demonstrated the beat.

Dancers may not have heard the musical chaos that first night, but one listener did: Elgin Edmonds. "He showed up," said Clay, "sat in the lobby. I felt sorry for the cat. It was pathetic." Clay's week stretched to four years.

Like the man he replaced, and unlike his new band mates, Clay was born in the North (Rock Island, Illinois, November 15, 1923). He'd earned his reputation around Chicago before moving east, and he maintained his contacts there through heavy touring. Freddie Crutchfield stopped by Muddy's gig to see Elgin and was in for a surprise. "I saw Clay and he was playing the blues real great with Muddy. I said, 'Clay!'" Freddie raised his voice to a squeaky high question mark. "'Whachou doing playing blues?' I always thought Clay was one of the greatest jazz drummers in Chicago." Indeed Clay was Mr. Bebop, the jazz man.

"We quit touring in January [1958]," Muddy said. "We got tired of it. We'd been on the road for five straight years, staying at home with our families about two months out of the year, so we decided we gonna cool it, gonna get work around Chicago and be at home with our families. The blues are so popular we can work six, seven nights just around Chicago."

While there's truth in it, Muddy's emphasis on the local gigs was a deflection from the loss of national jobs to rock and roll. But not touring meant getting local in a big way. Smitty's Corner was in the heart of the South Side, Thirty-fifth and Indiana, a corner property and somewhat larger than the other venues; its spaciousness made the diminishing jazz crowds feel all the more paltry. Owner O'Brien Smith "thought he'd try blues for a couple weeks and we stayed there about four years," said Clay. "Soon as we started, the place was packed. There were two lines, one two blocks long on Thirty-fifth Street, and one two blocks long down Indiana."

Smitty's was less of a shoebox than many of Chicago's other blues clubs. The stage — there was a stage — was elevated a couple feet. A bar ran down one whole side of the club, and the floor was filled with tables and chairs; there was little room for dancing. Muddy still played no guitar and did little singing, but the crowds continued to come.

In 1958, Muddy's brother Robert visited and, with Bo driving a Crown Victoria Cadillac, rode with Muddy to another regular gig he maintained, midweek at the F&J Lounge in Gary, Indiana. "Muddy played till past midnight, and then we headed back to Chicago," said Robert. "I thought we were going home to get some sleep, but he pulled into Smitty's Corner and at that hour of the morning they were waiting for him to arrive. He was there till daylight. We got home, he went to breakfast and I went to bed."

On Sundays at Smitty's, Muddy hosted a matinee show. The band played the first couple numbers, then began calling up guests, and players rotated on and off the stage. "If you was good enough, you could get up and play," said Willie Smith, a drummer who jammed there and later joined the band. "The music didn't ever stop, it would just steady turn over."

Like his girlfriends. When Dorothy found out Muddy was stepping out on her, she dropped into his gig at Ruby's Show Lounge — like a ton of bricks. She broke every window in the band's station wagon (she even broke the side-view mirror), which she had no trouble finding; on the side was painted "Muddy Waters and his Hoochie Coochie Boys."

When Muddy arrived, he and Dorothy got to fighting and James Triplett stepped in to break it up. The cops thought the men were doubling up on the lady and threw them both in jail. The band used that night's pay to bail them out. Muddy hid the station wagon so Geneva wouldn't see it but the *Chicago Defender* ran a photograph of the car the next morning. Muddy dispatched Cotton to buy every copy on the corner. "Here come a little lady walking down the street," said Cotton, "rang the doorbell. Muddy opened the door. She said, 'Is Mrs. Morganfield here?' Muddy said, 'Hey, Grandma, someone wants to see you.' The woman had the paper folded up under her arm. When Grandma got to the door, the lady said, 'I just want to show you what a rotten motherfucker you got,' and handed her the paper. And I left the house then, I got out the door."

"I sometimes thought Geneva saw Muddy less than anybody," said Mary Austin, a teenager he'd met in Florida who, when she accepted Muddy's invitation to move to Chicago, was installed on a cot in his daughter Azelene's West Side apartment. "I was nineteen," Austin recalled, "his daughter was in her midtwenties, and she began calling me Little Mama. She opened her arms to this little country girl and we really got along. She was jet black and pretty, looked like her daddy. Her boyfriend was J. B. Cooper, a good-looking guy, light skinned. They both dressed real well. One of the first things 'Lene told me, and she kept telling me over and over, was not to use drugs." While Mary's relationship with Muddy's daughter blossomed, hers with Muddy did not. Muddy rarely came around, and when he did it was usually to fight with Azelene. If Mary was too green to city ways to see what was going on, Muddy read the situation between his daughter and Cooper both for what it was and what it would become; Cooper had hooked Azelene on heroin and was pimping her.

"Right away Azelene and Johnny B. took me to this tavern in Jewtown," Mary continued, "and that was our spot. We went there every day. Later I realized that J. B. was working her out of there." Mary enrolled in a nursing school soon after her arrival. "Muddy was very jealous. When I would go out, if anyone would ask for a dance, he would come off the stage and it was a problem." Muddy rarely allowed her to attend his Chicago gigs, though he did take her on the road. When she needed to reach Muddy, she left a message for him at the Chess offices. "He'd told them I could reach him there. Muddy told me he was married, but he told me his wife was very ill."

When Muddy came by and Azelene was out, he and Mary made love on the cot. "Azelene was a lot like Muddy, very fiery. She looked just like him. One morning he came in there from a gig, I was sleeping in that folding cot — that cot was the only thing he ever gave me, he never gave me any money or helped with the rent — and he picked it up and tossed me and that bed, and Azelene jumped on his back. She was all over him. I carry a scar on my head from holding Muddy back from hitting her one time, she threw a plate at him and it got me. It wasn't that I wanted to live with him because once I got to Chicago I found out who Muddy was, and after I got pregnant, I really found out. When I told him I was pregnant, I don't think Muddy believed that the child was his son until after he was born. And then he couldn't say he wasn't 'cause he looked just like him." Mary was in the Jewtown tavern one day, pregnant, when a man sat next to her, looked her in the eye, and said, 'You don't belong here, come home with me.' Azelene knew him and approved, and Mary escaped. She maintained contact with Leola Spain, Azelene's mother, leaving her infant with her while she worked. "Leola had a lot of spirit," Mary remembered, "doing all she did and with only one hand — she'd had an accident at her factory job. But she knew what Muddy could be like. She knew."

◊   ◊   ◊

At Smitty's, Muddy hired his first electric bassist. Fender introduced the instrument in 1953 and it had been slowly gaining appeal. It was much more portable than the huge acoustic bass, and once amplifiers could accommodate the deep resonance, its popularity spread. Muddy announced an audition for a bassist, and Andrew Stephenson — "A. W." to his friends — showed up. "When James Cotton and Pat Hare saw I was from Memphis, they knew I could play." Stephenson waited his turn. "The tune was 'Hoochie Coochie Man,' it was the delay thing. You couldn't play right up on it. When it came my time, I didn't have a bass, I had to tune my guitar down. Muddy said, 'I done went through fifteen guys so if you play this tune for me, you got the job.' So, I played it. I had just made twenty-one. When I got with him I had to order an electric bass from Fender, and it took me six months before I could get it."

In August of 1958, Muddy cut his most down-home number since "Blow Wind Blow" five years earlier. "She's Nineteen Years Old," though credited to Muddy, was written by St. Louis Jimmy Oden, Muddy's friend and sometime housemate. Jimmy had lived in a rooming house operated by a mentally impaired, middle-aged woman and her mentally impaired son, who picked up change collecting returnable soda bottles. Inspired, Jimmy wrote a song called "She's Forty Years Old" that was about her ways, which were just like a baby child's. Muddy liked the song very much, but not as much as he liked nineteen-year-old women. So he changed that line, singing it like a man and a half, the kind who could keep a young girl satisfied. It's funny what a word can do.

The next song, "Close to You," became the single's A-side. It lacks the subtlety and feel of "Nineteen Years Old" — Muddy overworks a forced laugh, using it at the end of most every line — but it spent more than three months on the charts, Muddy's sixteenth and final appearance in the top twenty.

However solid Muddy made his tunes, rock and roll still seemed unstoppable. Needing another local gig, Muddy went to Johnny Pepper. Pepper's Lounge, a slight place, had opened less than two years earlier. At the start, they'd used proceeds from the early night's bar to replenish the late-night liquor. By the time Muddy came, Pepper's was hopping with a "twenty-five-cent night"; a quarter at the door would get you in to see Otis Rush and all your drinks were twenty-five cents. It wasn't the glory days, but it became Muddy's home through the early 1960s. "Muddy came to me and said, 'What about a job?'" recalled Pepper. "I said, 'You a big man, I don't think I can handle it.' I said, 'I only charge thirty-five cent on Thursday nights, and I couldn't make enough to pay you.' He said, 'Try me anyway. We'll get together on it.'"

Meanwhile, there was a young and beautiful waitress at Pepper's named Lois Anderson, and Muddy got together with her. "She was a flirty type woman," said Jimmy Lee Morris, who later played bass with Muddy. "She went from man to man, wasn't a one-man woman." She stayed with Muddy long enough to have his third child, a girl named Mercy.

At Chess, record sales were down for all blues. Leonard understood how this would affect his longtime artists, but, approaching his company more like a family than a business, he refused to let them feel the full impact. "My father and Phil would look through the royalty statements," Marshall said, "and I remember them once taking money from some artist and giving it to Wolf because Wolf's statement had zero."

But while Muddy was making the best of his thirty-five-cent nights, suffering with the diminishing loss of his American blues audience, his salvation was being orchestrated far far away. Across the ocean, some young men and women in England had heard Muddy. Like a coat from the cold, these British blues fans were about to extend a hand across the water.

CHAPTER 10

SCREAMING GUITAR
AND HOWLING PIANO
1958–1959

I t would be like going to a grocery store in Japan and trying to buy grits." That's how British jazz man Chris Barber described the difficulty he faced trying to find Muddy Waters in America. "You don't know what to ask for or who to ask." Barber played trombone, and his band was among the most popular for what the British termed "traditional jazz," a sound heavily influenced by American Dixieland. Barber's group was distinguished by their fondness for Delta blues; his trombone replicated the slide guitar parts. In a Mississippi juke joint that might have gone over like sushi, but it was all the rage in postwar English concert halls.

The Chris Barber Band was successful without importing American artists, but they savored improving their styles alongside authentic performers, and they enjoyed their company when traveling. They'd played with Sister Rosetta Tharpe, Sonny Terry and Brownie McGhee, and then Chicago's Modern Jazz Quartet. "The reason we had Muddy Waters in this country," Barber said, "is because the MJQ's keyboardist John Lewis told me, 'If you don't get Muddy Waters, then you're doing it all wrong.' And he offered to find him for us."

Muddy was skeptical about carrying his music so far away. He didn't know he had two four-song EPs available there, a mixture of his early Aristocrat material and more recent sides. In 1951, Big Bill Broonzy had toured England. He'd suggested Muddy make a similar trip, but the idea seemed so preposterous at the time that Muddy didn't even consider it; plenty of gigs were available nearer home. But in the post–Chuck Berry days — hey, a gig's a gig.

Cotton drove Muddy and Spann to the airport; Geneva came too.

"When Muddy got on the airplane, Dorothy and Mildred were standing there in the hall to see him off. Geneva didn't know them to recognize them. And when Muddy came back, I seen them then too."

"I was going overseas," said Muddy, "and I didn't know what to think. And that was a big surprise for me." The surprises seemed continuous and ever larger. They drove on the wrong side of the road, they called themselves talking English but you could hardly make out their words, and their money was funny. Muddy brought Spann to make sure someone on stage could speak his language.

They arrived Tuesday morning, October 14, 1958. This was their first international flight and likely their first airplane flight ever. They were surely tired, but excited British fans promptly knocked on their door. Among them were the writer Tony Standish and the guitarist Alexis Korner. "Right from the beginning," writes Standish in his 1959 *Jazz Journal* account, "I received the impression that Muddy was not interested in discussing old, half-forgotten recording dates and who played what on what session." Muddy did, however, obligingly unpack his white Fender electric guitar and pose for photographs. Learning that Korner played, Muddy handed him the instrument and said, "Play some for us, man."

"The experts were obviously pleasantly surprised," writes Standish. "'Aha, [Big] Bill learned you that,' chuckled Muddy."

Their first full day, Muddy and Spann filmed a Granada TV show, *People and Places,* then were taken to Leeds, where their first gig set the tour on an inauspicious start. The Leeds Triennial Music Festival was a stodgy bill sponsored by a cousin of the queen; it featured string quartets and the odd acceptable jazz group. Muddy played Thursday and Friday; the dates preceded the Barber tour. "Very few musicians in England would have had any idea how to play with Muddy, or any idea what this music meant," said Barber. "At Leeds, he played with Jazz Today, seven or eight good players. Kenny Baker was the leader — he later played trumpet for the Muppets. But the band didn't know what to do."

"They thought I was a Big Bill Broonzy," Muddy said. "I wasn't. I had my amplifier and Spann and I was going to do a Chicago thing.

We opened up in Leeds, England. I was definitely too loud for them. The next morning we were in the headlines of the paper, 'Screaming Guitar and Howling Piano.'"

Muddy joined Barber on Saturday at Newcastle-upon-Tyne for the first of ten dates. The show began at 7:30 and introductions weren't made until an hour before, leaving no time to rehearse. "We're white guys, late twenties, carrying trumpets, clarinets, a banjo," said Barber. "Muddy was nice, but he didn't say much. I asked Otis if Muddy began his shows with 'Hoochie Coochie Man.' He said yes, in the key of A." Each show began with a full set by the Chris Barber Band, then an intermission, and then the Barber Band returned for a few numbers before bringing on their guests. Muddy spent the first half of the evening subjected to Dixieland and wondered if anyone in the entire country of funny-speaking people knew anything about the blues or his music.

After an intermission and a brief warm-up by the Barber Band, the stop-time chords of "Hoochie Coochie Man" sounded. Muddy came out in a dark suit, the spotlight reflecting off the conk in his hair, and Otis wore a white tuxedo jacket with a spangled orangey-red bow tie and black trousers, a stripe down the side. The brass players departed, leaving the bassist and drummer. Unlike at Smitty's Corner, Muddy had no band to hide behind, no club to table-hop. He was on stage and he worked hard. Their sets varied each night, but this review of a later show at St. Pancras Town Hall, written by Tony Standish, reflects the attitude of those who embraced the music.

They began slowly, feeling their way before a quiet, listening audience. Gradually the music increased in depth and intensity, through "Nineteen Years Old," "Key to the Highway," and "I Can't Be Satisfied," and Big Bill's plaint from Parchman Farm, "Baby, Please Don't Go." By the time the spellbinding "Blues Before Sunrise" came up, Muddy had the audience hooked on the end of those curling blue notes that shot, shimmering, from the big amplifier box. Mr. Fender would be amazed at the sounds that Muddy Waters, out of

Stovall, Mississippi, can wrench from his usually fiendish in-
vention. And when Muddy slipped a short piece of brass pipe
onto the little finger of his left hand, the sounds were eerie and
yowling, a distorted electronic voice singing back at the intensely human one — answering, commenting, affirming.

Behind Muddy, Otis drove them down with all the facility
bred of fifteen years around the blues clubs of the Chicago's
South Side.

They did "Close to You, Baby," "Goin' Out Walkin',"
"Long Distance Call," "Mannish Boy," and "I'm a Hoochie
Coochie Man." Muddy was really working. The perspiration
rolled down his face, glistening in the spotlights as he threw
back his head to sing — with it now and not letting go or up.
Backstage, the ecstatic looks on the faces of the Barber Band
were an indication of the moving power of a real blues singer.
Keith Lighbody, the band's road manager, was hopping with
excitement, and my goose pimples were out in force. We were
all well within hearing distance of some pretty fabulous music.

The [Barber] Band trouped on stage to join in on a stomping "I've Got My Mojo Workin'." Muddy exulted through the
wonderful lyrics; he did a little buck and wing across the stage;
the band sat on a driving, wailing riff; and Muddy took it
away and out. The applause was a storm out there, but a short
encore was all Muddy could manage. He was exhausted from
playing and singing, and a lot of people, this writer included,
were exhausted from listening. It was a glowing, happy sort of
exhaustion.

Not everyone was glowing. Photographer Val Wilmer, who was
an enthralled teenager when she saw Muddy in 1958, explained,
"They wanted Muddy to be a folk musician, and electric guitar had
not really been heard, not loud. The chords yes, but not that kind of
wild playing." Harold Pendleton, Chris Barber's business partner, remembered that when Muddy Waters struck the first note on his electric guitar at St. Pancras Town Hall, one well-known critic and

several of his cronies got up and walked out. "[Muddy] fiddled with the knobs [of his guitar]," the review stated. "The next time he struck a fierce chord, it was louder, and I realized that this was the established order of things. As he reached for the volume knobs again, I fled from the hall."

"The artists this audience had seen were countryish, singing songs about plowing behind mules and telling a few anecdotes," British blues scholar Paul Oliver said. "For the time, it was screaming electric. It was what Muddy would be playing in Chicago clubs."

"I drove 'em crazy in fifty-eight," said Muddy. "I went over there and they went stone nuts! 'Where's he comin' from with all this noise?'" As the tour progressed, Muddy toned down his playing.

After each show, Muddy's dressing room was crowded with fans. "All the London blues mafia was there," said writer Frank Weston, "and Muddy was getting bombarded with questions from collectors — 'Was that really B. B. King who was on the Otis Spann 78 "Five Spot"?' and the like. Muddy was always a gentleman, lots of patience, always had time for the fans and collectors."

"When I wormed my way backstage, an eager sixteen-year-old, it was 'Good *morning* little schoolgirl!' all around," Val Wilmer recounted. "Doubtless glad of some female company after all those earnest record collectors with their talk of forgotten sessions and obscure locations, Muddy offered me a drink.

"There weren't many black people in this country then. Backstage, their bodies felt powerful because they had just come off stage. Sweat was coming through their clothes. They had Vaseline in their hair and their faces were all shiny from sweat. All the grown-ups seemed to me terribly matter-of-fact with them: 'How about another drink, Muddy, old chap?' The bottle of whiskey was there and Chris of course was there with his stutter and smiling face.

"Muddy was giving me the eye but he was giving everybody the eye. He was a great womanizer. There wasn't anything nasty about it. I felt like his attitude was, 'Oh well, you don't know what you're missing.' Over the years I realized that, because he came from a segregated society, to make an approach to a white woman in front of white men, even though it's not unsafe here, is still a taboo. He was reserved, which was quite nice. And Otis was very friendly. He squeezed my hand and gave me one of those looks and said, 'I hope to see you again sometime.'

"Then I asked them for their autographs. Otis wrote his and then he pulled out a stamp for Muddy's signature. Not realizing, I said, 'Oh, I want you to sign it,' and Muddy did but it was a great struggle because he could hardly write."

"We found that the American Negro artists could never believe their luck here," said Pendleton. "Chatting up the English girls was easy because there was none of the prejudice that there was in America. The jazz fans here had something like racial prejudice in reverse — if he was black, he could do no wrong."

In an interview near the end of his trip, speaking with Max Jones, a writer for *Melody Maker,* Muddy made his point that the blues — his blues — was an evolving music, though he expressed it without musical instruments or terminology. He used a wad of cash. In miles, the trip to Chicago from Mississippi was not as great as Chicago to London, but the money in Muddy's pocket symbolized a distance from his past greater than any that could be quantitatively measured. "There's no way in the world I can feel the same blues the way I used to," Muddy told Jones. "When I play in Chicago I'm playing up-to-date, not the blues I was born with. People should hear the pure blues — the blues we used to have when we had no money. I'm talking about when you couldn't even buy moonshine, a hot dog even. When you were making thirty-five cents a day." He dug into his pocket and waved the wad over his head. "How can I have that kind of blues with this in my pocket?" How did he explain it? The question came often, and the answer was always the same: he'd tap the side of his head with his forefinger and refer to his "long memory."

Muddy's tour of England was more than a significant landmark in his career. It revitalized him. The packed halls, the teeming dressing rooms, the questions and comments and praise from people so disconnected from the Mississippi Delta and from Chicago's South Side all bolstered his confidence. "I didn't play my guitar until about two months ago," he told Tony Standish, "but I'm gonna keep on playing now. I won't rest no more. Sometimes, when it comes up to a high tempo, I'm kind of slow — that's why I got the lead guitar player, let him take care of that business. I'm slow, but when it comes to the blues, why, I got pretty good fingers." He would soon buy a new guitar, a red Telecaster with a custom neck made of rosewood, strong enough to handle his heavy strings, and a raised nut to accommodate his slide. Before leaving, he told *Melody Maker,* "Now I know that the people in England like soft guitar and the old blues. Next time I come I'll learn some old songs first."

But the impact of Muddy's tour was more than a validation of his career: it became an investment in his musical future. Like the imitators who sprang up behind Chuck Berry, like those who followed in the path of Muddy's Aristocrat recordings a decade earlier, a number of the new fans at Muddy's British shows formed bands of their own. A young Eric Burdon stood up at the Newcastle College of Art and said he had tickets to the Chris Barber concert with Muddy Waters and wondered if anyone else was going. John Steel stood up and said he was. They formed a band, the Animals. "I realized I could play guitar," said Eric Clapton, "when I mastered this bit of Muddy Waters's 'Honey Bee.'" Davies and Korner heard confirmation in Muddy's music to crank up their own, and their group, Blues Incorporated, would evolve into another one called the Rolling Stones.

❖   ❖   ❖

Chuck Berry had made Chess Records a major player with the rock audience, and soon they found themselves selling not only a new style of music, but a new, more expensive format too: the LP, the long-playing, twelve-inch, thirty-three-and-a-third-RPM album.

Folk music was one of the first nonclassical styles to exploit the LP, being a genre that wasn't oriented around hits; an artist's repertoire was more important than how he or she played one particular song. The folk audience was predominantly white, and by the late 1950s, they were in their post-Levittown affluence. In 1958, a forward-thinking individual at Chess Records, sensing the new trend and realizing an opportunity, packaged twelve of Muddy's songs from his decade with Chess and released it as *The Best of Muddy Waters*. It was an ideal introduction for the new market of consumers, giving the uninitiated listener a taste of Muddy's breadth, ranging from his amplified Delta blues such as "I Can't Be Satisfied" to his early urban blues band sound — "Honey Bee" — to the recent piano- and harmonica-led songs such as "I'm Ready" and "Hoochie Coochie Man." The songs were immediately attractive to the budding Love Generation: song one, side one was "I Just Want to Make Love to You."

Alan Lomax, who'd spent the better part of the 1950s in England (after being tagged a communist at home), was aware of Muddy's acceptance there and put Muddy on the bill of a Carnegie Hall show he was producing. Lomax's "Folksong: '59" was intended to tell the story of American music in song. Muddy joined Memphis Slim, country singer Jimmy Driftwood, gospel artists the Selah Jubilee Singers, as well as bluegrass artists and New York folk interpreters. Bobby Darin was billed to represent the rebellious rock and roll, and he did so perfectly — by not showing up. After Muddy played Carnegie Hall, Chess went even more aggressively for the folk consumer's dollar. Big Bill Broonzy had recently died (Muddy was a pallbearer), and while Broonzy's fans mourned the loss, Chess offered them a replacement, an album titled *Muddy Waters Sings Big Bill Broonzy*. It pitched Muddy as a folksinger, as if "Hoochie Coochie Man" had never happened, as if he'd been raised in the coffeehouses that began dotting the northeastern cityscape.

The Broonzy album was recorded over two sessions in the summer of 1959. Francis Clay drummed on the first one; the second session introduced drummer Willie Smith, who would soon occupy the drummer's chair, staying for the better part of twenty years. "When I was little I used to dig Big Bill's stuff," said Smith. "Them was blues at that time." Issued early the following year, the album features a relatively unexciting batch of songs. The hard edges and angularity of Muddy's best work are replaced by an approachable, somewhat superficial, blues style. *Billboard* didn't mind: "A fortunate coupling —

Broonzy's material interpreted by Muddy. Blues fans will find this hard to put down."

And it seemed like after his trip overseas, there was a turn of Muddy's fortunes. Chuck Berry was indicted in 1959 under the Mann Act for transporting a fourteen-year-old Apache Indian girl across state lines for immoral purposes; before his trial, he was indicted again on a similar incident. Jerry Lee Lewis married his thirteen-year-old cousin and fell from grace, and Little Richard left rock and roll for the grace of gospel. Rock suffered another major blow with the airplane crash that killed Buddy Holly, Ritchie Valens, and The Big Bopper. Payola became national news, and suddenly Alan Freed was not the man he used to be.

While rock and roll seemed to be nosediving, blues was getting a boost. Sam Charters published his book *The Country Blues,* pointing the way for the blues revival that would sweep the 1960s. This trend was further foretold by the trickle of European visitors and American whites who began dotting the South Side clubs. Muddy and Leonard were surely not done trying.

When Chess producer Jack Tracy introduced Muddy to Nesuhi Ertegun at Smitty's at the end of the 1950s, the bluesman probably assumed the Turk another foreign fan. But Ertegun was a principal at Atlantic Records and had a lot of power in the music world. The meeting was casual but the music was extraordinary. Ertegun went back to New York and soon an invitation came from the coast that would propel Muddy to white America.

Meanwhile, the increasing numbers of whites — Americans and Europeans — who wanted Muddy's company intimidated him. "Muddy was scared to talk to them, so he sent me," said Clay. "I started telling him what to say. When writers would come in, he'd walk down off the stage and say [adopting a formal tone], 'Good evening, I'm Muddy Waters, welcome to Smitty's Corner.' He got it down fast, he delighted in it." Cotton remembered one night at Smitty's Corner when "in walks Paul Butterfield, Nick Gravenites, and Elvin Bishop. Muddy Waters thought they was the tax people. He owed some taxes, said, 'Goddamn, they've come to get me. That's got to be them.' Muddy hid in the office between sets." The three were not from the IRS; they were budding white blues musicians.

The writers, the musicians — Muddy realized that white America was on his tail. Before the decade's end, Elvis had recorded a song called "Trouble" in his film *King Creole,* and its striptease beat was very reminiscent of "Hoochie Coochie Man." "I thought," said Muddy, "I better watch out. I believe whitey's pickin' up on things that I'm doin'."

He was right.

CHAPTER 11

My Dog Can Bark

1960–1967

M uddy's tour of England laid the groundwork for the second half of his career, when he became the godfather of rock and roll and an icon for white audiences. His impact on the youth — electrified by his power and sensuality — sowed the seeds of the British Invasion, when rock and roll bands would remind America of its indigenous music.

But that would all be somewhat indirect. The terms of Muddy's personal acquaintance with white America were established at the Newport Jazz Festival, 1960. He played raucous, hard-grinding Chicago blues, his band like a tractor driving up a hill. When Bob Dylan would play similar music at the Newport Folk Festival half a decade later, the audience would boo. Such a ruckus was unacceptable to budding hippies and committed folkies in white New England when it came from one of their own. But Muddy didn't read Dylan Thomas or attend college; he shared neither this audience's background nor their foreground. He dropped in on the folk scene like a museum exhibit from the wild — jungle music authenticated by jungle men. In case of emergency, break this glass. Muddy shattered it.

The blues program was held Sunday afternoon, July third. The day before, more people than the venue could hold wanted to see Ray Charles and the vocal group Lambert, Hendricks, and Ross. It was summer and hot, and about 300 tipsy jazz fans realized that only a handful of cops separated them from swinging with Ray. So they rushed the cops, who pulled out tear gas and water hoses, and such a melee ensued that by midnight there were three companies of National Guardsmen on the streets.

Muddy's entourage saw the lingering mayhem as they arrived Sunday morning. They'd driven from Chicago the night before and would return the next day; a 2,000-mile one-night stand. James Cotton pulled the station wagon over when he saw John Lee Hooker standing on a corner, his guitar slung over his shoulder, no case. "You better get in here," he said, and they all drove to backstage safety.

The town's council, more comfortable with millions of dollars than thousands of marauding music fans, decided to terminate the annual party. George Wein, the event's promoter, quickly undertook negotiations. Arrangements had already been made with the United States Information Agency to film the Sunday show for promoting American culture overseas. The council recognized their patriotic duty, and as a compromise agreed that the blues program — but no other events — could go forward.

Before Muddy played, his band backed Spann, who stepped out as leader, and also backed John Lee Hooker. Around 5 P.M., Muddy strode to center stage. His band wore formal white attire, he wore black. Standing erect, keenly aware how distant his South Side joints were, and how white this audience was, and how large, Muddy was solemn as he introduced his first number — recorded only a month previously, not yet released, and thus completely unfamiliar to the audience: "I Got My Brand on You."

By the end of the next one, "Hoochie Coochie Man," these songs about sex and fun were hitting home. No one (but the band) minded when he forgot the words to "Tiger in Your Tank"; vamping with the title only drove home the image. These squealing record buyers were riding right with him when, using the colloquial names of the male and female mule, he sang in the hip-shaking "I Feel So Good": "I feel like a jack on a jenny / way over behind the hill."

They went absolutely nuts for "Mojo," clapping along and dancing to the best of their ability. Muddy, by this point, was completely comfortable, thrusting his hips and grinding as if he were on a familiar Chicago stage. "Lay it on me," he told the band, and Cotton led them in a shuffling good-time breakdown that would have made proud Lewis Ford, Muddy's rowdy levee-building partner from Stovall. Pat Hare's guitar sound was the envy of all the young rockers.

Drummer Francis Clay, among his kind at this jazz festival, embellished the rhythm; "Mojo" jumped as if newly mastered. "I wasn't a hand to dance," Muddy had told Lomax twenty years earlier, but during "Mojo" he showed Elgin movements, skipping over to Cotton, whisking him off his feet and into a fox-trot, then breaking into a jitterbug that defies every rumor and legend about Muddy's stoic stage presence. Returning to the microphone, he repeatedly thrust his hips, emphasizing exactly to which mojo he was referring, and just how it worked. His authority was casual and majestic; the crowd demanded a reprise. Muddy gave them "Mojo" again, hammering home four times, "Got my mojo working," because it was, and it did.

At the day's close, all the blues performers assembled on stage for a medley of blues standards, passing the lead vocal. The sight of these luminaries together, and the thought that opportunities to recreate it at Newport were no more, so moved poet Langston Hughes, a member of the Newport Board of Directors, that he composed a poem on the spot, grabbing a Western Union blank and writing on the back of it. He handed "Good-bye Newport Blues" to Spann, who could read, and Spann, sharing the feeling, quickly returned to the stage, joined by most of Muddy's band. Too drained, Muddy remained backstage; Spann sang lead, performing the poem as if he'd learned it from Friday Ford back in Belzoni. "It's a gloomy day in Newport," Spann sang, and in the next verse asked, "What's going to happen to my music?"

The answer to Hughes's lament is ironic. Muddy's set, filmed by the USIA, was released as a live album. "Got My Mojo Working" was nominated for a 1960 Grammy Award in the category "Best Rhythm and Blues Performance." In England, "Tiger in Your Tank" and "I Got My Brand on You" were promptly snatched up by Alexis Korner's Blues Incorporated. Spann's Newport set was released on album in Europe, and he, who had recorded only four sides as bandleader, returned to New York the next month for a session backed by Robert Lockwood Jr., initiating a side-career as bandleader. The successful marketing of Muddy's appearance established Newport as a blues commerce center. And, after a two-year hiatus, the festival resumed.

❖ ❖ ❖

Muddy might have had an inkling of this success when, the previous September, 1959, two French blues fans, Jacques Demetre and Marcel Chauvard, introduced themselves to Muddy on a Saturday night at Smitty's Corner. "Muddy expressed his joy, shook our hands, and presented us to his band: 'Hey fellows, look at these cats who've come all the way from France to hear us. You're going to have the time of your life.'" They recounted their experiences in a book titled *Land of the Blues*.

A sturdy man, Muddy talked without pausing for a breath, until he had to go back onstage. Then he introduced us to the audience, which consisted exclusively of black people, most of them apparently modest employees who sat around little tables and didn't dance. As soon as the band started, we were at the very root of the blues; theirs was the purest and most emotional music we had yet heard. Under the spell, we sat listening to them for four solid hours, enjoying this music that everyone seemed to understand perfectly.

After the gig, Muddy, concerned about their safety, insisted on driving the visitors back to their hotel. In the car, they inquired after blues singer Kokomo Arnold. Muddy had lost touch with Kokomo, but not with his passion for early blues. In the crisp night air of autumn, urban Chicago rolling past the windshield, he broke into song, Kokomo's "Milk Cow Blues."

Upon their return to Europe, the Frenchmen paid a visit to Paul Oliver (who had written the program notes for Muddy's UK tour) in England and inspired him to visit Chicago, which he did the week after Newport, 1960. Muddy was "incredibly welcoming" and insisted Oliver and his wife stay at the house. "I couldn't really believe that St. Louis Jimmy was actually living in the basement of Muddy's house," remembered Oliver. "I went down, saw all the waste pipes and plumbing passing through, and Jimmy was curled up in the corner."

Equally amazing were Muddy's other tenants: James Cotton was living upstairs with his wife and child, as was George "Mojo" Buford, who would soon join the band; Spann was still in and out of the basement, and Bo was often there; Muddy's uncle Joe Grant (which Oliver mistakenly heard as "Brant") also lived downstairs. Cookie, Muddy's four-year-old granddaughter, had moved in a year earlier, and Geneva's sons Charles and Dennis were part of the household.

"I was surprised how carefully the furniture was looked after," said Oliver. "All the big settees, big armchairs, all covered in sheet plastic and fitted like a shirt, the perfect suburban home. They didn't want to bring the South but they weren't really quite urban either. It was summer and, to keep the heat out, they kept all the curtains drawn and hardly any lights on so it was difficult to see until the evening when they could throw them back. It made the place rather gloomy whereas the cellar was actually the brightest. It was painted a curious lemon color."

On nights off, the whole house shut down by nine, stirring again between five and six in the morning — farmer's hours. Oliver stayed several days, keeping late hours at clubs and conducting interviews from Muddy's basement for his book *Conversation with the Blues.* "I think the thing that struck me most about Muddy," he said, "was he spent most of the time sleeping. He gave out so much when he was performing. He said to me once, 'You're not performing unless you're sweating.' . . . Muddy roared, leaped, jerked in fierce and violent spasms. When he came off the stage he was in a state of near trance and the sweat poured off him."

Little Walter was hanging out at Muddy's gig, interrupting Oliver if he spoke too long to Muddy, and generally creating confusion. "Walter would call for another round of drink and then the waiter would come up and Walter would say, 'I didn't ask for it,' and look at me with his eyebrows raised," Oliver recounted. "'Did you see me ask for that?' He had been shot in the ankle and it was heavily bandaged. When I expressed some concern he ripped open his shirt and he was just covered in scars from knives and God knows what. He courted disaster, I think he rejoiced in it."

After Oliver, Chris Barber showed up with his wife, vocalist Ottilie Patterson, off for a couple days from their American tour. "It was always amazing," said Muddy's granddaughter Cookie, "no matter how many of them came through or had to stay there, we always had room. Our dining room had a sofa in there, and in the living room there were two sofas. That's how Muddy was. We would have two or three people in there or any stray we would pick up, it wouldn't matter."

Muddy welcomed the Barbers like family, placing their wedding photograph on the living room mantle alongside photos of Little Walter, himself, and other family members. Geneva prepared pots of food. "Chris Barber asked me to meet him at Muddy's house," said Bob Koester, whose Delmark Records was recording the contemporary blues scene. "Mrs. Morganfield insisted I have some food and I was probably missing a few meals in those days." Stuffed full, he, the Barbers, and Muddy were driven by James "Killer" Triplett to the F&J Lounge in Gary, Indiana, where Muddy maintained a Tuesday-night gig.

The F&J Lounge was less a nightclub than a reception hall, densely packed with socializing people, the band an afterthought. "Muddy bestrode that stage," said Koester, "totally in charge. He had the entire audience in the palm of his hand." During one set, when the band announced Muddy, he tripped on some wires as he stepped across them. "There were all kinds of sparks and stuff flying," said Koester, "and Muddy was just calm as hell, as if it was planned."

Barber was wide-eyed watching Muddy strut about the stage for "I'm a Man." The audience shrieked like the background voices on Muddy's record of the song — "The ladies would swing their purses, saying, 'Sing it Muddy, sing it,'" another visitor remembered, "the whole crowd would just go nuts"— and it climaxed with Muddy pumping up his machismo and taunting the ladies, egging them to egg *him* to reveal his manhood until, when the tension rose and could be no longer restrained, Muddy would unzip his pants and let loose — a soda bottle fizzing over the top.

(After the show, Barber, Ottilie, and Koester went to a nearby diner for breakfast. They were the only whites and the waitress ignored them until they selected several plays from the jukebox, contemporary hits by Brook Benton and Muddy. Their order was taken immediately.)

Paul Oliver also went to the F&J, driven by Muddy himself. "He had the radio on real low, and if B. B. King came on, or Howlin' Wolf, then he'd turn it up to maximum volume and the whole car would fill with the sound and he would listen really hard. As soon as he heard Wolf's voice, conversation stopped and he focused on that. And he'd mutter for a while afterward."

❖   ❖   ❖

As the reigning king of Chicago blues, Muddy could have had his pick of musicians. Instead, he ran his band like a good ole boys club, letting members bring in friends. He wasn't looking for stars, just someone to fall in with his group and make the gig — dependability over musical ability. Spann stayed right by his side, but bass players came and went, rarely taking Willie Dixon's spot in the studio, but playing gigs and tours: Marcus Johnson, Mack Arnold, Jo Jo Williams, Smokey Smothers; only Jimmy Lee Morris stayed a while. "I didn't want to play Mud's old stuff," said Morris. "I was doing Bill Doggett, he was hot, or Jimmy Reed. But Muddy, Wolf, Jimmy Rogers — all that shit was dead." Cotton, who'd seen Jimmy Lee play in Gary, told the new guy he'd get to stretch out the better half of the night when Muddy was off stage.

Muddy took to Jimmy Lee and soon he was bandleader. Cotton didn't like that, and he turned over the driving and loading to the new players, warming up his throat at Lake Park Liqueors, where his friend was a bartender. One night, waiting out front for a bus and somewhat anesthetized, Cotton was shot five times by a crazed fan; when he recovered, he quit Muddy (he'd be back) to reprise his teenage position as bandleader. In the studio, he was replaced by a horn section; on gigs, the job went to George "Mojo" Buford.

Muddy brought Buford up from the "junior" band, a group that included Willie "Big Eyes" Smith on drums; they took Muddy's gigs when he was on the road. Buford, from Hernando, Mississippi, had been an upstairs tenant of Muddy's. Willie soon followed Buford into Muddy's band, replacing Clay. "At that time being a musician," said Willie Smith, "if you couldn't play Howlin' Wolf, Muddy Waters, Little Walter, and Elmore James, you couldn't get on nobody's bandstand." The young Muddy had played Son House, Robert Johnson, and Leroy Carr songs; by the end of the 1950s, he was part of the pantheon.

Smith had come to Chicago for two weeks in 1953 and never returned to Helena. Five years earlier, when he was about eight, he heard Muddy and the band broadcasting on KFFA. James Triplett had been his baby-sitter back then; it was Killer who introduced him to Muddy. Smith and Clay, and sometimes drummer S. P. Leary, traded the drummer's chair for the decade, until Smith settled himself in. Buford and Cotton traded the harmonica spot; Buford was in and out of Muddy's band over the next two decades.

The guitar position was also volatile, though not as volatile as guitarist Pat Hare. One December Minneapolis day in 1963, half tight and armed with a fresh half-pint and a pistol, Hare fired a few shots at his girlfriend. She fled but returned to throw him out; guns and Hare were not uncommon. Neighbors phoned the police when more shots were fired. "The two officers, with [officer James] Hendricks in the lead and carrying a shotgun, approached the apartment door, which they found unlocked. Hendricks opened the door and caught a glimpse of Hare standing behind it with an automatic pistol in his hand," the *St. Paul Dispatch* reported on December 16, 1963. "'Give me the gun,' Hendricks ordered." Instead of complying, Hare stepped around the door and fired three shots. Two of the .32 caliber slugs hit Hendricks in the chest and the other in the groin. Hendricks dropped to the floor and patrolman Langaard, immediately behind him, fired three shots from his service revolver into Hare's body at close range. "When the officers got there, Mrs. Winje [Hare's girlfriend] was lying moaning on a davenport."

Hare's 1954 recording, "I'm Gonna Murder My Baby," proved prescient. He'd killed his girlfriend with shots to the upper chest and abdomen. In the one-day trial he pleaded guilty to murder in the third degree and received a life sentence. In the pen, he formed a band, Sounds Incarcerated.

Hare's replacement was James "Pee Wee" Madison, a left-handed upside-down guitarist who'd been playing modern stuff with Jimmy Lee Morris. "I played a couple sets with Muddy," said Pee Wee, a demure, soft-spoken man with red skin, a quick grin, and a penchant for danger who'd come to Chicago from Osceola, Arkansas, and practiced guitar to Little Walter records. "That was my first real gig. He made the set easy for me, until I caught on." Nevertheless, Pee Wee kept small change taped to the front of his guitar, possibly so he'd have carfare home in case he got fired.

Also coming into the picture was Sammy Lawhorn. He was in his early thirties, but had matured impressively around Helena, Arkansas, rooting his modern guitar style in Muddy's Delta sound. He learned to swing with the beat, sway with the heat. There was just one thing: "He was a hell of a guitar player," said Jimmy Lee Morris, "but he had a sleep disease." Maybe.

"Did I have the impression that he was narcoleptic?" asked Elvin Bishop, who took lessons from Sammy. "No. You see a guy passing out, and a couple hours before, you see him drink two half-pints, narcolepsy is not the first thing that leaps to your mind."

"All of us was drinking," said Jimmy Lee Morris. "Everybody would be drunk. They'd call us the Muddy Waters Drunken Ass Band. Shit man, when you're playing blues all night long, that's life, man."

⬧ ⬧ ⬧

McKie's Show Lounge on the South Side was a new club popular with the younger African American set. To fill a week, they sometimes booked a blues band, though their crowd associated blues with their parents. Muddy took a gig there one Monday, and between sets, Willie Smith sat at a table with a couple young ladies. "Once you get in that position where pretty women are steadily flashing you, it's pretty hard to not touch," Smith said. "That's the way that was."

"I had just moved in that neighborhood, my first little apartment," said Lucille McClenton (then Lucille Dease). "I was seventeen. I had two children. Willie was already at the table. Muddy asked was this my first time down there, and he asked me how old I was because I looked real young to be in a lounge. I told him I was eighteen going on nineteen. And he bought me drinks. I was drinking pea pickers then, a lot of gin and a little lime juice. And we started seeing each other. About a week later he asked me did I want to go out of town with him, he'd pay for my baby-sitter and stuff."

Muddy had recently parted ways with Lois. Suspecting another mule in his stall, he told her he was going on the road, then opened her door to find her messing with his valet, C. D. (pronounced "seedy"). Under Muddy's nose, C. D. had been pushing heroin, Lois a recent customer. "C. D. was a little pimp on the South Side," said Cookie. "As I got older and was developing, I remember Muddy telling me, 'Don't ever go by that C. D. Don't ever have anything to do with C. D.'" Lois died a decade later from a drug overdose. "She was on furlough from prison," said Mercy Morganfield, her daughter. "It was self-inflicted. She was set outside by a hospital dumpster, where she was found."

For nearly all of the 1960s, Lucille Dease was Muddy's main road wife. She rode in the Cadillac to out-of-town gigs, was picked up in the Cadillac for local gigs, hung on Muddy's arm and hung out with his friends. "I think Muddy always had high regards and respect for Leola, that was probably the only one he respected," said Cookie. "But I think Lucille Dease was the love of his life. Lucille was his mistress all through my childhood. He was married to Geneva and she raised me, and just to see the hurt and the pain — how a man could do that to a woman who is supposed to be his wife — it was very disrespectful to Geneva and I felt he must have loved Lucille a lot to put Geneva through this."

"I learned a long time ago that the only thing a black man have is his lady," B. B. King reflected. "Nothing else. If he got his lady, he's happy — as long as that lady's happy. We still try to make some money because we know if we don't, somebody else will and she'll go over there. But I think from the days of slavery, the black male want to do everything he can to make her happy."

"He was amazed I'd never heard of him," Lucille said. "'I'm Muddy Waters,' and I'd say, 'So fucking what?' As the years went on, it hit me but then I didn't give a shit who he was."

❖   ❖   ❖

There were other changes in Muddy's personal life. He was in the South, March of 1962, when he got word that his father died. He'd visited Ollie the previous fall. With his brothers and a nephew, he was a pallbearer. "Ollie was a converted man when he passed away," said Robert Morganfield, Muddy's half brother. "He was a Baptist."

Not quite his son. In Muddy's household, "Geneva and I were at eleven o'clock church on Sunday," said Cookie. "Geneva was a very, very strong Christian believer. Muddy's grandmother raised him as a strict Southern Baptist. But I lived with him twenty-something years and I never seen him go to church or belong to church. But Muddy could quote the Bible. I think he still had the belief. When his cousins would come in, the reverends, there wouldn't be the drinking around the house or none of that."

In 1963, Muddy's uncle Joe Grant died. Uncle Joe lived in the basement, and though he was only three years older than Muddy, he was heavy and not in good health. "I was a little girl and Muddy had been out playing," said Cookie, who was five years old at the time. "The biggest thing in our home was when he would come in, we would make these big breakfasts. When I would hear that door open I'd get right up, it would be like a Sunday dinner right then. Geneva would always get up. Otis Spann would be there, his wife, and whatever band members that he would bring home. We were making pancakes, and I wanted syrup." She ran down the back stairs to her uncle's room and found him playing possum — awkwardly, half off the bed. She was several bites into her pancakes before she told Muddy. "Muddy went downstairs and he lost it."

Joe and Muddy had been raised as brothers on Stovall. Joe had come to Chicago first, given Muddy an electric guitar. Losing him was losing his hold on childhood, and his final grasp of his grand-mother. Muddy honored Uncle Joe with his next child, born to Lucille. "His uncle had just died, that was Muddy's heart," said Lucille. "Joseph was named after him. Muddy was crazy about those babies." Lucille made sure Geneva heard the good news. "Lucille was very brassy," said Cookie. "She would call, talk about it, put it in the paper if she can. She had no respect for our house."

Life had not improved for Azelene, Muddy's Mississippi-born daughter, Cookie's mother. His ex-girlfriend Mary Austin remembered the last time she saw her. "She was out of it, her mind was gone. She was standing on the corner, leaning against a wall and looked at me but didn't even hardly know me. By that time I knew about seeing tracks on your arm. Muddy had a disc jockey friend whose daughter overdosed from drugs. He was dead set against drugs." On June 18, 1963, Azelene died of a heroin overdose; J. B. Cooper was in jail. "Muddy hated him," said Lucille. "Muddy despised that man."

Mary had, by this time, sent the son she'd had with Muddy to her mother in Florida and was making a life of her own in Chicago; she had instructed her mother never to tell the child that his father was Muddy Waters. "Muddy had brought me to Chicago and fed me to the sharks. He threw me out there to drown and I would have drownded. I knew nothing about Chicago, nothing about the fast life. If it wasn't for Azelene first, and then that man in the bar — I named my child for him — I'd have been eaten alive."

"When my mother died," said Cookie, "Muddy was in his bedroom on Forty-third and Lake Park and he set on the bed and cried. Muddy was as much a family man as he could be. He felt he could do anything and get away with it. And he did. He did. But I'm grateful that he kept me and he kept my part of the family together." Geneva phoned Willie Smith, letting some of Muddy's friends know about his first child's death; she knew Muddy wouldn't tell them. Azelene Morganfield Cooper is buried in the same cemetery as her father, her grave unmarked.

◆ ◆ ◆

Muddy continued his march into white America one fan at a time. Students twenty blocks south of Muddy at the University of Chicago invited him to campus for dinner and a performance. His hair was pomped and he was dressed too slick to fool with crumbs and cafeteria sauce; he gave his dinner to Bo, who had accompanied him. Mark Naftalin, a keyboard player who would soon form a white blues band with Paul Butterfield, sat across from his hero. "He was immaculate as always, dignified as always," said Naftalin. "If we exchanged more words than this, I don't remember them. And in retrospect, of course, what I asked him was extremely naive. But I was sitting across from him and I asked if he'd ever heard of Robert Johnson. I'll never forget his response. 'My main man,' he said, and that was it. 'My main man.'"

It's hard to tell from his recordings of the time. Muddy had successfully transformed the emotional depth of Robert Johnson to the ensemble attack of Chicago blues, but his recent studio recordings had forsaken everything for a shot at the white mainstream's dollar. "The Muddy Waters Twist" (January 1962) percolates, but it's completely devoid of emotion, and emotion was what Muddy and the blues were about. He'd been made a mannequin, propped before a fad. There is no Mississippi in the song, there is no Chicago.

Muddy's willingness to be experimented on was indicative of his submissive relationship with Chess. During these same years, Howlin' Wolf was cutting classic sides: "Spoonful," "Down in the Bottom," "The Red Rooster," "I Ain't Superstitious." "Killing Floor" was yet to come. Even Wolf's novelty numbers, such as "Three Hundred Pounds of Joy," maintained a bluesman's integrity; he generally doesn't sound like he's wearing a costume and trying to pass as Johnny Rocker or Peter Pop.

"Muddy didn't have the drive, the initiative that Wolf had," said Billy Boy Arnold. "Muddy let Cotton run his show. Wolf wouldn't be sitting at no table with no woman. Wolf would be on that stage kicking ass all night long. Muddy was a great artist, but he became less of a draw in the Chicago clubs than Wolf, until the white audiences came along and rescued him."

Jimmy Rogers, too, respected Wolf. "Wolf was better at managing a bunch of people than Muddy or anybody else. Muddy would go along with the Chess company, Wolf would speak up for himself — and when you speak up for yourself you're automatically gonna speak up for the band. Muddy would go along with Chess because Chess was gonna give him the money to pay his car note if he needed to cover a bill."

The yoke of sharecropping — and the nominal protection it offered — never fit Wolf. A huge and hulking man, he moved about like he was breaking shackles: on stage, he seemed assembled from boxcars. "Wolf would be sitting in the corner with his spectacles on in intermission," recalled Billy Boy Arnold, "studying his book; he went to night school, he took music lessons, he was always trying to advance." Muddy had made a life in the plantation South. He played guitar, ran a bar, drove a car. His pockets jingle-jangled with silver and scrip. Muddy not only sought a relationship with the boss man, but was sheltered by it. It was how he lived.

"The difference was," continued Billy Boy Arnold, "if you played in Wolf's band and got fired or quit, you could draw unemployment compensation. If you walked up to Muddy and said something like unemployment compensation they'd think you were crazy — 'What the hell's that?'"

Smitty's closed in 1961, but at Pepper's more and more white faces appeared. Muddy's name was painted on the front of the building and the club was easily accessible from the Forty-third Street el stop. Charlie Musselwhite had come up the hillbilly highway from Memphis in 1962, and he saw the sign while driving an exterminator company truck. Poking around, he began to frequent the place and got friendly with a waitress named Mary, who, one Wednesday night, told Muddy that he should check out the honky on harmonica.

"So Muddy called me up to sit in," said Musselwhite, "and at this time, blues was out of fashion. I was eighteen and they thought it was funny I knew anything about it. So any time I was in Pepper's Lounge, he'd have me sit in and word got around. People started offering me money to play."

Musselwhite got to know everyone in the band, but was closest with Spann. If it was wet, Spann drank it, and Musselwhite was into that. "Spann liked me and would introduce me to women, 'Charlie, I want you to meet my wife.' It would be a different woman every night. And he was always fixing me up with other ladies and we'd go out. Pepper's was open until four in the morning, but there was a whole other scene that happened after that. There were these private clubs that were open till the next afternoon. Anybody could pay the door fare to get in, and they served alcohol. Then we'd get a hotel room and flip a coin to see who got the mattress and who got the springs. Spann and his lady would be on one and I'd be with my lady on the other. He called me his fucking-buddy."

Muddy was still consigned to black clubs, where the young audience considered him old-fashioned but where he was sought out by white kids who were exploring the roots of their music. White guitarist Elvin Bishop was led to Pepper's by the black cafeteria employees he befriended at the University of Chicago. "Muddy Waters was playing at Pepper's and man what a scene," said Bishop. "Completely packed, all the chicks up front, he had on a fine suit, a nice process, a little narrow mike, little narrow tie, sharp shoes, and he was sweating away singing 'Rock Me' and 'Mojo Working.' The place just rocked. He didn't do a whole lot of jumping around, but he was intense. He'd have a grip on that microphone, standing back the length of his arm — he had a powerful voice — and he was standing straight up, dignified, sweating from every pore. Every once in a while he'd jerk his body, *ja-pow,* he was one hundred percent into it."

The circle drew tighter and yet more diverse, whites and blacks, old and young. Charlie Musselwhite became friendly with Big Joe Williams, the rambling Delta blues guitarist who would record for Testament and Delmark Records. "I'd go in Pepper's with Joe," said Musselwhite, "and as soon as Muddy would see Joe he'd make a big fuss, get him a place to sit, buy him a bottle and have them bring over a setup, which was a bowl with ice and tongs and a couple little red cherries to make it classy. He'd announce from the stage that Big Joe Williams was in the audience and he wrote 'Baby, Please Don't Go.' Muddy would act like a little kid around Joe, and Joe loved to be treated like that."

Pepper's served home cooking, allowing patrons to fill up before tanking up. If the kitchen closed and you were still hungry, a man with a cart would appear out front selling pig-ear sandwiches. "That opened about midnight," said Elvin Bishop, "because the idea of eating a pig-ear sandwich doesn't get appealing unless you've been drinking till then."

◇   ◇   ◇

After "The Muddy Waters Twist," the next manipulation Muddy subjected himself to was overdubbing vocals on instrumental tracks by Earl Hooker, creating "You Shook Me" and "You Need Love." These, however, worked surprisingly well, due in large part to the musicians' shared background. Hooker was a Clarksdale native, younger than Muddy, who successfully adapted his slide work to the electric guitar. He stood out even among his peers, who included Buddy Guy, Otis Rush, Matt Murphy, and Freddie King; he recorded mostly instrumentals and thus his name recognition was as limited as his vocal range. These tracks move at tempos comfortable for Muddy, leaving room for him to build words from moans, to stretch his vocals like he would his guitar strings, and to add emphases and emphatic pauses. ("You Need Love" was later interpreted by Led Zeppelin as "Whole Lotta Love" and resulted in a lawsuit and payments to Willie Dixon, the songwriter.)

Muddy recorded one of his deepest blues in the spring of 1963, "Five Long Years." Maybe because it was written by Muddy's cousin Eddie Boyd, Muddy felt a kinship to the song. Spann's dark piano roll sets the mood. The pace is slow and unhurried. Cotton, back in the band, stays simple, playing accompaniment rather than lead. ("Phil wouldn't put reverb on my harmonica," Cotton remembered. "Said people wouldn't be able to tell me from Walter. That let me know I was doing pretty good.") The session continued well, and after a couple more tracks, everyone in good humor, Muddy dipped back to his youth and, like a band entertaining the boss man on Stovall, they cut "She'll Be Coming Around the Mountain."

A concert recorded by Chess a couple months later reveals the stylistic spectrum of blues at the time. The label's biggest tradi-

tional stars — Muddy, Wolf, and Willie Dixon (Walter was scheduled but didn't show, and Sonny Boy Williamson was actually recorded
later) — were backed by its upcoming bright light, Buddy Guy.
Guy's band segues the performances with instrumental riffs — taut,
slashing, and very electric — an emerging blues-rock style tagged the
"West Side sound." Chess ultimately packaged the same album with
two different titles and different artwork. First a more conservative
one *(Folk Festival of the Blues)* on Argo, the jazz and folk subsidiary,
and later a flashier one on Chess *(Blues from Big Bill's Copa Cabana)*.

Buddy Guy had come to Muddy's attention shortly after his arrival from Louisiana. Muddy had Bo drive him to the 708 Club, then
waited in the red station wagon while Bo fetched Guy. "I walked out
and he was sitting in a station wagon in the front seat, so I attempted
to get in the back," Guy writes in his autobiography, *Damn Right I've
Got the Blues*. "'Don't get in the back. Get in the front,' he said. So I
got in the front. And he's sitting up there eating a baloney sandwich.
'Go ahead on, get you some baloney,' he said. 'Make a sandwich.' So
I started thinking, 'This cat here is better than I thought he was.' I
thought he was going to be saying, 'Look man, I'm Muddy Waters.'
But he was down to earth and I thought, 'Wow, what else can you ask
for?'"

Chess remained anxious to capitalize on the folk craze; Muddy's
Folk Singer album, recorded in September of 1963, was probably
named before it was recorded. But now young whites looking for
more passion in their music increasingly turned toward the blues.
Rock and roll had dissipated from the force of "Great Balls of Fire"
and "Hound Dog" in the mid-1950s to "Itsy Bitsy Teenie Weenie Yellow Polka Dot Bikini" and "Let's Do the Twist" in 1960; the British
Invasion was still nascent.

Chess's next concept was to record Muddy with either a peer or
one of his mentors, both on acoustic guitars. For Leonard, it was a return to 1947, when he'd first recorded Muddy — something in the
Lightnin' Hopkins or John Lee Hooker vein. The idea must have appealed to Muddy, certainly more so than another twist record. Besides, he was returning to England in October and needed to brush

up on his acoustic guitar; he wasn't making the same mistake of play-ing a screaming guitar over there again.

The resulting album is an intimate, if imperfect, portrait of Muddy. The sounds are crisp, clean, and close; the microphones have been chosen and placed with care. Sensing the possibilities, Muddy accents his singing with hums and moans, the occasional side com-ment, and whispered lines. It is mostly great listening, though running underneath and surfacing occasionally ("My Captain," for example) is the sense that maintaining the conceit of his nearness has deflected Muddy's attention and diminished his feeling.

The next month, October of 1963, Muddy returned to Europe with the second American Folk Blues Festival, an annual tour that ran into the early 1970s. In London, the first of the seventeen dates — they'd also play Belgium, Germany, France, and Denmark — Muddy strode on stage and sat down. He strummed his acoustic guitar, per-haps mentioned how nice it was to be back, and then he moaned his way into the recently cut but as yet unissued "My Captain." Applause was not thunderous. Holding back nothing, he reached into his repertoire for a surefire winner and delivered a deep, solo version of "Rollin' Stone." Response was polite. Then the band joined him for quiet versions of "Five Long Years," "Blow Wind Blow," "Trouble No More," "My Home Is in the Delta," and "Mojo."

"Back at his London hotel after the concert, sharing a bottle of Johnny Walker with Memphis Slim, Matt 'Guitar' Murphy, and me, [Muddy] sat shaking his head in disbelief," recounted photographer Val Wilmer. "His wide, fine-featured face with its high New World Indian cheekbones seldom betrayed his emotions; now a look of gen-uine puzzlement disturbed it. Just what did they want, these [British] white folks? He'd brought along the acoustic guitar they'd de-manded. He'd given them the old down-home country blues this time — and now all they could ask him was, 'Why'd you leave the Telecaster behind?'"

Show after show he tried to win them over, but found that while Americans were digging the rootsier acoustic sounds, the British were still catching up with Muddy's *last* visit, buying electric guitars

and cranking their amps. Muddy's catalog had become widely available in England through an improved licensing and distribution deal
Chess struck with Pye Records in 1959. Muddy was unaware of his
influence; one British band (with David Bowie) was named the Manish Boys (maintaining the typo on the original release's label), another
was The Mojos, and a third was the Rolling Stones, who'd already
achieved a hit covering Chuck Berry's "Come On," with Muddy's "I
Want to Be Loved" on the flip side.

Anxious to crank his axe and rejuvenate his former image, he
readily agreed to return to England in the spring of 1964. This tour
would run a couple weeks, climax with a TV special, then hit Paris
for a night. Dubbed "The Blues and Gospel Train," it also featured
Sister Rosetta Tharpe, Sonny Terry and Brownie McGhee, Reverend
Gary Davis, Cousin Joe Pleasant from New Orleans, and Otis Spann.
Joe Boyd was hired as tour manager; he had just finished his studies
at Harvard, where, using the space beneath his dorm bed as a warehouse, he'd become the Boston-area distributor for Delmark Records.
Boyd went on to become a pioneer of folk-rock, producing artists as
diverse as Fairport Convention, Pink Floyd, Kate and Anna McGar-
rigle, and REM; he also founded the Hannibal label. "I've been associated with a lot of interesting things since this tour," he said, "but in
my view of my career in the music business, it was hard to top that
first job. I've never really been associated with anything that beat it."

Like the *Folk Singer* sessions that had anticipated the sound of his
1963 tour, the two songs Muddy cut a couple weeks before leaving in
1964 indicated this year's audience would find Muddy in top form.
"The Same Thing" and "You Can't Lost What You Ain't Never
Had" were a return to the blues that had put Chicago on the map.
"What make men go crazy when a woman wear her dress so tight?"
Muddy asks in the first line of "The Same Thing" (writing credited
to Dixon). The music is a perfect accompaniment, haunting and
dark, energetically restrained and full of latent power. Pee Wee
Madison makes his first studio appearance, his inexperience serving
him perfectly as a rhythm player; no sparks or West Side flash distract. There's also no harmonica player, which forces Muddy's slide

guitar to the fore. He shies not one bit from the challenge, establishing the song's mood with his opening guitar solo — exactly four notes, letting each one pierce like a knife puncture's pain, pushing the lingering sound with his slide as if twisting the weapon.

Less than three weeks later, on April 29, Muddy was on a stage in Bristol, a suburb of London, a crowd filling the large hall. For Joe Boyd, the tour's first night was a watershed experience. "Here were these guys who could barely fill a 150-seat coffeehouse in America and there the hall, with nearly 2,000 seats, was packed. Teenage girls were queuing outside the dressing room for Muddy's autograph. The kids were knowledgeable and really into it."

After a show at the Hammersmith Odeon, some students came backstage for autographs and invited the players to a party in the suburbs. Spann, always up for a good time, accepted when told there would be girls. Reverend Gary Davis too. Boyd joined them, and Muddy came along. "There were all these students gawking and for a split second I think Muddy got the idea that there might be some pussy here," said Boyd. "He started chatting with some girl but I think he realized that it probably wasn't on, that this was a bunch of innocent kids who were just blues fans. He always maintained this extraordinary dignity."

Spann began doing a featured spot, and on May 4, one of two days off, cut an album for English Decca, *Half Ain't Been Told,* backed by Muddy, Knowling, and Willie Smith (produced by Mike Vernon). A casual and relaxed session, the kinship between Muddy and Otis is easy to hear; with only a small rhythm section, the two exchange licks and riffs like old friends sharing a bottle, Muddy careful not to steal the spotlight. True to the Muddy band tradition, Spann cut a rocking version of the contemporary hit "Pretty Girls Everywhere," changing the verb from "see" to the more autobiographical "got": "Everywhere I go / I got a pretty girl there."

From outside, the blues world seemed small and intimate. But Joe Boyd realized from the start that the narrative he'd constructed about the artists was just that: a construct. "It came as a great shock to me that they didn't really know each other's music. Brownie and Sonny knew Gary from New York and from South Carolina but Cousin Joe was from another planet. The Chicago guys knew each other but Ransom wasn't that close to Muddy or Otis particularly. These were disparate universes that had no connection.

"The first morning in the hotel, Sister Rosetta and her manager/husband — she had a fur coat and he had a camel hair — she found herself sitting across the table from Reverend Gary. I thought, 'Well these two will get along because they're from this deep South gospel tradition.' Gary, he orders two fried eggs and he kind of feels the plate — he's blind — picks up one of the fried eggs and has yolk spilling down his front and drops it in his mouth. Sister Rosetta went, 'Puhlease!' She said, 'I don't ever want to sit at the same table as that man again.'"

Nevertheless, the disparate musicians began to draw together. On May 7, in an abandoned railway station, Granada TV staged a concert; it was Muddy's second appearance on English television within a year. "By the end," said Boyd, "Rosetta had done a 180-degree turn on Gary and decided he was the deepest man she had ever met. The last night she told me, 'When he does "Precious Lord," get me a microphone off stage.' He starts into this incredible version and Rosetta is on her knees backstage moaning right straight out of Arkansas, like she'd sang with her mother. Gary heard the voice and said, 'Sing it, Rosetta.' It was just incredible. And Muddy was in the wings watching all of this. I vividly remember him doing 'Long Distance Call' and he drew out that line 'another mule kicking in my stall' for ages, shaking his head from side to side. It was the height of the blues boom."

◊   ◊   ◊

Upon returning to the states, Muddy played some East Coast dates, dancing his jitterbug. "I have a feeling a white is going to get it and really put over the blues," Muddy told guitarist Michael Bloomfield in a 1964 interview. "I know they feel it, but I don't know if they can deliver the message."

Muddy had seen Bloomfield around South Side clubs since the

late 1950s, when the teenager used to take a bus and two trains to see — or hear — his hero. "From two blocks away, you'd hear that harmonica," said Bloomfield, "and then you'd hear Muddy's slide, and I'd be like a dog in heat." When the doorman refused entrance to the kids, they sat outside and listened. One time Muddy came out and shook their hands.

In England, there was a generation of kids who'd have relished being turned away from the door of a South Side club. All they had was the vinyl experience, none of the flesh, none of the smoke or the spilled drinks or the ladies hiking up their dresses and dancing dirty, cinder-block buildings made intimate by beer signs and precious little light.

"When we started the Rolling Stones, we were just little kids, right?" said Stones guitarist Keith Richards. "We felt we had some of the licks down, but our aim was to turn other people on to Muddy Waters."

Indeed, the band had formed after Richards bumped into Mick Jagger, who was carrying two albums: Chuck Berry's *Rockin' at the Hops* and *The Best of Muddy Waters*. "When I got to hear Muddy Waters," said Richards, "it all fell into place for me. He was the thing I was looking for, the thing that pulled it all in for me. When I heard him I realized the connection between all the music I'd heard. He made it all explainable. He was like a codebook. I was incredibly inspired by him as a musician."

The Rolling Stones named themselves after Muddy's song and began performing in 1962. Their first album included the lead track from Muddy's *The Best of,* "I Just Want to Make Love to You." (The success of the Stones' album meant a significant payment to Arc Music.) They toured the United States in 1964, stopping by the Chess studios to record in the same place as their heroes. At the time, Muddy was making his worst records; the horns on "Short Dress Woman" are heinous.

"We pulled up with the equipment," said Stones bassist Bill Wyman, "and we were out there putting the guitars in and the mike stands and amps. Muddy came walking down the street, and he helped us in with it. We were like [in awe]. And he was like, 'Come on boys. Gimme that. I'll help you.' A while earlier, we had been thinking, 'God, suppose we met Muddy Waters and those guys at the studio when we're there?'"

Richards's memory is slightly different. "We walked down the corridor and there's the assistant manager, here's the studio manager, over there some guy's painting the ceiling on a stepladder and as we're walking by our guide says, 'Oh, by the way, you might like to meet this guy — that's Muddy Waters.' And there's Muddy in overalls and he's whitewashing and I'll never forget the image, Muddy's great big beaming black face all splattered with whitewash and I'm looking at my man, right? This is America, right? This is the music business, right? We were going in to cut some of his songs in his own studio, but he ain't selling records at that time. He came down off the ladder, chatted for a bit — there was no animosity, no bitterness. He was such a gentleman." Muddy's matter-of-fact demeanor was the outgrowth of his sharecropping years; most anything, good or bad, that was happening to him in Chicago couldn't be as tough as the boss man's tub of silver dollars.

Unless he wasn't painting the ceiling. "That's some kind of Keith's fantasy, and I tease him about that," said Marshall Chess, who remembered the Stones "drinking straight whiskey out of bottles," which helps account for the differing memories. "If you knew Muddy Waters, he just wasn't in there painting the wall. Muddy was always dressed sharp as a tack. He wasn't about to be getting no paint spots on his Stetson shoes or his custom-made suit." (Several Chess employees find the painting story difficult to believe; one said, "Leonard would be the first one to say, 'Get your ass down, I don't want you falling off those damn ladders.'")

Meeting the longhairs meant little to Muddy at the time, though as their popularity grew, so did his respect and appreciation for them. Their first number-one song in the United States, summer of 1965, was "(I Can't Get No) Satisfaction," a title directly inspired by Muddy's "I Can't Be Satisfied." "The Rolling Stones created a whole wide-open space for the music," said Muddy. "They said who did it first and how they came by knowin' it. I tip my hat to 'em. It took the people from England to hip my people — my white people — that a black man's music is not a crime to bring in the house."

❖ ❖ ❖

Slowly but surely, gigs in white clubs were becoming more frequent. In Chicago, blues finally moved uptown when Big John's opened in a white neighborhood on the North Side. Paul Butterfield began building his reputation there, inviting South Side blues players to his gig. Soon enough, Muddy was there on Wednesday nights, Wolf took Thursdays, and Butterfield had Friday, Saturday, and Sunday. "I lived about four blocks from there," said Marshall Chess. "We would all sit around the table with Muddy. He was like a prince, this supreme, regal archetype bandleader. He was having his drink and looking for some pussy. He might not have said more than ten words. His presence — it's the feeling you got from him that was an immense thing."

From Big John's, the Butterfield Blues Band signed to Elektra Records and became stars with their song "Born in Chicago." Steve Miller saw an article about them in *Time* magazine and moved to Chicago. "Muddy had the best band, the best material, and it was always an event when he came in," Miller said. "I was in competition with him for the same gigs." Muddy got the sympathy vote in *Downbeat* magazine's 1964 Critics Poll: "Talent Deserving of Wider Recognition."

In 1964, a white guy working for Shaw Artists on the East Coast was looking at the company roster and was surprised to see Muddy among their clients. As rock and roll and then folk moved in, Shaw's involvement in blues gigs had declined; they'd virtually abandoned him. "I called Muddy to see what he needed for a week in a club," said Bob Messinger. "He said fifteen hundred bucks. He was very welcoming. He had already been to Europe, had a taste of the good life, and was interested in making progress. I started to get college dates for him right off the bat, one-nighters, which led me to believe the market was already there for him." Messinger landed him a week in Boston at the Jazz Workshop, seven nights plus a matinee — for $1,750. For that kind of money, Muddy added a sax player.

With Messinger at Shaw making the calls, glamour gigs on the East Coast picked up. At Muddy's first of two nights at the 1965 New York Folk Festival, held in Carnegie Hall, Muddy shared the bill ("The Evolution of Funk") with Son House, among others. House, who was tall and boney, walked backstage with his loose gait and one of Muddy's band members nudged another, then imitated the man's walk. "Muddy moved across to that guy quick," said Dick Waterman, Son House's manager. "Quick! And Muddy grabbed him. 'I seen you mockin' that man. Don't you be mocking that man.' And everybody fell back. He said, 'When I was a boy comin' up, that man was king. King! If it wasn't for that man, you wouldn't have a job. If it wasn't for that man, I wouldn't be here now.'"

Also in New York, Muddy squeezed in an Apollo gig with B. B. King, T-Bone Walker, Bo Diddley, and Bobby "Blue" Bland. Feeling good in the Big Apple, he bought Lucille a diamond ring — on the street. They rushed to a jewelry store to have it appraised. Muddy was an international star, but he was a rube country boy at heart: cut glass.

The big gig that summer of 1965 was Newport, a bill titled "The Family of Jazz." Muddy shared the lineup with Dizzy Gillespie, Memphis Slim and Willie Dixon, the Les McCann Trio, the Modern Jazz Quartet, Pete Seeger, and Big Joe Williams. His set included a jam with Dizzy Gillespie, but the real action took place with Butterfield, who upset folk stalwarts with his electric approach to blues. Introducing Butterfield, Alan Lomax lamented the band's lack of purity and bemoaned the future of the blues. His concerns were not shared by the audience ("We were boogying and totally blown out by the Butterfield Band," recalled blues artist Maria Muldaur) nor by Albert Grossman, who was managing Bob Dylan and about to sign Butterfield. The hefty Grossman took umbrage at Lomax's words, and in short order, the two gray-haired men were rolling and tumbling in the dust, fisticuffs.

In the blues arena, Muddy had settled the dispute over electricity and authenticity long ago in Chicago and in England more persuasively than he'd realized in 1958. Seven years later, America was coming to grips with its division and collision of cultures; what it meant for black people to bring their music — their lives — into white venues and white neighborhoods; and what it meant for whites to co-opt the culture. At a concert, this turmoil led to a fistfight; in the larger community, it led to riots. Martin Luther King came to Chicago in the mid-1960s, purchased an apartment building on the West Side, and began rehabilitating it. When Mayor Daley would not recognize him, he held a rally at Soldier Field, July 10, 1966; the 40,000 who attended got Daley's attention, but all he gave King was an audience. Two days later, police arrested West Side kids who were playing in a fire hydrant to keep cool, and the neighborhood, already steamed, blew its top; riots destroyed whole blocks. The city restored calm by promising movement toward open housing. A decade later the United States Justice Department found Chicago the most segregated city in America.

But in many ways, Muddy's black audience had aged with him; the next generation's black youth identified with the burgeoning soul sound. Electric or not, blues was stigmatized as their parents' music and, with Civil Rights assuming its just role in the era of black pride and nationalism, blues was shunned for its connection to slavery. For whites, the music's reach into the past validated it, giving it a vitality of generations. (B. B. King, too, was breaking into a white audience with his *Live at the Regal.*) The fact that it was the basis for rock and roll and allowed for solos that were emotional, fevered, and expansive — and soon indulgent — made it all the more alluring. Controversy put a sheen on it. Sizzling moments were naturally attractive to Bob Dylan, so he enlisted Butterfield and his drummer Sam Lay and guitarist Mike Bloomfield to accompany his sidemen Al Kooper and Harvey Brooks at the 1965 Newport festival. Together they put the rock in folk and ratcheted up the decade's energy level. The chain was direct: Muddy, Butterfield, Dylan.

❖ ❖ ❖

January of 1966 marked the release of Muddy's first LP in two years, *The Real Folk Blues,* a compilation of mostly electric and rocking material recorded — and released as singles — between 1947 and 1964. The concept, scrawled on the back of a menu at Batt's Restaurant across the street from the Chess offices, was the same as 1958's *The Best of,* and if it didn't cause as much sensation as that reintroduction had, it did reach its intended audience. The folkies were still catching up to the Muddy 78s and 45s that had predated their interest. The success of this album initiated a series of such compilations for other Chess blues artists.

In Chicago, his fans had an extra treat: Muddy took a job as a disc jockey on WOPA, where his old friend Big Bill Hill was king. He was on from two till four in the afternoon, playing blues, but he wasn't cut out for it. "I had a lot of people listen at me 'cause that phone jump off the wall when I got on the air with 'em. And I was playing it for them, too. But I couldn't make no disc jockey. I'm tellin' you I can't wear but one shoe. At night I'd be hoarse, so I give it up."

In the spring of 1966, the Shaw Artists Corporation closed its doors. Muddy was playing Boston and, with a line forming at the door, Bob Messinger approached him. He was clean, sharp, spoke with a Cape Cod accent. There was culture and money around him like Muddy hadn't known. Messinger proposed becoming his manager. "Muddy said, 'What you gonna charge me?'" recalled Messinger. "I said, 'Union says I can charge you fifteen percent. I'll charge you ten percent on nightclub dates, and fifteen percent on concerts and colleges.' He said, 'That's more than fair, you got a deal.'"

Muddy kept Messinger closed out of his business with the Chesses. "Muddy kept his relationship with them very personal," Messinger said. "Whatever went on there, it was his business only." Muddy got money and legal counsel, but most importantly, he got security, a furnish, from Chess — his bills would not go unpaid. With a manager, Muddy could create a more formal relationship with the label, but he was allowing no manager to get between him and the Chesses. So Messinger exploited his strength, which was booking.

Chess's latest idea was to sell Muddy to B. B. King's audience, which was older blacks and younger whites. King played uptown blues, his stinging guitar runs couched in urbanized horn arrangements. "I play cotton-patch music, cornfield, fish fry," Muddy said. "B. B. and Albert [King] are a different style, a higher class of people'd see them."

To attract that audience, Chess devised *Muddy, Brass, & the Blues,* a concept album that didn't change Muddy's cotton patch so much as tried to hide it. Muddy and the band recorded their parts — about a dozen tracks — on Wednesday, June 22, 1966, and the horns came in the next day. Like a second project laid atop Muddy's, they overdubbed on every song; an organ was also added on four. The brass is crisp and tight, with lots of flash, but it says nothing about Muddy Waters or the blues; the horns don't belong. The *Brass & Blues* sessions were Cotton's last with the band for about four years. It was obviously time to leave.

Sandwiched between the ill-fated *Muddy, Brass, & the Blues* and an insipid session with clarinets, Muddy unleashed a burst of independence, a song called "My Dog Can't Bark," a track so explosive it's like a telegram to Chess Records — with music, because he wouldn't say it with words — that he was a BLUESMAN, that trends would come and go, that some sounds would get popular and other sounds would fade, but his sound was drawn from the eternal well, that it could be played solo and slow or fast with a group, and in case you forgot what that sounds like, dig this — motherfucker. "Down through the years you're going to get a whuppin' and I got mine good," Muddy said. "'Cause those record companies will whup you to death. You believe me. I know." Recorded at a Chess session, "My Dog Can't Bark" chases bad blues up a tree. Muddy plays like he's actually got a tiger in his pants, not like he's just singing about one. Instead of Dixieland horns appended, Muddy revs and revives his slide, darts like a fishtailing skid. (It's the same slide guitar sound heard on Bob Dylan's "Highway 61," which came out ten weeks later, with Marshall Chess's high school chum Michael Bloomfield playing it.) Cotton's harp runs across his lips like each note is giving him electric shock. Muddy sings, "The people they're talking about me and you /

I done got tired, I'm gonna talk some too." But Chess wasn't listening and Muddy capitulated, making more of his career-worst records.

Muddy's music wasn't the only thing suffering. The rough life began to take its toll on the drinking and smoking Otis Spann. On October 9, 1966, while touring in California, he suffered a heart attack and landed in the hospital. A few days later, playing at the Troubadour in Los Angeles, Muddy was reunited with Pete Welding, who'd spent half a decade on the South Side and earned Muddy's trust, representing him in some business dealings when asked. (His Testament Records recorded some of Muddy's and his band mates' finest material.) Welding's review of the show in the jazz magazine *Downbeat* provides a window into Muddy's deep blues (a window Chess Records did not see):

> Earlier in the week, Otis Spann had suffered a mild coronary attack and had been hospitalized for a few days. He was eager to play, despite his weakened condition, but Waters forbade it — except for one feature, "Five Long Years," and Spann, though obviously shaky, turned in his usual impeccable job. . . . [Muddy's] singing was a revelation — strong and direct, refreshingly free of the artifice and gimmickry that has marred a good bit of his vocal work over the last few years. . . . His voice is still full of dark, smoldering power, bristling with emotion, with a sharp edge of pain to it. At the end of a superbly sensitive "Blues Before Sunrise," he surprised his listeners with two choruses straight out of Robert Johnson — sung in the high aching falsetto of that master of the Delta blues. They were a vivid reminder of Waters's own deep roots in the music of his native Mississippi.
>
> His bottleneck playing was excellent, recalling his prototypical work in this genre on his early commercial recordings in the late 1940s and early 1950s. . . . The high point of the evening was Waters's solo performance of "Country Blues," his personalized adaptation of Robert Johnson's "Walking Blues." On this piece, the bottleneck playing, in open tuning,

was by far the most compelling of the evening, harking back as it did to Waters's earliest and most expressive use of this old Delta technique.

Muddy's return to his early style was probably, in part, a direct nod to Welding. Welding's record label, Testament, was responsible for *Down on Stovall's Plantation,* an LP of most of the Fisk–Library of Congress recordings, reminding fans and newcomers alike of the depth of Muddy's blues. The release was set in motion a couple years earlier in Chicago, when Welding played Muddy three of the Stovall tracks from a blues compilation. "Muddy asked, 'Where is the rest of them?'" said Welding. "He told me he had done a whole bunch of those for Mr. Lomax on two separate occasions. Muddy didn't bullshit, so I believed what he said. We sent to the Library of Congress and requested a copy. A few weeks later we received them and had a listening party. Muddy said, 'We got to get this stuff out.' He thought it was wonderful. But Leonard Chess did not want to put it out. He thought the sound was terrible, it was too old-fashioned, and besides, he had lots of other Muddy recordings that he hadn't released."

What Muddy had done on a summer day a quarter century earlier was now of interest well beyond his old circle of Friar's Point and Rena Lara. People all over America and beyond were interested in hearing what he'd done. It made his life seem very very large, and also very very small. What had happened to McKinley Morganfield? The world knew Muddy Waters, bluesman, but what of Della's grandson, what of "Stovall's famous guitar picker"?

CHAPTER 12

ROLLIN' STONE

1967–1969

I n the editor's note of the first issue from late 1967, Jann Wenner
wrote about his new magazine directed at the mushrooming
youth market, "The name of it is *Rolling Stone,* which comes from an
old saying: 'A rolling stone gathers no moss.' Muddy Waters used the
name for a song he wrote; the Rolling Stones took their name from
Muddy's song, and 'Like a Rolling Stone' was the title of Bob Dylan's
first rock and roll record." To the un-generation, characterized by re-
bellion and rejection of their past (and expressing it across Chicago at
the 1968 Democratic Convention), Muddy presented a heritage far
from their suburban homes, a life of experience — unsuburban, un-
modern, unmanufactured: real. That didn't mean they preferred
buying his records over those released by the younger artists he influenced, but it meant both respect and increased sales.

Chess Records, in high-concept mode, realized that an album
cover with several of its stars' names could move some of this new
market's disposable income from their blue-jean pockets to the company coffers. At the start of 1967, Muddy, Bo Diddley, and Little
Walter created *Super Blues,* an album that rocked up the blues and
tried, unsuccessfully, to create an intimacy between the artists. "Hey
Muddy," thuds Bo, "my baby got a mojo." Walter rasps like he needs
medical treatment. The package was successful enough to repeat half
a year later, this time replacing Walter with Wolf. Though still not a
crowning musical achievement, the *Super Super Blues* album was an
improvement. Putting Muddy and Wolf in the same room was sure
to create sparks, and it did: Wolf begins taunting Muddy, "I'm the
king, I'm the king."

This new recording of old material was followed by another compilation of Muddy's old recordings. *More Real Folk Blues* focuses on Muddy's slide playing, and tracks such as "Sad Letter," "Early Morning Blues," and "Whiskey Blues" stirred not only the folk and rock fans, but Muddy himself. "One of the few times I saw Muddy come out of himself was just after the album *More Real Folk Blues* had been released," said writer Peter Guralnick. "A friend of mine had gotten the record at the Harvard radio station and he interviewed Muddy and played excerpts from it on the air. This was the first Muddy had seen of the record, and it stimulated both his engagement and his imagination. His performance at Club 47 later that night included songs and open tunings that he probably hadn't employed in ages."

Another fortuitous encounter came during a chilly October 1967 stint at a Montreal club. Local enthusiasts arranged to record Muddy and the band informally at their rooming house. With a kitchen there, and a relaxed sense of familiarity, the band was at ease, smoking cigarettes and drinking coffee while the recordists set up. In his liner notes to *Goin' Way Back,* Michael Nerenberg writes, "All eyes seemingly turned together towards the silhouette in the doorway as Muddy stepped into the room, a purple velvet house robe adding a certain majesty to his already imposing presence. Even the slippers and hair net little diminished the dignity of his bearing." Muddy strums a bit, is told it's all working, answers sleepily: "Crazy." He slides down a string, strumming a slow rocking rhythm, playing runs and falls, working the sleep from his voice on "Gypsy Woman" like he might have on a 1930s Sunday afternoon after a late night out. It's an acoustic session, and Muddy's in the mood. By the third song, "My Home Is in the Delta," his slide is going to town and back, Sammy Lawhorn accompanying him. Muddy addresses his final song to Lucille, who is sitting quietly while her man records; it's "Mean Disposition."

Later that year, Muddy recorded two studio sessions for Chess, producing an album's worth of honest material, Mud playing Mud. The songs are good and so is the music, which is probably why they were not released for four years — until Chess finally decided that an unmediated Mud might be better than a manufactured Mud.

❖ ❖ ❖

In February of 1968, Muddy landed in New York City short a harmonica player. Guitarist Luther "Georgia Boy" / "(Creepin') Snake"
Johnson, who'd recently joined, reminded him about the white guy
they'd met a couple tours back; he'd come to the Apollo's backstage
with a friend of the band, all jive and attitude, talking Harlem soul
stew. His name was Paul Oscher and he'd managed to emulate Walter's amplified tone without benefit of an amp. Hearing the kid's big
fat sound, Snake had whooped, "Motherfucker's got a tone."

So Snake called Paul, who'd recently turned eighteen, and Paul
ran to the club. He played "Baby Please Don't Go" and "Blow Wind
Blow" in a stairwell and Muddy told him, "I like the way you play,
man." Oscher recalled, "Muddy didn't speak too much, and he often
spoke with his finger to his lips, like he was reminding himself to
hush even when he was speaking. I got in this old Volkswagen van
with most of the band, some of their girlfriends. They all had pints of
gin. Spann says, 'Lucille, let me see my shit, baby.' And she hands him
his pistol. I'm thinking, 'I'm into this shit here.'" Indeed, Paul was in.

Perhaps not surprisingly, most white audiences thought it natural
that a white player was in the band; they'd come to Muddy through
the Rolling Stones and other blues-based rock groups. "I was really,
really crazy about Paul," said Muddy's granddaughter Cookie. "I was
just becoming a teenager when Paul came to the house. Other white
guys came around and were a little standoffish but Paul really clicked
with the family. We would laugh and look at TV and Daddy would
really be on Paul's case. 'I'm gonna fine ya, Paul, your shirt wasn't
clean.' 'I'm gonna fine ya, Paul, you was late.' I'd be like, 'Whoa, I'm
glad he's here today, I'm out of trouble.' Paul would walk up and
down the street and I would tell everybody, 'Don't mess with him,
that's my cousin, he doesn't have good sense.' But Paul was the only
white person I ever seen that had such a good rapport on the low
South Side. We'd sit on the porch and he'd laugh at my friends or
make jokes, start playing the harmonica. I would be so happy when
Paul walked in the door."

Adult guidance had not been plentiful in Cookie's life. She was thirteen, pregnant with Muddy's first great-grandchild; he was fifty-six. Muddy wasn't home when the doctor called with the results of her pregnancy test. According to Cookie, "Geneva went to the cabinet and poured herself a drink. She said, 'You are lucky, Cookie, because you slipped by.' She assumed positive meant *positively not pregnant.*" When Muddy came home, Cookie hid. "He started searching and calling my name. It felt like the whole house had crumbled. I left out the back door and went over to the lake — but I had a phobia about water. When I came back, Muddy looked like a monster standing on that porch. But he was very supportive. The one requirement for me was that I stay in school through the pregnancy."

Around Muddy, sex was everywhere. Not long after Paul arrived, he sat on Muddy's front stoop and a woman in the building across the street waved at him. "She was eating ice cream, she said, 'You want some ice cream?'" Paul recounted; he promptly moved in with Fannie Mae and her two little kids. "I told Muddy that she had a biting pussy," Paul said, "that she could clench and unclench it, so about a week later she said, 'Guess who was just on the phone with me? Your boss!' He was trying to get her to meet him around the corner." Paul laughed, then added, "I mean it was no exclusive situation. She was fucking her boyfriend on Saturdays."

Not everyone was so tolerant. Hanging with Muddy's guitarist Pee Wee Madison in front of their building, Paul was flirting with a girl from another floor named Barbara when a guy named Roy stepped outside and said, "This is for you, bitch," and shot her in the head. They thought he was shooting blanks until she slowly spiraled to the ground, began convulsing. Paul looked at Pee Wee. Pee Wee shook his head. Roy stood next to them, holding the gun. Like cartoon characters, Paul and Pee Wee zigzagged across the street. Muddy called the police, then retrieved his .38 snub-nose from the headboard of his bed, stuck it outside the waist wrap of his house robe, strolled out front where Roy was threatening witnesses, and announced, "Motherfucker don't scare nobody."

"Guns were part of the scene," said Oscher. "Muddy had a hatbox of guns, maybe six or eight, he kept in the hall closet. One was a Wyatt Earp special, it had a long long barrel, real old. And he had a Winchester .38. He used to carry the snub-nose .38 all the time until he switched that for a little five-shot .25."

He wasn't alone. Bo slept with a sawed-off shotgun next to his bed, which Paul found out when he moved into the basement after Fannie Mae froze him out. "When Bo would sleep, if he was drinking, he would start shouting shit like, 'Move, bitch, move, motherfucker, move, bitch.' And I knew he had a shotgun next to him."

Pee Wee was known to the cops. They'd slow when they saw him, and he'd raise his shirt, showing no weapons in his waistband. But he was a small guy and he kept his elbows at his side, a pistol in the crook of his back. One New Year's Eve, Muddy and Geneva were celebrating with Bo, Otis Spann and his girlfriend, and a few other close friends. "They were drinking and having a good time," said Cookie, who throughout her childhood believed Bo was Muddy's blood brother. "In a black neighborhood on New Year's Eve they sometimes shoot their gun. Muddy and Bo were in the little vestibule right in the front and Muddy fired. Bo said, 'Oh Lord, Muddy, you done shot me in the leg,' and I remember Geneva saying they couldn't call the police because they didn't want that in the paper. They took Bo in the basement and Muddy tells me to go get the pail with the water and I'm thinking, 'When people shot you're supposed to take people to the hospital.' Bo was a big burly man, really, really dark, and he kept saying, 'No, no, Muddy could get in trouble.' Muddy this, Muddy that. Otis Spann went to the store and got two-fifths, Old Granddaddy, 100 proof. And they put Bo in this room and fed him liquor." A week later, Bo climbed up the steps and returned to the world.

An undercurrent of danger ran through even the good times. The Blackstone Rangers, a "community service" group that carried weapons openly, set its territorial line at Forty-third and Lake Park — Muddy's block. South of Forty-third belonged to the Stones; the Devil's Disciples — the "Ds"— had the North. "My mom's boyfriend was a Blackstone Ranger," said Joseph, Muddy and Lucille's son. "A sign on the wall would tell me what kind of area I'm going into. Wherever I go, I always look at the graffiti."

"I used to tease Paul about the gangs and he'd say I was just try-ing to scare him," said Cookie. "Our house was a dividing point and the fighting would start there. One day I called him outside and said just stand in the doorway and watch." The sight remains etched in Paul's memory: "The Blackstones parading down the street chanting, carrying sticks and weapons, chanting, 'Who run it? We run it!'" Guns, guns, everybody had guns.

◇ ◇ ◇

Little Walter's life was a skeleton key to death's door, and he was al-ways rattling the lock. "Every time I seen Little Walter, he was con-stantly looking over his shoulder," said Oscher. "He must have did so many bad things he didn't know when the shit was going to happen." He'd book himself into three or four clubs a night, a different band in each, do a set at all of them, and get paid by all. But the sound of his small combo jump blues had become dated, while Muddy's Delta sound rolled on like a freight train. "I think he was sort of a broken man," said Oscher. "His music didn't have the endurance of Muddy's stuff."

"Daddy and them would talk about Walter, what he was caught up in or how he would start fights or be at a club and do something vulgar to a woman," Cookie remembered. "But when Little Walter came to Muddy house, he was just himself, not Little Walter. His guards were down. We'd be watching TV and he'd fall asleep, or something like that." With his oldest friends, Walter didn't have to act like a star.

"The last time I saw Little Walter," Blue Smitty, Muddy's early guitarist, told *Living Blues* magazine, "I knew he wasn't here for long. I hadn't saw him in quite a while. Oh man, he had wasted away to nothing. And he saw me, he didn't hardly recognize me. And he said, 'Smitty, I done been out there, man.' I said, 'Yeah, you done been out there, baby, but I don't think you're gonna get back.' And it wasn't long."

On Valentine's Day, 1968, Junior Wells ran into Little Walter. "We were still hangin' out together, over here on Forty-third and

Lake Park and down to Theresa's. Walter was over there like they do, shootin' dice on the street, and a man throwed the dice and hit Walter in the butt with 'em and went to get the money and Walter picked up the money. And the man asked Walter for the money and Walter wouldn't give him the money and he took a hammer and hit Walter in the head with it. And nobody thought anything about it. You know, it didn't sound like it was that hard a lick. He went on home and he told his old lady to give him somethin' 'cause he [said], 'I got a bad headache.' So the next mornin' she woke up, he was dead."

The harmonica is a breath away from the soul of a man, and Walter's soul was rambling, roaming, and adventurous. Only slightly more complex than blowing a blade of grass, the harmonica cupped in his hands soared, dove, and emoted longing and pain like teenagers in congress. And now, with barely a gust, he was gone.

◇ ◇ ◇

Despite everything, Geneva remained the backbone of Muddy's home. A van would pull up and Earl Hooker, St. Louis Jimmy, Johnny Young, Floyd Jones, Roosevelt Sykes, and Little Brother Montgomery would pile out, beginning a card game that might last hours or days. The band hung on Muddy's stoop, drinking. Cookie was in and out, getting ready to have a baby. Rarely did anything faze the woman they called Grandma. She stayed in the kitchen, queen of her domain, humming, sipping from a small bottle in the cupboard, sending Paul or another boarder out for replenishment. There was a lot of entertaining to do. "He loved putting out a big bash," said Cookie. "And a lot of the musicians would come by and eat. We would always have big dinners during the holidays."

Muddy's son William, the child he'd had with Mary Austin from Florida, was about ten when he found out who his father was, and telephoned. "I said, 'Daddy, I want to come see you.' He didn't say, 'I'm a married man and I got a wife and if you come here, she's going to know what's going on.' He hurt me, broke my heart, he said, 'I don't think it's a good thing to do right now.'"

Muddy was head of enough households. "He'd come around and check on us," said Joseph, who was being raised by his mom, Lucille, in her apartment around the corner from Muddy's house. "He'd bring us food and money. He had a blue Cadillac at the time and all the kids would run to his car. He had another home, we knew this, but he would come spend time with us, maybe take us grocery shopping, whatever we needed."

Lucille remained unabashed about her place in Muddy's life. She came unannounced to Muddy's house in need of cash. Finding her at the door, and with Geneva in the kitchen, Muddy introduced her as Bo's girlfriend. "Muddy would get in his Cadillac," said Oscher, "you'd know he was going to see his girlfriend."

"Hell yeah Geneva knew," said her son Charles, then in his late twenties. "She was a good woman. She stood by her man. Long as he taken care of the home, it didn't faze her. They'd argue about the women once in a while, but they'd make up."

"The day that I gave birth to my child, which I was only thirteen, I came home," said Cookie, "and the phone rang. Muddy and Geneva were very excited about my child, they'd bought a beautiful crib. It was Lucille calling. She told Geneva, 'You're happy because Cookie has a little girl. But I had a baby two days before for Muddy.' Geneva knew of every child that was born out of wedlock, the birth date, everything. I don't see how she did it. I would not have tolerated Muddy's shit."

⋄   ⋄   ⋄

The coffeehouse and folk boom had been good for Muddy; his appearance at Newport had launched him into a new audience. But the war in Vietnam again changed that audience. Somewhere in the decade, coffee gave way to psychedelics, electrics to electronics. Muddy described the Electric Circus, a New York psychedelic club he played, as "blinking blinking jiving jiving shit."

By now, it wasn't just Leonard who was making the musical decisions; Marshall Chess was coming into his own at his father's label. An acid man, Marshall launched a subsidiary label called Cadet Con-

Muddy's cabin was built by a hunter from hand-hewn cypress planks before the Civil War. When Muddy lived there, rooms had been added and it looked similar to the home in the left background. Photo © John Rockwood INSET: *Ollie Morganfield, Muddy's father, from a veteran's ID card, 1961. Courtesy of Robert Morganfield*

The Stovall Commissary, where Muddy was recorded in 1942. The farm office and post office are on the far side of the store; beyond that, visible through the porch, is the juke joint. Courtesy of Stovall Farms

"Son" Sims   Muddy Water

Working on his manuscript about the Delta, John Work III returned to Coahoma
County in June of 1943 "for the purpose of interviews to fill in certain gaps
in the materials and to obtain some pictures of Delta scenery." Muddy, thirty,
is holding a National steel guitar, the kind favored by his idol Son House.
That's Work's handwriting at the bottom; note the singular Water.
Courtesy of the Center for Popular Music, Middle Tennessee State
University/John W. Work III Field Collection

Settling into Chicago, mid-1940s. Front row, left to right: Muddy Waters, John Lee "Sonny Boy" Williamson, Lacy Belle Williamson, Andrew "Bo" Bolton. Back row: unknown boy, Eddie Boyd, unknown woman. Courtesy of Bill Greensmith

Muddy Waters and Big Bill Broonzy, Chicago, mid-1940s.
Courtesy of Jim O'Neal

Advertisement from the Chicago Defender, *April 16, 1950.*
The changing of the guard. Courtesy of the Ron Fritts Collection

The Muddy Waters Band at the Zanzibar, 1954.
Left to right: Muddy Waters, Henry Armstrong, Otis Spann, Henry "Pot" Strong,
Elga "Elgin" Edmonds, Jimmy Rogers. Courtesy of Mary Katherine Aldin

CHESS RECORDING
ARTIST

MUDDY WATERS
And His Orchestra

Direction
SHAW ARTISTS CORPORATION
565 Fifth Avenue
New York 17, New York

The Hoochie Coochie Man joins Shaw Artists, 1955.
Courtesy of Mary Katherine Aldin

On tour in Florida, summer 1956. Left to right: James Cotton, Muddy Waters, Otis Spann. Photo © Elga "Elgin" Edmonds, courtesy of D. Thomas Moon

Otis Spann and Muddy Waters, Chicago, 1959. Photo © Georges Adins, courtesy of Jacques Pescheux / Bulletin du Hot Club de France

Muddy Waters at home with his wife Geneva and his granddaughter Amelia "Cookie" Cooper, 1959. Photo © Georges Adins, courtesy of Mary Katherine Aldin

Hanging out in Muddy's basement, 1959. Left to right: James Cotton (cropped), Sonny Boy Williamson II (Rice Miller), Jimmy Rogers, Muddy Waters, Otis Spann (cropped). Photo © Georges Adins, courtesy of Block *magazine, the Netherlands*

Muddy with girlfriend Lois Anderson, 1959, Smitty's Corner. Chris Barber and Ottilie Patterson are next to Lois. Courtesy of Chris Barber

Muddy at Pepper's Lounge with Letha Jones (left) and unknown friend, circa 1960. Courtesy of Letha Jones and Jim O'Neal

On the road, early 1960s. Left to right: Francis Clay, Andrew Stephenson, Muddy Waters, James Cotton. Courtesy of Keith Richards

Muddy Waters and Otis Spann in England, October 1963.
Photo © Val Wilmer, London

Germany, 1963. Photo © Stephanie Wiesand,
courtesy of Axel Kustner

Mid-1960s.
Courtesy of Mary Katherine Aldin

Muddy with Lucille McClenton, backstage in Memphis, mid-1960s.
Photo © Sid Selvidge, courtesy of Don Nix

England, 1970.
Photo © Sylvia Pitcher

Backstage at Mr. Kelly's, 1971.
Val Wilmer: "Years before I'd
been taking a picture of Muddy
and he got really cross because
there was a bottle of whiskey next
to him. In the meantime, the
whole world had changed with
the Rolling Stones and everybody
wearing their hair long, and at
Mr. Kelly's Muddy didn't mind
being photographed in his under-
shirt with a bottle in his hand."
Photo © Val Wilmer, London

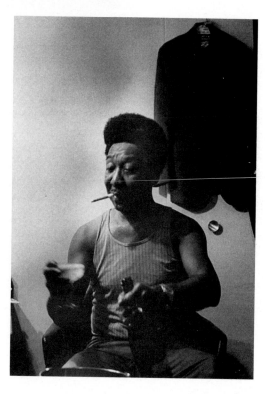

New Zealand, 1973. Left to right: Mojo Buford, Calvin Jones, Willie Smith,
Muddy Waters, Pinetop Perkins, Sammy Lawhorn, Pee Wee Madison.
Photo © Sal Criscillo

Muddy and Katie, about whom he sings on Unk in Funk, *circa 1974.*
Photo © Terry Abrahamson

*Suburban Mud: Westmont, 1978. Left to right: Muddy Waters,
great-granddaughter NaCherrie Cooper, great-granddaughter Chandra Cooper,
daughter Roslind Morganfield, playmate Lisa. Photo © Herb Nolan*

At the Bottom Line, New York, 1975. Left to right: Muddy, Bob Dylan, Paul Oscher. Photo © Willie Strandberg

The old school and the new: Muddy and Johnny Winter, 1977. Photo © Marc PoKempner

As soul music grew from the blues, new stars often came to pay tribute to the roots. This is Muddy and Stevie Wonder in the mid-1970s. Photo courtesy of Jim O'Neal

With the Rolling Stones at the Quiet Knight, 1978. Left to right: Mick Taylor, Muddy Waters, Mick Jagger, Keith Richards, Charlie Watts. Photo © Terry Abrahamson

Preaching the blues, England, 1977.
Photo © Sylvia Pitcher

cept, reaching out to his compadres on the mind-expansion trip. His first project, an album with Minnie Ripperton, sold a quarter million copies in the Midwest, making him a hero at home. Muddy referred to Marshall as "my little white grandson" and gave him lines to use on girls. "He would always ask me, 'Did you get any yet?'"

From his childhood on, Marshall had worked in the Chess facilities — office, studio, publishing, even operating the pressing-plant machinery. While still a teenager, Marshall went to Europe and arranged new and successful distribution deals for the catalog, also picking up on European fashions. "I was really into clothes and jewelry, just like blacks. My dad, too. My dad drove a new Cadillac every year, had the big ring on his finger, and he always told me that he would not be respected by his artists if he didn't. So I followed that. When I was thirteen I had a suit custom made, same tailor that these blues guys went to." In Paris, he'd been impressed by the shop of up-start fashion designer Yves St. Laurent, and modified the design for himself. "I had the wood walls of my office painted with shiny black epoxy paint, there was a gray rug, and the windows behind the desk were this black-and-white op art. It was high design. Chuck Berry dug it. I saw him decades later and he said, 'Man, that office. I knew you were a motherfucker, anyone who would have that office.'"

With his new power, and with the noblest intentions, Marshall attempted to bring that new audience he'd tapped to the blues, or at least to the bluesmen's bank accounts. "*Electric Mud* was a misunderstood project," he said of the album recorded simultaneously with France's May Revolution in 1968. "I came up with the idea of *Electric Mud* to help Muddy make money. It wasn't to bastardize the blues. It was like a painting, and Muddy was going to be in the painting. It wasn't to change his sound, it was a way to get it into that market." He tapped players from Chess's jazz label for the palette. "I put together the hottest, most avant-garde jazz-rock guys in Chicago for the album," said Marshall. "We were going to call them the Electric Niggers, but my dad wouldn't let me."

"I thought we were going to do a straight blues session when they said Muddy Waters," said guitarist Pete Cosey, who played lead guitar on the album. "I came prepared to play the old-time blues and found some electronic equipment there. So I hooked up into it and we took off. Muddy didn't have anything to do but be Muddy Waters and everything was swirling around him. He was going around the studio shaking his head. All through the session he said, 'I don't know, boy, I don't know.' He didn't get upset, or if he did, he didn't let it throw things off. But he was clearly confused."

Like on the farm, don't cross the boss. "A lot of people go in for [the effects] and I just tried to dedicate them a recording," Muddy said not long after the record hit the market. "Really I was shooting for the hippies with that." *Electric Mud* is remembered more for its over-the-top electronic effects than for its high points, which is not fair. True, the album is so full of screeching instruments and pulsating organs that it parodies the avant–Miles Davis sound it was emulating, but there are tracks, such as "I Just Want to Make Love to You" and "Herbert Harper's Free Press News," that achieve a unique artistry. If the record lacks subtlety, as a historical document it has a certain charm. Muddy's facial expression on the album's back cover is a Mona Lisa cipher; is he smiling or is he wincing?

(Pete Cosey was later told by Jimi Hendrix's valet that before he'd perform, Jimi would play "Herbert Harper's Free Press News" from *Electric Mud* for inspiration. "The first guitarist I was aware of was Muddy Waters," Hendrix said. "I heard one of his old records when I was a little boy and it scared me to death, because I heard all of those sounds. 'Wow, what is *that* all about?'")

Electric Mud became Muddy's first album to hit the *Billboard* (and *Cash Box*) charts, where it stayed for two months. *After the Rain,* recorded half a year later — soon after *Electric Mud*'s release — repeats the concept, though slightly toned down. "I'll never forget," said guitarist Cosey, "as soon as I walked into the studio for the follow-up and Muddy saw me, he threw his arms around me, said, 'Hey, how you doing, boy, play some of that stuff you played on that last album.'" On *After the Rain,* Muddy is given more of a voice and has Spann and Oscher in his corner; he is allowed lead guitar on several tracks. He contributes three new songs, though there is no recorded evidence of his ever playing them again.

Though *Electric Mud* shipped to retailers like a success and initially sold well, critics in America panned it. "It was the biggest Muddy Waters record we ever had at Chess," said Marshall, "and it dropped instantly. The English accepted it; they are more eccentric." The adulteration was so dense, the reviews so disappointing, and the warehouse returns so heavy that Muddy expressed his frustration, though he waited long enough — until 1970 — for whatever sales might occur to taper off: "They got this funny thing going, man. Every time I go into Chess to record, they are going to put some un-blues players with me. And it ain't that they're not good players, those boys can play just about anything, they some of the top-notch guitar players in Chicago, but they can't get that blues sound. And if you change my sound, then you gonna change the whole man."

Near the end of his life, he was even harsher: "That *Electric Mud* record I did, that one was dogshit. But when it first came out, it started selling like wild, and then they started sending them back. They said, 'This can't be Muddy Waters with all this shit going on — all this wow-wow and fuzztone.'"

Chess was not done conceptualizing, though their next effort was nearer to Muddy's mind. Instead of bending Muddy to fit the contrivances of the hippies, they would bring the hippies to Muddy. The idea for *Fathers and Sons* was conceived by Michael Bloomfield and producer Norman Dayron. Muddy and Spann were the elders, and in addition to Bloomfield, the accompanists included Paul Butterfield on harmonica, Sam Lay on drums — musicians from the Chicago scene with whom Muddy was familiar — and bassist Duck Dunn, from Memphis soul group Booker T. and the MGs. Every cut on the two-album set is a remake of a Muddy classic. Half the album was recorded in the studio over three days in late April of 1969, and half is drawn from a concert that the studio group performed the day after the studio session was done. "We did a lot of the things over we did with Little Walter and Jimmy Rogers and Elgin on drums," Muddy said during the making of the album. "It's about as close as I've been to [that feel] since I first recorded it." And, in fact, it is a real fine treatment. The "sons" had enough age and experience not to rush the music; when Muddy introduces the slow, slow tempo, they're dragging it right beside him. (Bloomfield's heroin habit, which soon would kill him, contributed to his leisurely crawl.)

They ably backed him at the live show. "Muddy's got everybody crazy," the reporter sent by *Rolling Stone* wrote. "He ends it, turns on his heel, and makes his way through the throng of musicians and followers who have come out of the wings and onto the stage. Pandemonium. He reappears. Chaos." For nearly ten minutes after he left the stage, the audience roared its delight. They stomped, shouted, clapped, whistled, screamed, jumped up and down in aisles and on seats. Backstage, Mud was heard to mutter, "It's just like Newport out there."

❖ ❖ ❖

During the making of *Fathers and Sons,* word spread that Leonard was thinking of getting out. He promptly received an offer from the General Recorded Tape (GRT) Corporation. They manufactured audiotape and were ready to own a catalog of material to stick onto that tape. They offered 6.5 million dollars plus 20,000 shares of GRT stock for Chess Records and its associated labels and hard assets (excluding the publishing arm of Arc). For that, Leonard was ready to move on. He'd accumulated three radio stations and his eyes were on bigger horizons. "My dad's plan with the GRT money was black TV," said Marshall. "He was going to leapfrog from radio to TV, starting with Chicago." Unlike at the radio stations, most of the executive staff at Chess Records was white, drawing intense pressure from the Black Power movement. "Jesse Jackson used to try to force me to hire more blacks," said Marshall. "That movement was centering on Chicago. But we gave back a lot to the black community. The radio station used to give tons — tons — of food away for Thanksgiving and Christmas. My father gave to the Urban League, NAACP, Martin Luther King's first radio show, scholarship funds."

"I made my money on the Negro," Leonard told the *Chicago Daily News* a couple years earlier, "and I want to spend it on him."

Muddy was a dedicated hand. The Chess family, like the Stovalls, would never let him starve, and that was Muddy's bottom-line concern. He'd seen starvation, in Mississippi and in Chicago. "I'll be with Chess as long as there's a Chess in the company," Muddy said at the time of the sale. New ownership seemed to affect him little; the push was on for *Fathers and Sons,* which was an expensively packaged double album. Muddy didn't need literacy to read the commitment in that. It wasn't famine on the farm, just progress. And the boss man was always available for a draw.

Leonard never got the chance to parlay his way into television. On October 16, 1969, driving to the radio station, he was hit with a massive heart attack and died behind the wheel. He was fifty-two years old. WVON ran a live tribute to its founder, and Muddy called in to make a statement. The host began, "You were one of the recording artists —" but Muddy interrupted. "I was one of the main artists. We got acquainted in forty-six, we were pretty close always down through the years. I think if he was livin', he would say what I'm sayin' now: he made me and I made him. So I lose a good friend."

The family cleaned out Leonard's office and found in the safe thousands of dollars in IOU notes. "I wish I had what we called the red book," said Marshall, "with all the advances in it. We used to say they hundreded you to death." In her biography of the Chess brothers, *Spinning Blues into Gold,* Nadine Cohodas writes, "What [the musicians] were paid was based more on what they asked for than what they might be owed under a contract." But with Leonard gone and GRT in charge, that wouldn't last.

Peter Guralnick visited the Chess offices while the company was in transition, late 1969 or early 1970. His interview with Phil Chess was interrupted by a phone call. "You know we sold the company," Phil said on his end. "Joe, Joe, you know we sold the company. No, man, we can't do that. I'm telling you, babe, we can't do that no more. No. I can't give you that kinda bread unless you come across with some shit first." Phil listened for a while, unable to get in a word, finally saying, "You know it ain't like the old days, it ain't like the old days, babe."

"[GRT] could have been in the tomato business just as well as the recorded tape business," said Malcolm Chisholm, a former Chess

210 ♦ *Can't Be Satisfied*

producer. Phil Chess was invited to stay, but when GRT named Marshall as Leonard's replacement, he could read the handwriting on the front door. Phil took over the radio stations. "They decided they wanted to get rid of my uncle," said Marshall. "That was stupid. They made me president and then they proceeded to destroy the company."

◇   ◇   ◇

However his recorded sounds changed, Muddy's live music stayed fundamentally the same. "The beat is almost like somebody falling off a bar stool," said Oscher. "It's not a straight, steady thing. The blues is like preaching, you mess with the time to draw people in. Muddy worked the audience, and he used time to do that. He'd sing, 'You say you love me baby . . .' and he'd wait, drag that shit out. There was no time there, you'd just wait on him. 'Please call me on the phone sometime.' He'd wait till he thought it was right to tell the story. When you're locked into that straight meter, you can't get your words out, you can't tell the story the way you feel it."

Concerts were booked through ABC Booking (which also booked B. B. King and Bobby Bland), while chitlin circuit gigs, Muddy's bread and butter, came through him directly. He'd stop a card game to answer the phone; others knew it was about a gig when he'd say, "When's this for?" And the next line was always the same: "Yeah, well you got to come up with a little more bread this time." Muddy's constant retooling of his lineup kept his band contemporary. Luther "Georgia Boy" / "(Creepin') Snake" Johnson had joined Muddy when bassist Jimmy Lee Morris returned to the steady pay of a factory job. Johnson aspired to guitar, which he played when Sammy was drunk or Pee Wee was on the outs. Snake would be the first to dress mod, to wear a big afro and small shades; his stage manner was so exciting that Muddy often kept all three guitar players.

Rehearsals continued to be infrequent and ill defined. ("Only thing like a rehearsal," says Oscher, "was him in the car making a humming sound, *aah ha ha hmm* to open up his voice.") When the band gathered, Muddy kept tabs on who was late and would leave the basement when it was time to play, hollering instructions from the living room. "We always knew if they had a big gig or were going out of town because then Muddy would stay down there," said Cookie. In summers, when the basement was too warm, they'd run extension cords out the kitchen door and play outside; Spann played his beat-up electric piano, a Band-Aid stuck on the top where he'd written his name. "When we were young we didn't think they were real musicians," Cookie said. "We'd be going, 'Oh god, they're playing this sorry stuff.' But if they picked up a little speed, we liked that. Otis Spann knew my girlfriends loved Aretha Franklin so he would have them play 'Respect' and that would drive us crazy."

Occasionally Willie Dixon would teach the group a new song. "One time Willie came to Muddy's house," Oscher recalled. "Then Spann's ex-wife Marie came by, said, 'I need to talk to Spann.' They went in the back room, had a big argument, Marie came out with a long butcher knife, said, 'I done killed that motherfucker.' And then left. Spann came out, his hands were cut up where he had stopped the knife. We rarely rehearsed, and that one only lasted about an hour till that shit happened."

On the road, twenty-three hours of the day were spent waiting for the one hour of work, and the grind could be maddening. Bo, as illiterate navigator, memorized roads, highways, and routes. Having previously entered Canada through Toronto, he turned a 500-mile straight shot from New York City to Montreal into a grueling 800-mile trip. "Everybody just twisting and turning, trying to get off of that ass," said Willie Smith. "You were riding two-lane highways all day and all night."

To pass the time, they'd talk trash. "Willie Smith said to me," recounted Oscher, "that when he was making love, he knows whenever he made a baby. I said, 'Willie, I don't think you can do that.' Willie said, 'Motherfucker, you ain't got nair child and I got thirteen children, you gonna tell me how to make a motherfucking baby?' I couldn't argue with that shit."

Nor could Paul argue with Bo's late-night jive. "Bo would go, 'Whoa! I see the moon and the moon sees me, God bless the moon and God bless me.' Then Bo would take a swig of gin, say, 'Wake up, motherfuckers, wake up, y'all sleeping while I got to work.' Then Sonny would say to Bo, 'Shut the fuck up, you ugly motherfucker. We the stars.' Then Bo would turn around to Sonny and say, 'Ain't but one star in this band and that's Muddy Waters.' And that's the way the motherfucking shit would go."

Doo rags on their heads, processes beneath, guns at their sides, the Muddy Waters band, integrated, was a sight to see. At a truck stop in east Texas, the whole room shut down when the band walked in; they opted for takeout. They stopped for gas in Michigan, late night, and the lady pulled down the shades. On their way to Tupelo, Mississippi, they passed a billboard in the middle of the night. Instead of THE ROTARY CLUB WELCOMES YOU or an invitation to a Kiwanis meeting, this one read, BEWARE! YOU ARE NOW ENTERING KLAN COUNTRY. A hooded figure sat atop a rearing horse. The silence in the van thickened.

They were much more welcome in St. Louis, where Muddy had a longtime friend, platonic, named Goldie B. Abram. She'd met him at a gig in 1964 and would often host him during his visits. "He liked fish," she remembered, "and I'd take him and Otis Spann and some of the other guys to a fish market. They'd get live fish, Spann would kill and gut them, and I'd fry 'em at my house. We'd have a little feast in the backyard."

"One of the first times I went to St. Louis," Oscher recalled about another kind of visit, "we pull up to a hotel on Delmar Boulevard, they got prostitutes on all the corners, they hike up their skirts, start shouting out, 'Muddy Waters in town!' After the gig we stayed up all night with those girls. There was a piano in the back of the place, Spann would play, we'd all be drinking tall glasses of whiskey, shooting dice."

Geneva paid him a surprise visit in St. Louis one time. "Grandma came all the way to St. Louis and had everybody running," said bassist Jimmy Lee Morris. "Mud had his girlfriend with him, her stuff in his room, we had to get her stuff out, stalling Grandma downstairs, and move her in with Spann." (He advised one of his band mates never to admit to infidelity even if caught in the act: "Who you gonna believe, me or your lying eyes?")

Sammy Lawhorn, who worked in a photography store when he wasn't traveling, had a talent for coaxing his dates to pose nude. In addition to his road shots of the band and their famous friends (a collection long since lost to poverty), he amassed a collection of his conquests, supine. "He was a camera bug," said Pee Wee. "He'd have your picture, you wouldn't even know it. He'd snap pictures of everybody. He'd show his naked ladies pictures in the hotel room." He also made movies, and he bought a voice-activated tape recorder, which he kept hidden under his bed.

Pee Wee had his own habits. "He used to antagonize other people," said Paul. "Pee Wee stepped on my mike cord in the middle of my solo, unplugging it. And when you're playing blues, if you want to fuck somebody up during the solo, you turn over too fast, short step 'em. He'd cut out my spot so there was nowhere I could go but follow him. Another thing, he'd learn my solos, play what I'm about to play, force me to jump to another place." At Symphony Hall in Newark, New Jersey, Paul and Pee Wee, who usually caroused together, drew guns and were circling each other when Muddy defused the situation: "First motherfucker that hits a lick is fired."

The band traveled down the East Coast to Washington, D.C. Alan Lomax, in 1968, was asked by the organizers of the Poor People's March on Washington to book "culturally relevant entertainment." Among those he hired was Muddy Waters. "He immediately agreed to come," Lomax writes in *The Land Where the Blues Began*. He quotes Muddy: "Sure we'll help out. We'll just drive on down overnight and get to town the morning of the concert." On the designated morning, Lomax spied a Cadillac parked in the shade, feet poking out the open windows. "Muddy was snoozing at the wheel. He looked up with that sleepy, crooked grin of his. 'Hi, Lo,' he said and we laughed."

Later that summer and back up the coast at the Newport Folk Festival, Muddy sat in for an ailing Son House and, as a tribute to his mentor, performed the celebrated "Walkin' Blues," a song that ran from House to Robert Johnson and Muddy. Bonnie Raitt brought it to a popular audience.

When the band flew to the Montreal World's Fair for a short set, the landing gear failed. In Boston, Paul Oscher and John Lee Hooker, shopping in Lord & Taylor, were trailed by store dicks, suspicious of a black man and white man together. In Austin, Muddy heard Johnny Winter opening the show and walked out front for a closer listen. "It was thrilling to me to meet him, he was one of the first bluesmen I heard on record," said Johnny Winter. "I was playing slide, had a National backstage, and he said he'd had one. I'd already learned most all of his licks."

Spann was on wife three, or three thousand three. Or three million three. His alcoholism was raging. "One time we were on the side of the highway in the desert, and I was helping Spann's Lucille get back into the van," said Oscher. "Spann was drunk. He lowered his head and looked through the top of his eyes, said, 'You fucking with my wife.' This came out of nowhere. His eyes were rolling out the side of his head. He looked so mean, so dangerous, terrible." Muddy's Lucille remembered a California trip when Spann brought his girlfriend; the two ladies skipped a gig and went out on the town. "When we got back she didn't have a chance to take her clothes off and Spann came home and he pitched a move and when she woke up she had a black eye. Spann talking about how she must have walked into the door."

Perhaps it was inevitable that with the explosion of interest in Muddy would come an explosion of his band. James Cotton had recently signed with manager Albert Grossman. That got Spann's attention, or his wife Lucille's anyway. After seventeen years of sitting quietly and taking it all in, Spann, in 1969, stepped out on his own — or as Lucille Spann's accompanist. Lucille had sat in on some of Spann's sessions, heard her voice on record, and wanted more of that. With Muddy, Spann had the best of both worlds — regular gigs through his boss and the opportunity to open many of the shows and to record numerous solo albums, establishing his own name. Muddy even shared billing ("Muddy Waters featuring Otis Spann" was typical). But Muddy wasn't ready to take Lucille — an unimpressive vocalist — into his band.

Muddy accepted Spann's departure as he'd accepted all his other sidemen's departures. "If you lose just an ordinary sideman you can pick them up anytime, but a real good man like Little Walter, Jimmy, and Otis, them was excellent men. It goes hard, man, but you have to get you another man, you just keep trying."

Muddy called on Joe Willie "Pinetop" Perkins. Pine was from the Honey Plantation outside Belzoni, Spann's hometown, not far from Rolling Fork. He was a man of Muddy's age and time, and shared Muddy's quiet reserve. The two had a quick affinity and developed a lasting affection. Pine had played with Robert Nighthawk, the King Biscuit Boys, Ike Turner, and Earl Hooker. "Pinetop," said Muddy, "he come from the part of the country that really know what he's doing with the blues."

Pinetop was in fourth grade when farmwork claimed him: "I made a tractor do everything but talk." He left home at seventeen, earning his nickname for his popular treatment of Pinetop Smith's "Pinetop's Boogie Woogie." He played a more gutbucket style than Spann, fewer notes, fewer fills, but he understood Muddy's sound and easily fit in. "I liked Spann's piano, but I played different," Pinetop said. "I played more of a bluesy type than Spann did. Spann put some jazz in his blues. I played more like Muddy's cousin, Eddie Boyd. I taught myself off records, Memphis Slim, them old piano players, then added to it. Yeah, hard and loud, beat it to pieces."

✧　✧　✧

Crowds on the road were good, and so was the pay — as high as $3,500 for a one-hour set. (And even then Muddy still hustled small change selling mojos — tiny textile sacks with a dried pea in them — to these young fans.) Stage restrictions loosened in 1969, while loose hair tightened. The natural came in, the process out. Muddy adapted to their fashion, dispensing with uniforms. He still favored a sports jacket and usually a tie, but he let his band unwind.

In the college town of Ann Arbor, Muddy and Wolf shared the bill at one of the larger blues festivals. The old rivalry seemed at rest, and the two were photographed together, laughing and drinking beer. Then Wolf took the stage — on a motorcycle. He played a fiery set, ignoring the stagehands and running past his time well into Muddy's. But thirty minutes on stage was just right for Muddy. He attacked the crowd with "Hoochie Coochie Man," and punch to punch, in a third the time, cut Wolf at his own game.

On the way to a show in Detroit, 1969, Muddy began bleeding from his nose. It kept up for a week, until blood came out of his eyes. Smoking, soul food, drinking, the wear and tear of the road — his blood pressure was out of control. "I used to be a good liquor drinker," said Muddy, "but when the doctor told me to come off the liquor, I said this is it, no more whiskey." He took up champagne. Clubs were told to have Piper-Heidsieck on hand, chilled, which Muddy could purchase as need be. "He was a champagne man, bought a whole truckload, put it down in his basement," said Pinetop. "Look like he was selling it." Muddy began to carry a penknife to whittle down the champagne corks so he could keep his bubbly fresh. His preferred pregig routine was to sleep three or four hours, then wake to a bottle of champagne. "Champagne for breakfast, champagne for lunch, champagne for dinner," Muddy told a reporter, "and champagne before bed."

On one October 1969 stretch, they'd been "up through Maine, up into Canada, back to New York," according to Muddy. "We ain't slept nothing but in the car. That's a grind." A Saturday-night gig in Covington, Tennessee was their last, and the home bed was nearly palpable. They had paid for hotel rooms, could have slept there, then pulled home refreshed. But sleeping in Covington would have meant unloading and reloading the equipment one more time.

John Warren, part-time driver, was especially anxious to see his wife. "Don't worry fellas," he said, sliding behind the station wagon's steering wheel on the last day of his life, "you're in good hands with Allstate." He had Pee Wee next to him in the front seat, Muddy behind him, and Pinetop behind Pee Wee. Bo and the others followed in the yellowbird Jeep van Bo picked up when the Volkswagen van wore out.

"Willie [Smith] said it was around six o'clock at night," said Oscher. "I thought it was real early in the morning." According to the police report, it was a bright, clear and dry 11 A.M. on October 27. The band was on Highway Forty-five, a two-lane road, not far from Champaign-Urbana and going north when a young couple — he was twenty-three and she was eighteen — coming the opposite way veered off the road, then overcompensated and nearly went off the other side. Muddy's brand-new Chevy station wagon had skidded sixty-three feet when the careening Pontiac struck it head-on.

"All you heard was a big loud noise, and then Bo shouted out, 'Lord have mercy!'" Paul remembered. "Then all that debris started coming over our van." Bo veered to the right of the accident, and the van halted in a field. His passengers, unhurt, ran to the scene. "We had to pull Muddy out of the wreckage," Oscher continued. "Warren was dead. The bone was coming out of his leg, the steering wheel was pressed up against his chest, and Pee Wee was smashed up against the windshield. Me and Sammy pulled Pinetop and Muddy out of the back and laid them on the grass. They were both conscious. Muddy was saying, 'I'm broken up real bad.' And I remember Muddy saying to Bo, 'Is my face messed up?'"

"That steering wheel knocked the breath out of Warren," said Pinetop. "I was in the hospital, these knees was all messed up. My head knocked on the ceiling. Brand-new car, man. Guy that hit us, he was driving sixty, seventy miles an hour, head-on collision. I couldn't see the girl in the front seat, she must have been going down on him."

Pinetop, fifty-six, and Pee Wee, thirty-three, were released two days later. John Warren, thirty-eight, was dead at the scene, as were the young lovers from the other car. Muddy, fifty-six, was taken to Carle Hospital in Urbana. Three ribs and his pelvis were broken, his hip shattered, his back sprained. Immediate surgery lasted three hours. Doctors told him he'd have to stay there for several weeks. "I ain't dying," he told a reporter, "but I ain't feeling so good." His hands were numb, he was unable to roll over in the bed, unable to feed himself. Muddy would remain hospitalized nearly three months.

"When Muddy had his accident, Bo was our rock," said Cookie. "He made sure that we got back and forth to see Muddy often. He was a very good friend to Muddy." Bo's shuttle service was also a screen, keeping certain parties from meeting in the hallway. "When he had that accident, I was pregnant with our third child," said Lucille. "I went to the hospital twice to see him."

"Muddy had the shorts — he was living week to week," said Messinger. "He asked us to get some money from Chess. I had never met either of the Chess brothers. I talked to Willie Dixon and Willie ran the ball. We arranged ten thousand dollars. Muddy's wife picked up the money and delivered it." There was a new family in the Chess big house, but the bills were still being paid.

CHAPTER 13

EYES ON THE PRIZE
1970–1975

M uddy stepped out of the hospital and into the 1970s on January 8. He moved slow, walking with a cane. His sides were sore, his knees weak, his hip held together with steel. He watched a scar form over his left eye. His left hand, on which the guitar made more demands, had suffered the greater injuries. "If I could get out and go around it would be okay," he said, "but sunup and sundown, sunup and sundown here in the house." But the swelling in his hands was diminishing, the numbness beginning to dissipate.

The hospital bills had all been paid by Chess Records. Muddy had no insurance, no safety money in the bank, just two decades of a working relationship with Len, Phil, and Marshall. Now Leonard was dead, Phil was gone, and Marshall had a few months left at the company; he departed in mid-1970 to start a record label for the Rolling Stones. (On his first visit to the band's rehearsal hall, he noticed a poster on the wall — from the *Electric Mud* album.)

Recuperating at home in February, Muddy enjoyed a Grammy Award nomination (Best Ethnic or Traditional Recording) for the *Sail On* album — containing material from as early as the 1940s. (Don't tell Muddy Waters *his* music don't last.) And if he listened at all to pop radio, he would have noticed something familiar in one of the contemporary hits. It was not a blues song per se, though some lyrics had been copped directly from his "You Need Love," especially the new song's catchphrase, "way down inside." Muddy may have heard Led Zeppelin's "Whole Lotta Love" like the English initially heard his 1958 tour: screaming and howling. But without him, it would not have come to be.

Within a couple months, Muddy began appearing in area clubs and was filmed for the documentary *Chicago Blues*. He hobbled in on crutches, requested a stool for the stage, and though his hands were not yet right, he played short sets. "I'm up and around, and I ain't runnin' yet," Muddy told *Rolling Stone*. "I only play about thirty minutes. My hands are all swollen, and the doctor said it'll take a while before they can be fixed."

Muddy's release from the hospital coincided with news about Otis Spann: the thirty-nine-year-old blues pianist was diagnosed with liver cancer. Peter Guralnick flew to Chicago on assignment for *Rolling Stone*: "When I arrived at Spann's home, a dilapidated apartment whose walls were covered with pictures of dogs, I sat in the living room talking to a woman and a male neighbor," Guralnick wrote.

> A skeletal-looking man in a bathrobe sat drowsily on the sofa half-asleep. We made small talk, I wondered to myself when Spann would be coming back, and then the man on the sofa, too weak to do anything more than mumble faintly, said something. It was only when I heard the ghost of his familiar, husky voice that I realized that this was Otis Spann.

A few days later, on April 24, 1970, Spann died in Chicago's Cook County Hospital. He'd played behind — or beside — Chuck Berry, Little Walter, Howlin' Wolf, Sonny Boy Williamson, Buddy Guy, Junior Wells, Johnny Shines, and many others in addition to Muddy. He'd shared his technique with sideman after sideman, stranger after stranger, giving away all he knew. He had a wife, he had three kids, and he had no money; he'd let his musician's union dues lapse so there was no headstone. "I remember walking by Muddy's car at Spann's funeral," said Charlie Musselwhite. Muddy's hip kept him car-bound. "He had the window down, looked really, really sad. I said, 'It's a sad day.' He said, 'Yeah, it is.' We shook hands through the window. And that's all we said. Everybody loved Spann. He was just drenched in blues. He was the blues walking and talking." Friends held a benefit to help defray funeral expenses; Muddy performed.

Gone was Little Walter. Gone was "Elgin" Edmonds, Big Crawford, Baby Face Leroy Foster, Johnny Jones. Of Muddy's early Chicago playing partners, only Jimmy Rogers and Sunnyland Slim were alive. "Muddy never showed his emotions," said Paul Oscher. "When Spann died, he must have felt that. He was with the guy seventeen years, but Muddy just said, 'There'll never be another Otis Spann.' Muddy didn't let you know."

"Muddy took it real hard," said Lucille. "He'd be sad, want to be by hisself. He mostly hold things tight."

So much feeling had gone from Muddy's bones into his early records, feelings that were hard to express unaccompanied by music. "He knew my music better than any man alive," Muddy said of Spann. "There is no one left like him who plays real, solid bottom blues like he does. We'd better raise another before it's too late."

❖ ❖ ❖

Muddy didn't need Spann's death to tell him it was a changing world. For that, he had his cane, a bunch of unmod suits in his closet, and bookings in small clubs, while younger white people played their versions of his music in massive arenas for big pay. The question repeatedly asked of Muddy was, "Do you think a white boy can play the blues?" The question was poorly phrased; what's meant is, "Why is it different when a white person plays the blues?"

"There are some beautiful white bands," Muddy explained, but he distinguished them as unauthentic. "[T]hey didn't go to the Baptist church like I went. They didn't get that soul down deep in the heart like I have. And they can't deliver the message. They're playing the white folks' blues. I'm playing the real blues. I'm singing the same thing the old master liked to hear when you're working for him."

Johnny Winter had recently made headlines signing his first major recording contract — for $300,000 (though reports were quickly exaggerated to a cool million). "Just one thing makes me a little mad," said Muddy. "These young white kids get up and sing my stuff, and other people's stuff that I know, and next thing is they're one of the biggest groups around and making that real big money.

Sometimes that makes me mad because we've been struggling so long, fighting for a little recognition."

As blues had seeped into other genres of music, losing its community, the bluesman or -woman no longer needed impoverishment or geography for substantiation. Lack of plumbing or a childhood in the cotton fields was no longer required to sing the blues; the style was enough. Muddy's popularity was curtailed by the same thing that made him king: the Delta soil that clung to him now threatened to inter him. He had become an institution. Institutions were honored, and forgotten.

There were black musicians younger than Muddy and Wolf who knew the blues and the commerce of music. Buddy Guy, for one, was raised under circumstances very similar to those of his influences and could play their style very well. But when it came time for Buddy Guy to make his own mark on the music world, the Muddy Waters style was claimed — by Muddy Waters. Guy could back Muddy and demonstrate his down-home chops, but to make his own statement, he had to respond to the new world. And that was a world of Eric Clapton and Jimi Hendrix, of James Brown and Creedence Clearwater, of blues licks on overdrive and blues licks on acid. That's where the spotlight — and the money — was.

In the spring of 1970, Muddy flew to Lehigh, Pennsylvania (the band drove). *Rolling Stone* covered his arena appearance at the Philadelphia Spectrum: "He strolled on stage with a crutch under his arm, put down the crutch and picked up his Fender, hobbled to a stool and opened with 'Hoochie Coochie Man.' He played a restrained, careful set, nothing fancy, and later told us that his hands were still partly numb from nerve damage. Doctors have told him that the deadening will go away at the rate of half an inch a month." Muddy Waters had big hands.

By year's end, Muddy was booked for three weeks in Europe. He'd begun picking up the pace and if he had to go out for a long haul, Europe was a better prospect: the drives between gigs were not so far apart, clubs treated the musicians better, and the audiences did too. The band parked the cars at Bob Messinger's New Jersey home, instructing him to send weekly payments home from the deposit he'd received. Muddy had checks sent to Geneva and smaller checks to Lucille.

The tour, which included Paris, Stockholm, and London, was well received. Muddy, still using crutches, was often asked about his accident. (He told his friend Max Jones, a British journalist he'd met in 1958, that his accident happened "a year and a month and five days ago.") The excitement of the tour distracted him from the pain in his hands and before the trip was over he'd taken to performing a solo version of "Walkin' Blues."

The English writer Charles Shaar Murray saw Muddy on a rainy night at a small club with a leaky roof, "in this filthy room with pools of water all over the floor." Thinking of how those who'd copped his licks no longer needed such gigs, Murray asked him "how he felt about being ripped off. I was thinking culturally, but he interpreted it as financially and said, 'If you don't rip me, he gonna rip me, and if he don't rip me, someone else will, so if you can't deal with that, don't get into the music business.'" Don't matter where you farm, the 'cropper's deal was never square.

"As we go to press," *Living Blues* magazine, the new bulletin board and blues family newsletter, wrote in its fourth issue, winter 1970–1971, "Muddy Waters has not yet been paid for his tour of England in November and December. Muddy is unable to contact his booking agent [*sic*], Bob Messinger, who was supposed to have met him in New York with the money. As a result, Muddy used personal funds to partially pay the members of his band."

It was bad timing to be screwed out of the tour money — it didn't make for a happy Christmas — but it gave Muddy a place to vent. So much had changed: the big house that had been Chess Records had turned cold. Machinations and whispers sprouted like bad plumbing leaks. Leonard and all the Chesses were gone and the cooks in the kitchen didn't feed the hands like they used to. Muddy was pissed off, confused, frustrated, and he had nowhere in-house to express it. When he wrote Bob Messinger on January 11, 1971, Muddy was fed up with being taken, was frightened of losing his furnish, felt he was owed the farm, and knew he was entitled to a piece of it. The hand-written letter — feminine script, Geneva's probably, or Cookie's — on notebook paper burns with rage, explodes like a letter bomb. So that he wouldn't be misunderstood, so that his intention and desire would be clear at that moment and clear decades later, he drove home his main point by printing in all capital letters: "I WANT MY MONEY!"

Breakups are not pretty. Exactly what happened is difficult to discern. Someone screwed Muddy out of some cash, and Muddy fired his manager. Those are facts. Messinger put the blame on the British road manager, then on the American promoter: "Apparently the road manager disappeared on the last day or next to last day of the tour. They came back with enough money to get home to Chicago and that was it." The missing money was a drag, and so was the resulting lack of management. "Muddy started booking dates himself," said Paul Oscher, who would soon quit the band. "We started going to the state of Washington, then Texas, then Montreal, to Virginia. We would go zigzagging all over the place."

In Muddy's personal life, Lucille had followed Lois, his previous girlfriend, down the poppy path, and the kids he'd had with her were taken by the state and put into foster homes. "Lucille got in the wrong crowd," said Willie Smith. "She was leaning pretty much in that direction. When you're dealing with that kind of people, you got to pay back one way or the other."

Muddy could find no comfort in the situation at Chess. The label had been moved to New York, the Chicago office was empty, the studio a rental facility for other labels. "They're all new people," Muddy said. "I don't know nobody and nobody knows too much about me."

The new Chess repackaged the old repackagings — *The Best of, Real Folk Blues,* and *More Real Folk Blues* — as *McKinley Morganfield AKA Muddy Waters*. Its liner notes, by Mike Leadbitter, the founder and co-editor of the British blues magazine *Blues Unlimited,* were scathing and captured the dire feeling of Muddy's traditionalist fans:

His friends are dead and gone and there is no competition. Competition led to the great Muddy Waters. Muddy's endless variations on old themes and lack of new material, coupled with a stage routine that has become almost mechanical, indicate that the great days are gone for good. . . . Perhaps whites put up with a lot of mediocrity when it is presented live, but this does not mean that they will buy it. Thus the great years of Muddy were between 1948 and 1958, a decade of varied, distinctive, amplified "country" blues. It is to this decade that we dedicate this album and when one plays it, the horrors of *Electric Mud* and the like are banished completely and we can really appreciate just why Muddy is, and was, one of the major blues artists of the postwar era.

A few days after writing Messinger, Muddy was given a document to sign by GRT, the new Chess owners. It was nothing he could comprehend, who knows what he was told — except that a check would follow soon after his signature. The bean counters at GRT had discovered that many of Muddy's compositions had never been published, and with the Rolling Stones and other million-selling bands covering Muddy's songs, they smelled money. The document put Muddy's publishing with their organization, Heavy Music, Inc.

The sharks at Arc, who still owned Muddy's publishing, went for blood. On March 3, 1971, while touring the East Coast, Muddy was told to appear at the New York offices of Arc Music, the longtime Chess Records publisher. What transpired there is described in the lawsuit filed on Muddy's behalf against Arc half a decade later. "Upon his arrival in the offices of Arc Music," the lawsuit stated,

> plaintiff [Muddy] was handed a check in the amount of $10,200.76, which purportedly represented the royalties due him for the six-month accounting period ending December 31, 1970, together with a statement which reflected the computation of the royalties. At the same time, defendants Gene Goodman and Philip Chess tendered to plaintiff a typewritten agreement and told plaintiff that this was "a new exclusive songwriter's agreement" and "the old one had run out." Defendants Gene Goodman and Philip Chess told plaintiff that

"this was more money than you ever got in your life" and that he was being "protected" and "looked after" and that they would "do right" by him and made references to the "big check" as proof of their good intentions.

According to the papers that Muddy couldn't read, signing made the songs the property of Arc Music. (Gene Goodman dealt with GRT's claim and soon had them convinced to "relinquish its claim in and to the musical compositions.") Muddy's status with Arc would be "employee for hire," implying that Arc Music had paid him a regular salary to compose songs. Lastly, the document was retroactive, dating back almost twenty-five years to grab the hits.

Muddy did what anyone working for shares would do if handed a check for ten grand: he signed the papers, signed away ownership of his songs. Again, what he was actually told is Merlin the Magician's guess, but it tells the power of money that they dared inform him the ten grand represented his earnings over the past six months. Muddy couldn't read or write, but if he was owed ten grand for that half year, he must have — MUST HAVE — been owed something for the half year before that, and each one previous. But he took the check and he didn't ask.

The Arc document refers to an attached schedule, which, had it had any writing on it — for it did not and was completed later — would have been a list of songs Muddy wrote and recorded. The defendants, the lawsuit stated, "feared that, although plaintiff was barely able to comprehend the written word, he may have been able to see a schedule consisting of many of the compositions composed by him . . . and thereby have made certain inquiries, the responses to which defendants wished to avoid."

◇ ◇ ◇

The lawsuit was organized by the man who had become Muddy's new manager. In the spring of 1971, a friend of Muddy's sought help through Scott Cameron at Willard Alexander, Inc., a booking agency strong on ghost bands such as Glenn Miller's, whose leader was dead.

"Asking do I want to book Muddy Waters was like asking a choco-holic if he wants a Hershey bar," said Cameron.

Cameron was raised in Madison, Wisconsin, where life was all Patti Page and the Mills Brothers until, fiddling with his radio dial one night, he picked up WLAC out of Nashville. That blew a new hole in his Swiss cheese. He cut a couple rock singles as a vocalist, but wound up in the hotel business, managing a unit in Omaha, Ne-braska. In the lobby one night he spied five guys with their hair painted silver, "and I was back in the music business in a heartbeat." In June of 1969, he took over Willard Alexander's Chicago office.

Scott phoned Muddy and they arranged to meet at the Chess building. Cameron was approaching the East Twenty-first Street of-fice as Muddy was getting out of his car. Cameron's distinguishing physical characteristic is his height: he stands barely five feet tall. "When I met him," said Muddy, "I'm looking to meet a MAN, I didn't look to meet a little bitty. And I was getting out of the car, and he was going in, and he said, 'You're Muddy Waters?' I said, 'Yes, I am.' 'I'm Scott Cameron.' Great big voice. I looked down, said, 'Yeaaah?'" Muddy laughs. "You hear him on the telephone, he sounds like he's a dynamo. He's roaring like a lion, *rrroarrr!* And I see this little fella, and said, 'Man, you wanna manage ME?'"

Cameron returned from Chess and phoned Willard Alexander in New York. "I was really excited. I told him I'd just signed Muddy Waters. Willard's response was, 'Great blues singer but he's a has-been.'" Cameron laughed. "I set out to prove him wrong."

Muddy's association with Cameron would last the rest of Muddy's life (and, contractually, through the lives of their descendants). "At the time, Muddy was at his real low ebb," said Cameron. "His only regular performance was at the Quiet Knight next to the el tracks for the door on Monday nights. My psychology was, it's because of this guy that we have *Rolling Stone* magazine, that's why we have the Rolling Stones — the common thread through all these guitar play-ers was Muddy Waters. And much to the chagrin of the blues freaks, instead of playing the forty-, fifty-, sixty-seat local blues club, I began putting him in the showcase room where the rock and roll bands were playing, getting him in front of the people that were buying records, associating with acts that spawned from Muddy Waters." Scott became a link to the other side. If rock stars were going to stand on the shoulders of giants, the giants were entitled — at least — to the runoff. Cameron lined up a spring tour of the East Coast. Fifteen months after his accident, Muddy was revitalized by his relationship with Cameron, and critics began to notice that something had changed. "Muddy emotes warmly and relates to his listeners in the opposite manner of B. B. King, who has allowed himself to become a professional, slick charade of himself," wrote one reviewer. "He was in as fine a form as I've seen him since the days of his legendary Club 47 appearances in the midsixties," wrote Jon Landau in the *Boston Phoenix*.

For the first time in years, he no longer confined himself to playing his best-known songs. In his first set he offered up a tune called ["Clouds in My Heart"] that had been recorded in [1955] and had never been issued as a single. He had completely reworked it. As Muddy talked about thunder and lightning, drummer Willie Smith and white harpist Paul Oscher created some special effects that worked perfectly.

In the second set, Muddy ran through the story of his accident — using the incident as the basis for a story: "Some of you may know that Muddy Waters was laid low with an accident a while back. Before it happened I had recorded this song. Didn't think much of it at the time. Afterwards, I thought better of it." The song was a rare nonblues for Muddy, "Goin' Home." Its melody line was reminiscent of "Bring It on Home to Me"— pure gospel. The band offered up a lowkey vocal response to Muddy's lead lines that created a wistful mood that fully expressed the frustration of the song. From there he moved into something more familiar, "Have you ever been mistreated / then you know what I'm talking about," and then into a fine "Live the Life I Love." With that over, he did a burning "Mojo" and was gone. Extended applause and a near standing ovation didn't bring him back. The set was a brief but successful tour de force.

After stepping up Muddy's road gigs, Scott Cameron coordinated a three-week stint at an old-school upscale Chicago club, Mr. Kelly's, which marked a turning point in Muddy's career. This was a venue on Chicago's Gold Coast, the expensive side of town. Frank Sinatra performed there, Lena Horne, Barbra Streisand. There was a doorman who wore a uniform and stood beneath a portico. There was valet parking, a sign that had all its lightbulbs, a marquee with letters as tall as a doorway. For twenty-one days in June of 1971, those letters spelled Muddy Waters. Pee Wee Madison, for one, was impressed. "Mr. Kelly's was a nice big club, expensive club. Lot of high-class people. Wasn't like the ghetto."

Paul Oscher knew something was unusual when Muddy called a band meeting before the first night. "Muddy took all of the guys into the kitchen and said, 'Now I ain't taking no alcoholic band into this gig so you guys better think about that.' So we were cool. The first set, Muddy was very laid-back, like he was afraid to sing. By the end of the night, he was doing his shit and people were going wild. Bill Cosby came down, Nancy Wilson was there." So was Bobby Stovall, who remembered the Chinese lanterns being hung at his father's house for Muddy's performance there in 1943. He sent a note up to the bandstand. "I had gotten divorced about that time," said Bobby, "so I would go see him and take a date. His way of finding me was to go through this drill from the stage where he'd say, 'Everybody has some luck in their life. Mine was living on a good man's plantation, he really took care of me, I remember him always, and his family is here, y'all stand up and take a bow.' The light would find us so he'd know where we were sitting. I told Muddy he did more for my sex life than he could ever know."

Mr. Kelly's was a beginning and an end. The Quiet Knight, the White Rose, Pepper's, the Urbanite, Silvio's — these were places that were about to become part of Muddy's past, his pre–Mr. Kelly's days. "I think I saw the last real regularly booked black Chicago club that he played," said Jim O'Neal, one of the founders of *Living Blues.* "It was New Year's night, 1971. I kept up with the club scene because we printed the listings in *Living Blues,* and the only time that I can remember that Muddy played at a black club in Chicago after that was if a film crew set it up."

Live (at Mr. Kelly's) was his first album of new recordings since *Fathers and Sons* two years earlier. It had been five years since Muddy recorded with his own band for Chess, and they'd been nearly obscured by brass. *Live (at Mr. Kelly's)* both countered the dire outlook of the *AKA Muddy Waters* liner notes and declared that Muddy had recovered from his accident. He is full voiced, plays stirring slide, and leads a solid band. Muddy was back.

◇   ◇   ◇

Not only was Muddy's career changing, so was the city. Chicago's white population, by the new decade, diminished by half a million, while the black population rose by 300,000. The city became nearly one-third black. The most momentous change on the expanding South Side came in 1970, when Congressman William Dawson died. This twenty-eight-year politician had maintained his control of the whole area's vices, including the policy game, and secured power that Daley's machine could not ignore. Upon Dawson's death, Daley restructured the district, thereby dividing the power and preventing a single African American from having such wide control. Gangs, especially since Martin Luther King's assassination, took a stronger hold and made the streets more dangerous; band members walked with their guns drawn at night. Shops, in the wake of so-called Urban Renewal, boarded up, and many neighborhoods were plowed under or irreparably split by the construction of highways on their spines.

In early December of 1971, Muddy went overseas for *The London Muddy Waters Sessions.* Accompanying him were guitarist Sammy Lawhorn, harmonica player Carey Bell, and producer Esmond Edwards from Chess's New York office. The band awaiting him was Georgie Fame on piano, Rory Gallagher and Rosetta Green on guitars, Rick Grech on bass, and drummers Mitch Mitchell and Herbie Lovelle; not everyone played both nights.

Sending Muddy to England was an expression of Chess's confidence in their original hitmaker (and would get them a good catalog item with steady sales). "It was basically a love session," said Edwards, who would return to London to produce similar records with Bo Diddley and Chuck Berry. "Muddy was so revered by those guys. Many may have had bigger names than him but they were in awe of being on his session. Their attitude was, 'Let's do what we can to make a great album for and with Muddy.'

"Muddy was a very quiet man. He would sit in his seat in front of his microphone and things would swirl around him. When I worked with Chuck and Bo, they were more imperious in their manner, much more outspoken than Muddy. Muddy might say, 'Maybe it's a little too sad or too slow,' something like that. But Muddy was easygoing and mellow, almost ignorant of the awe that the other guys held him in."

The *London Sessions* is a good meeting of the minds. Muddy's guitar parts are easily distinguishable from those of his guests; the generational disparity, the cultural difference is a significant part of the record's subject. But when the tapes were brought back to New York, what might have been a great album was degraded by overdubbed horns. In the mixes of the songs before they were made hip, the excitement between the artists is tangible, their blending of blues and rock, black and white, England and America. The sassy horns cover that like water on fire. (Several hornless mixes have been released posthumously by MCA / Chess.)

Muddy's return to the United States was more auspicious than that of his tapes: he won *Billboard* magazine's Trendsetter Award, which called him "a father figure of electric blues." There were other signs of his influence too, notably Etta James's answer song to Muddy's "Mannish Boy," "W.O.M.A.N." Three months later, after an album of previously shelved tracks, *They Call Me Muddy Waters,* won Muddy his first Grammy Award (Best Ethnic or Traditional Recording) and even before *London Sessions* was released, Chess put him back in the studio for *Can't Get No Grinding*. Again he was allowed to use his road band (with Cotton in the harmonica chair).

The album, which got a top rating from *Rolling Stone* (despite a grating electric piano) and was nominated for a Grammy, is decent midperiod Muddy, though it pales next to his classic sides. It establishes the standard for blues in the last third of the twentieth century: the performances are strong, but the emotion is pallid; you can't hear the artist falling to his knees, drawing power from the earth as he sends his plight heavenward.

Cameron continued to come through on the gigs, doing his best to expand Muddy's audience. The Mr. Kelly's gig led to performances at Carnegie Hall and a circuit of higher-class cabarets. In December of 1972, the Hoochie Coochie contingency found themselves at the St. Regis Hotel in New York, settling into suites for an extended engagement at the hotel's classy Maisonette Lounge. The accommodations lacked for nothing, but Muddy couldn't get comfortable. "For a blues band such as Mr. Waters's to make the transition from a blues club or concert situation to the more formal atmosphere of the Maisonette requires some adaptation on both sides," wrote the *New York Times*.

> Mr. Waters's only apparent concession is to play a relatively calm, couth set, avoiding the raw, boiling drive that he usually generates. He is not a vivid and visually communicative showman, such as B. B. King or Big Joe Turner. He simply sits down with his guitar and sings his blues, his round face almost expressionless except for an occasional rolling flicker of the eyes. . . . It is an uncharacteristically placid performance that is not helped by the lack of any verbal communication — by Mr. Waters, by his sidemen, or by anyone representing the Maisonette — which might help to draw the audience into an understanding of what Mr. Waters is doing.

By the time of his 1972 return to Europe, promoting *London Sessions,* Muddy was committed to the times: he was sporting an afro and wearing loud suits. A journalist for *Ebony,* a magazine directed at African Americans, described him as "the essence of the black man in Chi Town." He was able to carry the feeling overseas. "One of the best Muddy Waters shows I saw was at the 100 Club on Oxford Street," said Frank Weston, a writer and longtime British fan. "They were literally hanging from the rafters. It must have been the nearest thing England ever got to hearing what he sounded like playing in a Chicago club. That was the full band going full throttle. By then, there really was a blues audience, they were queueing out around the block. They had to turn people away that night."

The main event of the trip was an appearance at the Montreux Jazz Festival in Switzerland, but the highlight was an intimate recording made of a Swiss radio broadcast. The eleven songs, available on the posthumous Muddy compilation *One More Mile,* are as near to sitting around with Muddy Waters as anything since his early days. His slide work is full of personality and humor, his vocal phrasing is sensual and gripping. It's a side of Muddy not revealed on any other recordings of the era, nor in interviews. He sounds perfectly relaxed and comfortable, his electric guitar turned way down, accompanied by Louis Myers on acoustic guitar and Mojo Buford on harp. (Oscher had taken a sick leave from which he never returned; Sammy Lawhorn, a couple days before departure, pissed off someone and had both his legs broken. "They threw me out the third-floor window. I never had time to get right so I could land balanced. Would've been different if they'd thrown me out the fourth one, I betcha.")

They played Australia and New Zealand in 1973, a tour that proved them not only transcontinental but also transmorphic. In Canberra, the venue was a circus tent. Scott Cameron dragged him outside the tent to witness his newest fans. "It was the only time he laughed louder than when he first met me. There were these huge elephants that were chained to the ground but they were rocking back and forth like they were dancing to the music. Muddy went right down on his knees, laughing. Right on his knees."

The band returned to America and began a West Coast tour.

(They crossed paths with ZZ Top, a rock trio impressed by the band's backstage pastime: playing poker on a guitar case, each man's money next to his gun.) By this point, the road had finally become too long for guitarist Pee Wee Madison and he caught a bus to Chicago. Muddy quickly hired Hollywood Fats (born Michael Mann), who'd come to his attention through a stint with Albert King. Muddy's tunes, even his arrangements, were the standard fare for bands around the country; there was someone everywhere who could play Muddy's music Muddy's way. Fats fell right in, but didn't stay long; he wanted to be a front man. By then he'd switched bassists too, Calvin "Fuzz" Jones replacing Sonny Wimberley.

While Muddy's career was taking an upswing, blues that music couldn't cure came to his home. Gut pains had plagued Geneva, and as they got worse, the doctor's news came: cancer. It had spread from her bowels to her stomach. "That whole thing with cancer," said Cookie, "they never wanted to be educated about it. It was their belief, you got it, you're dead. Muddy was very distraught that whole time. I don't think he knew how to run the house — pay the bills, buy the groceries, and that was the first time I was really scared." Geneva suffered for about a year. Muddy took Dennis, her son, off the road and put him on duty at Lake Park. Charles, Geneva's other son, took his mother's illness very hard. "I felt sorry for Charles," said Cookie. "Geneva got ready to die, and I noticed a lot of changes in Charles with the drinking and not holding a job. Before then he wasn't nothing like that. A big change."

Changes were evident in Muddy too. His Boston friends noticed he was uncharacteristically drinking hard liquor, and hitting it hard. "I called Scott the next day and told him what was up," said Al Perry, who managed a radio station there. "He thought it was about Geneva. I took Muddy to a doctor, he gave a scrip. I said, 'Is there anything else he can do for himself?' The doctor said, 'Yeah, he can give up smoking cigarettes.'" Muddy never smoked another cigarette.

"With Muddy and Willie Dixon," said Cameron, "I found I was arranging hotel rooms, I was setting interviews up, I was doing everything but driving the van, and they weren't yet major income for Willard. So I had a meeting with both of them and we decided that as of February 1, 1973, I would quit Willard Alexander and I would go to managing them for a one- or two-year term, after which we'd assess the relationship. And it just kept going." Lacking a lawyer of his own, Muddy left it to Scott's to look over the agreement papers.

"Once I became Muddy's manager," Cameron explained, "everything came to me. He might talk business with people, but he never committed himself to do anything unless it was sent through me." At an early meeting in the Chess offices, Cameron made his presence known. "We walked into Ralph Bass's office," said Cameron, "and I'm looking at some of the stuff up on the wall, I see a Grammy nomination plaque and it was for Muddy's 'Got My Mojo Working.' Muddy never even knew he was nominated." The plaque went home with Muddy Waters.

Geneva died on March 15, 1973. Cookie distinctly recalls that Muddy was at home. "We were called to the hospital and Muddy and I went. Bo drove us in the Cadillac. Geneva was kind of delirious, going out of her mind. We took my baby at the time, Chandra, because Geneva really felt that that was her child, the little girl that she lost. By the time we got back home, the doctor called and said she was even worse and we turned back around and that night she died. Geneva made Muddy promise that he would take care of Chandra. He swore it on her deathbed. And two seconds later she was gone and Muddy began to cry."

Muddy bought a double plot in the Restvale Cemetery so he could be buried next to her. Geneva had purchased a dress she was hoping to wear to Cookie's upcoming high school graduation; she was buried in it. In addition to losing his wife, Muddy had also lost Lucille's kids; they were in foster homes. "After Geneva's funeral," said Cookie, "we had a conversation concerning those kids, that he wanted to take them into our home. They were wards of the state. If it hadn't been for him and my grandmother, we would have been in the same situation."

"I didn't know about Joe and Renee and Roslind until after Geneva died," said Scott. "He told me about them and he said that he wanted to formally adopt them and get them out of the situation they were in."

"I was put in the foster home for maybe two years," said Joseph Morganfield. "Then my dad finally got me out. I knew it was in the process. My social worker would talk to my foster parents and they would relay it to me. My sisters were in the same neighborhood, I'd see them going to school. It was kind of tough."

Spent and drained extracting Lucille's kids from the system (her mind still on dope), emotionally ragged from the death of his wife, and frayed by the road, Muddy must have thought it a blessing when Phil Chess called from the publishing company's Chicago office asking him to swing by and collect another "big check," $2,000 this time, and to sign a few more papers. On April 23, 1973, Scott drove Muddy to the John Hancock Building, waited in the car while Muddy went in. "He didn't tell me that he signed something to get the check," said Scott. According to the lawsuit filed three years later, Phil

> exhibited to plaintiff [Muddy] a check . . . in the sum of $2,000 and at the same time, defendant Philip Chess tendered to plaintiff a document which he informed plaintiff was "another exclusive songwriter's agreement" and that it was "that time again." . . . Schedule "A" . . . was again blank and was later completed by defendants in such fashion as to list thereon those compositions previously composed by plaintiff which defendants had omitted from the schedule annexed to the March 3, 1971, agreement.

The two grand was tendered as an annual "salary payment recoupable" against future royalties, making it not a salary at all, for he was being paid with his own money — thirty-eight dollars and forty-five cents per week. If he didn't sell enough records, he'd have a debt to the company.

◊ ◊ ◊

When Muddy finally got his Chicago children collected at home, he began looking for a new house. No one was comfortable bringing the outside kids into Geneva's home. Scott lived west of Chicago, in Clarendon Hills, and Muddy bought a house near there, paying the down payment from his increased savings; he rented Lake Park to Willie Smith.

The new home was on a large lot in the suburban, all-white town of Westmont, about an hour from downtown Chicago. White frame, it was unpretentious and thoroughly middle class. It had five bedrooms, a basement where Bo could live, a yard where Muddy could establish a garden, and, as cachet, a swimming pool. Muddy and Renee, his youngest, slept on the main floor; upstairs, Laurence (Muddy's adolescent grandson, Cookie's younger brother, who had been living with Leola and whose favorite songs were suddenly "Hoochie Coochie Man" and "Mannish Boy") and Joseph shared a room, Cookie had a room with her daughter (Muddy's great-granddaughter and his youngest daughter were the same age), and Roslind had a room. Birds sang in the trees, lawn mowers roared in summertime, church bells pealed on the hour. There was no bustle, no hustle, no hassle. The sand in this oyster was sugar. "I hated Westmont," Cookie said. "I was like, 'Where has he taken us?'" Charles stayed there the first week, then returned to the South Side. Dennis and his fiancée settled in as live-in baby-sitters and supervisors.

"In the beginning, I was really bitter toward the outside kids," Cookie said, "because I knew where they came from. I knew their mom. And I felt that Geneva had just died and we were disrespecting her. So there wasn't a lot of love in that house in the beginning. And just to hear them call Muddy 'Daddy,' it really threw me a loop. I felt they had no right. I'd been with this man through the neckbones, the chicken and dumplings, the no money, and now you bring your outside kids."

But in time, Cookie assumed a matriarchal role. "She kind of raised me," said Joseph. "She was there for us. Back then, she was all we knew. Bo and Cookie were in charge of everything, made sure we got to school, ate, whatever. Dennis would prepare all the meals, make sure everything ran smooth. Most of the outside work was my responsibilities, inside was my sisters'. Muddy didn't believe in the male washing dishes, vacuum cleaning, laundry. He was kind of old-fashioned that way. I had to cut the grass. I had to shovel the snow out of the path, and had to feed the dogs every day. We had two German Shepherds. Plus we had a pool I had to keep clean."

But the newfound lifestyle could only do so much. "Me and Muddy didn't get along," said Laurence, whose drug problems echoed his late mother's. "I was the only black guy in my high school and I didn't do typical sports that fit the old ways that he had. [Muddy's son] Joe played basketball and he went to every basketball camp that was. I was a swimmer and a diver. I was very good but I couldn't go to the university. In Chicago it was gangs and in the suburbs there was drugs. I got through high school, I didn't want for anything, but basically we didn't get along."

Cookie felt Muddy lost his "self-worth" when they moved to the suburbs. "The last few years, it was like there was another man there. When he got his outside kids, I think he thought that if he bought them things, they'd love him. The quiet time on Forty-third, when it was his cooling down time, those were good nights, you saw McKinley Morganfield. You didn't see Muddy Waters. You saw him laying around resting and joking and eating ice cream — those were good times. When we moved to Westmont, our life changed. When he was McKinley, it was one thing, but when he was Muddy Waters, he could do anything he wanted to."

❖   ❖   ❖

Chess Records had devoted effort and expense to Muddy's *London Sessions* and been rewarded with both a Grammy (Muddy's second) and strong sales. *Unk in Funk,* Muddy's next studio effort, was recorded January 29 and 30, 1974 — the same month that Muddy's additional tracks from London were coupled with Wolf's to create the album *London Revisited,* complete with expensive gatefold and *très* chic comic book liner notes. *Unk,* the first album since Cameron had assumed management, was the first to credit Muddy as a producer, sharing the duty with Ralph Bass. It also marks the appearance of Muddy's own publishing company, Watertoons. (Prevented by his contracts with Arc Publishing from putting his own name on his new company's songs, he used Cookie's name as author until the lawsuit was settled.)

Before the recording began at the end of January 1974, the band personnel changed again. While on tour in a small town in western Massachusetts, Sammy Lawhorn encountered a cop who noticed the illegal gun on his person. When Lawhorn's call for help came from jail, it went unanswered. "Muddy disbanded Sammy, left him in the air," said Pinetop.

For Lawhorn, this was the end of his career in the bright lights. He hung out at Theresa's, a basement blues bar on the South Side. "He had a drinking problem," said Bob Koester, "and Theresa would put up with him because he was so damn good. But the last set, he'd often be in a booth, sleeping." *Living Blues* writer Ken Burch encountered him in the late 1970s in Chicago, and Lawhorn was pimping his own daughter.

His replacement was Bob Margolin, a man in the right place at the right time. In the Boston area, Snake Johnson's band was Muddy's regular opening act, and Margolin (rhymes with "Steady Rollin'") had been a member since the early 1970s. "Bob could slide just like Muddy," said Pinetop. "Sometimes Muddy'd take the slide and give it to him." Margolin recalled, "Muddy used to say that there were two kinds of players: those who are born talented, and those you can 'build with a hammer and nails.' I'm sure Muddy was the first kind, and though I may have a little talent and a lot of desire, I'm the second kind. I am indebted to the carpenter."

Initially, Muddy showed little interest in tutoring — until he was baited by the sound of a guitar from the living room. "I started to play 'Can't Be Satisfied,' which was my favorite song long before I knew Muddy. Immediately I heard a huge 'Wrong!' from the kitchen. Muddy wouldn't pick up the guitar and show me, but he sang the corrections at me. As well as I thought I knew the song, there were subtle nuances I was missing that were critical to him."

Luther "Guitar Jr." Johnson (not to be confused with Luther

"Georgia Boy" / "[Creepin'] Snake" Johnson) had come up playing the West Side sound with Magic Sam, and had a high-pitched, soulful voice. His trebly, tightly wound sound added a distinct new texture to *Unk in Funk*. The album's harmonica duties were mostly given to Carey Bell, except for two tracks on which Mojo Buford plays, and the title track, for which Chess laid out money getting Paul Oscher to Chicago.

Muddy contributed several new selections, including "Katie," about a girl from the Chicago suburbs living in Boston; she'd been another blues singer's girlfriend till Muddy stole her. "When Muddy had a new song, he would specify a key and just start playing it," said Margolin. "We'd usually have it in a couple of takes. Occasionally there was a song where everyone would talk it through first. There was minimal arranging, just cues for solos."

"People ask if we wrote the lyrics or the melody," said Terry Abrahamson, who shares writing credit with Muddy on two of *Unk*'s songs. He was a twenty-two-year-old blues fan, transplanted from Chicago to Boston, who'd dug the Rolling Stones in college, which led him to Muddy in his own hometown, and a friendship developed. "Hey, it's the blues, all the melodies were written before I was born."

A couple months after *Unk* was recorded, Mojo Buford left the band to tend to his children. (Six years later he'd be back; bad pennies and good harp players — you can't shake 'em.) His replacement was a young player who'd befriended Paul: Jerry Portnoy. Portnoy had picked up technique from Big Walter Horton and made a name around Chicago accompanying Walter's former partner, old-school guitarist Johnny Young. Portnoy's father sold rugs at the Maxwell Street Market until the expressway ran him out in the early 1950s. "They'd send me down to Lyon's Delicatessen to get corned beef sandwiches for the store. Little Walter used to play right across the street."

Portnoy sat in with Muddy and three days later was hired. "I felt like a light was shining on me. You want to be a brain surgeon, there's a course of study. You get good grades, you take the right courses, it's not impossible given an ordinary set of circumstances. But Muddy's band, the harmonica has always been the centerpiece, and all the great players that went through there, and all of these millions of harmonicas they are selling to all these people all over the world — Muddy's band put you in the royal line of succession." Portnoy was the final component in the band that would carry Muddy into his comeback; this grouping lasted six years, the longest of the lineups.

◇   ◇   ◇

On July 18, 1974, Muddy anchored the debut of a new public television performance series, SoundStage. Augmenting his own band was a host of guest stars: Junior Wells, Willie Dixon, Koko Taylor, Johnny Winter, Dr. John, Phillip Guy (Buddy's brother), and a minireunion of the soulful Electric Flag, with Buddy Miles, Nick Gravenites, and Michael Bloomfield. Muddy was warming up as the guests began arriving, and the greetings were discreetly recorded and incorporated into the show. Caught sneaking a little Crown Royal backstage, Muddy told a *Rolling Stone* reporter, "You don't know how happy I am. It's the thrill of my life, man. Just to think that the kids didn't forget me."

Far from it. His fans came out in great numbers to hear him create the sounds he'd played in broken juke joints decades ago. The sound was bigger now — the band had grown in size and vastly amplified their volume, letting large arenas feel what used to reverberate off clapboards and echo from the space between the floor and the ground, where the wind howled.

The summer of 1974, Muddy returned to Europe. He played Montreux with an all-star band that featured Buddy Guy and Junior Wells, and members of the Rolling Stones and of Crosby, Stills, Nash, and Young's band. Stones bassist Bill Wyman called a rehearsal, but before they could even get through a whole song, Muddy said it sounded great and called an end to the ordeal.

The spirit hit one night in Reims, France, coincidentally the home of Muddy's beloved Piper-Heidsieck. "It should have been just another show on a European tour in the midseventies," remembered Margolin. "But somehow on this night, for no apparent external reason, the years fell away. A powerful, passionate young man in his prime sang from his big heart about his hard life. He pulled off his picks, slipped into his slide, and tuned his guitar to open-A, taking the Chicago blues he pioneered a deep step back toward Mississippi. Using the full dynamic range of his cranked amplifier, from a breath to a roar, he held his own voice up with full-bodied, percussive runs that were rock solid yet suggested swinging syncopation. His slide fills and solos were intricate, but raw and over the top both in volume and emotion. Then he put his guitar down and began to sing 'Still a Fool,' a rare and very deep song choice. Luther 'Guitar Jr.' Johnson and I came in with Muddy's 'Rollin' Stone' guitar licks. With the audience, the band followed the story in each verse and we were sucked into the depth of Muddy's singing. At the end of the verse where he sang, 'Well they say she's no good, but she's all right,' Muddy suddenly broke double time and began to chant: 'She's all right, she's all right / She's all right, she's all right' over the band's jumping, one-chord pattern. But every time Muddy sang the line, he sang it more intensely. He put progressively more power and meaning into the same phrase, over and over. For ten minutes, he built steadily until it seemed like we would all explode. When he cut his arm down and ended the song, we were all dropped back onto the ground, to pick up the shattered pieces of our little lives and go on as best we could."

Another night, with his band gathered in his hotel room to get paid, the mood was celebratory. The gig had been hot, the cash was all there, and drinks were flowing. Nobody remembers exactly how or why, but the effusive conversation turned to the old days and, specifically, a lecture from Muddy on how to make love in a Model T Ford. The positioning was the issue, and Muddy's experience taught that her butt needed to be out the door while he employed the running board for support. Seeing the puzzled faces on the youngsters in the band, Muddy launched himself on the bed, sent his fanny into wild gyrations, teaching by demonstration.

In addition to card games, drinking, and women familiar and unfamiliar, Muddy kept his sense of home by keeping Robert Johnson at his side. He might go from one strange European country to the next several days in a row, but he could lean toward anyone in the band and say, "Give me my shit," and instead of being handed a pistol, these days he'd get a cassette that had Robert Johnson on one side and Jimmy Rogers on the other. He amazed one European interviewer by casually pointing to the tape recorder and saying, "I got my favorite blues singer right on hand. I got Robert Johnson sitting on there now. And I play it about three or four hours a day, and sit back and listen to it. I like 'Crossroads,' 'Kind Hearted Woman,' 'Walkin' Blues,' 'Terraplane.' He got a few things that I'm not crazy about, but really I don't care what he plays." (Muddy was less fond of what he called Johnson's "ragtime" songs such as "Hot Tamales" and "From Four Until Late.")

Cameron was working his end too. Journalists continued to come, all given the same basic restrictions: not to ask Muddy how he got his name nor what he thought about the Rolling Stones. (Cameron: "If you didn't know the answer to those two questions, you don't know enough to interview Muddy Waters.") One interview, conducted by white journalists Margaret McKee and Fred Chisenhall, who were working on their book *Beale Black and Blue,* stood out. McKee had been raised on the McKee Plantation, near Stovall. "I'll have to tell the truth, you're from down in that way," Muddy said when they began talking.

"It's the black man and the white woman the ones they jealous of," Muddy told them, referring to the white men who rule society, especially in the South, especially in the old days. "But a black woman could work for a white man all day long, that's fine, nice. That's the way it was." Muddy had almost never spoken about racism in a public setting. Perhaps he didn't have to say anything. Perhaps it would have been like talking about gravity or the wetness of water. "I think they'll probably learn. About forty thousand years from now, maybe they'll learn better. They know more now, that's true. It's so much different. You could stay in most any hotel you wants. You'd be surprised how some people treat me now. I was in Tennessee — Murfreesboro — last week. Man, seem like it not no Tennessee — seem like Chicago."

Scott tried to keep surprises from Muddy, but Muddy managed to surprise him. "I learned about [Muddy's daughter] Mercy, she was probably fourteen, fifteen," he said. "I think we were in New Orleans and coming home. We stopped and saw her in Mississippi. Then I used to send her a check once a month." She soon visited him in Chicago. "He had a house full of people I didn't know, and I didn't know him really," Mercy said. "I had grown up so ridiculously horribly poor, to me his home looked like opulence. I was resentful. As the years went on, he saw I was resilient, that I would work and do something."

In Florida Muddy collected another of his progeny. "My mother said I was about two or three when I left Chicago," said Big Bill Morganfield. "I was raised by her mother. First time I remember seeing my daddy, I was around a teenager. He had came down to play the War Memorial Auditorium in Fort Lauderdale. My mother went, and I knew she was going to see him. They woke me up that night, came to the house. He was walking with a cane. I had a little plastic guitar, one of the strings was missing. He said, 'That's the E string.' We talked, and that night he got rid of the cane. I still got that cane. That was the first time I can remember laying eyes on him outside of a picture. I was hurt for a while, I was deprived of the chance to spend a lot of those years with him. Like any son would do with his father."

In Florida Muddy met a young lady who would also become part of his family. "We were playing in Gainesville," said Bob Margolin, "and Muddy asked me to run to the store for him. When I came back to his hotel room, the door was open and I stepped in. It took a second for my eyes to adjust to the dark, and there was Muddy sitting on the bed, surrounded by four hotel employees. He pointed to one, who turned out to be Marva, and said, 'Don't look at that one, I'm gonna marry her.'"

"My girlfriend had taken me to see his show the night before," the former Marva Jean Brooks recalled. She was nineteen years old and biding her time after high school working housekeeping. "At the hotel the next day, I was wearing an orange-and-white-striped miniskirt and we were all talking to Muddy. I went to his performance that night and it led from there. He started calling me Sunshine and we used to talk on the phone at night, and he told me point-blank, 'You was born for me.' I was a young kid and never thought a famous man like Muddy Waters would be interested in a young girl like me. I was a child, but he made me feel as a woman, as a woman should feel."

Muddy was strengthening other family ties, bringing his kids on some summer tours. At the show's end, he'd invite Renee, Joseph, Roslind, and Dennis and Charles (if they were around) to join him for "Got My Mojo Working." "It didn't sink in until I became an adult just how famous he really was," said Joseph. "To me, I was just with my father, having fun."

"Can you imagine growing up with this man and then seeing all these kids surface?" asked Cookie. "Mercy, Renee, Joseph, another boy — and me not knowing? It was hard learning the private side of Muddy. Joseph and Renee's mother got strung out on drugs. Mercy's mom was strung out on drugs. It made me see the man part of Muddy. Someone can be all dressed up and all cleaned up when you see the outside, but they made me see what Muddy was really about.

"I always think about Muddy's song, 'I'm a Man.' When he'd sing that song, he really meant it. He'd put his whole heart in it, you could see he really meant it. When I was younger, he was a god to me. As I have gotten older, and dealt with things, I will always be grateful for the things he did in my life, but as a person, he was not a very nice person."

◊   ◊   ◊

Touring emphasized to Cameron that the part of Muddy's career that did not involve Chess Records was doing very well, and the part that did involve Chess was not. Howlin' Wolf, not far from his death by kidney disease, had recently sued Arc Music, Chess's publishing arm, for $2,500,000, charging they had fraudulently induced him to sign over "sole and exclusive" ownership of all his compositions to the company and owed him for unpaid composer's royalties and profits. While Cameron was investigating the possibilities of leaving the company, calls were coming in that further confirmed Muddy's stature. Muddy cut a few songs for the Hollywood film *Mandingo* and recorded a Dr. Pepper radio jingle.

Levon Helm was the drummer in The Band, the popular roots music group that had backed Bob Dylan and enjoyed many hits of their own; Henry Glover was a legendary black record producer, involved in the early days of Syd Nathan's King and Federal labels: he produced hits with James Brown, Hank Ballard, and Little Willie John. Helm and Glover had recently formed RCO, "Our Company," and were hiring themselves out to labels to produce artists at a studio in Woodstock, New York. They wanted Muddy to be their first production and were excited about working with Chess Records. Levon's audience was exactly the one Scott wanted Muddy to reach. "Muddy had two or three options left with Chess," said Cameron. "I went to New York and met with the people running Chess Records. I told them we'd do the *Woodstock* album, but if it didn't sell, Chess would release Muddy from his contract. 'Oh, no problem, no problem.'"

In early February of 1975, Muddy and Scott flew to New York. Pinetop and Bob Margolin were coming the next day; they'd be joined in the studio by several people Muddy didn't know (including Levon's band mate Garth Hudson) and by Paul Butterfield, a familiar face. Glover and Helm wanted to cut a couple Louis Jordan tunes with Muddy, "Let the Good Times Roll" and "Caldonia." Glover had collected some new material that seemed like it might fit. "For 'Why Are People Like That,'" said Helm, "we just started going over it — head arrangements, a tempo that Muddy liked, and follow Muddy. It was like the music played us. And we knew Muddy had 'Fox Squirrel' and some more original songs."

The result was Muddy's best studio album to date, the players bringing a vitality that had been missing at least since Leonard Chess died. It wasn't Muddy's deepest blues, but it was relaxed and fun. Cameron was pleased, though he knew Muddy could do better. "Muddy was at the ultimate point of not wanting to make another record for Chess," he said. "He finds himself in a place that he wasn't familiar with, and he's with these musicians who think so much of him but have never played with him. We had a genuinely good time, but the musicians were a little bit in awe of Muddy and they folded in behind him instead of pushing him. Muddy's thing was get in there, get this done, and go home." Recording away from Chicago, however, distanced Muddy from his troubles. "Any problems between Muddy and Chess were far away from us, nonexistent in the studio," said Helm. "Not only was there none of that kind of tension, there was no tension."

The Muddy Waters Woodstock Album was on the streets three months after it was recorded, and Muddy hit the road. In New York City, he played a week at the Bottom Line. Bob Dylan, who was emerging from retreat, showed up several nights in a row, bringing a drunken Phil Ochs (a folksinger not long from suicide) and 1920s blues singer Victoria Spivey — who made everyone address her as Queen Victoria. She wore a flowing white gown decorated with snakes, and Muddy kept asking her to take it off; the snakes gave him the heebie-jeebies.

"Dylan came into our tiny dressing room with a group of musicians who were soon to become his Rolling Thunder Revue," said Margolin. "Muddy could tell he was someone important because of the intense excitement. It was arranged for Bob to sit in." Muddy, more acquainted with the gangster than the pop star, the gun than the poet, got the name mixed up. "Muddy announced to the audience, 'We have a special guest on harmonica, please give a nice round of 'acclause' (that's how Muddy pronounced *applause,* and no one ever corrected him) for . . . JOHN DYLAN.' A couple of people clapped politely, and most turned to their friends and asked, 'Who?' I leaned over and stage-whispered to Muddy, 'His name is Bob, like my name — *Bob* Dylan,' and Muddy repeated, 'Bob Dylan,' as though that's what he had said the first time. The audience went apeshit."

Rock stars didn't much impress Muddy because he didn't know who they were. When Rod Stewart had recently come backstage at a gig in Detroit, Muddy heard his English accent and couldn't understand why the musician would come to America to find an audience. He was more comfortable with the Allman Brothers, with whom he toured in the fall of 1975. One of their gigs was in New York's Central Park, and they stayed at the fancy Plaza Hotel. Songwriter Terry Abrahamson showed up and Muddy shared his room with him. "He didn't like air-conditioning, and we couldn't figure out how to turn off the air conditioner, so Muddy and I stuffed towels in the air-conditioning vents. I was always coming to his hotel rooms, bringing food and we'd drink champagne. Once I knew I had his ear, I'd usually bring him some lyrics. I never saw him pick up his guitar in his hotel room. We'd just hang out, usually have the TV on, he'd be wearing his black undershirt and black silk boxer shorts."

In the meantime, Cameron received the first accounting of Muddy's *Woodstock* album, claiming tens of thousands of copies sold. "I was a little suspicious because I hadn't seen anything really happen with the record. The end of twelve months comes along and now the number has gone even higher — with an extraordinary number of copies being held in reserve. It didn't make a lot of sense, so I flew back and said, 'You're going to take those out of reserve or we're off.'"

"Chess was by then a disaster, really," said Esmond Edwards. "The main problem was that the Chess mystique, without Leonard, was not there. Len and Phil had a relationship with the artists, even if it was calling everyone 'motherfucker.' GRT was a white-bread operation, with business grad people running it, they didn't have a feeling for the music."

In June of 1975, GRT closed the Chess's longtime studio in Chicago. They sold Chess Records in August to All Platinum Records, a label whose president, Sylvia Robinson, had had a hit with "Love Is Strange," which owed a debt to Chess's Bo Diddley. The sale, less than a million dollars, was said to be a tax write-off for GRT. All Platinum hired a young rock bassist to oversee the marketing of the new acquisition. Despite this kid's brave talk — "GRT was sitting on a gold mine and they were treating it like a pile of shit"— Cameron and Muddy wanted off. By November, All Platinum agreed to let them go. "That be the second time they sold me," Muddy said, "and I got tired of being sold to everybody."

Unceremoniously, and without any fanfare, Muddy concluded his twenty-eight-year association with Chess Records on November 20, 1975.

CHAPTER 14

HARD AGAIN

1976–1983

T his is a big time for me tonight," chuckled the birthday boy over the din of big Texas blues fans who packed Antone's blues club to help their main man celebrate in 1976. "I'm gonna be forty years old tonight, and I guess that makes me about the oldest young person I know of."

Midnight approached in Austin, Muddy would be sixty-three, but those awake were not concerned with counting, certainly not higher than twelve, as in twelve-bar blues, and if bars were the subject, the correct answer was one: Antone's. "You see a guy that's a king, an immortal from Mt. Olympus," said Clifford Antone, proprietor of the establishment, "first time I heard him play slide, it almost scared me. It touched something in me I didn't know I had. 'Please don't stop, keep playing.'" When Antone's opened in 1975, blues was not the healthiest of wild beasts. After the boom of the 1960s, the new sincerity gave way to the pyrotechnics of acid rock, theatricality, and — *hisssss* — fusion jazz. Disco's mechanized throb, sweeping the nation, was antithetical to the natural beat and sway of the rhythm of the blues. Few bluesmen wore high-heeled glitter boots (though many took to leisure suits). But hope was not lost. A new generation was arriving. "I did all my shows for five nights," continued Antone, "Tuesday through Saturday. Jimmie Vaughan was twenty-three, Stevie was twenty. We put Jimmie Vaughan on stage with Muddy, he played slide and Muddy's head snapped. He told me that Kim Wilson was the best harmonica he'd heard since Little Walter. The blues players had never seen no kids like this."

After a week in Austin, a bluesman felt like a player again. Several nights in one place meant when they woke, instead of packing, the band could go downtown and shop for plaid jackets and polyester clothes. It meant Pinetop could unpack his tool and grease up some bird. "Muddy would have a big room," said Antone, "and Pinetop would have an electric deep fryer. They'd be drinking champagne and eating fried chicken. I was twenty-five and in heaven. And the chicken was good."

The minute hand approached midnight. As Margolin led the crowd in "Happy Birthday," Austin gifted Mud with some of his own: Buddy Guy and Junior Wells strode onstage. Muddy's jaw dropped; you could have wiped him off the floor. "I raised these two blues musicians since they was only thirteen!" he shouted, and they ripped through "Got My Mojo Working."

How was the old bluesman surviving in the modern 1970s? Quite well. He owned a suburban home and was landlord over another, owned a couple suburban road vehicles, several cars. He had friends in high places and won his third Grammy a month earlier for the *Woodstock* album. He had dates booked across America and across the oceans. He was free, free, free at last from his withering record company and on a roll with a manager who had a vision and who exercised might. In his lifetime he'd gone from plantation scrip to an American Express card (and Visa, Amoco, and Dominick's Finer Foods cards). He'd inspired a top magazine and a top rock and roll band. And he was about to rise to a new height of stardom.

"I wanted Muddy on Epic and Associated Records," said Scott Cameron. "They had a real machine going and they seemed supportive with their artists on the road. Their marketing was second to none. Johnny Winter and the whole Blue Sky Records thing was really hot." It helped that the head of the label, Ron Alexenburg, was a fan; he'd entered the biz working for a record distributor in Chicago. It was a homecoming too; Epic was a division of Columbia, which was the label he'd done his second Chicago sessions for in 1946.

Muddy assembled a band in Westport, Connecticut, for a week's recording, October 4 to October 10, 1976. From his own group he brought Pinetop, Margolin, and drummer Willie "Big Eyes" Smith.

Pine, like Spann before him, had become an anchor to Muddy's sound. He'd learned to play in the same school as Muddy — a cotton field, where the conjugation was done with a hoe and the school lunch was a fish sandwich and homemade whiskey. If Pine brought the root, Margolin brought the licks. He'd seen a cotton field only on television, but he'd studied it, brother, watching Mud's fingers night after night, bugging him at Westmont, playing the old tapes. Big Eyes brought the delay, and that delay is what moved behinds. Muddy called him "the greatest Saturday-night drummer alive," and a Saturday-night record was his intention. Harp duties went to James Cotton, a natural choice.

"Johnny Winter inspired Muddy's band to push Muddy," said Cameron. "The studio we used was in Dan Hartman's house, an ideal setting, so relaxed. Johnny was, at that point, straight as an arrow and fun to work with. You'd see Muddy and him feed off each other with this excitement going from level to level to level because they'd just keep pulling each other higher."

Hard Again affirms the advice Muddy held dear since Big Bill Broonzy spoke it in 1943: "Do your thing, stay with it, man. If you stay with it, you goin' to make it." Muddy was true to himself. *Hard Again* is the culmination of Muddy's career, a modern and lasting interpretation of his achievement: it is an electric blues band that captures the force and emotion so much more easily achieved by a lone player baring his soul with just his voice and his instrument. The band becomes the instrument and Muddy plays them. "Every country has its own music," Muddy said, getting to the heart of authenticity, "and I got the Delta sound. There's so many musicians, they can sing and play the guitar so good, but they can't get that sound to save their life. They didn't learn that way. That's the problem. They learned another way, and they just can't get it."

Muddy's new treatment of "Mannish Boy" rivals his earliest hits for passion and power. He sings the lines over air, night air, dusty air, Mississippi in New England and champagne air. The instruments lay out, except for the slide guitar, which dares only to snake between the lines. The single string's reverberations hang like heat, shimmering and bending. Muddy's voice is cavernous, huge, so full of character it's impossible to believe he's ever recorded songs where he wasn't a hammer, and it's downright depressing to think how long it had been since he sounded so good. There's a quiver in his voice, the sound of the tones amassing as they travel up his chest and through his throat and out between his lips. The spiritual distance is even farther. There is no Leonard Chess on the receiving end, no Chess brother and no Chess son. The farm was sold and the straw bosses gone with it. Muddy was plowing old ground in the old harness with neither benefit nor burden of a furnish. On these tracks, and especially on "Mannish Boy," the lead track, Muddy sings like a man freed to sing for himself. There is pride in this voice, independence, a drive, a declaration: everything's gonna be all right this morning, yes I know.

And that is just the first four bars. The Telecaster — it's Margolin playing Muddy — hits a couple high notes, lingering like a question: band, are you ready? And like a freedman falling across the Mason-Dixon Line, their resounding answer is that there's no stopping us. Muddy chuckles — not with laughter but with strength, and the story begins, an old story told anew:

> *Now when I was a young boy* [and the band hits]
> *At the age of five,* [and the band hits again]
> *My mother said I was gonna be,* [it's music as boxing]
> *The greatest thing alive.*

His mother was right. These were the greatest living blues. And the players knew it. The song's close includes the studio jubilation that followed, the lightness they felt at realizing that the bleakness of the past couple years — the past couple decades — suddenly had lifted. Muddy yelled and clapped in the studio, grinned broadly, walked around with a bounce in his step. He said, "This stuff is so good, it makes my pee pee hard again." And an album title was born.

"What I really wanted to do as a producer," Johnny said, "was to make Muddy feel comfortable and make his music sound as good as it used to. I felt that the real, raw blues and some early nasty rock and roll hadn't been recorded right since recording techniques had gotten too good for that kind of music. We were all in one big room, there were almost no overdubs at all, practically everything was done at the same time, and there was a lot of room noise — instruments feeding through other instruments' mikes. Everything that the normal studio engineer tries to make sure doesn't happen, I tried to make sure that it did."

Perhaps most rewarding to Muddy was that the music achieved such a deep sound without his guitar. He had lived to hear his own legacy. Bob set up Muddy's Telecaster right next to his chair, and it was there for him every day, but Muddy never picked it up. Both Bob and Johnny were surprised, but song playbacks confirmed that he was well covered.

An inspired session under his belt, Muddy waltzed across the globe — Switzerland, France, Poland, Italy — while Levon Helm and fellow members of The Band planned their farewell concert. The concert, to be known as *The Last Waltz,* was set for Thanksgiving weekend in San Francisco, and featured some of the biggest — and most funky — names in popular music, such as Bob Dylan, Dr. John, the Staple Singers, Van Morrison. Muddy's performance, preserved in the Martin Scorsese movie of the show, was riveting. A single camera holds on him, head and shoulders, occasionally tighter, sometimes looser, but unable to let go. No edits. No cuts. Nothing but the blues, nothing but Mud.

"Muddy didn't want to go and boy I remember Paul Butterfield got really, really mad at me on the phone," said Cameron. "Begrudgingly, Muddy went. He wasn't happy about the show, but it did wind up being the very first royalty check from a record company he ever got. It was the first one. He got a royalty on the soundtrack album." A lifetime in the business, and finally a proper royalty check.

(Marshall Chess dissents: "When the Chess artist got their statement, there would be a page called Writer's Royalties, so if the record sold twenty thousand, he would get one cent, two hundred bucks, the writer's part of it." A payment of one cent per song per sale was, then, not an uncommon payment.)

◇ ◇ ◇

On December 23, 1976 (the thirty-fourth anniversary of Muddy's second marriage), before the release of *Hard Again* or *The Last Waltz,* Scott Cameron filed a lawsuit on Muddy's behalf in U.S. District Court against Muddy's publishing company, Arc Music. Cameron simultaneously filed one for his other client, Willie Dixon (who'd signed with Cameron at Muddy's suggestion).

The essence of the lawsuit is found in the section titled "The Conspiracy and the Acts in Furtherance Thereof," which states,

> [D]efendants Gene Goodman, Philip Chess, and Harry Goodman together with Leonard Chess entered into a plan and scheme to prey upon plaintiff's [Muddy's] inability to comprehend the nature and terms of agreements relating to musical compositions composed either in whole or in part by him, and to divest plaintiff of his rights therein and the benefits flowing from the commercial exploitation thereof. . . . Arc Music was formed for the purpose of divesting plaintiff of his rights in and to musical compositions composed by him. . . . [As for songs recorded by Chess artists on Chess or affiliated labels] no royalties would be payable to Arc Music with the result that Arc Music would make no payment to plaintiff. . . . any royalties which might otherwise be due plaintiff pursuant to his agreements with Arc Music would be substantially understated on or omitted from the royalty payments rended by Arc Music to plaintiff, and the amount of such underpayment would be retained by Arc Music for division among [the defendants].

The lawsuit also notes that, as for the $2,000 annual salary, "at no time since the initial payment on April 23, 1973, has plaintiff ever received any of the 'salary payments' by way of an advance of the sum of $2,000."

When Arc began there had been no real model to look toward.

The world of independent record labels had grown quickly and been thrust from the margins into the mainstream with little warning. When the Chess brothers first entered the business, they had no publishing agreement because they didn't know what it meant. There had been, however, plenty of time to rectify that. But proving the rip-off was not going to be easy; trying to make sense of the Chess family's peculiar accounting — taking from the hits to give to the legends, paying on demand rather than on schedule — was made impossible when GRT threw away the files that the company had accumulated. "Cartons and cartons and cartons of all the back shit that was up in the mezzanine of that building were trashed," said Marshall. (In their response, Arc denied most everything and stated, "It was the intent of the plaintiff and Arc Music to formally bring plaintiff into the employ of Arc Music. . . ," but failed to explain why they never acted on their intent.)

The lawsuit asked for a total of 7.5 million dollars and the absolution of the agreements between Arc and Muddy. Within five months it was settled out of court, the terms confidential. One result was apparent: when the copyright renewal came up, ownership of Muddy's songs went from Arc to Muddy and Scott's Watertoons Music. The victory, like everything else in Muddy's life, came on shares: Muddy received partial payment, the manager got the rest.

◇   ◇   ◇

In the early spring of 1977, *Hard Again* was released to wide critical acclaim. The package befitted the man. The cover photo was an exquisite black and white, a near full-body shot against a white background, Muddy in a camel hair winter coat and a three-piece suit — his buttons glimmering, his hat atop his head. It's from a large-format negative (taken by fashion photographer and portraitist Richard Avedon), so the detail on his face is intimate: the bristles of his graying mustache, the shaving bumps on his cheeks. His thumbs are hooked into his vest pocket and he's got slightly more than half a smile, as if he knows something, knows we know it, but knows we know only something less than half. The photograph is a kind of a capsule summary of his aura; it bespeaks elegance, and also hard work.

"I saw a whole new life breathe into Muddy," said Cameron. "He was finally getting crowds, he was finally making money. In the early seventies, you'd see fifty people in a club and the club owner's up there saying, 'You gotta give me a break, I'm losing so much money.' And later the same club owner was screaming about why he can't get him back because his club doesn't hold enough people."

In March, Muddy embarked on a *Hard Again* tour with the recording band. They were crackling, and Epic recorded many dates. (When Marva would join Muddy for several days on the road, Leola would come to the house to stay with the kids.) Portnoy and Fuzz were left at home, on retainer. "I got a band and they're on vacation now, with pay — and hell, I ain't never had a vacation with pay!" Johnny Winter, thrilled to be performing with his hero, remembered picking up Muddy's guitar. "You couldn't play his guitar to save your life," Winter said. "It was impossible. He had his strings so high off the neck, and he used such heavy-gauge strings too, you just couldn't play it. Muddy said to me, 'When you pick up somebody else's guitar it's like somebody else's woman that doesn't want you. The guitar is telling you, "Leave me alone, I don't want you."'" They sold out the Palladium in New York, a large hall known for rock acts. In Boston, Peter Guralnick went backstage to say hello and found Muddy talking to a woman whom he introduced as Robert Johnson's sister. "'Here, show him. Show him the picture,'" Guralnick remembered Mud saying. "From her wallet Anne Anderson drew a picture of a man with a guitar: it was indeed Robert Johnson. 'You see, man? You see?' said Muddy with a proud, almost proprietary expression on his face. 'Didn't I tell you? Isn't that really something?'"

Peter had his young son with him, who'd been allowed to bring a friend. They were thrilled to meet a celebrity and, reacting like many children do — and before Peter could stop him — the friend asked Muddy for his autograph. Graciously, Muddy asked if he had a piece of paper. The boy produced a bar napkin. Writing was not a simple task for Mud. He looked at the cocktail napkin, then at the kid, and pronounced, "That's a mighty shitty piece of paper you got there."

The band stayed on the road, playing Hawaii, Africa, and Europe. They played a tribute to the pop band Foghat, who'd rocked up Muddy's version of Dixon's "I Just Want to Make Love to You" and sold it to another generation. In October of 1977, they sold out 6,000 seats at Radio City Music Hall, sharing the bill with B. B. King, Albert King, and Bobby "Blue" Bland.

From Radio City, the band continued north, returning to Dan Hartman's studio in Westport to make another album with Johnny Winter, this one titled *I'm Ready*. Not long before, Bob Margolin had gone from Boston to Rhode Island to hear Jimmy Rogers, who was also enjoying a second career. "I had to call Muddy the next day, so at the end of the night I asked Jimmy, 'Is there anything you want me to tell him?' He said, 'You tell him anytime he wants to get together and play those old blues like we did, I'd like to do that again.' I got goose bumps — the combination of Muddy and Jimmy playing together is a large thing in my life. If you have a house or a car, this was bigger in my life than your house or your car are in yours. So when I told Muddy the next day, he said, 'Boy that would be great, I'd love to do that, maybe we could do a record with him sometime.' So I called up Johnny Winter, and he arranged for that to happen. While we were at it, I said, 'Little Walter's gone but Big Walter's still around,' and we got him too."

At the studio, Margolin set up Muddy and Jimmy's guitars. "I tuned them and set them for big fat heavy sounds. Johnny Winter was up in the control booth and he said to them, 'Guys, those are really distorted, is that the way you want them?' They both go, 'Yeah! Yeah, that's it, that's the shit.' They always used really big fat sounds — the sound of an amp turned all the way up."

"Copper Brown" was cowritten with Marva. "Any time a song would come in his head, he'd get me up," she remembered. "'Wake up, Marva, wake up, you gotta write.' I always kept a pen and a pencil by. He'd tell me what to write and I would write it. I'd be half 'sleep and nodding, but I'd be writing. 'Deep Down in Florida,' he did that with me, 'Who Do You Trust,' 'Copper Brown.'"

The mood at the sessions was similar to the previous year and achieved solid, though different, results. There's a restraint that makes this album a bit more mature, and a bit less powerful. With Muddy playing, there's another guitar sound woven in, and Jerry Portnoy sometimes joins Big Walter. ("I used to drink with Big Walter in Chicago," Portnoy said, "so recording together was a gas.") The sound, however, is less dense, more intricate. *I'm Ready* was released in February of 1978 — on the heels of *Hard Again* winning a Grammy Award, Muddy's fourth, and also winning street credibility with the *Rolling Stone* Critic's Award. *I'm Ready* would earn Muddy his fifth Grammy Award.

◇   ◇   ◇

On July 9, during a stint at the Quiet Knight, Terry Abrahamson was backstage talking to Muddy. "Willie Dixon was there," said Abrahamson, "and the backstage door opens, in comes Keith Richards and Ronnie Wood. I love the Stones — if I'd never heard the Stones, I'd have never gotten into Muddy. Keith Richards walked over to Muddy, kneeled down, and kissed his hand." Said Margolin, "Muddy knew Mick and Keith very well, but hanging out after the show, he kept addressing Charlie Watts as 'Eddie.' Charlie didn't correct him, and seemed really tickled to be around someone who didn't kiss his ass."

During an extended gig at the Cellar Door in Washington, D.C., Muddy's presence in town came to the attention of a fellow southerner who was also on an extended stay, President Jimmy Carter. He invited them to play the White House. "They wanted me and my band," a somewhat incredulous, and very proud, Muddy told a documentary film crew. "From where I'm from, a black man couldn't even get inside a white man's front room." So on a hot August afternoon, 1978, the vans drove through White House security, set up their equipment, and watched bomb-sniffing dogs smell their gear before they played. "Muddy Waters is one of the great performers of all time," said the president. "He's won more awards than I could name. His music is well known around the world, comes from a good part of the country, and represents accurately the background and history of the American people." The president and first lady were treated to, among others, "Hoochie Coochie Man," "The Blues Had a Baby," and "I Got My Mojo Working."

"We didn't know about the show until about a day before," said Calvin Jones. "We didn't get paid nothing. Shit no. I got pictures with Jimmy Carter and all of us. Somebody got paid but I don't know who it was. Playing for the White House, don't make no money — that's tough, ain't it? They didn't even give us good dinners, give us some hot dogs."

⬦ ⬦ ⬦

In the fall of 1978, Muddy announced a European tour had come together for the next month "with some rock guy," Margolin said. "When I got over the shock of realizing I'd have to change a lot of immediate plans, I asked Muddy who we'd be playing with. He said, 'I can't call his name — it's one of those guys who was on that *Last Waltz*.' I named off a bunch of them and when I got to Eric Clapton, he said, 'Yeah, that's the one.'"

The first few nights, Muddy returned to the hotel after his own set. "One day, over breakfast in Germany, he asked me about Eric's music," Margolin continued. "That night, Muddy stayed. Two things Eric played really nailed Muddy: he did a very soulful version of Big Maceo's Chicago blues classic, 'Worried Life Blues,' which the late Otis Spann used to play when he was with Muddy. And Eric did a killer open-G slide guitar 'Come See Me Early in the Morning,' in which he used a trademark Muddy Waters turnaround lick. Muddy got a big smile and said, 'That's *my* shit!' From then on, they were close, and Muddy used to call Eric 'my son,' his highest compliment to a younger musician."

The partnership worked well for both parties and was reconvened in North America on March 28, 1979, for a forty-seven-city tour. Muddy's label had issued *Muddy "Mississippi" Waters Live,* featuring live renditions of songs from the previous two albums — and the requisite chestnuts. The live material featured his touring band, along with three songs drawn from the tour with Johnny Winter and James Cotton. The crowd's reaction to Muddy's slide work — you can hear their eyes lighting up like Christmas trees — confirms the eternal power of his playing. Half a century before, he'd drawn the same reaction from a juke house full of field hands, the same way Son House had drawn it from him. *Going up the country, don't you want to go?* The live album won Muddy his sixth Grammy. The wide exposure brought by the Clapton dates promoted sales of his recent releases, which were readily available, and of the older material, which was slowly being repackaged and rereleased by All Platinum.

When Muddy played Atlanta, his son Big Bill heard about the gig on the radio. "My daddy had moved from Chicago to Westmont and the number I had was no longer any good. I thought my daddy changed his number and didn't want me to bother him. So for years I didn't try to bother him. I went to see him in Atlanta and he hugged me. His words were, 'You're Mary's boy?' I said yeah. He hugged me, said, 'Well you're my boy too.' I got goose bumps. I still get goose bumps. I sat there in the dressing room with Bob Margolin, Jr. Johnson, Pinetop Perkins, Jerry Portnoy, and they kept saying, 'Man, you look just like Joe.' My daddy sat there in his chair, he had a little lady on each side of him, he just sat there staring. Staring." Big Bill's words, which began fast and furious at the clear memory, slowed as the memory crept from the shadows, as its edges and wholeness came to light. Big Bill took a breath, but breath wouldn't come. Tears did, in a steady stream, and he buried his head in his hands. "Man, you know, it hurts. It's a hurting thing."

When the tour came through Memphis, Muddy arranged to have the day free. He and Bo took the white Cadillac down Highway Sixty-one, the road of Golden Promise, past their old stomping grounds and all the way to Issaquena County. A field hand named Robert from the Esparanda Farm remembered seeing the big white Cadillac pull up. "The farmer sent me in a pickup truck to find out who was looking around," he said. "It was Muddy Waters, and he was with Carrie Brown, his cousin who lived near Glen Allan. I was trying to like Carrie at the time. We all went up to Glen Allan after sun — we were working sun to sun — drank some beers, then he left for a gig." At home, horsepower had replaced the horse, but little else had changed.

On June 5, 1979, in Chicago, Muddy married Marva Jean Brooks. He'd sat up in bed a few mornings earlier and announced his intentions to her. "It was spontaneous," Marva remembered. "Me and Cookie were running around trying to get everything ready. It was a simple house wedding. I didn't want anything fancy and Mud wasn't that type." It was her twenty-fifth birthday, he was sixty-six. The small ceremony was held at Muddy's home. In addition to his band mates, his manager, and other friends and families, the party included Clapton and his entourage; Johnny Winter flew out for the occasion. Muddy ordered steaks from a butcher that Willie Dixon recommended, and there was lots of champagne on ice. "It was a big party. At the time, 'I Shot the Sheriff' was a hit, and that was one of my favorite songs," said Joseph Morganfield. "All my friends were riding bikes by, trying to peek through the fence. What stands out in my mind is Clapton went swimming in our pool in his underwear." What stands out in Eric Clapton's mind is Muddy "riding around on his tricycle and it was like, 'This blues singer is behaving like a clown.' He was just a regular guy at home."

During the Clapton tour, Muddy had joined the Rosebud Agency for booking, run by Mike Kappus. Kappus put champagne on Muddy's contract, a clause reading, "One (1) fifth of either Piper-Heidsieck Gold Label Brut (1971, 1973, or 1975); Krug (1971, 1973, or 1975); or Dom Perignon champagne, iced and with at least six (6) champagne glasses." Said Kappus, "The champagne on the contract rider was an extra stretch for promoters when Muddy's demand was not at its peak, but Muddy always wanted his champagne. Turned out, if they didn't have it, Muddy had several bottles that he would sell to them to give to him."

Though things were getting better for Muddy, the band was not sharing in the reward. "Muddy wouldn't say nothing about it," said Pinetop. "He was making plenty of money. He got a whole lot of money off Chess Records since Scott got in there."

"Conditions for us stayed about the same," said Fuzz. "Hotels were going up and up. The Holiday Inn in 1971 was something like twenty-two dollars a night, it got to be sixty or seventy dollars. We would get a double, wasn't able to be in no single." Muddy made no attempt to rectify the situation; he'd turned all his business decisions over to Cameron.

Muddy took a break from the road for about three months at the end of 1979, and the band put together a tour of their own, billing themselves as Muddy introduced them: The Legendary Band. They asked Muddy if they could use one of his suburbans; he refused. Squeezing into Fuzz's Cadillac, they hit the road for holiday money.

When they recorded in Westport in May of 1980, the tensions were high and the spirits were not. It was the road band (and Johnny) only, no substitutes, no guests. As if trying to get comfortable, Muddy, in addition to the full-on band, worked with smaller units. "Mean Old Frisco Blues" is inflected with rockabilly innocence, hearkening to Elvis's interpretation of another Arthur Crudup tune. "I Feel Like Going Home," pulled from the *Hard Again* sessions because there wasn't enough from this session to make a whole record, is all acoustic. The textural differences on *King Bee* were, to some degree, a result of the simmering feelings. Margolin remembers suggesting that less might be more on some songs and Muddy fired right back at him: fine, you sit out.

There was hardly a break between the sessions and the resumption of the endless tour. They started on the East Coast, went up into Canada, then down into middle America. They went to Europe in July, back to Canada, and over to Alaska, where Cotton's band opened their shows. One bleary night on the road, when somewhere felt like nowhere, Muddy got "belligerent" in the dressing room, according to Bob Margolin. "The uncomfortable business situation was the developing split. I stood up and elaborated on a problem, and he just quietly answered, 'Oh, I can understand that.' He drank a little more than usual that night after the show, and the band got in his two vans for the ride back to the hotel. Muddy and I were in one of the vans with Luther driving, and Muddy's depression overtook him. With Luther and me, caring friends, he ran down a long list of things with health, personal life, and business that were going wrong and really weighing on him. It was heartbreaking to see Muddy so down, and to know that all of his success and greatness and the world's love couldn't comfort him. He was coping fine by the next day, but his problems were real, and eventually they did get the better of him. Soon he did lose the band, and his health, and that is nothing less than tragic."

"We were playing a place called Harry Hope's out in Cary, Illinois," recalled Scott Cameron, "an old ski lodge. I think it was a Thursday, Friday, and Saturday and we were scheduled to leave on either the following Monday or Tuesday for Japan. The tour manager came up to the dressing room and said that the guys in the band would like to talk so I went downstairs and out to the van. I didn't have any idea why they were calling me downstairs. No idea at all. And they all demanded double the money or they weren't going to go."

"Conditions wasn't what it was supposed to be," said Willie Smith. "The real issue was, on our days off we had to pay our hotel. Muddy done got big so he was kind of picking gigs, getting the good ones, and you might be off two or three days. All we was asking for was half of the hotel fare, we'd all share rooms. But they didn't compromise. Scotty said it ain't a man here that can't be replaced. Everybody started getting in an uproar. He was right in a way of saying it, but a band has been with you so long through thick and thin and then all of a sudden there's no man that can't be replaced, there is a principle that goes along with that, too. Muddy didn't deal with it. And Scotty said, 'You take it or leave it.'"

New visas could not be arranged on such short notice, so the band got their double pay. But when they got home, Cameron, at Muddy's request, informed Jerry Portnoy, pegged as the ringleader, that his services were no longer required. "And within the next twenty-four hours," Cameron remembered, "I had a call from another member of the band saying if this member was gone he was gone. And then I had a call from another member of the band that if any of the members were gone they're all gone." And they were. As a bandleader, Muddy was like Duke Ellington: he turned out other bandleaders. The bands that backed B. B. King, Howlin' Wolf, and a host of major blues stars remained faceless musicians. From his first band to his last, Muddy produced stars. The Legendary Band followed suit, quickly recording an album and hitting the road.

Nonetheless, losing his longest running unit must have left

Muddy with a sense of isolation. Marva was there to brighten his dark moments, and old and new friends rallied 'round him. But there was hardly time for such thoughts. He called Mojo Buford, and within days a new band was assembled. Bassist Earnest Johnson brought the old feel of Smitty's Corner with him because he'd absorbed it there. Lovie Lee slipped onto the piano bench, occasionally replaced by Lafayette Leake, who'd recorded with Muddy in 1955. Buford played harp and Ray Allison quickly found his way to the drums. Guitars were handled by Jimmy Rogers, who forsook an East Coast tour to help out his old friend, and by the young John Primer, who mentored in Chicago with Sammy Lawhorn. (Guitarist Rick "Junior" Kreher assumed Jimmy's guitar spot after the tour.) Muddy Waters kept on rolling.

◇ ◇ ◇

Back home, Bo's breathing had become increasingly strangulated, and finally he consented to visit the doctor. "Bo was a veteran and I went with Muddy to take him to the VA Hospital," said Cookie. "They ran the tests and when they told him it was lung cancer, black people during that period, the word *cancer* was death to them. And Bo deteriorated really fast after that. I remember a sister of his came and they were going back and forth about who was going to pay this, and Muddy standing in the middle of the floor told the sister, 'How dare could you ask that? Everything will be taken care of,' and we buried Bo.

"Muddy took it very hard. It was the third time I'd ever seen Muddy cry. The first time was when my mother died, the second time when he took me to the hospital to say good-bye to Geneva, and then when Bo died in his Westmont bedroom. Those were the only times."

He had work to distract him. In April of 1981, *King Bee* was released, and Muddy set out again to promote the record on the road. His Beacon Theater show was reviewed in the *New York Times*. "It was hard to believe that the great blues master will be sixty-six [*sic*] years old on Saturday. Both vocally and instrumentally, he completely dominated his six-piece band and outshone his special guest, the Texas guitar virtuoso Johnny Winter." (At his birthday party that year at home, the centerpiece on the dining room table was a champagne fountain.)

In July, the new band played festivals and clubs across Europe, from Finland to the Hague, Austria to Italy; James Cotton opened a string of shows. In August, their blues festival gig was broadcast on National Public Radio. In September, they hit the West Coast, including a relaxed date on a mountaintop near Saratoga, California, at the Paul Masson Winery. "There was a winding road up there, and the stage was beneath a backdrop of a church brought over stone by stone from Europe, then partially rebuilt after the 1906 earthquake," said Mike Kappus, who booked the gig. Sharing the bill were Willie Dixon, John Hammond Jr., Sippie Wallace, Clifton Chenier, Albert King, and James Cotton. Johnny Winter flew in at his own expense. "I just wanted to be with him some more," said Johnny. "I liked Muddy, he was a good guy." The winery hosted the musicians at their chateau, complete with a pool and a chef. Muddy, particular about his champagne, snuck his own bottles in; when he sat by the pool, he'd hide the label because he didn't want to offend the hosts. "At the end," Kappus continued, "they broke out some estate-bottled champagne, shared it with all of us. When Muddy tasted it he said to me, 'Oh, if I'd known they had this I wouldn't have been sneaking in my own bottles.' "

That same month, Muddy was booked for a Mississippi homecoming, headlining the fourth annual Delta Blues Festival held at Freedom Village near Greenville. He'd taken the gig at the behest of his daughter Mercy, who was in college nearby and was about to graduate magna cum laude. The day before, he traveled to Jackson for a reception in his honor at the governor's mansion. Muddy wore a white suit with a Hawaiian shirt. The next month, he was inducted into the Blues Hall of Fame at the Blues Foundation's first ceremony.

When the Rolling Stones next returned to Chicago, arrangements were made in advance to film an unrehearsed jam with Muddy at Buddy Guy's Checkerboard Lounge on Sunday, November 22. The

club, at 423 East Forty-third, was housed in a former automobile repair shop and was next to a car wash. Muddy's band was playing, and
the Stones joined them for what would be the last time Muddy was
ever recorded. The meeting of generations was more than a passing
of the torch, it was a real fun time. Muddy holds the microphone for
Mick Jagger while the two hoochie coochie men share vocals on
"Hoochie Coochie Man," Keith Richards studies Muddy's fingers
while they share guitar duties on "Baby Please Don't Go." The music
is loose and fun, transforming the Checkerboard Lounge in Chicago
into a Mississippi Delta Saturday-night fish fry.

A couple of weeks later, Muddy was with Marva, Cookie, and Leola, shopping at his favorite South Side produce store. Without warning, he passed out in an aisle. "He came to within seconds," said
Cookie, "said he was okay, that I would have to drive home. He had
high blood pressure and said he'd been eating too much pork." He
went to the doctor for a physical and some tests, and just days before
Christmas the doctor asked him to come see an oncologist. "They told
him they saw cancer on his lungs. Cancer, that's the only thing I ever
saw Muddy afraid of, because Geneva died of cancer and she went
completely out of her mind towards the end, and then it killed Bo too."

"When Mud first found out that he had cancer in the lungs, it was
a shock for all of us," Marva recalled, "but he never felt defeat. He
was a strong man. He stayed in good spirits." Doctors removed part
of Muddy's cancerous lung, and he began radiation treatment. They
recommended chemotherapy too, but "he got up one morning and
said he wasn't going for chemo," Marva continued. "He had made
peace with the Lord and all he wanted was to be home with his
family."

Mike Kappus went to visit him during a hospital stay. Muddy was
lying in the bed, his back raised, and his spirits were high. "We were
talking about John Lee Hooker, and he was imitating John's voice
and joking about how each of them would try to one-up the other,
which was the first one to get a Cadillac, the first to get a Mercedes,
the first to get a phone in the car. The visit was really positive."

"I'd stop by the hospital," Rick Kreher, Muddy's last guitarist, remembered, "and bring him *Living Blues* magazines. He liked to look at the pictures, talk about the people, pick his spirits up. He always thought he was going to get better. He had that will to live, that kind of guy. He didn't want to give it up."

"I had no idea my daddy had cancer," Big Bill Morganfield said. "I talked to him after he got out of the hospital and I said, 'Daddy, what's wrong?' He said, 'I just had an operation, they cut me.' I said, 'What's wrong?' He said, 'It's all right.' He wouldn't tell me. I knew he was sick because he had a bad cough from deep inside him." Muddy had been unable to tell his son about his illness, and he asked his manager to keep the news from the public. "For some reason, Scott did not want the nature of Muddy's illness known," Kappus said. "We were not to say that he was ill and by all means not reveal the nature of the illness."

Muddy got a morale boost when Columbia Records, more than thirty-five years after the fact, released his sessions with Mayo Williams. When Jim O'Neal was given a tape of an old 78 that sounded like Muddy, even though his name was nowhere on it, he sent it to Westmont. It was the James "Sweet Lucy" Carter "Mean Red Spider" session, Muddy's first ever in Chicago. "He hadn't heard it," said O'Neal. "He said he didn't realize it had ever come out. He had forgotten all about it."

And there was more good news: doctors told him his cancer was in remission. By late spring of 1982, Muddy was feeling stronger and a new tour was booked. Eric Clapton was playing in Miami on June 30, and Clapton's manager arranged a surprise visit. Marva, Scott, and Muddy hopped a plane. Clapton had incorporated Muddy's "Blow Wind Blow" into his set, and when he began it, Muddy stepped onstage. "Eric was clearly in shock," said Kappus. "At the end of the song, Muddy left the stage and Eric said to himself as much as to the audience, 'That was Muddy Waters!' It was a tremendous surprise for him. We were thinking that Muddy was bouncing back, but he was not there yet."

Upon his return home, Muddy coughed up blood. The cancer had returned, but Muddy's body was not yet strong enough for surgery.

"If he had been able to build up his strength, maybe they could have operated again," said Kappus, "but his spirits were down. There had been an optimism that everything was going to be okay. After the Clapton show, there was a realization that that wasn't going to be the case."

"When they told him it came back, I think Muddy felt he couldn't fight it anymore," said Cookie. "He did the radiation, and took the medication, but he wasn't the same after it came back the second time. His clothes were hanging off him. I got him a suit that would fit, but he would just lay on the couch. My twins were nine months old, and I was raising Muddy's grandchild, the same age, and I brought them over there and I felt so bad. Here was their great-grandfather and he was so ecstatic, but I could see that he was unable to enjoy it."

"Even at the end we still had fun," said Jimmy Rogers, who phoned up his partner just weeks before his death. "I was getting ready to leave for Canada, a tour, and he told me he was getting better, that they were trying to build him up for an operation. He told me he'd be back as soon as the weather breaks. Around the first part of June he said he'd see me somewhere on the road. My wife was playing some of the records that we made down through the years, and he could hear it through the phone. He said, 'I'm getting ready to come back through.' I said, 'That's good,' but he never did make it out of there."

Muddy had his son Joseph living with him at Westmont. The gap between their lives was immense, and ironic. Joseph had gone from having nothing, like Muddy, to living the American dream: suburban house, swimming pool, basketball camps, spending money, educational opportunities. Materially, he was satisfied. Muddy provided him a furnish. To give him an understanding of the grit that had produced these pearls, Muddy arranged for Joseph to visit Willie Smith's mother in Mississippi. "His mom lived on a farm in Mississippi, and my dad let me go out there for a couple weeks. It was fun but it was weird. She had an outhouse with a bathroom. We had to get water from a well. She had a wood stove, you had to actually chop the wood. There was no electricity and the next house was maybe a mile away. It was pitch black and lots of mosquitos. I wondered what I'd got myself into. By the third night it was cool. Every day before I got up, I woke up to the smell of breakfast. That was great. I could buy firecrackers up in town, that was exciting. I never had drunk water from a well before or used an outhouse. I guess that's how he grew up and he wanted me to get a taste of it."

On his last birthday, his seventieth (though celebrated as his sixty-eighth), there was a party at his house. His band was there, lots of family and friends. Phone calls came in from around the country. Muddy mustered his strength and enjoyed himself, though it exhausted him. Over the next month, he slipped in and out of consciousness, but he stayed at home, his last days spent among his family and loved ones.

CHAPTER 15

THIS DIRT HAS MEANING
1983 and After

H e used to introduce me at his concerts," Marva said in her soft voice. "I always asked myself why, why he'd scooped me up. I am shy-natured, and I didn't like all those people looking at me. I hated it when he'd do that, but he'd say, 'You can do it, you can do it.' Now I know why. He was preparing me for representing him after he was gone."

Marva was next to him in their bed at home when Muddy breathed his last. He'd fought off the hospitals, avoided the chemotherapy, spent his time at home with his family. Late in the evening on April 29, his heart gave out. An ambulance took his body to the Good Samaritan Hospital in Downers Grove, Illinois, outside Chicago, where he was pronounced dead on arrival at 2:17 the morning of April 30, 1983. He was seventy years old. Cause of death was listed as cardiorespiratory arrest and carcinoma of the lungs. No autopsy was necessary.

"Geneva was a very, very big churchgoer and that's why, when Muddy died, I went to my church and asked if he could have the funeral service there," said Cookie. "I knew that's how his grand-mother had raised him." And so plans were made. On May 2, his casket was laid out at the Metropolitan Funeral Parlors on the South Side of Chicago. Muddy was dressed in a white linen leisure suit set off by a striped purple shirt and handkerchief. Thousands of fans made their way down church aisles overflowing with flower arrange-ments, great and small, sent by record labels, music publishing or-ganizations, and fans from all walks of life. The Rolling Stones sent one of the largest spreads, with a note that read, "In memory of a wonderful man dear to us all. We shall never forget you, Muddy." "I'm sure you never knew," said the card on the flowers sent by Hank Williams Jr., "but I loved your music and learned a lot from you." The Nighthawks, up and coming, ready to spread his word, sent a single rose. "This is overwhelming, an incredible outpouring of admiration," Scott Cameron told a reporter. "These were Muddy's stomping grounds. We couldn't close it to the public." The viewing lasted for three days. "I came from Europe to say good-bye," said James Cotton. "People were lined up for two or three blocks."

"I went to Muddy's wake," B. B. King remembered. "I sort of thought like they do in New Orleans, like you should cry at the incoming and rejoice at the outgoing. I remembered the days that I could talk to him, the days he tried to help me, the music he could play — I've got some with me right now — and I was sad to see him go, but relieved that whatever bad he'd gone through, he didn't have to do that anymore and whatever was good, these are memories we can all cherish."

"Mud was the type of person," said Marva, "he didn't want you to weep, he would want you to celebrate the way he was. His music was like that too. What went down with him when he was coming up, a lot of that went into his music, but he didn't let that get him down. He was a happy-go-lucky person. Muddy loved to entertain. When he got in front of a large crowd, he had more fun than the crowd did. When he came home, his family was his main priority. He liked to cook, he baked cakes, he loved being in the kitchen. Most everybody that came to the house, he was always offering something. That was him."

The funeral service on Wednesday, May 4, was held in a large hall that overflowed, leaving hundreds of friends and fans stranded outside. Some had come to pay their respects, others to gawk at famous entertainers during their grief. "No single event ever focused so much worldwide attention on the blues," Jim O'Neal reported in *Living Blues*. "It was all Muddy's manager Scott Cameron and the Morganfield family could do to prevent the funeral from becoming a circus, but amidst the overflow of mourners, they did manage to conduct the proceedings in a manner as dignified as the way in which Muddy himself had carried out his mission as the King of Chicago Blues."

The service commenced at 7:30 P.M. Reverend C. W. Hopson, who did not know Muddy, officiated. Muddy's family from Mississippi had come, from Michigan and elsewhere. There were his children, grandchildren, great-grandchildren, and stepchildren. Leola Spain was there. "They didn't want to let me in," said Lucille McClenton, "but I got in." Others in attendance included Willie Dixon, Buddy Guy, Junior Wells, Memphis Slim, and magician David Copperfield. Johnny Winter was so shaken, he couldn't speak. Pops Staples, another Mississippi Delta guitarist who'd made an impact on the world, sang "Glory Glory Hallelujah." Several of Muddy's recordings were played, including "They Call Me Muddy Waters" and "Got My Mojo Working." The guitar screamed and cried, and so did the mourners. The family wailed from the front, some of them fainted. The funeral closed with the playing of Muddy's "Hoochie Coochie Man," reminding everyone "the whole world knows who I am."

The next morning, mourners gathered at the funeral home for the ride to Restvale Cemetery. Like an Egyptian king, Muddy asked to be buried with his red Telecaster, a last favor that was not easily honored: the guitar kept the casket from closing, until the neck on it snapped.

The cavalcade of cars left the South Side and drove out toward Muddy's suburban home. Though the route had not been published, people knew, and the streets were lined with well-wishers out to pay their last respects. "It was like royalty," remembered Mike Kappus, who had been an usher and served as pallbearer. The remaining pallbearers were drawn from his last band and other business associates: Mojo Buford, Lovie Lee, Ray Allison, Rick Kreher, and Tim Rosner. "I'm skeptical about the supernatural," continued Kappus, "but this was quite amazing. We brought the casket to the burial site, and there was family in a semicircle around the vault. There were various flower arrangements in that area, they'd brought the larger ones near. As we set the casket on the support, there was a loud crack and the easel supporting this floral arrangement in the shape of a red guitar had cracked. Several of the women screamed."

That night, a spontaneous wake was held at Buddy Guy's Checkerboard Lounge. Fans overflowed the walls, grooving and gawking. Buddy Guy jammed with James Cotton, and read a telegram from the city's mayor, Harold Washington: "We know you're with us, Muddy, so let the music play on, and on and on." Hubert Sumlin was there, and Sunnyland Slim, who, at two in the morning, led an entourage to another club that was open later. Muddy's spirit lived on.

◇　◇　◇

Muddy was buried in Chicago, but his heart never left Stovall, never left the sound and feel of the Mississippi Delta where he was shaped and formed. Late in his life, when interviewed by Margaret McKee, he laughed when his success was mentioned, said, "I've never been a big shot and I never will be one. I'm just plain Muddy Waters from Clarksdale, Mississippi. We got the headquarters from Stovall. That's me." He'd been around the world, and he still identified himself by the plantation office where he'd been paid, such as it was, for his crop.

Sharecropping shaped Muddy, just as it shaped several generations. Richard Wright, in his 1945 introduction to *Black Metropolis,* asked, "What peculiar personality formations result when millions of people are forced to live lives of outward submissiveness while trying to keep intact in their hearts a sense of the worth of their humanity?" Muddy is but the study of a single person; however, his life proves a telling instance. His aspirations were never diminished, though how he achieved them was affected. He took where he could and left behind a path of destroyed relationships, women forlorn and desperate, family on unsteady grounding. He was a friendly, sociable guy who liked to be around people and play music for them. His determination to succeed sometimes diluted his artistic integrity, but his eyes never averted from the prize. He'd absorbed suffering and abuse at his emotional core, and the music that escaped from there resonated with feeling. He could not trust satisfaction, relying instead on immediate gratification, and he was worldly enough to know he was being shortchanged.

If gospel music is about the future of one's soul, blues music is about its present. Muddy began preaching the blues to a local congregation that needed temporary relief from oppression, and he found that the oppressed numbered well beyond his friends and neighbors. The passion in Muddy's music grabbed listeners, absorbed and enveloped them, transforming their here and now. "The blue are . . . intensely worldly," John Work wrote in 1943, adding, "The blues singer has no interest in heaven, and not much hope in earth." So now there was a little hope. Nineteen forty-three was the same year that Muddy left the South, and soon after, he changed the sound of the blues. Chicago was a promised land and for Muddy it delivered. He had to work at it, but he knew his goal was artistic success, even at the expense of all else, including money and family. Blue Smitty wasn't comfortable getting too far from his electrical work, Jimmy Rogers and Little Walter made too many concessions to the musical demands of the moment, and when that moment passed, so did those songs. For James Smith, one of Muddy's guitar mentors on Stovall — Muddy says he could play as well as Robert Johnson — other endeavors or interests kept him from making a record. Muddy had a goal, and he stuck to it, paying the price. In the end, he did get money and he lived his last years in a happy family environment. Through Muddy, the blues became a music of hope — not just escape. What had been the music of oppression became the music of liberation.

⬩ ⬩ ⬩

Towns in the Mississippi Delta are drying up and blowing away, the circle that Muddy swam in evaporating. Friar's Point, Belzoni, Rena Lara, Rolling Fork. Industry is drawing people from the smallest towns, and each departure leaves only emptiness. No one arrives to fill the void. A Wal-Mart opens, several town pharmacies close. The old five-and-dime with the wood floor shuts its doors. There is no new tenant. Dust gathers.

"My grandmother, Leola, got with Azelene's children and their kids, and with her sisters — it was about five vans of us, and took us to Stovall after Muddy died," said Cookie. "I always hated that she didn't do it while he was alive, but he never was a big one about going back there. We'd ask him to take us and he had no interest. She showed us the post office, wasn't big as a bathroom, and then the store and stories about that, and the church. Then she took us through the fields and showed us where Muddy used to play at. She showed us where they fished and where they would pick cotton, and where he used to play the guitar when they would call theirselves juking. Leola and her sisters were crying. If it hadn't been for my grandmother and her sisters being there, we wouldn't have known nothing about that area. We were really grateful that she'd taken us." Leola Spain Tucker moved to Defiance, Ohio, in 1992 and died there two years later.

Muddy's estate is divided among the children he accumulated after Geneva's death — his children with Lucille and with Lois. The children he raised — his grandkids and stepchildren — received a small lump sum and nothing else.

Cookie's children are off living their lives — in college or long graduated. Chandra, her oldest, recently purchased Muddy's South Side home from the estate and wants her mom to move in upstairs. Yet Cookie's suburban Chicago house, which should be quiet as an empty nest, rumbles with young children. She has taken in the children of Muddy's outside daughters. "I always knew that Muddy kept the family together, but I never realized how much until he died," she said. "I hear from these kids' moms maybe once a year. I've lost respect for some of the others, but there's no way I cannot love Renee and Joseph, because I raised them." Cookie is a nurse in the same hospital in which Muddy died. In the mid-1990s, she was diagnosed with uterine cancer. "When they first told me, I felt like them and I said to myself, 'Oh God, it killed Muddy and Geneva and Bo and they were so dumb with this I can't do this to myself.'" She has been cancer free more than five years.

Her brother Laurence lives several blocks away. He plays golf on Sundays, drives a fancy car, and is raising a house full of kids with his wife. "We was his grandkids that was there from birth and these [outside] kids got all his money," said Laurence. "I got some little animosity, but it's okay. They have nothing. And I was the one that was going to be nothing. My house is fine, I'm fine. And my sisters came out okay."

Mercy Morganfield, Muddy's daughter with Lois from the Smitty's Corner days, has become an executive with a major pharmaceutical corporation. "I inherited my determination and drive directly from him," she said, "the need to succeed." During Muddy's last years, he enjoyed placing two stacks of American green cash on his kitchen table, one for him, one for her — Miss College — and then racing to count the money. "You're smart, Mercy Dee," he'd say, "I don't have to worry about you," though he always, gleefully, won the cash-counting contest.

Several of Muddy's children have wrestled substance abuse. Joseph recently remarried and showed up to hear Big Bill Morganfield and Bob Margolin play together in Chicago. He is studying to be a preacher. Charles continues to hang out at Forty-third and Lake Park. He's taken a room in the area and still lords over the gang of fellas in front of Muddy's old house.

Big Bill Morganfield has reconstructed his relationship with Muddy through music — the only way he could get to know him, the only way most anyone could get to know him. Bill's debut recording, *Rising Son,* features accompaniment from Pinetop Perkins, Bob Margolin, Paul Oscher, and Willie Smith. They perform five Muddy Waters songs and several of Bill's originals. "He knew he had a son that played, but to tell you the truth," said Bill, "I stunk. After he died, I went and locked myself in a room for six years, a woodshed, and I learned it. Note by note. Measure by measure. All my dad's records, I learned them. Maybe if I'd been there with him, I'd have been like the rest of them. None of his other kids are pursuing it. But I got it down." Bill Morganfield was named Best New Artist at the 2000 W. C. Handy Blues Awards.

◇　◇　◇

Maxwell Street on a Sunday at noon. Seagulls circle overhead, scouring the empty streets for hot-dog-bun tips. The sidewalk stinks of urine — fifty-year-old urine. The buildings are bombed out. Plywood covers the windows — "Windy City Board Up." Vagrant men hawk still-sealed porno tapes from plastic grocery sacks on their arms.

"If I coulda made thirty bucks, I'da been rich," said Jimmie Lee Robinson. He's the Mississippi guitarist who came to Chicago in time to watch Muddy break out, and later accompanied Little Walter. He plays guitar today with spurs on his boots, because he can't find good washboard accompaniment. He walks down Maxwell Street and sees a world that no longer exists. "Levitt's put a kosher dill pickle in the bun with the hot dog and boy I liked that taste." His city is punctuated by hot dog stands, and he discusses the past with relish. He is something like the inversion of Muddy Waters. He's done well enough as a performer, releasing a number of albums and touring in America and Europe, but not having achieved the level of Muddy's fame, he does not have to authenticate himself every night he plays. His lament — "coulda made thirty bucks" — could have been Muddy's in 1943, prior to leaving the South, an unknown blues musician plowing a field behind a mule or atop a tractor and dreaming of the possibilities, the blues falling all around him.

The nearby place where Jimmy Rogers lived when he heard Little Walter playing on the street is now beneath the foundation of the University of Illinois at Chicago's Physical Education building. Polk and Ogden, where Muddy and Jimmy first gigged, is part of the Chicago Medical School. Hy Marzen's Zanzibar became a church, but since a fire, the roof has been propped up by two-by-four boards. Muddy's first flop, at 3652 Calumet, is erased, a vacant lot in a row of stone buildings, three floors and a basement. Fences in the alley bear flowers, and plots of land are planted, a country feel in the city. Several of Muddy's old clubs are beneath an urban renewal expressway. Smitty's Corner is a currency exchange. The ghost of Maxwell Street past grows ever more transparent.

Several of Muddy's former players — the lineup is malleable — reunited in 1993 as the Muddy Waters Tribute Band. They've continued to do occasional tours in America and Europe. In late 1994, they recorded an album, *You're Gonna Miss Me (When I'm Dead and Gone)*, which was nominated for a Grammy Award.

Willie Smith, Calvin Jones, Jerry Portnoy, and Pinetop Perkins, calling themselves The Legendary Band, released seven albums and toured heavily. "Once we was in Charlotte, North Carolina," Calvin Jones said, "and we played at a college there. Eric [Clapton] played some big place, he came over where we were playing at, sat in, and we had a good time." One by one, the original members departed, leaving Willie Smith to rename the band and continue on. Calvin eventually moved back to Mississippi and lately divides his time between Senatobia and Memphis, touring when the calls come and playing sessions.

Pinetop Perkins, well into his eighties, has flourished with his solo career. Winner of eleven Handy Awards, he has released a steady flow of his own albums. "I have been up against it in my life," he said. "I have played with many a person. But I liked Muddy like a brother."

James Cotton's successful solo career was interrupted in 1994 by a bout with throat cancer. Treatment was successful, and he soon resumed his recording career. His 1996 recording, *Deep in the Blues,* won a Grammy Award, and more recently he and Mojo Buford have been touring together, dueling with their harps, Buford singing the vocals.

Following his break with Muddy, Portnoy toured with Eric Clapton's All-Star Blues Band for several years and recorded with him on *Blues from the Cradle,* one of the most successful blues albums ever. Portnoy has since developed a successful harmonica instruction booklet. "Playing with Muddy," he said, "has made me as comfortable talking to the president of the United States as I am talking to a wino at the corner of Sixty-third and Cottage Grove." Muddy as de Tocqueville: if the president can get the blues, the lowest of the low-down can get to be president.

Though his career has been plagued by missteps and bad juju, Paul Oscher has enjoyed renewed success. In the late 1990s, he formed a new band and began touring. With a very modest budget he recorded the excellent CD *The Deep Blues of Paul Oscher.* He recently dreamed that Muddy Waters came at him with a Coke bottle, trying to break his tooth. For two days following, he had pain in that tooth — though the nerve had been long removed. "The sound that comes out of the guitar is nothing without the person playing it," Oscher said. "It's just an instrument. But when you put your weight into it, to make it come out with that basic, deep sound — it's not the guitar. There's a spiritual connection."

The road became a home to Bob Margolin while he was with Muddy, and he's continued touring and recording ever since. In 1994, he attended the unveiling of Muddy's postage stamp in Greenville, Mississippi. "I got off the bus early and went to the food tent, and sitting there eating in a cotton field in Mississippi, a young man who looked exactly like a young Muddy walked up to me and said, 'Hi, Bob, nice to see you again.' The second before I realized it was Joseph scared the shit out of me." At an Antone's nightclub all-star anniversary party, Margolin played a solo set of Muddy's songs. "When I came into the dressing room," Margolin said, "Buddy Guy told me, 'Those are big shoes to fill. . . .' Shit, I'm just trying to keep 'em shined."

Scott Cameron continues to manage Muddy's estate, and unless there are unforeseeable changes, Scott and then his descendants will continue to collect money earned by Muddy's songs and share it with Muddy's descendants. "When MCA acquired Chess, they had Muddy Waters far in the hole on unrecouped advances and recording costs," he said. "I sat down with their business affairs people and I said this has gone on long enough. You've got to erase those balances, and you've got to give an appropriate royalty fee in line with today's standards. At that point MCA was going through all kinds of bad press, and I said, 'There are two choices, we either cut a deal or you get more bad publicity.' In addition to Muddy's estate, I represented Howlin' Wolf's widow, Jimmy McCracklin, Lowell Fulson, Memphis Slim's widow, even contemporary artists like John Brim, Koko Taylor, and Buddy Guy. We got them all an up-to-date royalty rate and anybody who had debt, the balances were thrown out and they all wound up getting royalty checks and they have ever since."

Marshall Chess assumed control of Arc Music Publishing in the 1990s when Gene Goodman retired, and in 2000 he reentered the record business with a label named for the original spelling of his family's name, Czxy Records (pronounced "Chess"). As for returning to the biz, he cited a statement his father often made: "Once you've had the experience of a gusher, you miss it."

Jimmy Rogers was seventy-three years old when we met in his South Side home. Several weeks later, he learned he had cancer; a few months after that he was dead. Such is the tenuousness of Muddy's early history, of a life in an oral culture. That evening, he was just back from a southern tour and feeling fit. His living room was well appointed, with contemporary, comfortable furniture protected from our cognac spills by fitted plastic like that Muddy had in his South Side home. He smoked long thin cigarettes and spoke in a voice like the tickle of worn sandpaper, weathered without sounding rough. "I keep big pictures of Muddy right there at my bedside, him and Sonny Boy," Rogers said. "They're the first thing I see in the morning." He was working until his death on December 19, 1997. Atlantic Records released an album that was finished posthumously, *Blues Blues Blues,* which featured friends such as Eric Clapton, Lowell Fulson, and members of the Rolling Stones. Less than a month after Jimmy died, Junior Wells also passed away.

Mary Austin, the mother of Muddy's son Big Bill Morganfield, ultimately settled in suburban Atlanta. She remains an active member of society and, after recently retiring, has taken up modeling. Lucille McClenton was living in a government senior citizen's center on Muddy Waters Drive when I first met her. Her apartment overlooked the South Side and the lake. She saw cool blue water and the white sails of boats, but there was no breeze inside. She had a grand view of the projects and of Muddy's former house. After a few minutes of talking, she got fidgety and began to wring her hands, picked things up and put them down. She looked young to be in a senior center; her room was in someone else's name. The lobby of the building stank of urine, the elevators were the slowest in the world. The sign out front, MUDDY WATERS DRIVE, had been warped and bent by the wind. On a later visit, she'd moved to the north side of town; she said she'd gone drug free and was trying to change her environment.

Marva Morganfield moved back to her small hometown in

Florida not long after Muddy died. "I was beginning to live my life and he had lived his'n," she said. "I was just a country girl, maybe I brought out what he was searching for all those years, what he missed after he left from Clarksdale. Mud was my father, my mother, my brother, my sister, he was all of that to me. I loved him deeply. I hurted when he hurted and there was nothing I could do. He'll always be here. You're not going to see him physically, but he's always here."

The blues may have come to Muddy on a dusty road while fixing a "punction" on a car, but an audience will always exist that understands "I can never be satisfied / I just can't keep from crying." On Friday, August 2, 1985, the street that ran by Muddy's South Side front door was permanently renamed Muddy Waters Drive. On January 21, 1987, Muddy was inducted into the Rock and Roll Hall of Fame. That same year, the "You Need Love" lawsuit against Led Zeppelin was settled out of court; payment to Muddy's estate was said to be around $200,000. In Rolling Fork, the town near Muddy's birthplace, a plaque and a gazebo were erected in his honor on April 21, 1988. That night, at Clarksdale's Civic Auditorium, ZZ Top headlined a fundraiser for the Delta Blues Museum's Muddy Waters exhibit, unveiling Muddywood, an electric guitar made from a cypress plank taken from Muddy's Stovall cabin. A thousand fried-fish dinners were sold outside the auditorium — Muddy always did appreciate a fish fry — and the event jumpstarted the city's interest in its indigenous music. *Hard Again*'s "Mannish Boy" was used in the Hollywood film *Risky Business,* on a Miller Genuine Draft Beer commercial, and in advertising jeans in England. In 1984, a theatrical play entitled *Muddy Waters (The Hoochie Coochie Man)* was produced by Chicago's Black Ensemble Theater Company and drew crowds for several months. In 1986, it was revamped for a two-month run, hosted by the Beacon Street Theater. At the 1992 Grammy Awards, Muddy Waters was recognized with the prestigious Lifetime Achievement Award. In 1998, his song "(I'm Your) Hoochie Coochie Man" was welcomed in the Grammy Hall of Fame. In April of 2001, Muddy was inducted into the Mississippi Musicians Hall of Fame. He would have surely appreciated the use, that same year, of "I'm Ready" in a commercial for the male stimulant Viagra. Muddy Waters was gone, and Muddy Waters was everywhere.

A generation has been born and matured since his death, and the testament to the endurance of Muddy's music is his power over those experiencing a world he never knew. His legacy is as strong as it's ever been. His culture — the blues culture — had an impact in the twentieth century that was, arguably, second to none. Duke Ellington evokes a cosmopolitan sophistication. Harry Belafonte's catalog captures the breadth of African influence on Western song. Louis Armstrong conjures America's melting pot. But Muddy's achievement is the triumph of the dirt farmer. His music brought respect to a culture dismissed as offal. His music spawned the triumphant voice of angry people demanding change. This dirt has meaning.

⬧   ⬧   ⬧

A coatrack full of empty hangers. A potbellied stove with no flame. The first chill of winter in Chicago's September air.

Dusk lingers, evening fending off night. This is the light when reflections are translucent, when a window reflects one's own image as easily as reveals what's beyond.

A shop front on Chicago's South Side, the start of a new century. Two old men in their seventies, or maybe their sixties and hard living. The room is scattered with more objects than either will be able to repair in this lifetime. Which bothers them none as they sit and play guitar.

A TV on its side. Two-thirds of a three-way mirror. A curious white wax apple smudged with auto grease, a refrigerator covered with a 1960s psychedelic pattern. "Your fingers are a little stiff," says the one who is not picking. His fingers are, in fact, palsied.

This room is long and deep. The ceiling is high, with fluorescent light fixtures hanging down several feet, and still way out of reach. The bulbs in most no longer even flicker. The sounds of glasses tinkling, patrons milling, matches lighting cigarettes, and old friends from the South stumbling upon each other in the North — these are all absorbed into the empty space now the domain of spiders.

The address of this shop is 706 Forty-seventh Street. Chicago.

The South Side. This block is a series of shop fronts, old buildings with common walls. Next door, they sell furniture and bicycles, dining room suites with gold-painted aluminum frames, clear Plexiglas table tops, and padded chairs, the fabric of which will fray sooner than expected. The address of that shop is 708 Forty-seventh Street. It used to be a club, the 708 Club, and Muddy Waters played there. Regular. Howlin' Wolf, once he began to attract attention, played there. Before them, Memphis Minnie played the 708 and after them, Buddy Guy played there, new in Chicago and thinking about returning to Louisiana.

The man and his companion at 706 lean back in their old office chairs, roll a little bit on the wheels. The chair arms are worn through, and foam stuffing seeps out. A young woman opens the front door and asks for spare change so she can buy drugs. No one gives her any money, but she sits down and listens to the guitar. They make her welcome.

"The blues were around way before I was born," Muddy said. "They'll always be around. Long as people hurt, they'll be around."

ITINERARY OF THE 1941 AND 1942 FISK–LIBRARY OF CONGRESS COAHOMA COUNTY STUDY

The Fisk–Library of Congress Coahoma County Study is a significant landmark in America's appreciation of its African American art and culture. In a report to the Library of Congress after the 1941 trip, Alan Lomax wrote, "So far as I know this study marks the first occasion on which a great Negro university has officially dedicated itself to the study and publication of Negro folk songs. . . ."

The trip yielded many resources and was itself well documented. When recordings from the trip have been cited, the dates have usually been approximated. Through correlating journals and correspondences at the Fisk Library, the Alan Lomax Archives, the Library of Congress, and The Center for Popular Music at Middle Tennessee State University, I have determined the itinerary of the recordists.

In the 1941 report, Lomax also wrote,

> The type of musical study which is herein projected and laid out will lay the basis, it is believed, for contemporary music history, for a new approach to the field of folk music, for a practical working knowledge of the musical life of people, which will be equally useful to scholars, professionals, and administrators in the field. The projected fieldwork will result in a study, jointly edited by Dr. [Charles S.] Johnson and his assistants, and by Alan Lomax, which will be published under the sponsorship of Fisk University.

The study was not only never published, it was misplaced, its hunt the subject of correspondence since 1945. During research in the John Work Archives at Fisk University, I located the complete study, along with complementary manuscripts by Lewis Jones, Fisk Department of Sociology, and Samuel Adams Jr., one of Jones's students. Hopefully, these works will finally be published.

1941

The 1941 traveling party included John Work III, Alan Lomax, Lewis Jones, and a Dr. Ross, from the Fisk Drama Department. The sociologists and musicologists apparently split up while in Clarksdale.

April 29   Alan Lomax at Fisk University to emcee a night of the school's fiftieth-anniversary celebration

July 30   Lomax writes to Dr. Charles S. Johnson, director of the Fisk Department of Social Science: "A number of people have suggested that southwestern Tennessee, which is slightly more stable than the Delta area, would be a better region for work than the one we have thought of already."

Aug. 22   John Work writes Fisk comptroller, proposing a trip to Ripley, Tennessee (four days), and Carthage, Mississippi (eight days), leaving on August 27

Aug. 23   Lomax writes to Work from Washington, D.C.: "I shall see you the morning of the twenty-fifth, ready, I hope, for our trip to Ripley."

Aug. 24   Lomax in Nashville [The destination was finally determined at a conference in Nashville. Dr. Charles S. Johnson, noting the density of the African American population in Coahoma County, swayed the others.]

Aug. 27   Recording #1a: Spirituals, Congregation Maple Springs

Aug. 29   Sleep in Clarksdale; travel to Hollandale, Mississippi, to record more spirituals

Aug. 30   Recordings at Mt. Airy Church; recordings at Morning Glory Baptist Church

Aug. 31   Recordings at Stovall with Muddy Waters

Sept. 1   Recording a baptism service in Money, Mississippi

Sept. 2   Recording in Mound Bayou with Mr. George Johnson, who'd been a slave of Jefferson Davis

Sept. 3   Recordings at Lake Cormorant, Mississippi, with Son House and Willie Brown

Sept. 7   Lomax in Rugby, Virginia, returning to Washington, D.C.

Sept. 20–22 Lomax in Nashville for Fisk's student-training seminar

Sept.–Dec. Two student field-workers remain in Coahoma County and are visited periodically by Lewis Jones and Dr. M. H. Watkins from the Fisk Ethnology and Cultural Anthropology Department

Oct.   John Work and his assistant, Harry Wheeler, begin musically transcribing the recordings

1942

The 1942 traveling party included Alan Lomax, Lewis Jones, and several of Jones's students, including a Ms. Worley and a Senor Eduardo. Lomax worked alone in Coahoma, regrouping with the others periodically.

July 11   Lomax departs a folklore conference in Bloomington, Indiana

July 12   Bowling Green, Kentucky

July 13   Nashville

July 16   West Memphis

July 17   Recordings at Clarksdale with Son House, who then takes Lomax to meet Robert Johnson's mother

July 18   Coahoma County sheriff detains Lomax; he sends a telegram, to Dr. Harold Spivacke, chief in the Library of Congress's Division of Music: "Please rush very official letter of identification mentioning Fisk Field Helpers General Delivery Clarksdale." Later, Lomax hears David Honeyboy Edwards performing as "Big Joe" on the street in Friar's Point

July 19   Lewis Jones and co. arrive in Clarksdale; they record Turner Johnson, a blind harmonica player, and then Miss Chapman, a white piano teacher

July 20–22 Recordings with David Honeyboy Edwards as "Joe Williams"

July 23   Recordings in Clarksdale with Rev. E. M. Martin, and toasts from M. C. Orr

July 24–25 Recordings at Stovall's store with Muddy Waters and the Son Sims Four

July 26   Recordings with Asa Ware and "old McClennon," followed by "ice cream and cake with a young Negro planter"; recordings that evening in a sanctified church

July 27   Recording date with Muddy postponed while Lomax fixes the recorder

July 28   Recordings and interviews with Alec Robinson, Annie Williams (Friar's Point), Jaybird Jones

July 29   George Adams and Mr. McClellan discuss old and bloody Delta days; interview with Charley Idaho/Aderholt; Lomax conducts the Family Report interview with Muddy and his family

July 30   Before leaving for Dallas and a personal visit, Lomax meets with teachers at the County Agricultural High School in preparation for a program of recording and presentation upon his return; he departs for Memphis

Aug. 8   Lomax returns to Clarksdale from Dallas, reunites with Lewis Jones; that evening they record the stories and songs of a section-gang singer

Aug. 9   Lomax records a public ceremony, Clarksdale, honoring the Negro soldier; meets with Coahoma County high school teachers

Aug. 10   Records game songs with Coahoma County high school teachers

Aug. 11   Records and films with Coahoma County high school teachers; meal at Ruby Harris's house

Aug. 12   High school demonstration; includes a lecture by Lewis Jones

Aug. 13   Clarksdale to Hollandale and back

Aug. 14   Clarksdale to Como and hill country

Aug. 15   Recordings near Como with Sid Hemphill; then Lomax departs for Nashville

Aug. 16   Arrives in Nashville at noon

Aug. 17   Nashville

Aug. 19   Recordings in Nashville at the Church of God Tabernacle

Aug. 20   Recordings at Smithville Church

Aug. 22   Sacred Harp Singing Convention in Birmingham, Alabama

Aug. 25–27 Nashville to Bowling Green to Nashville

Aug. 28   Lomax departs for Washington, D.C.

1943

June   John Work returns to Coahoma County; photographs Muddy

MUDDY'S DELTA RECORD COLLECTION AND REPERTOIRE

On July 29, 1942, Alan Lomax conducted the Family Report interview with Muddy and his family at their cabin on Stovall. In his journals, Lomax noted both the records in Muddy's collection and Muddy's repertoire. They follow as he listed them.

MUDDY'S RECORD COLLECTION
Arthur Crudup, "Black Pony Blues" / "Kind Lover Blues"
Arthur Crudup, "Death Valley Blues" / "If I Get Lucky"
Peetie Wheatstraw, "Sweet Woman Blues"
Tony Hollins, "Crawlin' Kingsnake"
Sonny Boy Williamson, "Bluebird"
Jay McShann and His Orchestra, (no title)
Elder Oscar Saunders, "Conqueror" / "Preaching"

MUDDY'S REPERTOIRE
"You Are My Sunshine"
"The House"
"Dinah"
"St. Louis Blues"
"Country Blues"
"Texaco"
"Deep in the Heart of Texas"
"Home on the Range"
"I Be's Troubled"
"Take a Little Walk with Me"
"County Jail Blues"
"Thirteen Highway"   Walter Davis
"Angel Blues"   Walter Davis
"Thirty-Eight Pistol"
"Down South"   Sonny Boy Williamson
"Sugar Mama"   Sonny Boy Williamson
"Bluebird Blues"   Sonny Boy Williamson

"Canary Bird Blues"   McKinley Morganfield
"Burr Clover Blues"   McKinley Morganfield
"North Highway"   McKinley Morganfield
"Ramblin' Kid"   McKinley Morganfield
"Rosalie"   McKinley Morganfield
"Boots and My Saddles"
"What You Know, Joe?"
"Missouri Waltz"
"Be Honest with Me"   Bill Monroe
"I Ain't Got Nobody"
"Corinna"
"Down By the Riverside"
"Chattanooga Choo-Choo"
"Blues in the Night"
"Dark Town Strutter's Blues"
"Red Sails in the Sunset"
"Bye-Bye Blues"

How to Buy Muddy Waters and Other Related Recordings

Essential Muddy Waters Recordings

Any *Best of* Muddy
Can't Be Satisfied
The Complete Plantation Recordings

Hard Again
Hoochie Coochie Man (Laserlight)
Live the Life

Also Recommended

The Aristocrat of the Blues
The Blues World of Little Walter
Bottom of the Blues (Otis Spann)
Chicago Blues Masters Volume One
Collaboration
Electric Mud
Fathers and Sons

Half Ain't Been Told (Otis Spann)
Hoochie Coochie Man (Just a Memory)
I'm Ready
Live (At Mr. Kelly's)
Muddy Waters at Newport
One More Mile
Woodstock Album

To gain a deeper feel for Muddy, I researched many filmed performances and interviews. A documentary was a natural result and, with Morgan Neville, I made *Muddy Waters Can't Be Satisfied*. This video features the best performances by Muddy and interviews with many of the people featured in this book. It's an excellent companion piece and, following its TV broadcast, the tape will be available through Wellspring Video (www.wellspringvideo.com).

Muddy's *Billboard* R&B Chart Hits

(According to *Joel Whitburn's Top R&B Singles, 1942–1955,* www.recordresearch.com.)

TITLE	DEBUT DATE	PEAK POS.	WEEKS ON
"I Feel Like Going Home"	9/18/48	11	2
"Louisiana Blues"	1/13/51	10	1
"Long Distance Call"	4/14/51	8	1

TITLE	DEBUT DATE	PEAK POS.	WEEKS ON
"Honey Bee"	7/14/51	10	1
"Still a Fool"	11/24/51	9	3
"She Moves Me"	2/23/52	10	1
"Mad Love"	11/21/53	6	2
"Hoochie Coochie Man"	3/13/54	3	13
"Just Make Love To Me"	6/5/54	4	13
"I'm Ready"	10/23/54	4	9
"Manish Boy"	7/30/55	5	6
"Sugar Sweet"	12/24/55	11	2
"Trouble No More"	1/14/56	7	6
"Forty Days and Forty Nights"	5/5/56	7	6
"Don't Go No Farther"	9/8/56	9	2
"Close to You"	10/20/58	9	13

Buying Muddy Waters

Through the prime of his career, Muddy's music came out on singles, two songs at a time. In 1958, his first album, *The Best of Muddy Waters,* was compiled from these singles, and it remains one of his strongest releases. Since then, Muddy's hits and most famous recordings have been packaged and repackaged, and most any way you mix them up, they're great listening.

Under the direction of Andy McKaie at Universal/MCA Records, Chess has enjoyed a revitalization befitting its original accomplishment. Currently, the Muddy compilations available through MCA are *His Best: 1947–1955, His Best: 1956–1964, Rolling Stone: The Golden Anniversary Collection* (a two-CD set that focuses on his Aristocrat and Chess recordings through 1952), and *The Millennium Collection: Twentieth-Century Masters* (a career overview). Any of these is a good place to start. *Muddy Waters: The Chess Box* is a three-CD set that spans his Chess career and includes some obscure tracks and remixes. *Trouble No More* focuses on Muddy's latter 1950s releases, a period that mixes some of his best with some of his worst recordings.

When I compiled my companion CD to this book, *Can't Be Satisfied,* I assumed all those hit tracks would be easily accessible and I focused on the rest of Muddy's catalog. I drew from non-Chess as well as Chess recordings, establishing Muddy's versatility within the deep blues form. It shines a light into dark corners, and hopefully the deal being negotiated for its release will have been consummated and you'll have no trouble finding it.

Muddy's first recordings, done for the Library of Congress, are available on MCA's *The Complete Plantation Recordings.* This release features not only the acoustic versions of some songs he later electrified, but it also contains the interviews Muddy and Son Sims did with John Work and Alan Lomax. The tracks where Muddy plays solo give a sense of the foundation upon which electric blues and rock and roll are built; the group tracks are in the string-band tradition, earlier and more ragtimey sounding. Though not the place to start listening to Muddy, this music is easily accessible and enjoyable even to the neophyte ear. The interviews are intimate and thrilling. The title, by the way, is a misnomer; there is another disc of recordings from 1942 on file at the Library of Congress (AFS 4770), about which a staff engineer informed me, "Broken but . . . repair appears very good, as if the grooves were lined up with the aid of a microscope."

In Chicago, before recording for Leonard Chess's Aristocrat label, Muddy recorded the one-off "Mean Red Spider" and three tracks for Columbia. The only release I know of "Mean Red Spider" is on the imported Document CD *Muddy Waters: Complete Recordings 1941–1946*. That CD contains all the music, but not the interviews, from *The Complete Plantation Recordings,* as well as some bonus tracks. The three Columbia recordings Muddy did in 1948 have been released on the Testament Records LP *Chicago Blues: The Beginning,* and on various Sony Legacy compilations, none of which is currently in print.

All of Muddy's first recordings for Leonard Chess on the Aristocrat label are available on a great two-CD set titled *The Aristocrat of the Blues.* It gives a real sense of the Chicago music scene in the late 1940s. This includes issued and unissued material, blues and jazz, Muddy as sideman and Muddy as leader. His tracks are excellent and, against the fabric of what others were doing, it's easy to hear why "I Can't Be Satisfied" and "I Feel Like Going Home" were so exciting when they came out.

Muddy Waters Sings Big Bill Broonzy (1958) was Muddy's first album conceived of as an album. Big Bill's style was more subdued than Muddy's, and this album is appropriately less intense. My favorite track, "I Feel So Good," gets a much more exciting treatment on Muddy's next album, *Muddy Waters at Newport* (1960). This is the release that introduced Muddy to pop culture and it remains a favorite of many of the people I interviewed. Most of Muddy's set was filmed that day, and someone really should marry the images to the audio and release a DVD or videotape of the set. Seeing Muddy dance across the stage during "Mojo" is one of the most exciting stage moments I've ever witnessed. There's a British CD, *Good-bye Newport Blues,* that combines *Newport* with several other great live tracks from later in Muddy's career.

The *Folk Singer* (1964) album is as intimate sounding as you could ask for, but the performance seems removed, as if the players were concentrating on the intimacy and not the music. It's never much moved me. (This album is available on a CD conveniently coupled with another of my least favorites, the *Big Bill* album.)

In 1966 and 1967, Chess compiled more of Muddy's early recordings, initiating their *Real Folk Blues* series with Muddy, and then following up with another round, *More Real Folk Blues.* Both are excellent, though I prefer the latter; it favors more of Muddy's great slide material. Sandwiched between was the album *Muddy, Brass, & the Blues,* to be avoided. (Some of these tracks can be heard without horns — on the *Chess Box* and on *One More Mile* — and are so much more listenable as a result.) The *Super Blues* album also came out in 1967, Muddy in the studio with Bo Diddley and Little Walter. A better idea than a record, its follow-up, *Super Super Blues* (which replaced Walter with Howlin' Wolf), comes nearer to fulfilling the potential, but these kinds of records are hard to pull off.

I came to a new appreciation of *Electric Mud* (1968) after rapper Chuck D. told me how the sounds of it first attracted him. There are great sounds on this psychedelic blues album and on its sequel, *After the Rain* (1969), but they can also be grating experiences. These musicians set out to push the envelope, and they succeeded mightily. Don't fear them, don't scorn them, but try to borrow someone else's copy before you buy your own.

The *Fathers and Sons* (1969) record is among the better of Muddy's latter Chess recordings. It combines good studio performances with live recordings. He's ably backed by younger, sympathetic musicians, and his songs, all remakes of earlier versions, are rendered honestly. It's true that the remakes lack the strength of the originals, but sometimes one hears a song anew when it's done differently. For the CD, the original tape was remastered, and three previously unreleased studio performances were added. Some of the original tracks were compiled with some of Wolf's from his *London Sessions* and are available on the misleadingly titled *Muddy and the Wolf.*

Three records came out in 1971. *They Call Me Muddy Waters,* all good blues, is built from recordings that had been previously shelved. *McKinley Morganfield AKA Muddy Waters,* no longer in print, was a repackaging of several previous *Best of*s. Muddy's *Live (At Mr. Kelly's)* is a fine, often overlooked record. His first post-car-wreck recording, this album announced his return to form, to unadulterated blues form.

The London Sessions, in the years prior to Muddy's comeback recordings, consistently proved a good entry into blues for the basic rock and roll fan. Recorded with British rock musicians, it brings a modern sensibility to Muddy's blues, updating his updated blues. (Of Chess's *London Sessions* series, the one that works best is Howlin' Wolf's.) Outtakes of Muddy's and Wolf's London recordings were issued on an LP titled *London Revisited,* without the horn overdubs that get in the way of the earlier release; Muddy's four songs are quite good.

I've never much liked *Can't Get No Grinding,* though it's often praised. I can't get past the electric piano, which dominates the mix. *Unk in Funk* is not a bad record, but neither is it memorable. Muddy's last record for Chess, the *Woodstock Album,* is a decent parting statement. With Levon Helm and Henry Glover producing, the sound achieves a modern, rooted groove. There's enough studio banter on the record that you can pick up the fun they had making it. For those trying to ease into blues, this is not a bad place to make the tentative first step. (But really, does *easing in* work? When the water feels a bit cold, don't you adjust faster by diving in headfirst? Go on, pick up a *Best of.*) If you are a completist, or are writing a book about Muddy, shop for the out-of-print, nine-CD box set from Charly Records in England, which includes everything Muddy did for Aristocrat and Chess through 1967.

As my text makes clear, I'm a fan of Muddy's CBS / Sony recordings, especially *Hard Again.* For the popular music fan unfamiliar with traditional blues, this is the perfect transitional record. It plays like rock and roll, but sounds like blues. *I'm Ready,* the follow-up, lacks the punch of *Hard Again* but is a more intricate, complex recording. *King Bee* and *Muddy "Mississippi" Waters Live* round out the Sony material and probably are best left for completists; you can sample tracks from them on the Sony compilations *Blues Sky* and *King of the Electric Blues.*

Some of the best Muddy is heard on Otis Spann recordings. *Live the Life*

(Hightone, www.hightone.com) compiles several different live dates recorded by Pete Welding in the 1960s, with Otis and Muddy taking turns leading; hard-hitting and deep. Three Spann albums from the 1960s are worth seeking out: *Half Ain't Been Told* (Decca / Black Cat) was recorded during the 1964 European Blues and Gospel Train tour. Muddy lets Otis lead, adding gorgeous slide guitar. A couple tracks from that session were included on the 1960s compilation *Raw Blues* (London Records). *The Bottom of the Blues* is a studio album, Muddy and his band backing Otis. Great stuff, it features a couple tracks written by Muddy not heard anywhere else; "Looks Like Twins" makes this album worth seeking out.

Before Leonard Chess would accept Muddy's band, they made a few recordings in various phases of formation. The earliest, with Walter singing lead, came during a Sunnyland Slim session that also included Muddy, Baby Face Leroy, and Floyd Jones. These two tracks are on a Dutch Sunnyland Slim Compilation, *The Devil Is a Busy Man* (Official), and also, though I have not seen it, a Nighthawk LP. The band got together behind Jimmy Rogers, delivering a more formed sound for his first rendering of "Ludella"; this appears on a 1992 Biograph CD of Regal recordings — *Memphis Minnie: Early Rhythm and Blues, 1949*. On *The Blues World of Little Walter* (Delmark, www. delmark.com), there's the entire 1950 renegade "Rollin' and Tumblin'" session. Jimmy showed up for some of these tracks, which best represent the earliest Muddy band sound. Lastly, though Muddy's not on it, there's good Jimmy Rogers with Sunnyland Slim doing an early "That's All Right" on the Delmark CD *Sunnyland Slim House Rent Party*.

MCA Records has done a good job of mining Muddy's unreleased tracks, outtakes, and even recordings not originally under the Chess auspices. I love the 1972 acoustic radio broadcast that makes up much of the second CD on *One More Mile*.

There's been a slew of live Muddy released. Much of it comes from the latter years and the recordings tend to blend. *Collaboration* is the title given to the only known recording from Muddy's first English tour, 1958. The recording was made from the soundboard, through which Muddy's guitar was not miked; his Telecaster went out to the room through his amp. So the sound on the disc is nothing like what the audience heard, but I find fascinating the general feel and vibe of Muddy and Spann in a foreign country that long ago. Muddy's Carnegie Hall performance with Memphis Slim makes up part of *Chicago Blues Masters Volume One* (Capitol). There's good music here; it's worth seeking out. Another of my favorite live releases is *Muddy Waters and Friends* (Just a Memory, www.justin-time.com), recorded one morning at a Canadian rooming house. After Muddy plays his few songs on the acoustic guitar, the instrument gets passed around; even Spann plays it. There's a companion to that disc, *Hoochie Coochie Man* (Just a Memory). The show is hot but so is the recording — distorted. Another live CD titled *Hoochie Coochie Man* (Laserlight, www.deltamusic.com) is notable both for its raucous slide guitar and its interesting set list (including "Rosalie," an obscure track from the Library of Congress recordings). Recorded in 1964, the CD captures Muddy at his mightiest; during "Tiger in Your Tank," when the guitar is about to overcome the vocals (as it rightly should, growling), the soundman abruptly adjusts it — it pains me every time. Nonetheless, among Muddy's live discs, this one's the one.

Avoid *Muddy Waters in Concert* (Classic Sound); it's horribly distorted. The CD *Muddy Waters Blues Band Featuring Dizzy Gillespie* is misnamed; Diz is only on one track. Fortunately, the set is not bad, but still, one hates to be tricked. The *Muddy Waters Story* (Chrome Dreams) is another deception. Labeled "spoken word biography," it's Muddy's story, but told by a dulcet-toned British man. It's not very compelling.

Many labels are reissuing a lot of great music, and it's possible to hear what Muddy would have heard as he was coming up in Mississippi and Chicago, and also to hear how his influence shaped music that followed him.

You could do a lot worse than starting with the Delmark Records catalog (www.delmark.com, or visiting their Jazz Record Mart at 444 N. Wabash in Chicago). They offer plenty of Mississippi Delta blues, and even more Chicago music. In addition to the previously mentioned Little Walter and Sunnyland Slim CDs, they have an extensive Junior Wells catalog, and such goodies as Morris Pejoe and Magic Sam. For a sampling of their modern releases, try Lurrie Bell, Rockin' Johnny, Little Arthur Duncan, or the Tail Dragger.

The Testament label has enjoyed an extensive reissuing through the HMG / Hightone label (www.hightone.com). Pete Welding made sure he got in the right place with the right people. In addition to his great Otis Spann recordings (which feature Muddy), look for Robert Nighthawk, Houston Stackhouse, Jimmy Rogers — or sample several of these artists on one of the many compilations (my favorite, today, is *Chicago Blues at Home*).

Alligator (www.alligator.com), Rounder (www.rounder.com), and Rooster (www.roosterblues.com) are good sources for modern and reissued blues. Rooster has reissued *And This Is Maxwell Street,* extensive audio recordings from a 1964 documentary that capture the sound of the street. Note Alligator's Elvin Bishop and Little Smokey Smothers collaboration *That's My Partner,* and their *Deluxe Edition* series of "best-ofs," especially Johnny Winter and Hound Dog Taylor. Old and new on Black Top include the late Freddie King and the recent Rusty Zinn, who gets a 1950s sound in the twenty-first century. Earwig (www.earwigmusic.com) has good Honeyboy Edwards and Sunnyland Slim; Blind Pig (www.blindpigrecords.com) has Big Bill Morganfield, Bob Margolin, and Magic Slim; check Silvertone (www.silvertonerecords.com) for Buddy Guy. Catfish Records (www.catfishrecords.com), an English label, has issued *The Roots of Muddy Waters,* a great compilation of songs that Muddy drew from.

Vanguard Records (www.vanguardrecords.com) has become a contender in the blues reissue market. In addition to their compilations from Newport Festivals and their pretty decent and reasonably priced thematic compilations (*Blues with a Feeling, Great Harp Players, Frett'n the Blues*), they have reissued the *Chicago / The Blues / Today!* series in one package. There's good stuff under the Fantasy umbrella (www.fantasyjazz.com) from a variety of labels, especially Bluesville, Takoma, and Stax. Ryko (www.rykodisc.com) was issuing much of the Tradition and Everest labels; Putumayo (www.putamayo.com) has combined some African roots with its blues legacy, such as the compilation *From Mali to Memphis.* Dig Birdman Records, Smithsonian / Folkways, Easy Baby, Amina, Acoustech, Document, Yazoo, and Arhoolie (John Littlejohn's *Slidin' Home* belongs in every home).

These addresses are good places to get started for Muddy Waters and blues on the Internet:

www.blues.org (The Blues Foundation)
www.bluesworld.com
http://theblueshighway.com
http://bluesnet.hub.org
http://blueslinks.tripod.com
www.muddywaters.com

NOTES

GENERAL READING SUGGESTIONS

For a broad history of the blues, the best place to start is Robert Palmer's *Deep Blues*. Get to know the players by reading their profiles in Peter Guralnick's two collections, *Feel Like Going Home* and *Lost Highway*. His *Searching for Robert Johnson* is also a good macroview of the Delta. (Guralnick's *Sweet Soul Music* is the best place to learn about soul music, which evolved from blues.)

My feel for Delta life was greatly enhanced by *The World Don't Owe Me Nothing*, the recent autobiography of Honeyboy Edwards. Other good sources for insight into early blues include Henry Townsend and Bill Greensmith's *A Blues Life* and Mance Lipscomb's autobiography, *I Say Me for a Parable*. James Agee writes beautifully about the sharecropper's life in *Let Us Now Praise Famous Men*. David Cohn's *Where I Was Born and Raised*, though somewhat paternalistic (or perhaps because of that), was a well-written overview of 1920s Delta life from a white perspective. Gayle Dean Wardlow's *Chasin' That Devil Music* includes much of the author's research about early blues artists and life in Mississippi; it's fascinating reading, comes with a CD, and is probably best appreciated after gaining an introduction to the musicians elsewhere. Sit in on interview after interview with the greats in Jim O'Neal and Amy van Singel's *The Voice of the Blues: Classic Interviews from* Living Blues *Magazine* (Routledge), new in 2002.

Paul Oliver has written extensively about blues. The text to read first is *Conversation with the Blues*, a mosaic compiled from his firsthand accounts of growing up with the blues. It has been recently republished, with many photographs added, and comes with a CD of his field recordings.

For a history of Chicago blues, Mike Rowe's aptly titled *Chicago Blues* has a lot of information and a lot of pictures. The best factual account of the Chess Brothers, and also a good history of the recording scene in Chicago, is Nadine Cohodas's *Spinning Blues into Gold*. Finally, there are two books that focus on Muddy Waters. *Bossmen*, by James Rooney, is essentially an oral history, told almost solely in Muddy's words. *Muddy Waters: The Mojo Man*, by Sandra B. Tooze, uses an extended Muddy discography as its foundation, tracing his life through his recordings.

Muddy Waters was a decade and a half dead when I began this book, and many of the people from his early years had also passed away. I am indebted to the many researchers and writers who documented the lives and careers of Muddy and his cohorts. While working on this book, I was never without the pressure of time: a month after I met Jimmy Rogers, he found out he had cancer, and a few months later, he was dead. Junior Wells followed weeks thereafter.

For Muddy's voice, I relied heavily on several key interviews, graciously provided by Peter Guralnick, Jim O'Neal and Amy van Singel, Margaret McKee and Fred Chisenhall (on file at the Memphis–Shelby County Public Library and Information Center), Link Wyler and Russ Ragsdale (provided by Richard Chalk), the estate of Pete Welding, Charles Shaar Murray, and Paul Oliver. Also, Paul Trynka, John Brisbin, Larry Lasker, Nadine Cohodas, Matt Sakakeeny, Stanley Booth, and Jas Obrecht were kind enough to share their interviews of Muddy's cohorts with me. I drew from many other printed interviews, all cited herein. Reading interviews with Muddy for more than five years, I saw many of the same questions asked of him repeatedly. I have documented the instances when I have combined answers from different interviews on the same subjects.

Unless otherwise noted, all quotes from the following people come from my interviews: Terry Abrahamson, Goldie Abram, Georges Adins, Billy Boy Arnold, Mary Austin, Chris Barber, Bruce Bastin, Bill Bentley, Elvin Bishop, Joe Boyd, R. L. Burnside, Scott Cameron, Marshall Chess, Francis Clay, Amelia "Cookie" Cooper, Pete Cosey, James Cotton, Freddie Crutchfield, Terry Cryer, Chuck D., Carl Dugger, Esmond Edwards, Honeyboy Edwards, Mary Emerson, Peter Guralnick, Buddy Guy, Levon Helm, Magnolia Hunter, Pete Hunter, Manuel Jackson Jr., Calvin Jones, Mike Kappus, Robert Koester, Alan Lomax, Pee Wee Madison, Bob Margolin, Lucille McClenton, Bob Messinger, Bill Morganfield, Elve Morganfield, Joseph Morganfield, Marva Morganfield, Mercy Della Morganfield, Robert Morganfield, Jimmy Lee Morris, Charles Shaar Murray, Charlie Musselwhite, Dave Myers, Mark Naftalin, Nate Notkin, Jim O'Neal, Paul Oliver, Paul Oscher, Harold and Barbara Pendleton, Pinetop Perkins, Al Perry, Sylvia Pitcher, Jerry Portnoy, Barbara Purro, Keith Richards, Beulah Richardson, Richard "Harmonica Slim" Riggins, Jimmy Rogers, Bobby Rush, Otis Rush, Dick Shurman, Willie Smith, Little Smokey Smothers, Andrew "A. W." Stephenson, Bobby Stovall, Willie Strandberg, Dick Waterman, Marie Stovall Webster, Norma Weiland, Frank Weston, Charles "Bang Bang" Williams, Val Wilmer, Johnny Winter, and Bill Wyman.

INTRODUCTION

xiii   "They done found out I'm sellin' whiskey": O'Neal and van Singel, "Muddy Waters."

xiii   "I went there, I said, 'Yassuh?'": Ibid.

xiii   "I couldn't figure it out": Ibid.

xiii   "I couldn't handle this white man": McKee and Chisenhall interview with Muddy Waters.

xiii   "Same cup I drink out of": McKee and Chisenhall, *Beale,* pp. 234–235.

xiv   "He brought his machine": Ibid., p. 234.

xv   "We got his stuff out of the trunk": O'Neal and van Singel, "Muddy Waters."

xv   "So I just went along": Jones, *Melody Maker.*

xv   "When he played back the first song": Palmer, "The Delta Sun."

xv   "Man, I can sing": Standish, "Muddy Waters in London" part 2.
xviii "I wanted to get out of Mississippi": Guralnick, *Home,* p. 67.
xix   "I been in the blues all of my life": Harris, Liner notes to Otis Spann's *Bottom of the Blues.*

1: MANNISH BOY *1913–1925*

Muddy's Father: Ollie Morganfield and Berta Grant never married. Ollie's first wife was named Sissy, and their son was Freddy. Ollie later married Gertrude Crayton and had ten more children: Dave, Ollie Jr., Robert, Matthew, and Ellis were the boys; Luella, Mary, Gertrude, Fannie, and Annie were the girls. "He sharecropped and leased on Magnolia Plantation till 1947, then he moved closer to Rolling Fork," Robert Morganfield told me. "When he retired, he was renting somebody else's land and farming cotton on it." Muddy has been quoted as saying he was born on the Kroger Plantation. The interviewer probably misunderstood Muddy: *Kroger* was the name of the farm manager on the Magnolia Plantation.

The "long-lived resident" mentioned on page 3 was named Beulah Richardson, whom I met while knocking on doors looking for old people near Jug's Corner. In 1933, Beulah Richardson hired Ollie to play a Christmas breakfast at her home. She'd killed hogs, prepared meats, made sausages, and was fortified with "whiskey on up." The party would have been a smash, with Ollie taking home five or six dollars, had she not stayed out the night before carousing and riding in a convertible. "I had pneumonia by morning. The doctor came and saw all that food, said, 'Someone's going to have to fix me something to eat.' And he sat and ate before he tended to me." She had no memory of Muddy's mother or grandmother.

Stovall Plantation, and Cotton: Stovall was — and is — a 4,500-acre plantation; it's actually the Belmont, Waterloo, Prairie, and West End plantations combined. That's a substantial territory, with its own mule barn, hay barn, dairy barn, and a blacksmith shop the size of a barn. It sits on Oak Ridge, next to the Mississippi River, and follows the bank of the Little Sunflower River, a flood stream. The Stovall land nearer the river is some of the Delta's finest.

During high water, flood streams take the Mississippi's water — and all its silt, sand, and collected topsoil — and dump it on the high bank. The water drains away from the flood stream to a drainage stream; the heavy sandy soil is dumped first, and the finer silt is carried further. Sandy loam (the ice cream soil) produces the best cotton; the heavier soil is called buckshot, so named because its clay content makes pellets hard enough to shoot. (At the time of the great flood of 1927, rows had been cut into the fields by mules. A flood in 1995 carried away much of the sandy topsoil, and the rows in the buckshot ground from 1927, and the mule tracks, were still evident.)

Stovall was timberland when originally settled by Colonel John Oldham in the 1840s. The Choctaw had cleared one area and were raising corn, and they cleared a track nearby for pony races. Oldham named his farm Prairie Plantation. When his great-grandson-in-law, Colonel William Howard Stovall, inherited the land around the time Muddy and his grandmother arrived, the Stovall Plantation had grown to its full size. In a 1930 aerial photograph of Stovall, the oval shape of the pony track is still evident in the fields. ("Neither my daddy or grandmother sold off or bought much property," said Bobby Stovall, who was raised there.)

"My daddy used to ride a horse all over the plantation, he never rode a truck," Marie Stovall Webster said about Colonel Stovall. "He'd be out till at least seven o'clock at night." Some people have reported that signals on Mississippi plantations were sent across fields by blowing on conch shells, but Bobby Stovall found that laughable. "Signals like that would have been given with a cow's horn. They were also used in fox hunts, and for cows. Most everyone I knew could blow one. Where the fuck are they going to find a conch shell in the Mississippi Delta?"

Over time, mechanization increased. In addition to the technological advancements, the transition from hand labor was also influenced by the enforcement of minimum wage in the Delta. "After that, you couldn't afford to chop cotton," said Norma Weiland, today's office manager at Stovall Farms. "When you were paying thirty cents an hour, it was a lot different than when you were paying two and three dollars an hour. You could pay the children lesser wages and the minute they changed all that, the children ended up being left at home. The farmer could not afford it. Farmers had to take advantage of the technology to stay in business."

Pete Hunter, Stovall's contemporary farm manager, explained, "It gradually transformed from sharecropping to where the farm had all the mules, harnesses, etcetera, kept them in one area, and these people were paid so much a day or an hour. I can remember during the midfifties, in the era of tractors, a person hoeing or chopping cotton was paid two dollars a day, and a person driving a tractor was paid four dollars a day. Money was paid in cash out the window of a pickup at the end of the day."

Norma continued, "Everyone says farmers are the biggest gamblers of all. I'm not sure they're not the biggest fools of all. If you were going to put a pencil to it, no way would you invest the amount of money it takes to grow a crop with the hope of a return so little. Why do people farm? It provides them with a way of life. It gets in your blood, you have to watch things grow."

It's said to be just coincidental that 1916 was the year of both Mississippi's first boll weevil infestation and the inauguration of infamous, racist governor Theodore G. Bilbo.

4   Born October 20, 1890: This date comes from a military ID issued to Ollie in 1961. For the 1920 census, taken in April, Ollie listed his age at his last birthday as twenty-eight, indicating a birth year of 1891.

4   There is no record of Berta: Berta Grant has been virtually erased from history. When researching her, I also tried other names associated with the Grant family: Preece (and its various spellings) and Jones.

4   April 4, 1913: According to the 1940 census, John Work's treatise (Fisk Archives), Alan Lomax's notes (Lomax Archives), and the Lewis Jones manuscript (Fisk Archives), Muddy's birth year was 1913.

4   at least twelve years old: Assuming the age of childbearing begins at twelve, if Berta were born to a twelve-year-old Della, she was twenty when she had Muddy; if Berta was twelve when she conceived Muddy, she was born in 1901.

4   McKinley A. Morganfield: Middle initial per Lomax correspondence, January 27, 1942, though I've never seen the initial used anywhere else.

6 The Delta had been a swampy jungle: Joe Willie Wilkins said that one night, while his father was out playing music, he and his mother were "home alone when a panther smelled food cooking and tried to enter the house through the cat entrance in the door. He could only get a paw in; Mrs. Wilkins cut it off with an axe." (Hay, "Wilkins," p. 8.)

6 three sons: Ollie's brother Lewis Morganfield wound up on Stovall; he became a preacher, and raised a family there and later in Clarksdale. Eddie Morganfield died before he was thirty. "He was happy-go-lucky," said his nephew Elve.

7 less weight equals less pay: Each cotton sack is weighed at day's end and then emptied into a cotton house, a shed on wheels that shuttles between the field and the gin. A 500-pound bale requires 1,300 pounds of boll. The seed accounts for the difference. It takes a lot of seedless cotton to create some weight.

8 A plantation was a privately owned small town: Not that the black people living in Mississippi's towns were any better treated. Blues musician Johnny Shines summed it up: "Down South, it was open season on black folk. Kill 'em anywhere you see 'em." (*Can't You Hear the Wind Howl,* produced and directed by Peter Meyer.)

8 "brozine": Many plantations used their own scrip, a tender good only at their plantation store. Among the items available there — at prices set above market value — were kitchen staples such as flour and lard, basic hunting and fishing supplies, and coal oil, clothes, stick candy, and hair straighteners.

9 "she furnished for me and my uncle": McKee and Chisenhall interview with Muddy Waters.

10 "I never did see my dad": Welding, "An Interview."

10 People grew what they ate: "We had our own horses, mules, cows, goats, and chickens, and I watered 'em from the time I was a kid," Muddy told Robert Palmer in *Deep Blues* (p. 100). "I had to pump the water, and that pump would put blisters in my hand. Even for one cow, you got to pump a lot of water. She'd take two draws out of those big tubs and that'd be it."

12 "I started early on, burning corn stumps": Wyler and Ragsdale interview with Muddy Waters.

13 "they didn't give you too much schooling": Oliver, *Conversation,* p. 30.

13 Reverend Willie Morganfield: Lewis Morganfield's seventh son was Willie Morganfield, who, along with two of his brothers, followed his father into preaching. And, like his first cousin, the Reverend Willie Morganfield also became a singer, though his million-selling hits were gospel, not blues. "What Is This," recorded for Jewel Records in 1959 (a company run by friends of the Chess brothers), is perhaps his best-known recording, although many of his songs and sermons remain in print. He was born on Stovall and was raised there and in Clarksdale, moved away in 1945, and returned in 1975. He has lived in bigger and smaller cities, preached from some of the nation's largest pulpits, and is currently pastor at Clarksdale's Bell Grove Missionary Baptist Church. He spoke from behind the desk of his church office, a basement room adorned with plaques, letters of commendation, and gold records. He has had three heart attacks and continues to smoke heavily.

14   The blues began taking shape: The blending of the African American and Scots traditions explains the plethora of lyrics and melodies common to both blues and bluegrass. For more information, see Tom Mazzolini's "A Conversation with Paul Oliver" in *Living Blues*.

14   the lyrical shape of AAB: John Work's unpublished manuscript includes this note about the AAB lyrical structure:

> In the singing of the blues there is seen an intense subconscious esthetic demand that the third line — the punch line — have a rhyming last word. The entire thought of the singer most often is expressed in this last line. The first line and its repetition may contribute to it, but more often it does not. The prime aim of the singer therefore is to provide preliminary lines with a rhyming last word for the end of the last line. Frequently these preliminary lines are "nonsense" in their relation to the last line. Here are several illustrations extracted from Delta blues: "Brook run into the ocean, ocean run into the sea / If I can't find my baby now/somebody going have to bury me." "Minutes seem like hours / hours seem like days / Seems like my baby / would stop her low down ways." "You know the sun is going down I say / behind that old western hill / You know I wouldn't do a thing / not against my baby's will." (Work, Fisk Archives)

14   "delay singer": Palmer, *Deep Blues*, p. 102.

14   The earliest description of blues: Peabody, "Notes on Negro Music," p. 149. Another interesting note from his article states: "In their refrains ending on the tonic, they sometimes sang the last note somewhat sharp. So frequent was this that it seemed intentional or unavoidable, not merely a mistake in pitch" (p. 151). And:

> The long, lonely sing-song of the fields was quite distinct from anything else, though the singer was skillful in gliding from hymn-motives to those of the native chant. The best single recollection I have of this music is one evening when a Negress was singing her baby to sleep in her cabin just above our tents. She was of quite a notable Negro family and had a good voice. Her song was to me quite impossible to copy, weird in interval and strange in rhythm; peculiarly beautiful. It bore some likeness to the modern Greek native singing but was better done. I only heard her once in a lullaby, but she used sometimes to walk the fields at evening singing fortissimo, awakening the echoes with song extremely effective. I should not omit mention of a very old Negro employed on the plantation of Mr. John Stovall of Stovall, Mississippi. He was asked to sing to us one very dark night as we sat on the gallery. His voice as he sang had a timbre resembling a bagpipe played pianissimo or a Jew's harp played legato, and to some indistinguishable words he hummed a rhythm of no regularity and notes apparently not more than three or more in number at intervals within a semi-tone. The effect again was monotonous but weird, not far from Japanese. I have not heard that kind again nor of it. (p. 152)

16   "Our little house was way back in the country": Palmer, *Deep Blues*, p. 100.

16 "On Stovall, there's a church and on up the road to Farrell": Lasker interview with Myles Long.

16 "more churches than stores and schools combined": Jones, "Folk Culture Study," p. 4.

16 "My grandmother told me when I first picked that harmonica up": Rooney, *Bossmen*, p. 105; also New York Radio interview, 1966.

17 the church was losing influence: Samuel Adams Jr., a sociologist who lived in Coahoma County in 1941, wrote

> The spirituals can no longer be said to be "the natural expression of the mind and the mood of the plantation Negro" of today, for the "natural idiom of the Negro proletarian, the blues," is used to express the plantation Negro's mood of the present. In the past the plantation Negro sang of "the Pearly Gates and Dem Golden Slippers" as compensation for the hard life of this world, but now he expresses the realities of today by singing:
>
> ... Done worked all the summer
> ... Done worked all the fall
> And here come Christmas
> And I ain't got nothing at all
> I'm just a po' cold nigger. (Adams, Manuscript, Lomax Archives)

The church's diminishing sway was also evident in children's songs. One older version was:

> Turn to the east
> Turn to the west
> Turn to the one you love the best.

But approaching midcentury, the words had been changed:

> Shake it to the east
> Shake it to the west
> Give it to the young man you love the best.

17 "The spirituals are choral": Work, *Negro Songs,* p. 28.

17 "You get a heck of a sound": Welding, "An Interview."

17 "Can't you hear it in my voice": Palmer, *Deep Blues.*

2: MAN, I CAN SING *1926–1940*

Muddy's First Guitar and Influences: Muddy told many stories about acquiring his first guitar, including the tale that his grandmother sold a cow and shared the money with him; he told James Rooney, "I saved nickels and dimes until I got two dollars and fifty cents, and I bought it from a young man named Ed Moore." (Rooney, *Bossmen*, p. 105.)

In addition to learning from Scott Bohaner, Muddy mentions "this other cat," referring to James Smith, a local player. Muddy told Guralnick in 1970, "Several boys around there could use the slide and I'd say they were just as good as Robert

Johnson, the only thing about it is they never had a chance to get a record out." (The same applies today. Give a listen to the field recordings on the recent collection from Music Maker Records *Expressin' the Blues,* which documents contemporary unrecognized blues talent.) Muddy remained friends with Bohaner, who had a child, Esther Morganfield, with Muddy's cousin Lois. Jim O'Neal verified the spelling "Bohaner" in the Social Security Index, though Robert Pruter found it as "Bohanner" in Chicago telephone directories. Scott's description in the text comes from Richard "Harmonica Slim" Riggins. Elve Morganfield remembered Bohaner from Stovall: "Scott was a brown-skin fella, nice head of hair, wore a mustache. Always kept a smile on his face."

When Muddy was buying 78s, record stores per se didn't exist in rural areas like the Mississippi Delta. Phonographs were large instruments, standing tall and made of heavy wood, occupying a significant place in a room. Hence, they were sold primarily in furniture stores; as a result, records were also sold there. In smaller towns, furniture was sold in a general store. "Really, in the little town I was around they didn't have just a definite record store," Muddy told *Living Blues.* (O'Neal and van Singel, "Muddy Waters.") "They'd sell everything like shotgun shells, and pistols and cartridges, something like a hardware store." One interesting consequence was that many furniture retailers became early talent scouts. H. C. Speir, in Jackson, Mississippi, was perhaps the most famous. He ran auditions, where he "discovered" Robert Johnson, Charlie Patton, Son House, Skip James, the Mississippi Sheiks, and Tommy Johnson, among others. He claimed to have become a talent scout only so his store would have good records to sell. Another retail scout was Lillian McMurray, who ran the Trumpet label out of her Jackson, Mississippi, furniture store in the early 1950s. She was the first to record Sonny Boy Williamson II (Rice Miller), and she also recorded Joe Willie Wilkins, Elmore James, and Willie Love.

Charlie Patton: Despite the occasional issuing of his records with "Charley" instead of "Charlie," Patton, who could not read or write, could sign his name, and did so with an "l-i-e." A brief list of Patton's students is something like a "who's who" of early blues: Son House, Tommy Johnson, Willie Brown, Howlin' Wolf. The list of those he influenced — from Robert Johnson to Houston Stackhouse, from Tommy McLennan to Muddy — would fill a book. Revenant Records has released a fascinating and beautiful box set of Patton's recordings and those influenced by him, *Screamin' and Hollerin' the Blues: The Worlds of Charley Patton.* In Revenant's fine fashion, it includes an extensive hardcover book; one entire CD is devoted to interviews with those who knew Patton. Other sources for Charlie Patton include *King of the Delta Blues: The Life and Music of Charlie Patton* by Stephen Calt and Gayle Dean Wardlow, and the collaborative *The Voice of the Delta: Charley Patton and the Mississippi Blues Traditions.*

Country Boy, City Lights: Honeyboy Edwards told me that Muddy lived for some time in Mayersville, on the river near Rolling Fork. It's possible that was in 1930; although I found other early census reports on Muddy, I could not locate him in that year. I tried Stovall and Blytheville, Arkansas, where Muddy told Lomax his family lived for a while. Edwards claimed, "Muddy stayed out there, my uncle lived out there, too. That's why I know that. Then he moved up about ten or twelve miles further, out from Rolling Fork. If they stayed here and didn't make any money this year, then they say I'm going back over here." Mayersville, the county seat, is also a jail.

Reverend Morganfield remembered covering for Muddy when his playing took him far from Stovall. "He'd be gone, playing the guitar. Sharecropper, they'd leave it up to you to make sure you got the work done. Muddy had two small mules, and we would plow and take care of things for him when he had something else to do." Muddy's early ventures to Memphis remained indelibly etched in his mind, especially Handy Park on Beale Street. "They had some people in that park that was running rings around us," he told McKee and Chisenhall. "Them people in Memphis was baaaad, man. Big Shaky Head Walter was the harp man." A 1941 interview quoted a resident of the Stovall-neighboring King–Anderson Plantation: "I likes Memphis this way: there ain't as much prejudice. You don't have to merry bow as low there to the white man as you do in Mississippi." (Adams, Manuscript, Lomax Archives.)

When Honeyboy Edwards first met him, Muddy was working his traps. "Joe Williams took me to meet Muddy Waters in 1939," Edwards told me. "Joe knew everybody! Muddy was staying out in the country at the time. He was a trapper. He would catch coons and possums, minks. We went to his house and his wife was there. [I think this would have been Leola.] She said, 'Muddy, he's in the woods pickin' up his traps.' We waited for him and he come back, wearing those hip boots. He had a gang of possums and threw them in the corner. His wife fixed supper for us. He had a lot of game, gravy, biscuits. Some people come buy half a pint from him, wasn't but about fifty cents. I don't know whether he was making it, but he had plenty of whiskey in his house. Muddy hustled all kinds of ways out there."

Muddy sold whiskey but probably did not run his own still. "Brownie Emerson," he told Margaret McKee, "he was making good whiskey. John McKee at [the neighboring] McKee Plantation, I used to buy whiskey off of John McKee. It costs two dollars and fifty cents a gallon. I used to sell it off for twenty-five cents a half-pint. You had sixteen half-pints." The other popular drink, even cheaper, was Sterno, or "canned heat." One side effect of canned heat was the jake leg, a paralysis of the limbs. Mager Johnson, brother of bluesman Tommy Johnson, remembered his brother's frequent use: "That canned heat, it was red. It was in those little old cans. When you open it, take the top off the can. He'd strike him a match and burn it, burn the top of it. And he'd put it in a rag and strain it. It's got juice in it. Squeeze the juice out of it into a glass. And then get him some sugar and put it in there. And then some water. And there he'd go. Oh, he started I don't know how many people around here in Copiah drinking that stuff." (Evans, *Big Road Blues,* p. 57; this book is an excellent source for more information on Tommy Johnson.)

19 "ramshacked it on out": Rooney, *Bossmen,* p. 104.

19 "All the kids made they own git-tars": Oliver, *Conversation.*

19 "I was messing around with the harmonica": Welding, "An Interview."

19 "But I got hold of some records with my little nickels": Ibid.

19 "Texas Alexander and Barbecue Bob": McKee and Chisenhall interview with Muddy Waters.

20 "I wanted to definitely be a musician": O'Neal and van Singel, "Muddy Waters."

20 "Yeah, of course I'd holler too": Oliver, *Conversation,* p. 30.

20 "Muddy would always be humming": Lasker interview with Myles Long.

20 "When I was comin' up": Oliver, *Conversation.*

21 "I was playin' harp then": Welding, "An Interview."

21 "cabaret nights": Welding, "Afro Mud."

21 "Everybody used to fry up fish": Welding, "An Interview"; O'Neal and van Singel, "Muddy Waters."

22 "Twelve o'clock you'd better be out of there": McKee and Chisenhall interview with Muddy Waters.

22 "They would have the parties": McKee and Chisenhall interview with Muddy Waters.

22 "You'd find that house by the lights shining in the trees": Edwards, *The World,* p. 51.

22 "When you were playing in a place like that": Welding, Interview with Johnny Shines, p. 24.

22 "seem like everybody could play some kind of instrument": Oliver, *Conversation.*

23 "I stone got crazy": Gibbs, "The Entertainers: Muddy Waters," p. 23.

23 "I used to say to Son House": DeMichael, "Father and Son," p. 12.

23 "I should have broke my bottlenecks": Ibid.

23 "I sold the last horse we had": Palmer, *Deep Blues,* p. 101.

23 "The first time I played on it": Aldin, Liner notes to *The Complete Plantation Recordings.*

24 "I saw Patton in my younger life days": Murray, *Shots,* p. 179.

24 "I worked for fifty cents a day" McKee and Chisenhall interview with Muddy Waters.

25 "We made the whiskey in canal ditches": McKee and Chisenhall, *Beale,* p. 234; McKee and Chisenhall interview with Muddy Waters.

25 "I'd have my own Saturday-night dances": Palmer, "The Delta Sun."

26 "how that music carries": Palmer, *Deep Blues.*

26 "wild and crazy and dumb in my car": McKee and Chisenhall interview with Muddy Waters.

26 "I didn't ramble that far": Palmer, *Deep Blues.*
    In his song "Burr Clover Blues," Muddy sang of a town fifteen miles away as "way up in Dundee." He never set foot in Helena — a swinging town twenty miles from his home — until KFFA began broadcasting blues from there.

26 "I knew Robert Nighthawk": O'Neal and van Singel interview with Muddy Waters.

27 "I played with Big Joe Williams": Guralnick interview with Muddy Waters.

27 "pal around with him": Ibid.

27 "Big Joe made Muddy quit coming around with him": "Blewett Thomas Interview," *Blues Access.*

27 Asian descent: The possibility of Muddy being partially of Asian descent is not wholly unlikely. A Chinese population had been in the Delta since 1879, brought in to build the railroad lines.

28 "Every girl I met mistreated me": McKee and Chisenhall interview with Muddy Waters.

28 "Robert Nighthawk played at my first wedding": O'Neal and van Singel interview with Muddy Waters.

 Muddy was known to favor a party. A house band led by Robert Nighthawk is no slouch act. Muddy had known Son House for three years, Big Joe Williams was regularly passing through, and Charlie Patton was still alive. Other possible guests included the elusive James Smith, Brownie Emerson the bootlegger, Myles Long before he was saved, and Andrew Bolton in his youth — oh, but for a wedding photographer!

29 "They was high-time through there": McKee and Chisenhall interview with Muddy Waters.

29 "Anytime they's in my vicinity": O'Neal and van Singel interview with Muddy Waters.

29 "Kinda like a saw": Wardlow, "Henry Sims."

29 "We played juke joints": Guralnick, *Home,* p. 66.

29 "My boss really liked that kinda carrying on": O'Neal and van Singel interview with Muddy Waters.

31 "I loved [Robert Johnson's] music": Ibid.

31 "People were crowdin' 'round him": Murray, *Shots,* p. 181.

32 "Memphis, M-E-M-P-H-I-S": McKee and Chisenhall interview with Muddy Waters.

32 "Robert Nighthawk came to see me": Palmer, *Deep Blues,* p. 15.

32 "I got big enough to start playing for the white things": McKee and Chisenhall interview with Muddy Waters.

33 Silas Green: Muddy discusses the Silas Green show in his *Living Blues* interview. (O'Neal and van Singel, "Muddy Waters.")

34 "I went to St. Louis": O'Neal and van Singel interview with Muddy Waters.

3: AUGUST 31, 1941 *1941*

 The 1941 Fisk–Library of Congress Recording Trip: It is often written that the purpose of the 1941 trip was to find Robert Johnson. Lomax, however, had known of the bluesman's death for at least two years — since the December 23, 1938, "Spirituals to Swing" Concert at Carnegie Hall. There, Lomax's cohort and friend John Hammond played two Johnson songs from a phonograph onstage as a memorial to the artist so essential to the evening's narrative — "Walkin' Blues" and "Preachin' Blues."

 To boot, Muddy was very nearly not discovered; three weeks before the August Fisk–Library of Congress Coahoma County Study, Lomax suggested they work in "southwestern Tennessee, which is slightly more stable than the Delta area." (Lomax, Library of Congress, July 30, 1941.) On August 23, Lomax wrote John Work: "I shall see you the morning of the twenty-fifth, ready, I hope, for our trip to Ripley [Tennessee]." The Mississippi Delta was finally settled on, its population of African Americans being the densest in the nation.

 Once they arrived, the recordists were careful to keep their subjects comfortable. When recording, "It was important to keep the machine out of the picture," Lomax wrote in *The Land Where the Blues Began,* "so I generally sat between it and the singer and flipped the discs with my back to the turntable. . . . Every side could hold fifteen minutes of sound. This meant long events — church services, games, storytelling, work scenes, extended reminiscences — could be documented. Every time I took one of those big, black, glass-based platters out of its box, I felt that a magical moment was opening up in time. . . . For me the black discs spinning in the Mississippi night, spitting the chip centripetally toward the center of the table, also heralded a new age of writing human history — and so it proved."

When Muddy was being recorded, Carter Stovall happened to be home from Yale; he saw the strange car on the farm and rode over to investigate. They proceeded with his blessing. According to Lomax's invoice, the cost of the nineteen-day recording trip in 1941 was $580 ($100 records; $130 per diem, twenty-six days [$5/day]; $200 mileage, 4,000 miles; $150 needles and payment to informants).

For a great sense of the Lomax family's times, read Benjamin Filene's *Romancing the Folk.* He traces their careers from Leadbelly to Bob Dylan. Well written. Check out John Cohen's CD *There Is No Eye: Music for Photographs* (Smithsonian Folkways, 2001), on which Lomax performs a soulful "Love My Darling-O."

A good start for further information on the research of Alan Lomax's father, John, is Nolan Porterfield's book *Last Cavalier: The Life and Times of John A. Lomax.* Another interesting resource is the Library of Congress American Memory Web, which offers online material from the John and Ruby Lomax 1939 Southern States Recording Trip Collection: http://memory.loc.gov/ammem/lohtml/lohome.html.

John Work's field recordings have never been compiled, but such a project has been under discussion at Revenant Records. These recordings are, in many ways, a missing link in the history of field recordings; they are among the few made by a black recordist of black artists. John Work III died in 1967; he was sixty-five.

35 Fisk Jubilee Singers: Fisk University was founded soon after the Civil War's end with the purpose of educating freed slaves. The university's touring chorus, the Fisk Jubilee Singers, was formed around 1871 and found quick public acceptance, raising enough money in America and abroad to build the school's permanent home. John Work II recorded with them as first tenor and leader in 1909.

36 "I would like very much to have the opportunity": Work correspondence, Fisk Archives, June 21, 1940.

37 "Everywhere we went": Lomax correspondence to Jerome B. Wisener, Library of Congress, September 5, 1941.

38 "Burr Clover Blues": Burr clover was planted in fallow cotton fields to replenish the nitrogen that cotton sapped from the soil; Colonel Stovall had a contract with the Rose Seed Company to plant and grow the seed, giving his farm a second cash crop. "['Burr Clover Blues'] is a song of admiration for the fertility of the land on which [Muddy] lives," Lewis Jones wrote in "The Mississippi Delta," his unpublished account of the trip, "and incidentally it is a blues inspired by no hard luck, disillusionment, or unrequited love."

38 "You get more pure thing": New York Radio interview, May 21, 1966.

38 "Country Blues," "My Black Mama," and "Walkin' Blues": John Cowley does an in-depth comparison of these three songs in his article "Really the Walkin' Blues."

42 "What's the name of that tuning": When playing slide guitar, Muddy applied Spanish tuning, also called open G. The tuning is: D G D G B D, low string to high string. Other regionally common tunings Muddy mentions include vestapol tuning (open D: D A D F# A D, low string to high string) and cross-note tuning (open Em [E B E G B E]), which was used by only a few blues artists, notably Bukka White and Skip James.

43 The tension, documented in Lomax's field notes: Lomax, for example, would soon write about Work: ". . . trying to work out his problems — mostly of incompetence, laziness, and lack of initiative on his part."

46 Muddy in both the audience and the spotlight: Lomax reports on the next day's exhaustion in his field notes, following the recording of a baptism service: "By this time we had grown so sleepy, so thirsty, and the mosquitoes so energetic that we had to say good night. The meeting broke up to hear the records, everyone asking anxiously, as usual, where they could buy copies. They were completely delighted by the recordings, laughed and slapped their sides with pleasure over the shouting and moaning."

46 he couldn't see a big city in his future: Welding, "An Interview."

46 The whole encounter took about seven hours: McKee and Chisenhall interview with Muddy Waters.

50 "Gradually, I began to see Delta culture": Lomax, *Land,* p. xiii.

How, in *The Land Where the Blues Began,* is John Work III represented? He merits one mention, in the preface (p. xii): "The composer John Work agreed to do the musical analyses."

51 "The fatal error made by many writers": Work, *American Negro Songs,* p. 9.

Later in his introduction, on page 38, Work illustrates one of the uses — needs, even — of music in African American society:

The Reverend Israel Golphin tells of his employment with a gang laying railroad tracks in Arkansas because he was a good singer. He had just asked the "boss-man" for work and had been refused. He watched the gang work for a while and noticed that they were in difficulty because the singer or "caller," as he is sometimes termed, was inexperienced and was timing them wrongly. The men were grumbling. Golphin offered to "call" for them. The gang so appreciated him that they went to the "boss-man" and requested that he be hired — and he was.

4: COUNTRY BLUES *1941–1943*

The 1942 Fisk–Library of Congress Recording Trip: The recordists' return was delayed a couple times. The 1941 cotton harvest proved unusually large and necessitated the first postponement. Wages went from seventy-five cents per hundred pound to two dollars. "Not since 1926 had the wages reached that level. Everybody was in the fields," Lewis Jones writes in *The Mississippi Delta.* "All day white women were driving through the Negro residential district seeking someone who would work for them." The second delay was a result of the cold weather settling in.

During the delay, Lomax wrote a long and warm letter to Jones in which he described his "attempt to develop a genuine approach to history for radio, and what might possibly be termed a democratic type of propaganda in which a free people has the opportunity to explain for itself in its own terms the nature of its own life." (Lomax Correspondence, Library of Congress, January 21, 1942.) I thrill to Lomax's "democratic" ideals, the sense that communication is supposed to be *of* the people. In a discussion once about his recording "Blues in the Mississippi Night," he told me, "My story is the discovery of what you can do with a recording machine to democratize communications. Television networks and Hollywood maintain their control by keeping budgets too high to match. They set quality rules which can keep producers of small means off air. This is a way of excluding everybody that doesn't have big bucks. It turned into a one-way street, from up to down, with receivers that are very inexpensive, and transmitters terribly terribly expensive. It's an equation of the present communication system. Technically, you can't get that kind of quality with a documentary, unless you have the cameras on dollies and all the bullshit. That's what I represent. Oral history was aimed at the general objective of giving ordinary people a voice."

Honeyboy Edwards remembers Lomax showing up in 1942. "He was driving a brand-new forty-two Hudson Super Six. That's six cylinder, dark green, never will forget it. He drove up in the yard and my gal's auntie come out. He got out of the car with a book under his arm — people in the country, a man gets out of a big car, got on a suit — she was scared."

During the 1942 recordings, "Joe Turner," sung by Lewis Ford, introduced the subject of old songs. "Son Simms [*sic*] recalled that the earliest blues were 'Joe Turner,' about the long-chain man who took prisoners off to the work camps," wrote Lomax in *The Land Where the Blues Began,* "and 'Make Me a Pallet on the Floor.' 'That's how these women will do you, when you're off from home,' said Simms [*sic*]. 'They don't want to get the bed nasty with them and their kid man, so they put some old quilt down on the floor so they can do their business.' 'And their good man will never know,' Lewis chimed in."

During the 1942 questionnaire, Muddy's family tells Lomax they've been at Stovall nineteen years, which would date their arrival to 1923; however, they were at Stovall in 1920 to answer the census, which suggests they sojourned elsewhere. They tell Lomax they spent a year farming in Arkansas, a town he heard as "Blairsville" but is actually Blytheville. (Muddy's second cousins lived there; Honeyboy Edwards remembered meeting Muddy on Ash Street there.)

The publication of the Fisk–Library of Congress Coahoma County Study's findings never saw fruition. John Work completed his manuscript, "consist[ing] of 158 transcriptions of folk songs; a folk sermon found among the Negroes of Coahoma County; a catalogue of the disposition of the records (whether transcribed or not); and a treatise consisting of ten chapters, bibliography, two indexes (general and classified); a biographical appendix; and a preface describing the transcribing process." (Work correspondence with President of Fisk University Dr. Thomas Jones, Fisk Archives.) It was sent to the Library of Congress and to the president of

Fisk, but was misplaced by all parties until discovered during research for this book. Lewis Jones also wrote a treatise, as did his student Samuel Adams, who spent three months doing fieldwork in Coahoma County during 1942.

One concrete result of the Coahoma County Study was a seminar at Fisk for ten students during the spring semester of 1943. It drew from a regional pool of national talent, including Professor Thomas Washington Talley (author of the 1922 study *Negro Folk Rhymes, Wise and Otherwise*) and Dr. George Pullen Jackson (whose controversial 1943 book, *White and Negro Spirituals,* emphasized the "European" sources in African American spirituals). Fisk offered nineteen seminars, ranging from "Characteristics of a Folk Culture" to "Dance Music and the Blues," which covered "Sex and love in the culture. The family pattern and lovemaking conventions. The red-light district." ("Folk Culture Seminar," Fisk Archives.) This seminar represented a dramatic change in the focus of African American academia. Previously, Fisk's focus had been so Eurocentric that lightness of skin tone had long been rumored a prerequisite for admission. John Work's interest in blues — a music considered not only a low art but also a sin — sparked a cultural reawakening, initiating movement away from Bach and "the classics" and toward the African American tradition.

54 "We did the very first show": Harvey, "Growing Up with the Blues."

54 Sonny Boy II: Rice Miller never waxed a record until John Lee Williamson was six feet under God's brown earth. (He did claim to have recorded in 1929, but the song has never been found.)

In Mississippi, Tom Freeland introduced me to Carl Dugger, an octogenarian from northwest Arkansas. "Out here in the country, we used to walk about eight miles to see Sonny Boy," Dugger remembered. "Had to pay a nickel to go in. This was back in the nineteen thirties. He had seven or eight harps around his belt, he could put two harps in his mouth at the same time. They put Sonny Boy in jail in the town of Sardis, him and his partner. They played inside all night, let 'em out the next morning, carried them down to a little one-room café. They played around, took up money with a hat, and went on to other places."

Lockwood and Williamson's ramblings affected the radio show. "We set some good speed records getting back to the ferry," Robert Lockwood Jr. told *Living Blues.* "Sometimes Captain Johnson would wait on us if he knew we were coming, but we missed it a few times and had to sleep in the car until six or seven o'clock before he started again." (Harvey, "Growing Up.") KFFA announcers have said they were often concerned they'd give the cue for King Biscuit Time and nothing would happen.

55 "He'd [announce] every spot": O'Neal and van Singel, "Muddy Waters."

56 "Sr. Eduardo": Lomax field notes, Lomax Archives. Further described as "the keen dapper Brazilian sociology student."

57 "How it come about that [Robert Johnson] played Lemon's style": Lomax, *Land,* pp. 16–17.

57 "General Musical Questionnaire": This document is on file at the Library of Congress, as is an interesting forerunner. In September of 1941, Lewis Jones made a list of the songs on five jukeboxes in Clarksdale, giving a great sample

of what was popular at the time and what was familiar to Muddy; that list is most easily accessible in Tony Russell's "Clarksdale Piccolo Blues." Russell notes that the list is overwhelmingly urban. One-fifth of the titles are blues, only two of which are country blues; the remainder of the songs are big band-ish and swing. Interestingly, Louis Jordan, Count Basie, and Fats Waller were found on all five jukeboxes.

61   "how long to make twenty dollars": McKee and Chisenhall, *Beale,* p. 235.

61   "I carried that record up the corner": Palmer, "The Delta Sun."

    The mistaken belief that Muddy had his own jukebox may stem from this quote in the O'Neal and van Singel *Living Blues* interview: "I taken one [record] and put it on my jukebox." (O'Neal and van Singel, "Muddy Waters.") "My" jukebox does not refer to one in his home, where, without electricity, it would be useful only as a table, but rather to the jukebox Muddy favored, which was down the road toward Farrell — "before the hill," according to Magnolia Hunter. That's where he put his copy of the Library of Congress recording, about which he told *Living Blues,* "I'd slip and play it, you know — I didn't want 'em to see me."

62   "an old cotton picker was asked whether or not the people sang": Adams, Manuscript, Lomax Archives, p. 51.

62   The machine was ready to take the jobs of men: Agribusiness boomed in the early 1930s. According to Smithsonian historian Pete Daniel, the USDA was excited by the decline of small farmers' fortunes, because that cleared the way for the larger farmers to absorb them and to more efficiently use the burgeoning mechanized equipment. Federal policies combined with science and technology to expedite agribusiness. The 1933 Agricultural Adjustment Act, which paid farmers to plow up portions of their crop and evolved into payment to landowners for not planting, further eradicated the need for field hands. (See Daniel, *Lost Revolutions.*)

63   "two different repertoires": This quote comes from Lewis Jones's "The Mississippi Delta"; however, there are sections of Jones's manuscript that include, verbatim, John Work's handwritten notes. So I'm surmising that this is Work's information from his 1943 trip, when he took the picture.

64   "I was doing the same thing": McKee and Chisenhall interview with Muddy Waters.

64   a suit of clothes and an acoustic Sears Silvertone guitar: Hollie I. West, *Washington Post,* September 24, 1971, Sec. B.

5: CITY BLUES *1943–1946*

Arriving in Chicago: Muddy came north on the Illinois Central Railroad. That link to the North had been established in 1858 as a freight and passenger steamboat line. By 1885 it ran as a railroad from Jackson, Tennessee, to New Orleans. The rail line shifted Mississippi's development from towns along the river to those along the railway. Clarksdale, previously a nothing town, assumed prominence over Friars Point, which had once been the most important port for trade and travel. The Illinois Central Railroad directly linked the Delta to its terminus in

Chicago, connecting the Mississippi farms to the Great Lakes shipping industry. (See Corliss, *Main Line of Mid-America.*)

Reverend Willie Morganfield, who visited his cousin frequently, said about Chicago, "Chicago, you don't play in Chicago. You have to be very cautious there. But I walked the street, went where I wanted to go, because I know a little about Chicago." A. J. Liebling, writer for *The New Yorker,* spent several months in the city in 1951, and he also learned a little about Chicago, noting the inverse pride citizens had in how bad things were, whether it was civic corruption or the weather. "The contemplation of municipal corruption," he wrote, "is always gratifying to Chicagoans. They are helpless to do anything about it, but they like to know it is on a big scale." (Dedmon, *Fabulous Chicago,* p. 347.)

Entering the Chicago Music Scene: When Muddy arrived in Chicago, the recording industry was crippled by more than the Petrillo ban. Charlie Gillett, in *The Sound of the City* (p. 8), notes: "In April of 1942, the War Production Board had ordered a 79 percent reduction in the nonmilitary use of shellac and implemented a regulation which required the exchange of old records for every one purchased. To survive the shortage, the six major record companies, Columbia, Victor, Mercury, Decca, Capitol, and MGM, concentrated almost exclusively on the predominantly white popular music market." (See also Gelatt, *The Fabulous Phonograph: 1877–1977.*)

When Muddy eventually found club gigs, the money was not extraordinary. According to contracts discovered by Jim O'Neal dating between 1942 and 1944, Memphis Slim and Big Bill Broonzy were paid seven dollars and seventy-five cents each for midnight shows at the Indiana Theater. The pair split thirty dollars for Friday, Saturday, and Sunday nights for four months at Ruby's Tavern, and Slim alone, for five nights a week at Rudy's Chicken Palace, took home thirty-six dollars a week. Broonzy was prominent at the time. Jimmy Rogers said about him: "I really admired him, hair stand on my head to see that man. Big Bill gave me a lot of points on what was going down in this blues field." (Trynka interview with Jimmy Rogers.) Muddy told McKee and Chisenhall that he met Broonzy in 1944, the same year he met Memphis Slim, Tampa Red, Lonnie Johnson, Sonny Boy I, and Lee Brown. "I played with Lee Brown after 'Bobbie Town Boogie' came out," Muddy told O'Neal and van Singel. "It was sellin' pretty good, but it wasn't sellin' much as he played it. He did 'Bobbie Town Boogie' four times a night! It wasn't but just him and [guitarist] Baby Face Leroy and me. That's where I met Baby Face Leroy. We didn't even have a drum, not the biggest part of the time. Lee Brown introduced me to a record agent, Mayo Williams." Williams got Muddy on his first Chicago session.

Muddy's early repertoire included two Big Joe Turner hits, 1940's "Piney Brown Blues" and the next year's "Corrine, Corrina." (Muddy recorded his own version of the latter on his *Woodstock* album.) His voice, though gruffer than Turner's, was as big, and both were declamatory. The slow drag of Turner's "Piney Brown Blues" suited Muddy's mercurial manner; it was a staple of his repertoire around the Delta and a favorite for his audience when he got to Chicago. He told *Living Blues,* "I used to sing good 'Piney Brown.' 'I been to Kansas City, everything is really all right.' I used to drown that, man, I used to put that in water and drown it." (O'Neal and van Singel, "Muddy Waters.") He may have been singing that song the night that Calvin Jones stumbled onto him in Chicago at the Boogie Woogie Inn, Roosevelt and Paulina. Calvin remembered the harp player was not Walter and not Jimmy. Muddy told O'Neal and van Singel, "Little Johnnie Jones used to play harp with me too, the piano player." Muddy and Johnny (on piano) later recorded together for Aristocrat.

Stories about the formation of the early band abound. In addition to the account at the end of Chapter 5, the following elements of evolution also seem credible. Muddy told Charles Murray, "Then Blue Smitty left us and Jimmy got a job, and this left me by myself. I got a guy named Baby Face Leroy. He played drums and guitar, but he and I was playing git-tars together." (Murray, *Shots,* p. 184.) He told Bill Dahl in the *Illinois Entertainer,* "Me and Baby Face Leroy started to playing. He played guitar. We said, 'Hey! We need another piece.' And we went and found Walter and got him to come with us. Then Jimmy Rogers came back to the band. That made four of us." (Bill Dahl, "Muddy Waters Reigns As King," *Illinois Entertainer,* May 1981.)

Jimmy elaborated on his business relationship with Muddy in the early days: "Muddy as a boss," Jimmy told Paul Trynka, "we got along real good. Only thing he was short on was asking people for money. And Muddy was a kind of shy guy of big cities — he wouldn't get around too much. He'd talk to people if they talked to him, he'd go to work, come home, and that was it. Chicago to me was just another big city. I'd been around Memphis and places, and I knew you had to stay on your toes and watch the people you associate with." (Trynka interview with Jimmy Rogers.)

When Muddy met Lester Melrose, for whom he cut his second Chicago sessions, Melrose was at the end of a long run of success. He'd entered the music business selling instruments, sheet music, and records, but soon grasped that the money was in publishing. By developing connections with performers, he became a talent scout and record producer, his control of the sessions furthering his publishing interests. Over time, with one man overseeing so much of the recording, his sound developed a certain sameness. The scene was changing around him, in front of him, but he was too entrenched in the old sounds to see it. (See Koester, "Melrose.")

67   "I was thinking to myself": Welding, "An Interview."
67   "The Great Northern Drive": The editorial ran on October 7, 1916, cited in Drake and Cayton's *Black Metropolis,* p. 134. The statistical information comes from Rowe, *Chicago Blues.*
67   "I went straight to Chicago": Standish, "Muddy Waters in London" part 2.
68   "If there was no one to meet [the arriving passengers]": Spear, *Black Chicago,* p. 147. This quote is also cited in Mike Rowe's *Chicago Blues.*
69   "I had some people there": McKee and Chisenhall, *Beale,* p. 236; McKee and Chisenhall interview with Muddy Waters.
69   "the heaviest jive you ever saw in your life": Rooney, *Bossmen,* p. 109.
69   "Work there eight hours a day": McKee and Chisenhall, *Beale,* p. 236.
69   "During the last war": Drake and Cayton, *Black Metropolis,* p. 91.
69   "I never did go get good jobs": McKee and Chisenhall, *Beale,* p. 237.
69   "I got a job at the paper mill": Oliver, *Conversation.*

70   "tell this man at the [draft] board": McKee and Chisenhall, *Beale,* pp. 236–237.

70   "The blues Waters found": Welding, "American Original."

70   "The vigorous, country-based blues": Welding, "Afro Mud."

71   "My blues still was the sad, old-time blues": Welding, "An Interview."

71   "You'd go in": Rooney, *Bossmen,* p. 110.

71   "I played mostly on weekends": McKee and Chisenhall, *Beale,* p. 237; McKee and Chisenhall interview with Muddy Waters.

72   Dan Jones: His address was 1857 West Thirteenth Street.

72   "I call my style country style": Standish, "Muddy Waters in London" part 2.

73   "You done made hits": McKee and Chisenhall, *Beale,* p. 237.

73   "she was a Christian-type woman": O'Neal and Greensmith, "Jimmy Rogers," p. 11.

74   "They was men then": Ibid.

      Rogers remembers meeting and playing with Sonny Boy II, but places it around 1939 or 1940. He attributes the radio show, however, as his reason for seeking him, so it must have been after November 1941.

74   "small change": Ibid, p. 12.

74   "My favorite men": Ibid.

74   "I could feel [racism]": Melish, "The Man."

      In an excellent *Living Blues* cover story about Jimmy Rogers in 1997, "I'm Havin' Fun Right Today," author John Brisbin mishears Rogers say that a "state senator" brought Muddy to his house. "There wasn't no senator that drove him over there," Rogers told me. "He came over there with somebody that Jesse knew."

74   "started jamming over at his house": Rowe, *Chicago Blues,* p. 67.

74   "I knew what I was listening for": Melish, "The Man."

75   "I just harmonize it": Author interview with Jimmy Rogers.

75   "nobody home but us musicians": Ibid.

75   "start this house-party deal": Rowe, *Chicago Blues,* p. 67.

75   "One night it was raining": O'Neal, "Blue Smitty" part 1.

76   "I went down in Jewtown": Ibid.

77   "He really learnt me some things": O'Neal and van Singel, "Muddy Waters."

77   "It was a very, very good improvement": Wheeler, "Waters–Winter Interview."

77   "I was playing with Smitty": Voce, "Jimmy Rogers."

77   "If Blue Smitty wasn't there": Brisbin, "Havin' Fun."

78   "We'd call it scabbing": Rowe, *Chicago Blues,* p. 49.

78   "So one day I was going to get a haircut": O'Neal, "Blue Smitty" part 2.

      Muddy told Pete Welding the tavern was at Polk and Ogden Streets on the West Side.

79   "We were playing our little clubs": Guralnick interview with Muddy Waters.

79   "My uncle Joe [Grant]": Oliver, *Conversation.*

79   "It wasn't no name-brand": Murray, *Shots,* p. 182.

79   "It was a very different sound": Obrecht, "Bluesman."

79   "He wanted me to play like Johnny Moore": Welding, "An Interview."

80   "He got his paycheck": Brisbin, "Havin' Fun," p. 21.

80 "Musicians, blues players": O'Neal and Greensmith, "Jimmy Rogers."
80 "He had that particular little twinkle": Obrecht, "Bluesman."
81 "Why don't you sing one": O'Neal and van Singel, "Muddy Waters."
82 "I remember that session": O'Neal, "Muddy's First."
83 "When we discovered what was going down, then I said, 'Wow, man! We got something here!'": N.p., n.d.
84 "That country stuff might sound funny to 'em": Obrecht, "Life and Times."
84 vaulted for almost a quarter century: Muddy's Lester Melrose tracks were first released in 1972, on Pete Welding's Testament LP, *Chicago Blues: The Beginning.*
84 "You gotta have something": Guralnick interview with Muddy Waters.
84 "People interested in people selling": O'Neal and van Singel, "Muddy Waters."

6: ROLLIN' AND TUMBLIN' *1947–1950*

More on the Band's Formative Years: Honeyboy Edwards gives a great account of Walter's arrival in Chicago, after falling in with him in St. Louis: "We had heard about Maxwell Street. That was where the happening was. Musicians come to Chicago from everywhere just to play on Maxwell Street. They could make a living there. [Walter and I] hitchhiked from East St. Louis to Decatur, Illinois. So we hit the streets in Decatur, and found a little whiskey house and played a while there. Then we played at that train station, Walter playing that harp loud. I had my guitar and little amplifier. And we made enough at that station to buy tickets to ride to Chicago. We rode the cushions!" (Edwards, *The World*, p. 150.) When Jimmy went outside to hear Walter, a rainstorm sent them scurrying to Jimmy's nearby apartment. Walter went home wearing Jimmy's dry clothes. "He'd come to my house every day," Rogers said, "wake me up. We'd talk and sit down and rehearse." (Melish, "The Man.")

Though no one else was home when Muddy, Jimmy, and Walter began rehearsing at Muddy's, they "wouldn't never blast the volume," Jimmy told me. "The distortion would get in the way. You keep it down where each individual can just about hear where the next one's going." He told Jas Obrecht that music "was the most serious thing that I had going in my life. Every day we would do that. We'd meet over at Muddy's house. I could walk from my house to Muddy's in about ten minutes. It was a long ways to walk, but it wasn't worth paying a streetcar fare to ride down there." (Obrecht interview with Jimmy Rogers.) Jimmy Rogers lived at Twelfth and Peoria, twelve blocks from Thirteenth and Ashland.

There are many variations on the story of Muddy getting to his first session. One excuse Muddy remembered giving to his superiors was that his cousin had been found dead in an alley. Also, some versions have Muddy stopping at home and learning of the session, and turning over the truck and the rest of the deliveries to his childhood friend Andrew "Bo" Bolton (Bo is the mysterious "Antra Bolton" mentioned in Rowe's *Chicago Blues*). It probably was not Geneva with whom Sunnyland conspired because it's unlikely Muddy had met her yet. (In the 1955 *Chicago Defender* he stated he was already successfully recording when they met. [Alfred

Duckett and Muddy Waters, "We Got a Right to Sing the Blues," *Chicago Defender,* March 26, 1955.]) The versions that have Muddy driving his uncle's coal truck or driving a junk truck for Chess seem to be plain misunderstandings.

John Brisbin, who specializes in extended articles written in his interviewee's own words (a genre requiring persistence and patience), got the following from Sunnyland Slim, who was notorious for confusing stories:

> A visitor found patience rewarded when, out of Sunnyland's whispery
> mists, came a clear, comprehensible version of that story, told as if it hap-
> pened yesterday: "Leonard Chess and Phil Chess, they wanted me to make
> this record. They wanted me to bring one of them old soul guitar players.
> I tried to get 'em one, get 'em Lee Cooper or Johnny Shines. Couldn't do it.
> My wife said, 'What the hell. Why don't you go and get somebody to make
> the record 'cause the man done left the paper there.' It was eighty-two dol-
> lars, union. . . . So I went and paid nine cents streetcar fare. Bessie didn't
> have but fifty-four cents to give me. I went over to Eighteenth Street and
> met Bo, Muddy's cousin. And I never will forget. We went on back to
> Canal Street. Muddy wasn't there see, but we talked to his boss. We told a
> lie. I said my daddy was fixin' to die, Muddy's mother was a little sick. We
> just conned the boss so we could get Muddy off the next day. . . . The man
> went for it. I played for a show that night. Big Crawford, Muddy, and I. It
> sounded so good. Muddy sounded good, good! We went to the studio the
> next day and Leonard Chess asked me, 'Hey man, can your partner sing?'
> I said, 'Sure, man. Set it up!' You know, to help Muddy out. But, you see,
> the thing were we had to square up things 'cause Muddy wasn't in the
> union. We had to go through some changes, you know, to get him in."
> (Brisbin, "Sunnyland Slim," p. 54)

Blue Smitty, however, remembered being taken to the union, with Muddy and Jimmy Rogers, by Eddie Boyd in the mid-1940s.

Jimmy Rogers remembered Big Crawford fondly. "He was the nicest guy. He was a big and tall guy — weighed about three hundred-and-some pounds and stood about six feet five inches. He was a huge guy, like Willie Dixon. I'd see him all the time, and we would talk and crack jokes and fool around together." (Obrecht interview with Jimmy Rogers.) Rogers also recalled Muddy's reluctance to record without the band. Though solo country blues were popular — Lightnin' Hopkins had sold well with his spare "Katie May," Big Joe Williams was attracting attention, and John Lee Hooker's "Boogie Chillen" was in the wind — Muddy "didn't want to play by himself. Sunnyland kept urging him. At that time, his bills was kind of gettin' high, his car note and he had to pay his rent. Muddy was kind of a tight guy with them pennies, man. So he tried it." (Brisbin, "Havin' Fun," p. 23.)

Though Muddy and Jimmy continued to play in clubs together every week, two more years would pass before they would record together for Leonard. Jimmy, in conversation in his later years, spoke disparagingly of Leonard. ("Leonard was pretty slick," he told me. "Those guys was gypping you as far as your money or tak-ing your material.") Jimmy signed to Apollo Records in New York in 1949, before finally acceding to Chess's dominance in Chicago. ("[Chess] was too heavy. You couldn't get no place unless you come through him." [O'Neal and Greensmith,

"Jimmy Rogers."]) For Baby Face Leroy, stardom never came — he liked music only when it was exciting. Though he would later record for the small Chicago label J.O.B., he mostly got out of music. By the decade's end, he was dead from tuberculosis.

Early Success: "My earliest memory of Muddy is when we were living on the West Side," said Charles "Bang Bang" Williams, Muddy's stepson and Geneva's second child, who was seven when his mother moved in with Muddy. "I came home from school, and he was listening to one of his records with a fella that lived across the street." Geneva moved to Muddy's with Charles; her other son Dennis soon came up from Mississippi, and Bo found his own place. Charles rode with Muddy on deliveries and remembers him preparing for gigs. "Muddy would slick his hair back, have bangs, the way black people used to wear their hair, tuxedo grease. But he wouldn't miss no days from work. I don't think he stopped working on the venetian blinds truck until the early 1950s."

Billy Boy Arnold, then an aspiring harmonica player selling newspapers in front of the South Side's Persian Hotel (and later an accompanist to Bo Diddley and Fats Domino), remembered the heat around Muddy's 1949 hit "Screamin' and Cryin'." "The Persian Ballroom was in there, and I saw all kinds of people there, Joe Louis, T-Bone Walker, I saw Ella Fitzgerald in the beauty shop getting her nails done. People were talking about 'Screamin' and Cryin'.' Muddy was hot then. I spoke to him when he was getting out of the car. He had a pretty black convertible, nineteen forty-eight Buick. It was a sleek new car and I walked from his car to the Persian Hotel with him. I'd ask every man with a guitar did they know Sonny Boy. He said, 'Yeah, Sonny Boy was my partner.' I told him I played harmonica. He said, 'Oh, that's good, keep it up.'" Muddy told Billy Boy he was going in to talk to his manager; I've tried hard to positively identify who that might have been, and can only conjecture that it was Big Bill Hill, the disc jockey who also had an agency.

Muddy's Stint in Helena: "We was just going down to be doing something," Muddy told *Living Blues.* "We wasn't going to stay down there, no way." (O'Neal and van Singel, "Muddy Waters.") Locals told me the band played Helena's Owl Cafe, the Cotton Club in Forrest City, the opening of the New Roxy movie theater in Clarksdale, a schoolhouse in Coahoma County where dances were held, and Will McComb's café on the same road as Muddy's old Stovall home.

Muddy's longtime Chicago gig at the Zanzibar had a heavy impact on the future of blues. One youngster who lived behind the club was future blues star Freddy King. He would slip in the side door, too young to be in there, to watch the band. "He was big and husky," Jimmy Rogers told *Living Blues* (O'Neal and Greensmith, "Jimmy Rogers"), "but was nothing but a boy. He'd sit right at the bar, next to me, watch every move I'd make on the guitar." King later made Jimmy's "That's All Right" and "Walkin' by Myself" part of his regular set. Otis Rush also had his blues epiphany at the Zanzibar. He was fourteen and visiting his sister in Chicago in 1948; she took him to see Muddy, and he decided, "This is what I want to do."

85 "I heard this harmonica one Sunday": Melish, "The Man."
86 "It was amazing": Voce, "Jimmy Rogers."
86 "He had a bass player": Melish, "The Man."

86 "Walter was wild": Brisbin interview with Jimmy Rogers.
86 "What really made me choose [harmonica]": Wilmer, *Jazz Beat,* pp. 14–15.
86 "playing around a few shoeshine stands": Guralnick, *Home,* p. 73.
87 "I told Muddy I met a boy": Voce, "Jimmy Rogers."
87 "Muddy and I could hear": Melish, "The Man."
87 "When I met him he wasn't drinking": Guralnick, *Home,* p. 75.
87 "He didn't have very good time": Murray, *Shots,* pp. 184–185.
87 "He'd get executing and go on": Brisbin, "Havin' Fun," p. 22; author interview with Jimmy Rogers.
87 "There were four of us": Obrecht, "Bluesman," p. 54.
88 "patrol buy": Trynka interview with Jimmy Rogers.
88 R. L. Burnside: Annie Mae Burnside had come up from Marks, Mississippi. "When I got to Chicago in nineteen forty-six, my dad was up there, staying on Fourteenth Street, and he told me, 'Muddy live right over there.'"
   "Their apartment on Thirteenth had two bedrooms, a dining room, and a kitchen," R. L. told me. "I hadn't started to playing out in the public then. I was playing around home and juke joints, house parties. I'd go over to Muddy's house about every other night and watch him play."
89 "We used to just do it for kicks": Voce, "Jimmy Rogers"; O'Neal and Greensmith, "Jimmy Rogers"; Brisbin, "Havin' Fun," p. 22.
90 "Aristocrat [Records] was doing all white stuff": Aldin, Liner notes to *Aristocrat.* For more on Aristocrat Records, see hubcap.clemson.edu/~campber/aristocrat. html.
90 "every porter, Pullman conductor": Brack and Paige, "Chess."
90 "[Leonard] had Goldstein [*sic*], a black guy": O'Neal and van Singel, "Muddy Waters."
   Sammy Goldberg had previously been a talent scout for Herman Lubinsky's Savoy label and the West Coast's Philo / Aladdin labels, among others. "Yeah, I remember Sammy Goldberg," Phil Chess told Mary Katherine Aldin. (Aldin, Liner notes to *Aristocrat.*) "He was a New York talent scout, and then he went to the West Coast and then he came to Chicago. He knew beaucoup of black talent." As for Lonnie Johnson not wanting to let Muddy use his guitar, he ate crow a couple decades later when the two shared the bill on a European tour. "Big Lonnie Johnson, he forgot his guitar in New York," Muddy recalled. "So after they finished that night I said, 'Lonnie, maybe you remember when I wanted to use your guitar in the union hall before I started recording and you really didn't want me to do it.' Lonnie just looked at the floor. He thought he had the world in a jug and the jug in his hand. And I mean he was strong! But you don't supposed to be like that, I don't think. 'Cause today your day, tomorrow somebody else's day comin' around." (O'Neal and van Singel, "Muddy Waters.")
91 "Hell man, go get him": Ibid.
91 Westerngrade: The name was confirmed in a period Chicago phone directory by Robert Pruter. The warehouse was at 2201 S. Ford Avenue.
92 "Let me do one": O'Neal and van Singel, "Muddy Waters."
93 "What the hell is he singing?": Collis, *Chess,* p. 10.

93 "he didn't know": Guralnick interview with Muddy Waters.
93 "He didn't like": Welding, "An Interview."
93 "Evelyn Aron, she dug me": O'Neal and van Singel, "Muddy Waters."
94 "couldn't get one in Chicago nowhere": Ibid.
94 "But I'm the man": Obrecht, "Life and Times."
94 "Then Chess began to come close": Welding, "An Interview."
94 "Come down and let's have coffee": O'Neal and van Singel, "Muddy Waters."
94 "He did a lot for me": Golkin, "Blacks, Whites, and Blues" part 1.
95 "I could hear that record": O'Neal and van Singel, "Muddy Waters"; Rowe, *Chicago Blues,* p. 70.
95 "Muddy couldn't pay his car note": Brisbin, "Havin' Fun," p. 23.
96 "I'd come across many, many women": Alfred Duckett and Muddy Waters, "We Got a Right to Sing the Blues," *Chicago Defender,* March 26, 1955.
98 "One morning there, Little Walter and myself": O'Neal and Greensmith, "Jimmy Rogers."
98 "We did a couple of little gigs in Helena": O'Neal and van Singel, "Muddy Waters."
99 "Muddy came up to the house where the party was": Lasker interview with Myles Long.
99 "I couldn't leave": McKee and Chisenhall interview with Muddy Waters.
99 promotion at the 708 Club: *Juke Blues,* summer 1997, p. 29.
100 Not pleased at having his star artist help a rival: Leonard also prevented Muddy from playing a session behind Lazy Bill for Chance Records, exerting the exclusivity clause of their handshake contract.

7: ALL-STARS *1951–1952*

Maxwell Street, Little Walter: "The union don't want you to play down on Maxwell Street 'cause it's scabbing," said Jimmy Rogers. "They can't get any money out of it. But on Saturdays, maybe on Sunday evenings, Walter could make more money on the street than he could at a gig 'cause you'd have thousands of people walking up and down Maxwell Street. Harry Graves, that was the musicians' union president, he would have field guys out there watchin' that stuff. They'd put a fine on you or blackball you. Walter, we'd quick run down and tell him, 'The hawk is out!'" (Brisbin, "Havin' Fun.")

Walter reveled in the openness of playing outside, the closeness of the crowd, the beer on their breath, and the sweat on their clothes. There was always an audience on Maxwell Street, and it was as much fun when the crowds were small as when the street was teeming with activity. Walter's friend would drop an extension cord out the window, and Walter plugged in the possibilities. "I had a heck of a time gettin' Walter off the corner," said Muddy. "That boy, I had to chase him out of Jewtown regular. He'd see me coming, and grab his mike and gone!" (O'Neal and van Singel, "Muddy Waters.")

"Juke" and Its Aftermath: In legend, "Juke" was recorded as an afterthought, once the other tracks were done. But the master numbers indicate it would have been recorded first. Jimmie Lee Robinson, who would later play guitar on some Little Walter sessions, said the song came from an old jazz record. "The recording was slower," Robinson told me. "Walter would play it all the time on the windup Victrola. Then he speeded it up and changed the rhythm a little bit." Jimmy Rogers attributed the song's roots to two prior songs, one by Snooky Pryor and Moody Jones titled "Snooky and Moody's Boogie" and one that Sunnyland Slim used to play as his theme, "Get up the Stairs, Mademoiselle." Sales reported at a thousand copies a day were most likely exaggerated; pressings usually began with five hundred, which was probably how many it took to break even. "Juke" was released on Chess's new subsidiary, Checker, because radio stations did not like a playlist dominated by one label; companies were establishing multiple entities under one umbrella.

Dave Myers's version of the Walter–Junior Wells switch played his band as innocents: "What happened with Junior was unbelievable to me. We was playing seven nights a week, we had it going. But one night Junior never showed up. People was lining up outside as usual, so we got up and played. At the bar, there stands Little Walter, he was supposed to be with Muddy and they was supposed to be gone three weeks. [After Walter told him he'd left Muddy,] I said, 'Look, man, that's y'all's business, I need a harp player, can you play with us?' And boy, we loaded him up and he loaded us up too."

Another version of Walter's departure has him playing at the Zanzibar gig when a woman wanted to hear "Juke." As was the custom, she enticed them with tips. She laid a quarter on Muddy's knee, a quarter on Jimmy's knee, and then for Walter, all she had was a thin dime. His big head popped, and he pulled out. As Junior Wells pointed out, "She didn't even have no money to give Elga." (O'Neal, "Junior Wells," p. 16.)

The musical difference between Walter and Muddy was laid bare in some early tracks Walter cut with the Aces. "Boogie," (which remained in the vault for decades) propelled by the unmistakable (and inimitable) energy of youth, replaces the jazz horns with guitar parts. "That was like us starting everything new in Chicago," Dave Myers told me. "Once we got that swing music where we could utilize it, we was tough boy." Louis Myers, Walter's guitarist, told *Living Blues,* "Listen, boy, them chicks fainted, boy. I ain't never seen people faint over music. Just stood up and hollered, 'Whooo!' And then, boom! When the music is good to them, man, they had what you call a fit. At that time [early and mid-1950s] we had a sound that the other cats didn't have. Everywhere we went, boy, they called us hell and destruction." (Lindemann, "Little Walter and Louis Myers.")

A Little Walter performance from the early 1950s was remembered by Max Kincaid in Mike Leadbitter's *Nothing but the Blues* (p. 12):

> I only saw Little Walter once and that was back in the early fifties at Dallas, Texas. The crowd that night was sluggish; you know, drunk and talkative and not digging the music. When Walter came on after the intermission he rode in on a big stud's shoulders and brought the house down with that amplified harp. Man, the show he put on! It was a night to remember! In those days they strung a rope down the centre of the dance floor to keep white and coloured [*sic*] apart, but before Walter was through that rope was down and things were right. Even the law was too hung up on the scene to keep control!

Though just a kid, Junior Wells stepped right into Walter's place. "Standing Around Crying" is a great cut (even *Billboard* recognized it with four stars, its highest rating). Wells's personality comes through clear in his *Living Blues* interview; here he is on the army:

> They had us out once, policin' up the area and they told us, "I want you to fall down on 'em and get those cigarette butts up." And they started gettin' down on their knees on them rocks at Camp Robertson. I stood up and I said, "No, you're not talkin' to me, if you're tellin' me that I gotta get on my knees and pick up some cigarette butts. I'm not gon' do that." So, they put me on restrictions. . . . I just right flatfooted told 'em that I'm not a soldier. I'm a musician. That's it. (O'Neal, "Junior Wells")

There's loads of good stuff in the article.

Big Walter "Shaky" Horton replaced Junior. His technique was more traditional than Little Walter's and Junior's, less reliant on the amplifier than on his own manipulations. Big Walter liked his nip, and he'd often boast that he was a direct descendant of Christopher Columbus's manservant. He is probably the harp player on Muddy's January 1953 session. Wherever and whenever "She's All Right" is heard, the record transforms the walls to cinder block, thickens the air with cigarette smoke and spilled whiskey, dims the lighting to the glow of beer signs and weak Christmas lights, and places you absolutely on the South Side.

Otis Spann: In Belzoni, Mississippi, Otis Spann learned well from a local, Friday Ford, and won a talent contest at the Alamo Theater at the age of eight. "Mr. Alamo, he used to send for me to play for the vaudevilles," Spann told Peter Guralnick. "Man, I had a little tuxedo and hat, it was really something." Spann claimed to have held regular club gigs by the time he was fourteen. He also claimed, however, to have served in the army for five years beginning in 1946, ranking as a second lieutenant upon discharge. Blues researcher Alan Balfour, after a correspondence with the U.S. Army National Archives, found no Spann enlisted at that time; several musicians, in fact, remember the bluesman at the piano in various Chicago clubs during those years.

By the late 1940s, he'd earned a regular gig at the Tick Tock Lounge, Thirty-seventh and State Street, leading a large band that included horns. "I saw Spann in the Tick Tock," Billy Boy Arnold said. "He was standing up playing like Little Richard, and I said that's the greatest piano player I ever heard in my life. A few months later he was with Muddy and I wasn't surprised because he was great."

Jimmy Rogers heard about Otis from West Side pianist Johnny Jones, who knew that Spann's band had broken up. "We needed a piano player," Rogers told John Brisbin. "Spann was playin' with [guitarist Morris Pejoe] over on the West Side of Chicago. Morris Pejoe had a day job and Spann would just be fussing around." (Brisbin interview with Jimmy Rogers.) Spann said, "Muddy kept putting me off, putting me off — 'Yeah, we'll see about it' — and finally he told me to come down one night. I played, they signed me up. (Standish, "Muddy Waters in London" part 2.) Once in, Spann became something of the Chess's house pianist, playing sessions with Bo Diddley, Sonny Boy Williamson, Howlin' Wolf, Chuck Berry, Buddy Guy, Jimmy Rogers, and Little Walter. "When I was growing up," Muddy's granddaughter Cookie said with a laugh, "I thought that Otis Spann was Muddy's brother."

105 Muddy left his day job: Guralnick, *Home,* p. 69.

105 summer of 1950: Walter began recording in June of 1950, Jimmy in August. Though the date of Walter's session is unspecified, the time has been determined by the known dates of the master numbers that surround it.

106 Jimmy recorded all his material at the end of Muddy's sessions: The day Muddy cut "Louisiana Blues" and "Evan's Shuffle," he and the band also backed Jimmy on two cuts ("Going Away Baby" and "Today, Today Blues"); the workday was not concluded. Muddy stepped aside, and the band slipped back into their musical overalls to play behind Johnny Shines.

106 "Muddy was never a binding man": Aldin, Liner notes to *Jimmy Rogers.*

106 "I know when you make 'em a star": O'Neal and van Singel, "Muddy Waters."

106 "Bo was a nice boy": Author interview with Pinetop Perkins.

107 "Seven nights a week": Guralnick interview with Muddy Waters.

107 "My first memory of Muddy": Charles "Bang Bang" Williams shared these stories about his childhood: "One day my girlfriend at school wouldn't give me no notebook paper. I put a Hopalong Cassidy ring on my finger and I jumped on her. The teacher called my mother, and they whupped me. And one day I told a young boy to get his ass back in the house at Forty-third and Lake Park. I didn't know Muddy was sitting in the car, but he didn't whip me, he made me stay in the house." Muddy found advantages, too, in the young sons. "When I was about ten, eleven years of age," Charles remembered, "I had girlfriends and they'd come over and he'd give them a dollar if they'd kiss him. And around that same time, I remember him putting me on his knee and teaching me how to drive."

107 Drummer Elga Edmonds: "Elga" is confirmed by phone books and also by the research of D. Thomas Moon, who befriended members of Elga's family and met a nephew named for his uncle: Elga Edmonds. (Moon, "Elga Edmonds.")

108 "scufflin', sleepin' in cars": Brisbin, "Havin' Fun," p. 26.

109 "All that stuff came to me": Welding, "An Interview."

110 "Evans Shuffle": Sam Evans hosted a show on WGES. The few other prominent blues deejays in Chicago were Al Benson, also on WGES, Jack L. Cooper on WSBC, Herb Kent on WVON, and, later, McKie Fitzhugh on WOPA.

110 "I tried to give Tampa a few dollars": O'Neal and van Singel, "Muddy Waters."

111 "My drummer couldn't get that beat": Golkin, "Blacks, Whites, and Blues" part 1, p. 27.

111 "You sure worked for your money": Cushing, "Behind the Beat."

111 "Blues is nothing but the truth": Guralnick, *Home,* p. 227.

112 "Leonard calling people a motherfucker": Trynka interview with Jimmy Rogers.

An example of Leonard's intermediation in the studio is preserved in the false starts that precede "Blues Before Sunrise," from Muddy's October 1958 session. Before Muddy can deliver his second line, Leonard breaks in. "Hold it, Muddy," he says three times. "Say, Guitar Tucker, when he said, 'The blues before sunrise,' you ought to come in with a figure after that." Leonard sings an example of what he means, not great, but enough to inform Tucker, who, once the track is under way, livens that spot in each verse.

"Chess would sit there with his eyes closed in the booth," said Odie Payne. "If it hit him, he'd say, 'That's it, man,' but I heard him say many times, 'Man, you got to make me feel it.' The man would say, 'I doing the best I can,' and [Leonard] would say, 'Yeah, but I don't feel nothing.' He'd work you to death." (Golkin, "Blacks, Whites, and Blues" part 2, p. 27.)

In June of 1959, Leonard didn't hear what he wanted as Muddy began "Take the Bitter with the Sweet"; studio tapes captured their exchange:

"Preach the son of a bitch," Leonard told Muddy.

"I can't preach on the first beginning, baby. Can't talk shit on the first beginning."

"Talk shit like I'm your baby."

"I got to get into it, baby, first," said Muddy.

Leonard admonished him. "Got to get into it from the first word. It's not a broad that you can sit there for two hours and bullshit with her."

"I make her hot and then get her. Make her hot and get her, baby." Then Muddy turned to the band. "Slap it good. Slap it behind."

The master take came next.

113 "The Muddy Waters blues": Francis Clay, who would replace Elga Edmonds by decade's end, was playing jazz at the Heat Wave, a large club. "Muddy's band played there on our off night. The owner told me to come in when they played, and they had more people on an off night than we had the rest of the week!"

114 "This is where the soul of man never dies": Palmer, *Deep Blues,* p. 233.

115 "At one time there was a wide gulf": Gart, *First Pressings Vol. 2.*

115 major labels began jockeying for position: Paramount first revived Okeh Records, dormant a decade, in the spring of 1951 to compete in the R&B world. Soon after, Paramount wrested Okeh's distribution from several of its company-owned branches and delivered it to area independents.

115 "We were sitting down": Trynka interview with Jimmy Rogers.

115 "We would build it and then": Walters, Garman, and Matthews, "Jimmy Rogers."

115 "At the time we called it the jam": Trynka interview with Jimmy Rogers.

116 "If you couldn't play that song": O'Neal and Greensmith, "Jimmy Rogers."

116 "All my best records": Lindemann, "Little Walter and Louis Myers."

116 "He said, 'What's that?'": Brisbin interview with Jimmy Rogers.

117 "Little Walter flashes": Gart, *First Pressings Vol. 2.*

117 "When we got back to the hotel": Brisbin interview with Jimmy Rogers.

118 Shaw Artists: The agency was founded in early 1949 by Billy Shaw, who was working as a booking agent for Charlie Parker and other bebop artists; he'd been VP of Moe Gale Agency and resigned to start Shaw Artists. (Howlin' Wolf was with the Gale Agency in the 1950s.)

118 "You wasn't at no blues joint": O'Neal, "Junior Wells," p. 12.

118 "from one end of the line": Ibid., p. 119.

119 "I raised Junior Wells": Gelms interview with Muddy Waters.

119 "Every time we'd look around": O'Neal and van Singel, "Muddy Waters."
119 "We was running in and out of town": Walters, Garman, and Matthews, "Jimmy Rogers."
120 "If somebody can shine": Guralnick interview with Muddy Waters.

8: HOOCHIE COOCHIE MAN *1953–1955*

Muddy and Wolf: Not only did Muddy host Wolf, but he also helped him get a band together. Drummer Earl Phillips remembered Muddy coming to his gig: "Muddy came by there one evening and says to me, 'How about getting with my man and help him, and you can go somewhere?' Just like that, Muddy did. I goes over on Greenwood Street to see Howlin' Wolf. This was in 1954. And he got to talking and he decided he wanted me to work with him. So we started rehearsing, sometimes in Muddy Waters's basement because Spann used to be with us sometimes." (Cushing, "Behind the Beat.") In the early 1960s, Little Smokey Smothers played with Wolf and also sat in with Muddy on guitar. "Somebody would always tell Wolf and he'd say, 'I heard you been hanging with them Muddy Waters boys. Them ain't nothing but drunks. I don't want my guys hanging with them guys.'" Calvin Jones, who also played with Wolf for several years before joining Muddy, doesn't recall Wolf ever making such demands. The documentation of the union conflict between Muddy and Wolf was found by Scott Dirks in the papers of Local 208, archived in the Music Research Department of the Harold Washington Library in Chicago. I know of two Wolf biographies and two documentaries in the works.

Arc Publishing: When short on money, many artists — not understanding the long-term value of their work or unwilling to gamble that its value would rise — sold their rights to the publisher. Marshall told me: "Publishers often helped out their clients by buying songs from them. Goodman bought some songs from Memphis Slim. There are letters in the file from Memphis Slim thanking him. Arc had bought the Jimmy Reed catalog, and years and years later they did a lawsuit against Arc. So we hired a detective to find Jimmy Reed's lawyer from that time, we knew his name. He's retired in Florida, gives us a sworn affidavit that not only the Reeds needed the money, the IRS was going to take everything, they were thrilled, they were kissing feet for being able to get the money."

Arc Music's original domain was only international rights and versions of Chess artists' songs remade by people outside the company. Domestic publishing stayed within Chess; that is, instead of Chess paying Arc and Arc paying the Chess artists, the record company paid itself. The artists received nothing, or nothing like what they were supposed to receive, until they began filing lawsuits against Arc in the 1970s.

Band Personnel: Little George Smith was soon to be George "Harmonica" Smith. In the early 1950s, while working as a film projectionist in Itta Benna, Mississippi, Smith discovered that he could remove the machine's amplifier and speaker and play his harmonica through them; on his own, he'd developed a style similar to Little Walter's. He was leading a little band, but he leapt at the chance to join Muddy Waters, quitting his day job as a janitor at the Twentieth-Century Theater. Days,

Spann went through the drill with George Smith, and they were so busy at night that he was quickly on top of the songs.

Joining Muddy's band was the fulfillment of James Cotton's dreams. "I was married to this woman, Ceola," he told me, "and she bought me a record player and every record that Little Walter and Muddy had ever made. She used to get up in the morning time, write me a note, leave me ten dollars on the record player. 'Learn this song.' She knew Muddy's songs better than I did. And when I'd play, she'd say, 'Well, you missed that part there.'" Ceola's regimen served Cotton well; when he joined Muddy, he was instructed to play the harp parts as they'd been recorded. "The blues didn't get too low-down for us," Cotton continued. "We didn't stand back from any musicians." In June of 1955, Muddy battled Ray Charles, the blind keyboardist who took his blues roots in a more jazzy, orchestral direction, at the Trianon Ballroom, a lavish South Side dance palace that had only recently begun allowing black patrons to enter. The house was packed, the gate was a record, and the battle was a tie. The Trianon scheduled a rematch. The verse James Cotton contributed to "Rocket 88" begins: "V-8 motor and this smart design . . ."

Music was changing in 1955 and Muddy's lineup was affected. Through the rock and roll of Bill Haley and Little Richard, the saxophone was enjoying a revival, honking and shouting its modernity. (Haley's 1956 hit, "See You Later Alligator," was written and originally performed by Chess's Bobby Charles and brought Arc a substantial payment.) Straight blues, deep blues, no longer satisfied a full house. "We was playing them black dances and it's kind of hard just to play a dance with a harmonica and guitars," said Muddy. "I added on a horn or so, and we could play at a club and dance, too." (O'Neal and van Singel, "Muddy Waters.") Muddy went through several players — Bob Hadley, Eddie Shaw, a Memphis player named Adolph "Billy" Duncan, J. T. Brown, Earl Brown, Bobby Fields, and Marcus Johnson, who also doubled on bass; Johnson played neither instrument expertly, but he kept Muddy's cars washed. Bob Hadley was not a good traveler; his legs tended to swell. He soon became a plainclothes detective and slept nights in his own bed.

122 "The piano is made for both hands": Hentoff, Liner notes to *Otis Spann*.

122 "I put a little swing into [the blues]": Cushing, "Behind the Beat."

123 "There was quite a few people around singing the blues": WKCR newsletter.

123 "I was in the men's house": Robert Frank Gelms, *Illinois Entertainer,* June 1983.

124 "Oh man, the people went crazy": Ibid.

124 "He done it two or three times that night": Brisbin interview with Jimmy Rogers.

124 "Hoochie Coochie Man": Benjamin Filene, in *Romancing the Folk* (pp. 105–106), offers this interpretation of "Hoochie Coochie Man"'s success:

> To these migrants, Dixon's songs offered some of the same consolation that Waters's statements of yearning in "I Feel Like Going Home" had provided for earlier settlers. Joining familiar down-home holdovers with new urban styles, the tunes achieved formally the sort of juxtaposition that the migrants themselves were grappling with in their own lives. To hear evocations of their southern customs in the context of the

vibrantly urban sound appealed to their longing for all they had left behind and their eagerness to merge the old and new. . . . Dixon's songs could appeal to newcomers from the South, but his language and imagery suggest that he was primarily speaking for and to migrants who had been settled in the North longer.

124 "We're so happy with Muddy": Gart, *First Pressings Vol. 4,* p. 20.

125 four thousand copies: Ibid., p. 21.

128 Muddy's move brought Leola: Cookie remarked on the relationship between Muddy, Geneva, and Leola: "Geneva really accepted my grandmother. I was raised that that was our network. Geneva was my grandmother's best friend. She would have Bo or anyone go pick her up. They would spend the weekends together, do the shopping. When Muddy really started out there cheating and stuff, that's who she would confide in. They were really good friends. If Muddy was going out of town, Leola would stay with Geneva. I never saw them have bad words toward each other. Muddy would go by Leola's and she would cook for him. They had a competition of cooking." Muddy's move to the South Side brought Geneva's mother, known as M'dear, to Forty-first and Greenwood. Geneva and Cookie visited her regularly. "Muddy always made sure that M'dear had whatever she needed," said Cookie. "Not that he would deliver it, but he would have someone to do it."

128 "I had Chicago sewed up": Guralnick interview with Muddy Waters.

128 "I know the peoples thought we hated": O'Neal and van Singel, "Muddy Waters."

129 "I'd say this is a song for Muddy": Dixon with Snowden, *I Am the Blues,* p. 149.

130 It was yellow and green: Some people recall the first car Leonard gave Muddy as red.

130 "Chess would get him a car": Trynka interview with Jimmy Rogers.

131 "So I got him home": Brisbin, "Havin' Fun," p. 25.

132 "you couldn't get a job without a harmonica player": Rowe, *Chicago Blues,* p. 88.

132 "Are you ready?": Tooze, *Muddy Waters,* p. 125.

133 "Willie Dixon got credit": Trynka interview with Jimmy Rogers.

133 "Pop Music Rides R&B Tidal Wave": Gart, *First Pressings Vol. 4.*

134 "I had done got Junior": O'Neal and van Singel, "Muddy Waters."

136 Band members earned: For a sense of what a club would have paid in 1959, contracts show Wolf was paid a $250 guarantee for him plus a band of four, with further payments of half the gate over $500.

138 The South was where racism held: Louis Myers was traveling with Walter in the 1950s. "I went in this place in Atlanta and I was just looking for a guitar and he said, 'Don't put your black hands on all the guitars up and down this line.' And I said, 'I'm just looking for a guitar.' 'No, no,' he said. 'We got white peoples coming in to buy guitars.'" (Lindemann, "Little Walter and Louis Myers.")

138 The South was also home: Robert Morganfield said, "He got back in touch, started to visiting with us, and we started visiting him. Always when he would come, he would make our sister Luella's home his stay place. He loved her biscuits and the way she made steaks. He'd visit around a couple days, then be gone."

139 "Somebody with a gun": Baysting, "Bluesman."

139 Lake Park Liqueors: Spelling as per Chicago telephone directory.

140 Nate Notkin: "One of the songs that made Muddy famous, I'm gonna put my tiger in your tank, he put his tiger in a lot of tanks. There was one case that stands out. This was a beautiful woman, she was married, she claimed that Muddy was the father, and that there wasn't any chance it was anybody else. So we got on two telephones in my office. Muddy said, 'Hey babe, how about if I come over now?' She said, 'Oh, my husband is home.' When it came to trial, I had an associate representing Muddy so I could be a witness. She had, as further proof that Muddy was the father, a notarized statement by Muddy acknowledging paternity. Well, Muddy couldn't read or write, except for his name, which was a hell of a job for him. The notarial public seal was there, but no 'subscribed and sworn' or the date, just the seal. She tried to introduce that in evidence, and the assistant state's attorney — it's a quasi-criminal charge — said this notary is a cousin of mine. So the case was continued until the cousin was brought in. He was a used-car salesman. She came to buy a car, she was in his office alone while he went out to attend to some other customer, and while he was gone for five minutes, she evidently used his notarial seal. The judge threw the case out."

Notkin also quashed a rumor that persisted, and took various forms, throughout my research. I heard several times that Muddy (sometimes it was Jimmy) ran over a child, possibly while driving drunk. Notkin said he never heard of it. "If Muddy had been involved, I'm sure I would have heard. He trusted me with his life."

141 "Muddy was kind of jealous": Louis Myers, Little Walter's guitarist, told Dick Shurman that one night he stopped in at the 708 Club on his way home. Muddy was playing. Louis saw a childhood sweetheart and didn't know she was Muddy's girlfriend. They embraced and chatted excitedly, unaware that Muddy was watching from the bandstand, stewing. Later, Myers was watching the sun come up from his front porch when a car came screaming around the corner. He watched, amazed, as it halted in front of his house. Muddy jumped out, holding a gun, saying, "I'll kill you, you motherfucker." Louis hastened, "Wait. Wait. Wait," and explained the old friendship.

141 "Only a few artists": Gart, *First Pressings Vol. 5.*

141 "Mannish Boy": The spelling on the original release was "Manish Boy." Unlike the suggested transformation of the man in the evolved spelling of Muddy's name, this seems to be simply a mistake.

142 "Muddy wanted to take 'I'm a Man'": Trynka interview with Billy Boy Arnold.

142 "Bo Diddley, he was tracking me": Bill Dahl, "Muddy Waters Reigns As King," *Illinois Entertainer,* May 1981.

Diddley's "I'm a Man" features Otis Spann on piano. Change did not come quickly at Chess. Leonard — and Muddy — did not mind stasis. "Evil," which soon followed "Mannish Boy," reworked the formula of "Hoochie

Coochie Man." Earlier, after the success of "I Feel Like Going Home," Muddy had cut both "You're Gonna Miss Me" and "Walkin' Blues," which were built on the same melody.

142 "some things come out all different": Obrecht, "Bluesman."

9: THE BLUES HAD A BABY *1955–1958*

Jimmy Rogers Retires: Even while blues greats were leaving the field, new ones were entering, and this second generation was profoundly shaped by Muddy. His heavy, declamatory vocals were the model for singers such as Big Boy Spires and Floyd Jones. Otis Rush, whose harrowing singing and playing on 1956's "I Can't Quit You Baby" announced a major talent, named Muddy as his inspiration. The reason he wasn't on Chess, the musicians knew, was because Leonard found him too close to Muddy in style.

Hubert Sumlin: Hubert Sumlin played with Muddy from May or June until sometime in December 1956. He began meeting with Spann in Muddy's basement. "Spann and I would work for two hours down there every day. He learned me a lot, man. Muddy wouldn't even pick up a guitar while I was with him." (Trynka interview with Hubert Sumlin.) He recalled his trek to Chicago: "[Wolf] calls up, tells me the train leaves at so and so time and you are going to be met by Otis Spann. I packed my little suitcase, gets on the train, and finally arrives at the big ol' Illinois Station on Twelfth Street. Otis Spann met me, man, I got to see all these big lights, and I got scared, so we went straight back to Leonard Chess's daddy's apartment building. Wolf had his own apartment there, he got me an apartment there and had done got my union card and everything. So the second day, me and Wolf we done had lunch, and he starts to telling me how this worked, how that worked." (Trynka, "Howlin' Wolf," p. 44.)

Later, when Hubert joined Muddy, "We were coming back from Florida, Spann had stopped and bought him a pistol — Saturday Night Special. So we all bought them. I got me a little old gun, it just fit in my coat. We had made it almost back to Chicago, Muddy had went on — he always did drive separate with his chauffeur. The police pulled our car over. He got Spann out of the car and come up with his gun, so then he hauled us all out. They pulled a gun from every man in that car. They called for another car, kept their guns on us the whole time. They thought they had captured the black mafia or something, and we all got thrown away in jail. We'd be there today without Muddy. He came down as soon as he found out and made them let us go. But they kept the guns." (Trynka interview with Hubert Sumlin.) Hubert went back to Wolf, and they enjoyed an eight-year run of hits, carrying a black audience into the 1960s well after Muddy's had faded and his appeal was mostly to whites.

"Elgin" Edmonds Gets Fired: "I had to find me a drummer that would *drive,*" said Muddy. "My drummer was straight right down — *bop bop bop bop.* I had to part from him 'cause he just couldn't hit the backbeat." (Palmer, *Deep Blues,* p. 168.) Freddie Below, the obvious replacement, was making it in the Chess studio and, any time he needed the road work, his commitment was with Walter. Cotton remembered the group running through five or six drummers before finding Clay.

"It was funny to me," Cotton said, "because all the other drummers brought their whole set of drums, Clay come to audition with just a snare drum." But Clay said, "No, I didn't audition." Marcus Johnson, whom some band members called "Marcus Garvey" because of his politics, got in a fight and out of the band. According to Cotton, "Marcus thought that Clay owed him something because he got him into the band. We played Gary, Indiana, one night, we loaded the instruments into the back of the station wagon, and Marcus knocked Clay down. And I gave Marcus a good whupping for it." Said Clay, "He'd get hot-headed sometimes." Clay also did not care for Triplett: "Pat Hare was always a pleasant person, but he loved to play with guns. He would have his gun on his bed, taking it apart, putting it together. He got in trouble one time in Texas, he shot at Triplett, who was an asshole anyway. He irritated everyone. He thought he was out of this world. The cops came, but they didn't arrest anyone, they were used to things like that."

Scott Dirks, researching union documents in the Music Research Department of Chicago's Harold Washington Library, found these American Federation of Musicians minutes of January 16, 1958:

> Members Elga Edmonds and McKinley Morganfield appeared before the Board as notified re: the claim of Edmonds against Morganfield for eighty-three dollars, representing seventy-five dollars for three days' wages plus eight dollars transportation. Morganfield stated that he gave Edmonds a notice in Florida on November 24 and he played with the band until a day or two before he left Chicago for Cleveland. He explained to the Board that he definitely told Edmonds that he would not go to Cleveland. Edmonds stated that he had been given notices many times before but that they were always taken back by Morganfield. He figured that this would happen with the last notice. He also admitted that Morganfield did not want him to go to Cleveland. He explained that after talking to President Gray, he did drive to Cleveland under the impression that perhaps Morganfield had not been able to obtain the services of a drummer. When he arrived on the job, Morganfield was surprised, and, having a drummer, he would not let him play. Instead of him returning to Chicago the next morning, he stayed for three days and Morganfield gave him some money but not enough to buy gas and oil for the round-trip from Chicago. President Gray explained his position in the matter and stated that he simply tried to act as mediator in the case. After Edmonds telephoned him from Cleveland, he talked to Muddy Waters and asked him to pay Edmonds's fare back to Chicago, which Morganfield agreed to do and gave him fifteen dollars. Edmonds stated that it cost him twelve dollars and seventeen cents each way, which included the price of gasoline and oil and turnpike fees. Muddy Waters agreed to pay an additional ten dollars to Edmonds as the balance due for transportation cost. On motion, the claim of member Elga Edmonds against member McKinley Morganfield was disallowed.

Francis Clay modernized Muddy's sound, making it rhythmically more complex without losing its essential backbeat. "Clay, by him playing the beat, he was a help to me and Spann," said Cotton. *Blues and Rhythm* wrote of Clay: "He was able to achieve more rhythmic flavor by doing such things as playing on the tom-toms and cymbals in unison with the melody, and also adding counter rhythms, all the while maintaining a basic backbeat on the bass and snare drums. Favors a small timbale-like tom-tom, used it for twenty years." (Leadbitter, *Nothing but the Blues,* p. 109.)

Luther Tucker: The rotating guitar spot soon fell to Luther Tucker, whom Muddy stole from the increasingly erratic Little Walter. Tucker was in his early twenties and ready to kick ass. His fiery style was reflected by his personality: he'd been kicked out of Memphis, his hometown, as an adolescent, and had come to Chicago, where he promptly stole a police car and landed in a juvenile detention center. His mother, in tears, put him in the care of Sunnyland Slim, and another career was born. Tucker's playing was fluid, and his solos slithered like wet snakes. He and Hare gave Muddy a sound rooted in blues but with a contemporary appeal, and that served him well on his next two sessions, including "She's Nineteen Years Old." The rooming house St. Louis Jimmy lived in was at 3300 S. Calumet. Big Smokey Smothers also claimed authorship of "She's Nineteen Years Old."

145 "He was my favorite singer": Berry, *The Autobiography,* p. 98.

145 "Yeah, see Leonard Chess": O'Neal and van Singel, "Muddy Waters."

146 Sharecroppers, which had numbered: Daniel, *Revolutions,* p. 7, as per *Historical Statistics of the United States, Colonial Times to 1970.*

146 "Fuck the hits": Lasker interview with Malcolm Chisolm.

146 "It was a trend": Guralnick, *Home,* p. 234; originally Lydon, *Rock Folk.*

146 number one on all three of their R&B charts: September 10, 1955. (Gart, *First Pressings Vol. 5.*)

147 he was not long from his first heart attack: Leonard had his first heart attack at the end of January 1957. By March of 1957, *Billboard* noted, "Len Chess, starting to show up at the Chess-Checker offices every day, says, 'It sure is good to be back.'" (Gart, *First Pressings Vol. 7,* p. 39.)

147 "The stuff that really started him": O'Neal and Greensmith, "Jimmy Rogers."

147 "Rock and roll kind of took over": May 1956, in *Billboard:* "SIGN OF THE TIMES: Jukeboxes at the MOA Convention in Chi last week blasting forth with R&R all day, no matter what booth it was." Same month:

> R&B GOING STALE?: The past two years have seen the American disk-buying public — in reality, the entire disk-buying world — discovering what many in the business have always known: that the rhythm and blues field is one of the most fertile, honest, and dynamic sources of song material. It has explored the emotions frankly and directly, and it has voiced some penetrating views of society. And always, underneath it all, there has been "The Beat." Today, it's hardly a secret that R&B is the big thing in our popular music. But there are indications that the music that revitalized the business is now in danger of going stale. (Gart, *First Pressings Vol. 6*)

"I was playing in the clubs with Muddy in the late fifties," said Billy Boy, "and Muddy didn't do nothing but sing — he had Pat Hare playing guitar. Muddy would sit in the audience with his lady, and his bodyguards and valets and strong-arm men, and he would come up and sing three or four numbers. He had put his guitar down because things were changing and he felt nobody wanted to hear that dang stuff."

148 "Forty Days and Forty Nights": This is a big, bold record. Hare contributes a

Chuck Berry–esque riff that may have inspired the Beatles' "Revolution." The song is similar to "Mystery Train," which had been a hit for Junior Parker in 1954 (and to Arthur Crudup's "Mean Old Frisco" from 1942). Cotton and Hare made "Mystery Train" part of the band's pre-Muddy set, and when Muddy saw the audience's reaction, he reworked the words and claimed the song.

148 the sound was quite different: "Don't Go No Further" was the sound of the urban blues club, the very electric guitar propelling patrons up and over the South Side cinder-block top. The flip side, "Diamonds at Your Feet," is a radical reinterpretation of "Take Sick and Die" from Muddy's Library of Congress recordings. The dirge is here made jubilant; instead of mourning his baby's passing, Muddy anticipates the occasion as a moment to celebrate her life. The session is rounded out by "Just to Be with You," one of Muddy's personal favorites.

149 "Got My Mojo Working": Ann Cole recorded hers on January 27, 1957, for an April release. Muddy's was recorded a month or so earlier. The week of April 27, 1957, *Billboard* made Muddy's version a Buy o' the Week: "This version of the tune is locked in competition with the Ann Cole disk. Most areas show it practically even with the latter." (Gart, *First Pressings Vol. 7*.) "We played with her a couple times after that," said Cotton, "once in Philadelphia at the Uptown Theater. We had a big hit on 'Mojo,' she asked Muddy not to sing it, so he didn't. We let her do it because it was her song in the first place."

Around the time of "Got My Mojo Working," Muddy went on a tour that featured Sarah Vaughan. Researching the date of the tour only resulted in conflicting accounts. Cotton told me, "That was the big tour. Nappy Brown, Sarah Vaughan — it was her tour — the Moonglows, Ray Prysock, Arthur Prysock, Al Hibbler, Jimmy Witherspoon. We got booed the first day, in Washington, D.C., at the Howard Theater. They were there to see Sarah Vaughan."

149 "So I told Muddy I couldn't play out the night": Trynka, "Howlin' Wolf."

150 "McCoys": Trynka interview with Hubert Sumlin.

151 "We quit touring in January": Standish, "Muddy Waters in London" part 2.

155 "I only charge thirty-five cent": For the musician, the money from a hit was in the gig pay. "A blues record," said Marshall Chess, "if it sold seven or ten thousand in Chicago it was a hit. At eighty cents a record, that's six or seven thousand dollars in a few weeks. The artist's royalty I think was two or three percent, let's say it was even five percent. It was complex 'no rules' time. There was all this payola going on to get the record played and that wasn't a recoupable investment, the label took care of all that. Songwriters' royalties were two cents per cut. The writers' portion was one cent. Let's say the most you would do was forty thousand. Four hundred bucks worth? These guys liked it when Chess got the record on the radio in Chicago, all of a sudden you could get four or five hundred for a weekend at a club."

Leonard Chess recalled for the *Chicago Tribune* how Chess responded to the payola charge. "We were the only company that refused to sign a cease and desist order. I was advised not to. Payola was standard practice in the industry and I told them I wouldn't stop unless everyone else did. At least I was doing it honestly — make a deal and send 'em a check and at the end of the year report it on a 1099 form." Leonard bought his first radio station in 1959. (Golkin, "Blacks, Whites, and Blues" part 2.)

155 he refused to let them feel the full impact: Chess's Robin Hood accounting method was consistent with Guralnick's interview with Marshall thirty years earlier: "Oh sure, we done a little padding. Sometimes when royalty time came around, let's say that he had one group that was very big, my father might cut their royalty by five hundred bucks and add it to Wolf's statement. But he didn't ever put it in his own pocket." (Guralnick, *Home,* p. 233.) Also, Nadine Cohodas recounts a story from the early 1960s: "[Producer Jack] Tracy was speechless during one meeting when Leonard was preparing the royalty checks. He looked at the statement with Jamal's royalties, which were considerable, and at [Ramsey] Lewis's, which were much smaller. He went over Jamal's earnings again and then told the accountant, 'That's too much money for him — give some to Ramsey.'" (Cohodas, *Gold,* p. 170.)

10: SCREAMING GUITAR AND HOWLING PIANO *1958–1959*

Muddy, the English, and the Electric Guitar: "Lomax had lived over here for about six or seven years and he played a lot of the Library of Congress recordings on the BBC radio," Paul Oliver said. "Anyone who had heard Muddy Waters would have heard him playing acoustic. When he played electric, it was a surprise. I felt rather thrilled by it, because he seemed right up to date. A lot of people still thought of blues as part of jazz, so it didn't quite match their anticipations."

"Muddy's guitar wasn't loud," Chris Barber stated with affirmation. "No one complained to me, and if they had, I'd have told them to get out. We were paying Muddy and Otis ourselves. We'd got them there for our pleasure. We had toured with Sister Rosetta Tharpe, and she played quite loud. We'd toured with Sonny and Brownie, and Brownie played amplified acoustic guitar. I didn't think Muddy played very loud." There's a CD of one date, midtour in Manchester (*Collaboration,* Tomato Records); Muddy's not shocking the ears.

He did, however, rock and roll at his unofficial gig at the Roundhouse, a small London pub run by Alexis Korner and Cyril Davis, two musicians who'd begun exploring blues before Muddy's arrival. When Muddy and Otis strolled into the packed, smoky upstairs room around nine in the evening, they smelled spilled beer and felt the sting of thick cigarette smoke — aah, home. They were immediately offered the stage. Korner remained to accompany the two on his steel guitar. "At the concert [halls], [Spann] had suffered from poor amplification, but at the Roundhouse there was no trouble," wrote Tony Standish. He continued:

> The left hand rolled them, huge and blue, and the right hand hovered, making it sing, and then swooped and soared, showering us with piano blues such as we had never heard in the flesh. . . . Muddy mopped his perspiring brow and laid aside his guitar. And suddenly there was another Muddy, a Muddy who sang as he must for his own people, in another world than ours. . . . He sang with his whole body — gyrating, twisting, shouting — preaching the blues chorus upon hypnotic chorus, weaving a pattern of quivering tension around and over an enthralled audience. (Standish, "Muddy Waters in London" part 1)

"At the Roundhouse," said Paul Oliver, "Muddy was closer to the audience and I think he was just rather more comfortable with it. He coped with the big concerts quite adequately, they were closer to the way he played on the first recordings he made for Aristocrat. It wasn't tremendously heavy. But I think he liked the club atmosphere. That prepared me a little bit for my visit to Chicago the next year. But I couldn't reckon with the kind of power and ferocity of his playing and performance on the South Side."

Session Notes: "She's into Something" is one of Muddy's most uncharacteristic songs. In his basement, Muddy had mentioned that he was interested in trying something different. At the Broonzy session, the band played him "She's into Something" with Spann singing, but Muddy cut them off before they could even get going, said, "Hold it, hold it, I don't do no cha cha cha."

"Clay could play a beat," said James Cotton. "He said, 'Let's put a little cha cha on it.' Pat Hare had his part. We picked it up like that." Muddy was won over.

I was discussing Little Walter's majestic harmonica sound from the January 1959 "Blues Before Sunrise" session with Chicago harmonica player and music interlocutor Dave Waldman, and he sent me this harmonica lesson, which he has allowed me to share:

The harp-player on the "Blues Before Sunrise" session was playing an octave harp. This would be a harp where, by blowing or drawing into one hole, you get a note and also the same note an octave higher. It's not the same thing as a chromatic. As far as I can tell, the harp player on the session uses such an octave harp for the entirety of "Crawling Kingsnake," except for the closing lick. This last lick is played on a normal ten-hole diatonic (probably a Marine Band) tuned in the key of A. (Note: the song is in the key of A, as are the other two songs from the session.) The octave harp also makes a brief appearance on "Mean Mistreater." There, the harp-player plays the first two verses of the song using a Marine Band (or something like it) tuned in the key of D. (Playing a harp in this way — a fifth above the key that the harp is tuned in — is by far the most common approach to blues harp.) After the last line of the second verse ("because you got that on your mind"), the harp-player picks up a Marine Band in A and plays that for most of the next verse. (Playing a harp that is tuned in the same key as the key of the song is sometimes called "straight harp.") However, in the middle of the last line of this verse ("Well you know you had the nerve to tell me"), the harp-player comes in with the octave harp. You'll notice that when he first comes in, the harp-player does not seem to have completely found his bearings on the octave-harp and plays a few notes that don't seem to fit with the key in which he's playing. And indeed very soon afterward in the song, the harp-player abandons the octave-harp for something more conventional. In the middle of the second line of the next verse (between "ain't it lonesome" and "sleeping by yourself"), the harp player comes back in with a D Marine Band and plays that for the remainder of the song. The octave harp on this session is the only use of such a harp that I'm familiar with in blues music.

157 without importing American artists: The British and the American musicians' unions each forbade the other to play in their country for fear that local musicians would lose work. "There wasn't a demand for British musicians in America," Chris Barber told me, "but there was a big demand in Europe and Britain for American music. People leapt on boats to Dublin. My band chartered a plane to see Louis Armstrong in Paris in 1956. We tried to arrange a British Louis Armstrong tour backed by us. The British union was communist run and the union guy actually said to me, 'Americans, bah! Why don't you get a Russian trumpeter?'" The stonewalling broke when the British union wanted to import Paul Robeson.

157 two four-song EPs: The first English EP was on Vogue, entitled *Muddy Waters with Little Walter,* subtitled *Mississippi Blues,* and it contained "I Can't Be Satisfied," "Feel Like Going Home," "Evans Shuffle," and "Louisiana Blues." The other was on the London label, named *Mississippi Blues: Muddy Waters and His Guitar,* and it featured "Young-Fashioned Ways," "Mannish Boy," "All Aboard," and "Forty Days and Forty Nights."

158 "I was going overseas": Guralnick interview with Muddy Waters.

158 "They thought I was a Big Bill Broonzy": Rooney, *Bossmen.*

159 "They began slowly, feeling their way": Standish, "Muddy Waters in London" part 1.

161 "I fled from the hall": Fancourt, Liner notes to *The Complete Muddy Waters.*

161 "I drove 'em crazy": Bill Dahl, "Muddy Waters Reigns As King." *Illinois Entertainer,* May 1981.

161 "When I wormed my way backstage": Wilmer, "First Time," p. 87.

161 "There weren't many black people in this country": Author interview with Val Wilmer.

In England, through great difficulty, Paul Oliver had acquired a photograph of Muddy, which he presented for an autograph. Muddy whipped out his rubber stamp and inkpad to hammer his signature. The ink was dry so he stamped it again, and several times more, until he'd covered the photograph in stamped signatures.

162 "I didn't play my guitar": Standish, "Muddy Waters in London" part 2.

163 red Telecaster: "A guy in Chicago made me a neck for it," Muddy told Tom Wheeler, "a big stout neck with the high nut to raise up the strings for slide. I needed to strengthen it up because of the big strings." (Wheeler, "Waters–Winter.")

"We went through a chain of amps," Jimmy Rogers told me. "Gibson was first and then we went from that to Fender and went from that to Standells. I like a Fender better than any amp that I've played. The sound of the Twin is clean and it's slick. I can dirty it up as much as I want, but I like for it to be clean."

163 "Now I know that the people in England": Palmer, *Deep Blues,* p. 258.

163 "I realized I could play guitar": Trynka, *Mojo* (April 1998).

Muddy left England on Monday, November 3, an eleven o'clock flight. He and Otis changed planes in New York, then on to Chicago. They arrived in time to make their regular Wednesday-night gig at the F&J Lounge in Gary. According to a note in *Billboard,* they made recordings during their New York layover: "Muddy, recently returned from Europe, will dish out some of the tunes he recorded on his return stay in NY." (Gart, *First Pressings*.)

163 post-Levittown affluence: By the decade's end, the Second City theater group, with Elaine May, Mike Nichols, and Ed Asner, was putting on a new, progressive kind of comedy show in Chicago.

164 "Folksong: '59": At Lomax's "Folksong: '59" in Carnegie Hall, April 3, 1959, Muddy brought Spann and Cotton and was provided a New York rhythm section. He did "Hoochie Coochie Man," then belted out "Walkin' Through the Park" before being joined by Memphis Slim, who did an instrumental that featured he and Spann trading licks on two pianos. Muddy stayed for Slim's two remaining numbers, providing sinuous backing on Slim's mellow interpretation of "Rollin' and Tumblin'" and a lonesome slide feel to "How Long Blues," the Leroy Carr song he'd told Lomax was the first he'd tried to learn. He leaves no doubt that he's mastered it. The songs were originally released on the 1959 United Artists album *Folk Song Festival at Carnegie Hall,* and have since been reissued as part of the Capitol Blues Collection (*Chicago Blues Masters: Muddy Waters and Memphis Slim*) on a CD that includes a set of studio collaborations the pair recorded in New York a couple years later.

164 "Big Bill Broonzy had recently died": Broonzy died August of 1958, and Muddy, along with Spann and Clay, had been among the pallbearers. Brother John Sellers, Tampa Red, and Sunnyland Slim were the other pallbearers.

165 Atlantic Records: Following Ertegun's visit to Smitty's Corner, Atlantic engaged Chess in a discussion about Muddy recording two dozen tracks with Atlantic's John Lewis; each label would release an album. (Gart, *First Pressings Vol. 8.*)

165 "increasing numbers of whites — Americans and Europeans": The winter before, in 1957, the Belgian fan Yannick Bruynoghe and his wife documented their prolonged stay in Chicago.

166 "I believe whitey's pickin' up on things that I'm doin'": Murray, *Shots,* p. 187.

11: MY DOG CAN BARK *1960–1967*

Newport: Richard Kurin, in *Smithsonian Folklife Festival* (p. 105), provides a brief history of the Newport festivals:

The Newport Folk Festival evolved from the Newport Jazz Festival. The Jazz Festival was initially an idea of Elaine and Louis Lorillard — tobacco heirs — to enhance the summer life of Newport's residents. They enlisted jazz impresario George Wein to produce the festival, beginning in 1954. After years of successful festivals, Wein, interested in the roots of jazz and in attracting college-student fans of popular folk groups such as the Kingston Trio, held the first Newport Folk Festival in 1959. Festivals in 1959 and 1960 were thought by people such as Pete Seeger to have too many city, professional performers and not enough folks. The Newport Folk Festival was reorganized in 1963 as a nonprofit foundation, with a board of directors including Seeger, Peter Yarrow, Theodore Bikel, Jean Ritchie, and others.

"[By the late 1950s], they started offering gigs at Carnegie Hall and Newport,"

Francis Clay remembered. "Muddy had never heard of them. He said, 'Man, you're driving me crazy with that Newport stuff.'" A festival atmosphere was not Muddy's normal environment, nor was the outdoors, nor was the daytime, nor the Northeast. The little pay barely made the great distance worth it. He was convinced by the other names on the bill: John Lee Hooker, Jimmy Rushing, Sammy Price, and fiddle and guitar duo Butch Cage and Willie Thomas.

European Friends: The Frenchmen Demetre and Chauvard were in America from September 10 to October 10, 1959. In a review of their book on its republication, Alan Balfour wrote, "Just how much information they gleaned from all those with whom they spoke is astonishing; information which laid the foundation for all future research into Chicago blues." (Balfour, "Land.") (*Land of the Blues* by Jacques Demetre and Marcel Chauvard is available through Soul Bag / CLARB, 25 rue Trezel, 92300 Levallois–Perrett, France. 176 pages, 94 photographs. Price: 190 French francs [postage included] payable by IMO or Visa / Mastercard.)

A longtime friendship was established the same year between Muddy and Georges Adins from Belgium. Adins had followed Muddy's 1958 British tour, talking with him in hotel rooms. Arriving in Chicago from the South — he'd hung with Lightnin' Hopkins in Houston and Sonny Boy Williamson in east St. Louis — Adins was invited by Muddy to stay at the Lake Park house, and he spent two weeks there. He fell right in, traveling to gigs with Muddy, joining him after Smitty's to visit a Jimmy Rogers set at Pepper's, then coming home to eat Muddy's corn bread and eggs in the wee hours. Muddy made him Cookie's godfather.

Georges and I hit it off quick; in September of 1998 he wrote, "I have of course a lot of family shots as well as pictures taken at club appearances in case your book would contain any pictures. Most of my collection is pasted in albums. . . . Maybe you can let me know how many you want for the book, if you prefer family pictures and others, if you want them glossy or matte, and also what size." News of his death came in May of 1999, as our friendship was blooming. I have tried, diligently but unsuccessfully, to locate his trove of material. Muddy's estate, Muddy's family, and various of Georges's friends have some of his photos, but these amount to a small percentage. Fellow researcher Robert Sacre has also tried to find the family, and he holds money in escrow as he searches.

Paul Oliver remembered Muddy's pride during his interview. "He didn't use any complex language but he'd stop and think and reply in a very considered way. It wasn't exactly spontaneous but I got the impression that it was important to him, and he respected the fact that I was a BBC reporter; he knew what the BBC was because he'd visited England." Oliver had further observations about other band members: "At the Tay May I became aware of how well Pat Hare played. His face was kind of scrunched up and he looked very, very mean onstage. I thought he was about fifty and actually he was about thirty-five; it was something deep-seated in his personality. Muddy liked to maintain the tension in his performance, Pat Hare worked up to it and then dropped back. Cotton also wouldn't play all the time. He liked to take two steps forward and cup his hand around the mike and scream out the choruses and then step back. When I saw Little Walter, he wouldn't stop playing. Walter came alive through his harp. He was difficult the rest of the time."

On Chris Barber's American visit, he sat in with Muddy in Gary, Indiana. "I knew how to play those blues," he said. "At the end of the first set, I put my trombone down, and this elegant black girl — the only people in America who looked smartly dressed to us Europeans were black people, everyone else wore Bermuda shorts and floral shirts — she leaned back in her chair and said, 'Say, are you Chris Barber?' I said yes. She said, 'Is that your record, "That Petite Fleur"?' I said yes. She said, 'I don't like it.'" Robert Koester also remembered Barber sitting in. "I went to the washroom and a guy came up to me and said what the hell is that strange horn that guy is playing?" Barber remembered: "Another funny thing, Muddy bent down on one knee, and he hitched up his trouser so it wouldn't get dirty, but he hitched up the wrong one. Also, Muddy would always talk confidentially to you, covering his mouth with his hand, but he'd cover the wrong side, blocking his mouth instead of concealing it."

Barber and Ottilie were also at Muddy's Carnegie Hall show in 1961 and followed the band to their penthouse suite at the Theresa Hotel in Harlem. "They were playing up there till five in the morning," said Barber. "Muddy sent his bodyguard [Bo] out to buy food periodically, and they got Ottilie to make bacon and eggs." When they'd slept it off the next afternoon, the musicians drove back to Chicago the way they'd come out: directly. Just another one-night stand.

Harold Pendleton, Barber's partner, also visited Chicago: "Our drummer Graham Burbridge was asking Francis Clay about triplets, because no one over here knew how to play them. As a result of our trip to Chicago, we left skiffle — Lonnie Donegan was by then singing songs like 'Does Your Spearmint Lose Its Flavor on the Bedpost Overnight.' We found Cyril Davies, who played mouth organ in a folk club, and we found Alexis Korner, who understood blues, and we added them to the Chris Barber Band for a blues set at the Marquee on Wednesday nights. Because our clubs were not licensed [for alcoholic beverages], an evening had two sets, with an interval set in between, so the main act could go to the pub. But the twenty-minute interval kept getting extended and we eventually gave Cyril, Alexis, and Long John Baldry Thursday night. Alexis could never find a drummer, Graham Burbridge was the only one who could play that style — because he'd been trained at Smitty's Corner. They did eventually find a drummer in the name of Charlie Watts. The Rolling Stones became the interval group on Thursday nights."

Europe in the 1960s: Willie Dixon told this great Sonny Boy story in his short-lived column, "I Am the Blues," in *Living Blues*:

Sonny Boy had a big coffee pot and this particular coffee pot he used for cookin'. One mornin' in Baden-Baden [1963], we just played a concert and we was intending to eat but wasn't no other place open. Just about time we were beginning to sleep, we smell something reeeal good. Somebody cooking onions or garlic and everybody was hungry anyways. So people went down to the restaurant, thought maybe the restaurant had opened back up. So finally everybody got to sleep. Then I heard a rumbling in the hall, everybody goes to the door, some of the guys have knives. Sonny Boy got a little short German feller by the collar in one hand, his knife open in the other hand. This little guy he's tryin' to explain to Sonny Boy that he's the hotel detective but Sonny Boy can't understand. Sonny Boy said, "This guy a peepin' Tom, because this guy is goin' around peeping through the key-

holes." He was smellin' around the doors to see if he could find out where
it is the aroma was comin' from. Finally they pry Sonny Boy aloose from
this guy and tell him, "Man, he's the house detective and he's tryin' to find
out somebody cookin' around here." This guy had on a little red tie. He's
much smaller than Sonny, he's pullin' back, he's tryin' to explain. This guy
was pullin' so hard. Sonny Boy took this guy's tie with his knife and cut it off,
right up to his neck, and this guy tumbled backwards down the steps. . . .
So about time it got good and quiet again . . . this aroma is still smelling
gooood. So I ease up and pull the door open real slow and look down the
hall, there was Sonny Boy barefoot in a night shirt — it was just about up
to his knees. And he beckons for me to come over there. "Hey, come on in
here, man, get some of these pig tails." This guy, in this very big coffee pot
of his, he's cookin' pig tails in beans. With onions and everything.

Joe Boyd visited Chicago a month before the 1964 tour and saw Muddy at Pepper's. "We were the only white people in the place. That tour was right along a cultural fault line for the blues. Within a year or two, the black audience fell away and
the white audience soared and that cannot help but change the music."

In a 1978 backstage interview, Muddy was asked by a reporter for *Dark Star*
magazine about the Rolling Stones. "They helped turn the white people around in
America," Muddy answered, "recording our records and putting our names on
them. When I first came out on records, white people didn't want their kids to buy
my records, called it 'nigger music.' Said, 'Blues is nigger music.'" The interviewer
interjected, "Race music," and Muddy answered, "They wouldn't say 'race,' say
'nigger.'"

Paul Butterfield and Newport: An Elektra Records executive flew to Chicago to
hear Butterfield's band at Big John's on New Year's Eve, 1964–1965. The group was
racially mixed, with Elvin Bishop, Jerome Arnold, Sam Lay, and, in short order,
Michael Bloomfield. "I heard the most amazing thing I'd ever heard in my life,"
Paul Rothchild said. "I said to myself, 'Here is the beginning of another era. This is
another turning point in American music's direction.'" (Von Schmidt and Rooney,
Baby, p. 248.) They promptly cut "Born in Chicago," which sold 200,000 copies and
established the band's reputation.

"What we played was music that was entirely indigenous to the neighborhood,
to the city that we grew up in," Butterfield said. He continued:

There was no doubt in my mind that this was folk music; this was what I
heard on the streets of my city, out the windows, on radio stations and
jukeboxes in Chicago and all throughout the South, and it was what people
listened to. And that's what folk meant to me — what people listened to.
Lomax implied in his introduction that this was how low Newport had
sunk, bringing an act like this onto the stage, and our manager, Albert
Grossman, said, "How can you give these guys this type of introduction?
This is really out of line. You're a real prick to do this." They got into a fistfight, these two elderly guys, right there in front of the stage, rolling in the
dirt while we were playing and I was screaming, "Kick his ass, Albert!
Stomp 'im!" There was bad blood rising, you could tell. (Ward, *Bloomfield,*
p. 44)

Butterfield's first album, recorded directly after Newport 1965, included Muddy's "Got My Mojo Working."

Shortly after Newport, Butterfield played three nights (one hundred bucks each night) at a Cambridge coffeehouse, Club 47. "He told me that I should get some of the other bands from Chicago, starting with Muddy Waters," said Jim Rooney, who was managing the club. The afternoon of opening night, Rooney phoned Muddy at the Hotel Diplomat. "I said, 'What kind of coffee would you like?' and he said, 'TSIVAS.' I said, 'What?' 'TSIVAS.' 'What?' 'TSIVAS! Tsivas Regal!' And I said, 'You've got it.' That night he got a bottle of Chivas Regal and everything was straight." (Von Schmidt and Rooney, *Baby,* p. 270.)

"[At Muddy's show] I walked into the men's room of the Club 47," said Peter Wolf, later vocalist with the J. Geils Band. "I had heard about Butterfield through the grapevine. In person, it was incredible. It seemed that all the Chicago bands started coming to town. . . . and there was Cotton, Spann, and S. P. Leary all gathered around a pint. They are my idols, so I picked up my cue real good and ran out and scored a couple of pints, and after the next show they were all over me, and my apartment was only four blocks away." (Ibid, pp. 268 and 272.)

1966 Gigs: In January of 1966, Muddy brought most of the band to Toronto for the taping of a CBC–TV special, "Bell Telephone Presents the Blues." In addition to performing, Muddy and Spann informally exchanged stories with Willie Dixon and Sunnyland Slim. The highlight of the performances is Spann solo, the whiskey on his breath nearly tangible, singing "Tain't Nobody's Business (If I Do)." A motto, clearly.

In April 1966, while touring with Big Mama Thornton — also managed by Bob Messinger — the band stopped at Coast Recorders in San Francisco to back her on *Big Mama Thornton and the Chicago Blues Band,* some of which has been compiled on her CD *Ball and Chain* (Arhoolie CD-305). A feisty woman who knew about being screwed by the music business — she'd recorded the original "Hound Dog," but because she hadn't written it, she received nothing but an honorable mention when Elvis's version became an international hit — she drew a hard edge from Muddy's band.

The band took three gigs over 1966 at New York's Cafe au Go-Go: May, August, and November. At the August date, Muddy's band did triple duty, backing Spann on the opening set and then backing John Lee Hooker as well as Muddy. The August dates yielded two BluesWay albums, one for Spann (*The Blues Is Where It's At*) and one for Hooker (*Live at the Cafe au Go-Go*), though Hooker's tracks may have been recut later. Spann's album is some of the best-sounding Muddy from the 1960s. Hooker, best heard alone, is ably backed by Muddy's ensemble; they understood the boogie groove at the core of Hooker's style and knew not to count bars and change chords until he did — if he did. In November, they were part of "The Blues Bag," a series running hot at the club that featured several name acts doing short sets in rapid sequence. There were matinees for younger kids, where the club sold ice cream instead of liquor; most kids snuck in their own bottle. Despite the cold rain, the line at the door was four people deep and ran around the block. One critic noted Sammy Lawhorn's "speed of execution that is breathtaking." (Kunstadt, *Record Research.*) While in New York for the November date, the band cut an album for Victoria Spivey's Spivey label as The Muddy Waters Blues Band; only Muddy was signed to Chess, so they were free to step out. Muddy participates on some tracks, credited as "Main Stream." This record is hard to find and generally worth the search.

In the wee hours, after a night of the May gig at Cafe au Go-Go, Muddy and Spann went to a nearby FM radio station for an interview, recorded by Bob Messinger. After the disc jockey's rambling start, a decent interview evolved, along with some real good music.

Band Personnel: One night, when the band happened to be in St. Louis, a gunman came into Smitty's, fire in his eyes and a firearm in his hand. "If we'd been sitting on that bandstand, we'd all be dead," said Cotton. "He said that everybody was going with his wife. And then he shot up into the ceiling. We heard about that, got kind of scared, and soon everybody had a little gun. And then it cooled off. So I'm standing up on Forty-third Street one night waiting on a bus, had a few drinks. And I look around and he is there with a .38 in his hand and he says, 'How come you treat me like you did?' And he pulled the trigger on it. Five times I got it. Never did nothing to him in my life. It scared every musician in the city. If he hadn't gone to jail right away, he'd'a been killed."

When Cotton left, he was replaced by George "Mojo" Buford. Buford was born in Hernando, Mississippi, in 1929 and began singing in spiritual groups before he was ten. He moved to Memphis in 1944, where he was exposed to more urban blues artists such as B. B. King and others on WDIA. He got to Chicago around 1953 and wound up in a group that got busy on the South Side. Spann heard them, sent Muddy by, and Buford's group became Muddy's "junior" band, filling his gigs when he'd travel out of town. (For more background, see Wisner, "Buford.")

Pat Hare was notoriously jealous. He'd often run to the phone between sets to make sure his girlfriend was home and not out being unfaithful. When she didn't answer one night, Hare took a Winchester rifle to her apartment and demanded to be let in. There was, of course, no answer. He fired through the front window. Ever the dutiful bandleader, Muddy helped him hide out; when the heat didn't let up, Muddy got him to Memphis. In May of 1963, when the scene cooled, Hare left Memphis for Minneapolis and a band with Mojo Buford. "Me and Jojo Williams went to Arkansas to pick him up," said Buford. "He was working on a farm, picking cotton and driving tractors." (Darwen, "Buford," p. 11.) He murdered his baby in Minneapolis six months later. (For a comprehensive account of Pat Hare's life and demise, see Hahn, "Blues Guitarist.")

168 Spann, who stepped out as leader: The labels for which Spann recorded include Fontana, Storyville, Prestige, Arhoolie, Decca, Spivey, Testament, Vanguard, Blues Horizon, Bluestimes, and Delmark, for which he employed, in addition to Muddy's band: Johnny Shines, Junior Wells, Johnny Young, and, later, younger white players such as Eric Clapton, Paul Butterfield, Michael Bloomfield, and Fleetwood Mac. A recently published Spann discography is marvelous. Begun by the late Bill Rowe, it features an excellent introduction by Alan Balfour and makes for informative perusal. (Available through Micrography Discographical Publications, Wkoestduinstraat 84, NL–1058 TJ Amsterdam, The Netherlands.)

170 "A sturdy man": Demetre and Chauvard, *Land of the Blues,* p. 59.

170 Kokomo Arnold: Ibid., p. 128.

171 "Muddy roared, leaped, jerked": Leadbitter, *Blues,* p. 11.

172 Bob Koester, whose Delmark Records: While Chess, unwittingly playing the role of Lester Melrose, was packaging Muddy in costumes that didn't fit, new blues fans were following the lead of Aristocrat two decades earlier and forming their own labels. Before founding Delmark Records, Bob Koester sold 78s through the mail from his St. Louis dormitory room. His first jazz release was in 1953; he moved the label to Chicago in 1958 and, after meeting Big Joe Williams and Speckled Red and helping recover Sleepy John Estes and Yank Rachel from oblivion in the early 1960s, began releasing blues.

176 his valet, C. D.: Jimmy Lee Morris knew him and said, "He got both Muddy's ladies strung out on drugs. And he's supposed to have been his friend. He was pushing that shit, had a pocket full of money. C. D. lived in the neighborhood."

177 "the reverends": Reverend Willie Morganfield, whose father — Muddy's uncle — had been a preacher on Stovall, was staying in Muddy's house in the early 1960s. He'd scored a major gospel hit in 1959 with "What Is This?"

"Muddy was a person like this," said Reverend Morganfield. "He respected my father. My father was a minister. And he knew my father wouldn't appreciate if I was singing rock and roll or blues. So Muddy didn't really encourage me. But when I got a call from a company that was going to give me forty-six thousand dollars to do two rock and roll songs, he said, 'They wouldn't have to ask me twice, I'd go right on and do it.' But my father had written a song for me entitled 'I Can't Afford to Let My Savior Down,' and that's what stayed with me all night, it just worried me and worried me, so the next morning I got up and told the guy I couldn't do it, it wasn't in me. Muddy wasn't churchy. That was his business."

178 Life had not improved for Azelene: After Cookie, Azelene gave birth to four more children, dispersing them to others. "We have one brother we don't know anything about," Cookie said, "because she was on drugs and left him in the hospital."

179 "The Muddy Waters Twist": Though Muddy's version was something of a reach, the dance had its redeeming value: it got the girls shaking. At a 1961 Ole Miss University dance, that, however, led to a step back in time. "The twist was out, and none of them girls ain't studying about no color," Muddy told McKee. "We were playing that music, they were getting down doing the twist. Them girls down, their little white panties showing. I was scared to look anyway — I had my head over, looking like a pump handle. So help me Jesus Christ, they put them lights out! If I'm lying, I don't want to say another word to you — they put them lights out!" (McKee and Chisenhall interview with Muddy Waters.)

Willie Smith also remembered the incident: "Just like it always was, they didn't want us to see those white girls shaking their booties so they had us to play in the dark. The one that put the lights out wasn't nothing but kitchen help. She was an old white woman, sixties or seventies, nothing you could do to change her ways. She did everything she could to disturb what was going on, but everyone was drinking moonshine and having a good time. It was raining cats and dogs when we were through and she put us out. We knew she wasn't nothing but help in the kitchen but she was white and we didn't want to start no trouble, so we obeyed. We was used to rain anyway. Sat in the car till the man got the check. He apologized. If you was black, you stayed back — at that time."

179 "Muddy let Cotton run his show": Trynka interview with Billy Boy Arnold.

179 "Wolf was better at managing": Trynka interview with Jimmy Rogers.

180 "unemployment compensation": Trynka interview with Billy Boy Arnold.

180 Charlie Musselwhite: He was raised in Memphis, on a road that dead-ended into a creek and a field. Said Musselwhite, "I'd hear people singing blues in those fields. I'd be a little kid playing in the creek, and I'd hear that music — that singing — and man, it just wrapped itself around me." (Bill Ellis, "Charlie Musselwhite: The Blues Overtook Me," *Memphis Commercial Appeal*, June 9, 1997, Sec. C.) Musselwhite moved to Chicago and drove an exterminator's truck; he told me, "I got to know the whole city right away. I remember around the Maxwell Street area, seeing a sign for Elmore James. And I'd go back at night and it was such a thrill. I didn't connect Chicago with blues at all. To me, it was a big city up North where it was easy to get a good-paying job. I'd see these friends of mine going up the hillbilly highway in these old jalopies and then come back a year or two later in a brand-new car. So that looked good to me. Especially after I had been digging ditches over in Arkansas for a buck an hour." After appearing with Big Walter Horton on a Vanguard Records anthology, Musselwhite released his first solo record, *Stand Back!*, on Vanguard at age twenty-two. He left Chicago in August of 1967.

180 Pepper's Lounge: When the music quit around four, Willie Smith usually hit the basement for some gambling. "That's where the dice game was," he said. "The cops used to get in on the game. We knew all the cops on the beat. Some of them later moved off the street into headquarters, and sometimes we'd recognize each other there from Pepper's basement."

182 "You Shook Me": The track was released as an instrumental for Earl Hooker, "Blue Guitar," on the Age label.

183 *Blues from Big Bill's Copa Cabana*: Buddy Guy said, "Jeff Beck and Eric Clapton, every time I see them they'll bring that album up and say, 'This is what turnt me around with the blues.' They'll show me those little licks I was doing." In the 1990s, Clapton had Guy re-create his track "Don't Know Which Way to Go" on the soundtrack to *Rush*. "I came up with the song," Guy said, "and come to hear they gave Willie Dixon credit for writing it." Around the time of the Big Bill recording, Muddy appeared on two Chicago TV programs, one entitled "For Blacks Only," and the other, "Jazz Supports the Symphony."

Buddy Guy, a sharecropper's son born in 1936 in the country about sixty miles from Baton Rouge, was raised on acoustic blues. "The first electric guitar I seen in my life was Lightnin' Slim. I didn't know what the hell that was. He came out in the country, plugged into a storefront, and started playing

John Lee Hooker's 'Boogie Chillen.' I had my allowance, thirty cents, and I put it in his hat. I got to know him." In 1956, Guy climbed atop his high school roof to watch Muddy's "Mojo Working" tour.

183 *Folk Singer:* A return to the earlier style probably appealed to Leonard too. His interest in the record label and recording was fading as it became more complex, and he began to branch out. In 1963, he purchased WVON radio, selecting the call letters because they stood for "The Voice of the Negro."

184 "Back at his London hotel": Wilmer, "First Time," p. 87.

187 Upon returning to the states: Writer Peter Guralnick drove from Boston to Hunter College in New York for his first opportunity to see Muddy perform, even though it meant staying up all night to drive back.

> Muddy, when he declared that he had a black cat bone and a mojo too, and when he tilted his head to one side, assumed that quizzically stolid look, and roared out, "I just want to make love to you"— Muddy might just as well have been eight feet tall, he was so majestic. On the last number of the set (it was his signature tune, "Got My Mojo Working,") he corkscrewed out one leg, hitched up his pants, and abandoned himself to a jitterbug, dancing with a concentration all the more remarkable in so stoic and ungainly a man. The crowd went wild. (Peter Guralnick, "Muddy Waters, 1915–1983," *Boston Phoenix*, May 10, 1983, Sec. 3)

Guralnick wrote of Otis Spann:

> . . . a mournful, diminutive, and slightly bewildered-looking man. From his familiar position, half-hidden and pushed into a corner by the oversized grand piano, he would hold court, carrying on a running conversation with the tables around him and offering well-meant, gratuitous advice to an audience that could barely pick up his words. He played with his head flung back, swinging his legs loosely off the floor and facing that piano at an angle with a fine disregard for the microphone. (Guralnick, *Highway*, p. 289)

187 "a white is going to get it": Bloomfield, "An Interview with Muddy Waters," p. 7.

188 "From two blocks away": Ward, *Michael Bloomfield*, p. 21.

> Marshall Chess said of Mike Bloomfield: "When my dad started making money around the time of Chuck Berry's 'Maybelline,' we moved from the South Side of Chicago to the northern suburbs. Bloomfield went to the same high school, I was a couple of years older. Mike Bloomfield must have been fourteen, and I went over to his house and he had a cherry red Gibson and he was playing Chuck Berry riffs and asking me about Chuck Berry and about music. I brought him a slide from the studio. He had never had a slide."

188 "When we started the Rolling Stones": Obrecht, "Muddy, Wolf, and Me."

188 "When I got to hear Muddy Waters": Bockris, *Keith Richards*, p. 38.

> The Stones left Chess with an album's worth of material, initially released as the EP *Five X Five*. "The Stones had one album out," Marshall Chess remembered. "I always was a Stones fan, they had something of Chess Records in their sexuality. I felt very comfortable with their music. At that time no one recorded at Chess but Chess artists. Andrew Oldham called me and said, 'We

are coming to America, can we record?' And I talked to my dad and we let them record. They came to Chicago and I was shocked. They were drinking straight whiskey out of bottles, and Brian Jones had the longest hair. Muddy came by, I remember Willie Dixon, because we were trying to hustle songs to them, by then we understood we could sell hundreds of thousands getting our song in. I took Brian Jones back to his hotel in my 1964 red Porsche convertible. No one in Chicago had ever seen a man with long hair. People started screaming, 'You homos.'" Marshall does not remember Muddy ever painting a ceiling at Chess. He also discounts stories of the family hiring Muddy to bartend at private parties during his lean years.

188 "We pulled up with the equipment": Guy and Wilcock, *Damn Right,* p. 57.

189 "get your ass down": Cohodas interview with Billy Davis.

189 "The Rolling Stones created a whole wide-open space": Murray, *Shots,* p. 188.

190 "Muddy had the best band": McCulley, "Father and Sons."

190 "Talent Deserving of Wider Recognition": Recognition wasn't going to feed families, and there were more personnel changes. Willie Smith initially quit in the mid-1960s to make more money hustling a cab. Clay came back, locked horns with Muddy, and left for the final time around 1967, which was when Willie Smith returned. In May of 1963, James Cotton returned to the band, replacing Mojo Buford, who, in his first of several stints, had seen more of the inside of a station wagon than he'd imagined possible. Cotton's year off proved a learning experience. "I found out during that time I wasn't a bandleader and people didn't know who I was, so I went back to Muddy to learn a few things." When he left again in 1966, George "Harmonica" Smith returned to replace him.

191 Muddy squeezed in an Apollo gig: "I met Lou Rawls at the Apollo and Gladys Knight and the Pimps (*sic*)," said Lucille. "Gladys Knight's brother thought I was Muddy's daughter, asked Muddy if he could take me out. Muddy told him, 'This is my wife!' Sammy Lawhorn got drunk, started cussing and act like he was fixing to jump on Muddy and Bo jumped on him. Bloodied his nose. Muddy cussed him out. Muddy was good for cussing."

191 "We were boogying": Von Schmidt and Rooney, *Baby,* p. 253.

192 basis for rock and roll: Buddy Guy toured Europe with 1965's American Folk Blues Festival, and after playing a song as close to James Brown's funk as to Muddy's blues, Buddy explained: "That's a little touch of the blues," but then he corrected himself and added, "or should I say Chicago blues," and then he considered that that definition wasn't accurate either and added, "with the beat to it." He used the same words Muddy had used when differentiating his style from his antecedents.

193 Batt's Restaurant: "We didn't have a coffee machine at 2120," Marshall Chess remembered. "I walked across that fucking street fifty times a day, for my father and Phil, bringing the coffee. We'd go to Batt's all the time. It was a Jewish restaurant. Chuck would order strawberry shortcake and then bacon and eggs, all backwards. If Muddy came in at lunchtime, 'Let's go get a sandwich.' And we'd walk across the street. We were regulars, every waitress knew us, we had our own tab."

193 "I had a lot of people listen at me:" O'Neal and van Singel, "Muddy Waters."

194 *Muddy, Brass, & the Blues:* Most of the songs get in an unadulterated verse or so
before the parade comes through. Several of the tracks have, over the years,
been issued as "hornless remixes," and nothing makes plainer how unneces-
sary the overdubbed instruments are. Spann plays chunky piano parts, knowing the horns will be all over the songs' turnarounds and spaces; the guitars
mostly lay back. "Black Night" breathes like a moonless sky, Cotton's harp
sounding like a distant cicada hopping trees until it's in Muddy's backyard.

194 "My Dog Can't Bark": The song was recorded on May 18, 1965, and "Highway 61 Revisited" was recorded on August 2, 1965. Bloomfield was living in
Chicago and went to New York for the Dylan sessions.

194 "you're going to get a whuppin'": Jones, *Melody Maker,* p. 29.

12: ROLLIN' STONE *1967–1969*

Electric Mud, After the Rain, **Marshall Chess, and the Players:** "Look," the Chess
Records advertising manager said in 1967, pointing to the inside front cover of a
successful teen record magazine. "There's my first Muddy Waters ad for the teeny
boppers." (Brack, "No Credibility Gap," p. 62.) Teeny boppers never really happened for Muddy, but the hippies did, a youth market that Marshall Chess reached
out to. Marshall was raised in the business. His earliest memory is being tossed by
his father to his Uncle Phil when shooting broke out at the Macomba. Wolf urged
Marshall early to get laid. "Wolf once told me — and I remember this because I
was so little and it was so shocking — 'The best pussy is wino pussy. You want
to take them in the alley and fuck them and then you leave. They don't be bothering you.'"

Before producing *Electric Mud,* Marshall had previously packaged straight
blues albums in psychedelic covers "to get them into the blues." The goal was similar for *Electric Mud* and *After the Rain,* though the methodology was inverted. The
low-key, black-and-white covers don't hint at the non-Muddy content within, except perhaps for the hideousness of the frog and slime showered on Muddy for *After the Rain.* (The inner spread of *Electric Mud,* however, is very nearly worth the
price of admission: a black-and-white photo essay of Muddy having his hair
processed at a parlor that boasts, "World's largest in beauty." He is regal even with
rollers in his hair.)

When the finished *Electric Mud* was presented to Muddy, he couldn't get past
the idea that, if it became popular, he would be unable to replicate the sounds from
the stage; how, in 1968, could he re-create the backward tape on "Mannish Boy"?
Then again, "Chess thought they could make some money off of those," said
Muddy, "and hell I could use some money too." (Murray, *Shots,* p. 190.)

Between the two Muddy sessions, Wolf was brought in for his psychedelic album, an experience he hated. Guitarist Pete Cosey recalled, "When we did the
Howlin' Wolf session, the Wolf was outraged at all those electronics. He was angry.
He didn't consider that the blues. During the sessions he would scowl. Phil Chess
came in and tried to console him. Wolf dropped a real good lug on me. I had a real
long beard, my shades, a big natural. The Wolf looked at me and he said, 'Why
don't you take them wah-wahs and all that other shit and go throw it off in the

lake — on your way to the barber shop.' He just wiped all the shit out in one stroke." Cosey continued, "Charles Stepney's arrangements were beautifully tight, yet open enough to let the guys do what they do. He had the patterns written; the groove on 'Herbert Harper' was locked. The other things were relatively simple by comparison. I did a lot of overdubbing on *After the Rain,* where on *Electric Mud* I only overdubbed once or twice. I got to use the bowed guitar on *After the Rain,* as I did with the Howlin' Wolf album. I did a little solo bowed guitar on 'Bottom of the Sea' and 'I Am the Blues.' 'Rambling Mind,' when Muddy did that before, he played traditional blues. But Charles utilized a line from a classical piece as a turn-around. The song was in twelve-bar blues, but when we came to the turnaround, instead of using the fifth and the fourth, we played the classical line. That was a really funky groove."

Bassist Louis Satterfield told Matt Sakakeeny, "The spirit that we came with — me, Pete, Charles Stepney — we were talking about being free and that's what it is. Free. When you're recording music, all you can put on a record is vibrations. How you vibrate determines how well people will receive it. They can't see you, they don't know nothing except how they feel when they hear it. We did not deviate too far away from the original, but we did stretch it out. You listen to it, Muddy was coming real strong. He hasn't changed anything in how he's singing. We called it preaching, how exuberant he was, how he could reach out and touch people. Muddy was a very witty guy. He would sit there, always positive, always dressed up. Sometimes when he would really get sharp he'd put on a blue suit and a white shirt and a red tie and red socks."

The photo session for *After the Rain* still rankles Cosey. "They sent us to Victor Screbneski, a famous photographer in Chicago known worldwide for doing fashion layouts. They wanted us to pose nude from the waist up and with creatures. Satterfield and myself refused to do it. They had some sort of liquid they wanted to smear the body with. We didn't think that was in good taste. Muddy did it for the cover. Phillip Upchurch was into snakes, so he took a picture with a snake and used it for his own album."

Electric Mud is Muddy's most polarizing record. It attracted a new audience in the hip-hop era. "To me it's a brilliant record," Chuck D. told me. "I've played it a thousand times. The voice and the character of Muddy Waters stand above the new music. Muddy's vocals *project.* That's what created a hook for me to get into it: these vocals are actually pulling the music. *Electric Mud* introduced me to other Muddy Waters stuff. It took me a while to warm up to traditional blues. A whole new world. But the automatic thing that struck me right away was the *Electric Mud* thing."

Fathers and Sons: "Bloomfield," said Marshall Chess, "he was always emotionally a basket case. During *Fathers and Sons,* he was so scared of playing with Muddy a couple of times that he took heavy tranqs. He had a lot of soul but he was a troubled, pained person, like a lot of blues singers are. And he liked drugs and alcohol, just like them."

The Thursday-night show at Chicago's Auditorium Theater drew an almost all-white audience of 2,800. Billed as the Cosmic Joy–Scout Super Jam, it blended deep hippie culture with deep blues. As fans found their seats, a lone musician plucked an African finger piano. According to Don DeMichael's review in *Rolling Stone,* "His ping-a-dinging sounded like there was a little air in the radiators." After the hippie mish-mash speech that followed ("thousands of years ago there were one people, one tongue, and three Faces. . . .") came a group so bad (The Ace of Cups) the critic wondered if it was a put-on. (DeMichael, "Muddy Waters Week," pp. 12–13.) Finally the *Fathers and Sons* band took the stage and warmed the house. Then Muddy toasted it. He was playing to a younger audience, many seeing him for the first time. "On 'Mojo' he put his guitar down," said Marshall Chess, "he did a dance and he was Rudolf Nureyev for fifteen seconds. It was like he was a ballerina, lightness on his feet."

In their excitement, Chess overestimated the market and shipped many more records than they would sell. Crates were being returned well into the next year, and one warehouse employee grumbled, "Who put out this stiff? Who put out this fucking stiff?" (Guralnick, *Home,* p. 238.) It was an ignoble coda to an otherwise successful effort.

Band Personnel: Born August 30, 1934, Luther "Snake" Johnson stopped picking cotton in rural Davidson, Georgia, when Santa Claus brought him a guitar. In Chicago, he did stints behind Howlin' Wolf and Junior Wells before realizing his boyhood dream of backing Muddy Waters. He was in the band when Bob Margolin joined: "He used to do endless versions of Wilson Pickett's 'Don't Knock My Love' as well as soul groove originals like 'Give Me My Check' (a welfare song) and 'Pull Out Your False Teeth, Baby, I Wants to Suck on Your Gums.'" Jimmy Lee Morris remembers, "Snake got scalded. His wife throwed some hot shit on his ass, lye, and burned him up, man. Every so often that stuff would rise up on his arms — big old water blisters, come up, go down, come up and go down."

When Luther Johnson moved to guitar, Lawrence "Sonny" Wimberley assumed the bass. Drummer S. P. Leary (born June 6, 1930) returned in 1967 for his longest stint with the band. An old-school drummer, he'd backed T-Bone Walker in Texas before he was old enough to drive. He came to Chicago around 1954, later joined Jimmy Rogers, and eventually played with most of Chicago's blues greats, including a long stint with Wolf. He'd recorded several sessions with Muddy as early as 1964 (including "The Same Thing"). S. P. could pull out his brushes, keep it firm when he played soft, letting Muddy whisper "Nineteen Years Old" and "Five Long Years."

Getting in Muddy's band had always been easier than getting out; when S. P. was too drunk to play, Snake assumed the drums and Muddy picked up the slack on the guitar. When Snake stepped out on his own, S. P. Leary was thrown out the open door. Willie Smith reassumed the drummer's chair, though slowly. First he took a single gig at the end of 1968; a tour offer followed. "We started talking about money. I was driving that cab hard, fourteen or fifteen hours a day. Muddy guaranteed me a certain amount, so I took a chance on it. But I kept my chauffeur's license up for about five years just in case."

Clay left the band for good by the end of the 1960s. While there's probably some truth to the following anecdote, I found Clay's stories colored by his resentment or dislike of Muddy. Clay says that when the band was nearing Chicago after a tour, he phoned his girlfriend. "We'd pull up, she'd be waiting for me at Muddy's house. Muddy would get mad every time he'd see that. I was getting my clothes out of the station wagon, next thing I know, jealous cat, Muddy whipped out his black-jack and was coming toward me. He didn't have any girlfriends who cared anything about him, they just wanted to take and take and take."

Also back on the scene, not in Muddy's band but with his encouragement, was former sideman Jimmy Rogers. "They was all worryin' me about hittin' the road again. Europe was somethin' I was wantin' to see anyway. That started me back up. I don't mind travelin' just as long as I got 'my train fare home.'" (Brisbin, "Havin' Fun," p. 27.) Freddie King, who used to sneak into the Zanzibar to watch Jimmy's fingers, brought his mentor to Shelter Records, a label run by young blues enthusiasts (including Leon Russell).

Other Recordings: When the Chess brothers visited the *Super Blues* session, Esmond Edwards, who'd been producing jazz records, had rarely seen them in action. "Phil and Leonard came up there and sat around," said Edwards, "urging them on. 'Hey motherfucker' this and 'What's wrong with you.' It was the revelation of an entirely different studio milieu than I had been accustomed to. You don't talk to jazz artists that way. But the guys took it. I don't know if it was a plantation thing or what, but no one got insulted. Muddy just grinned."

In November of 1967, Muddy's manager Bob Messinger put the group in the studio for a label run by Alan Douglas, who had recorded Jimi Hendrix. Contractually restricted from recording for anyone but Chess, Muddy was made producer. "Muddy was featuring Georgia Boy and he was all for recording him," said Messinger. They recorded about twenty tracks, then spread them across two albums. *Chicken Shack* featured Luther Johnson, *Mud in Your Ear* featured Mojo Buford, though everyone — Spann, Lawhorn, Wimberley, and Clay — had his say. Muddy did not cherish the producer's role. "It ain't too cool for me, man, 'cause you trying to tell someone something, and maybe they'll think your ideas is too square. I'd rather for them to have their own ideas and let someone else do that work and I'll do my real job." (Guralnick interview with Muddy Waters.)

Some of the best Muddy on record from this era is on the Otis Spann album *The Bottom of the Blues* for ABC's BluesWay label, also recorded in November of 1967. Muddy contributed two songs. The unlikely "Shimmy Baby" is set to S. P. Leary's wicked marching beat, with a strong New Orleans parade feel; it sounds much more like Spann's swinging knee than Muddy's foot tapping. "I haven't been writing much," Muddy told Guralnick, hastening to add, "All Otis's stuff, I wrote it also." Spann would soon part company with Muddy. The album's other outstanding track is also claimed by Muddy and is much more likely by him. A deep blues number, "Looks Like Twins" features his slide guitar; it's about lovers staying together because they look so much alike, making it a mate to Muddy's "Kinfolks Blues," a contemporaneous recording wherein Muddy breaks off an incestuous relationship because of the gossip.

Muddy accompanied Otis Spann at a memorial concert for Dr. Martin Luther King, assassinated in Memphis in April of 1968. With little to interfere — Willie Dixon is the only other musician — the affinity that made these two call each other "brother" is easily heard. They can be heard on the *Live the Life* album, which also includes intimate live recordings of Muddy leading his full band.

East Coast and Beyond: While on the East Coast, the band was treated to one of the highlights of Muddy's relationship with manager Bob Messinger. "I negotiated a deal with Guild Guitars to get them all guitars, basses, amplifiers. Guild was over in Jersey City, and we drove there. We were so happy that day. Muddy got three guitars." (Setting aside his Telecaster, Muddy picked up a Guild S-200 Thunderbird guitar, which he held during the photo session for *Electric Mud* — not that he played any guitar on the album.)

At the 1969 Newport Folk Festival, Muddy shared the bill with Son House, Sleepy John Estes, Yank Rachel, Jesse Fuller, Buddy Moss, Taj Mahal, and Big Mama Thornton. "Big Mama had her Cadillac in the parking lot backstage, and she cooked for the black acts and sold them soul food," said Bob Messinger, who was managing her as well as Muddy. "She had a butane stove. I didn't pay much attention to it because I had booked her on the job and I didn't want to be associated with it. George Wein, who always demanded quiet backstage and decorum, never said a word."

In Boston, kids not old enough to drink could attend shows as long as they didn't sit at a table. Like hawks on mice, Muddy, approaching sixty, and Spann, forty, hovered over that section. "When I was fourteen, into the Stones, a friend told me to listen to Muddy," said Barbara "Candy" Purro. "He came to the Jazz Workshop and I went with my girlfriend. We had to sit on the side, and Muddy and Spann started talking to us. Muddy was a total gentleman. Otis drank a lot. Every time they'd come to town, they'd get us into the shows, and Muddy would always dedicate 'Nineteen Years Old' to me."

In a Boston club, Paul got impatient waiting for a patron to get off the phone. "I said, 'Man, can you get off the phone, I got to make a phone call.' He said something smart to me, I was drunk, and I punched him. Then Muddy took me to the side, slapped me, said, 'What the fuck is wrong with you?' It was a light slap on my cheek. I didn't mind that Mud slapped me, I considered him a father. But what was weird, the next day he got real close in my face and said, 'I never touched you, I never touched you.'"

In Austin, Muddy heard Johnny Winter: Bill Bentley, now a Warner Brothers Records publicity executive, drove up from Houston, August 2 and 3, 1968: "This was back when nobody yet knew who Johnny was. He opened the show and smoked Muddy, blew him away. But the second night, Muddy's band came out and nailed Winter to the ground. They pulled out all the stops: Oscher was playing on his knees, Muddy played a version of 'Long Distance Call' I can still hear note for note. S. P. Leary, during one of the stop-time songs, would jump up and spin around. Later in the night, after he got loaded, he jumped up and he spun and fell. I'll never forget the look Muddy gave him."

Nor will Johnny Winter forget his visit from Oscher: "He came to my hotel room. Paul seemed to put on an act, like he was from the country. He asked if it was safe being that high, and we weren't but on the twelfth floor. In Chicago, I'm sure he must have been in some elevators. We were doing an interview, and he asked me if it was safe to talk on a tape recorder. He'd done records, so I can't believe he'd really be scared of a tape recorder. He was a nice guy, but he was funny."

Oscher was enjoying the road. "I'd learned these three-card monte games, now I wanted to try 'em out. So Jerry Portnoy and I go to this place where these big-time card hustlers are. We're going back to this traveling salesman's motel room and I tell Jerry, 'When I put my hand on this pocket it's the card on the right, if I put my hand on this pocket it's the card on the left.' So I'm fading the money and we're beginning to gamble and I put my hand in this pocket and then Jerry goes —" Portnoy interjected: "I'm facing Paul: his right or my right?" They blew the hustle.

"I was really into the lifestyle of the guys in the band," Oscher continued. "People would come into the dressing room and say 'Oh, man, that was a great show,' and I'd say 'Hey, you ever seen this?' I was hustling them for like ten, twenty dollars and it was really wrong because the real hustle I had was blowing the fucking harmonica. That was the real get over."

Muddy went from the East Coast to a string of University of California dates, then way east for an October / November European tour — billed as "The Story of Soul" — stopping in England for Jazz Expo '68 and the BBC's "Jazz at the Maltings," then heading to Paris, and eventually landing at the Montreux Jazz Festival in Switzerland. (Paul McCartney hung out with the band at Aynsley Dunbar's club, where Muddy's group was sitting in. "We hung out, drank," said Oscher. "Not really anything.") In Germany Paul asked for written directions to an electronics store. Walking around Berlin, he'd hold out his paper and ask for help, until someone said, "Do you know what this note says?" Paul wagged his head. "It says, 'Send this boy to a barbershop, he needs a haircut.'" Coming back, at U.S. Customs, Snake nudged Paul, said, "Hold this for me, will you?" and handed him his radio. Later Oscher watched with surprise as Snake retrieved the .32 snub-nose he'd taped inside.

"Snake was dangerous," said Oscher. "I saw him pull a gun on a bus driver right on Forty-third Street. Snake had a five dollar bill and he wanted to board, it was like two in the morning, me and Snake. And the bus driver said you gotta have exact change. Snake pulled a gun. 'Drive, motherfucker.' The bus driver hit the headlights and the police locked him up, just like that." In New York, walking across Washington Square Park, the claustrophobia of the big city overwhelmed Snake and he broke it open with a taste of the frontier, whipping out his pistol and shooting at S. P.'s feet. "Dance, motherfucker." But Snake's danger also had a charm. His pickup lines in bars were infamous. He'd say, "Could I kiss you right there?" and he'd touch the pretty girl's toe, then "Could I kiss you right here?" and touch her knee, and work his way up to her wicked midnight.

198 "open tunings that he probably hadn't employed in ages": Muddy had stopped traveling with two guitars, and when he played slide, instead of retuning to Spanish, he played in the standard tuning in which he picked; the effect was still powerful, but less gut-wrenching.

199 short a harmonica player: Birmingham Jones played harmonica for Muddy immediately before Paul. (See "Birmingham Jones, an Introduction" by Len Kunstadt.)

201 The Blackstone Rangers: The Rangers were formed earlier in the decade in response to The Woodlawn Organization's two attempts to upgrade the neighborhood; see Lemann, *Promised Land*. The Civil Rights Bill had passed on July 3, 1964, but the lack of actual change brought riots back to the West Side.

202 "The last time I seen Little Walter": O'Neal, "Blue Smitty" part 2.

Willie Smith, however, remembers Walter getting it together not long before he died. "Walter was at the Red Onion, I was with Muddy and we were talking about how strong Walter was and how he was getting back to his normal self. Muddy said he was fixing to have Walter back in the band. And that was the last time I saw him."

202 "We were still hangin' out together": O'Neal, "Junior Wells," p. 20.

203 Geneva remained the backbone: Once, on Geneva's birthday, everyone in the family — along with those in the house and some from outside the house — was sitting around the kitchen with guitars and harmonicas. "Muddy believed birthdays were the most special day of the year, because that's your day," said Cookie. On Geneva's day, she asked, "Old man, you gonna sing me a song?" And Muddy began "Rock Me." Cotton accompanied on harmonica. ("I realized what a powerful voice Muddy had," said Paul. "That whole house shook. It made me understand how Son House and those guys working without microphones could be heard.")

204 "They'd argue about the women": One night, Muddy's two ladies ran into each other. "Muddy was playing at Pepper's," said Lucille. "I was mad at him and left. Muddy told me, 'You stay off Lake Park.' I said I'm going where I want to go. And I came walking down there and it was in the summertime, me and my girlfriend. Geneva was on the corner and Dennis was with her, and Dennis say, 'Momma, there's that bitch that goes with daddy.' And she popped me upside my head and we got to fighting and afterwards I went back to the club and told Muddy, 'You had better go see about your wife, I just whipped her ass.'"

Lucille and Muddy also fought. "He hit me once," Lucille continued. "I was supposed to have been there at my house, but me and my girlfriend had went out and I was coming in at five o'clock in the morning and he was sitting outside the house in his car. He was calling me and I kept on walking like I didn't hear him. He went to slap me and I ducked and he hit my head. His hand swole up. So the next day he had a little miniature baseball bat, said, 'I'm going to beat your ass with this bat, I gotta make a living with these hands.' But he was just playing."

204 "blinking blinking jiving jiving shit": According to Stanley Booth.

206 "A lot of people go in for [the effects]": "Muddy: The Man Who Urbanised the Blues."

206 "shooting for the hippies": Jones, *Melody Maker,* p. 29.

206 Jimi Hendrix's valet: His name was James Finney.

206 "The first guitarist I was aware of": Murray, *Traffic,* p. 132.

207 "They got this funny thing going": Guralnick interview with Muddy Waters.

207 "that one was dogshit": Wheeler, "Waters–Winter."

207 "We did a lot of the things over": DeMichael, "Father and Son."

208 "Muddy's got everybody crazy": DeMichael, "Muddy Waters Week," p. 13.

208 Leonard was ready to move on: "No one got rich on the sale of Chess Records," Marshall told me. "We got a tremendous amount of stock worth seven dollars a share that we couldn't sell for five years. When I sold mine it was for one dollar and seventy-eight cents a share. And my mom and Phil, they never sold theirs. They waited until it was bankrupt."

208 "I made my money on the Negro": Dean Gysel, *Chicago Daily News,* June 1967.
209 "I'll be with Chess": Guralnick, *Home,* p. 233. Cookie remembered the Chess brothers: "The oldest used to always bring me candy. I think he thought if he bribed me it would be easy with Muddy and it worked. And I used to love bananas so he would come in with a bushel. And I would go there with Muddy and Muddy would come back to the car cussing up a storm about something they didn't do. 'Those goddamn Chess brothers!' They had almost like a family relationship."
209 IOU notes: One report stated $150,000 worth of IOUs were found in Leonard's office.
209 "What [the musicians] were paid": Cohodas, *Spinning,* p. 228. On page 229, Cohodas quotes Leonard saying he'd never give Sonny Boy a large advance. "He'd be broke tomorrow. . . . I'll make sure that he lives and his rent is paid." Cohodas also writes on page 229: "Some days the first-floor hallway at 2120 looked like the line at a bank teller's window."
209 "You know we sold the company": Guralnick, *Home,* p. 217.
209 "[GRT] could have been in the tomato business": Golkin, "Blacks, Whites, and Blues" part 2.
210 "they wanted to get rid of my uncle": Collis, *Chess,* p. 187.
    A brief history of Chess Records ownership: Len Levy, formerly of Epic Records, replaced Marshall and moved Chess to New York. Marvin Schlacter, from Janus Records, became president in 1971. He stabilized the company by merging Chess, Janus, and GRT, but by 1975 the game was over and Ralph Bass was charged with shipping all Chess masters to storage in Nashville. In England in the 1970s, Phonolog had the license and was actively reissuing the catalog, including the *Genesis* series of three boxed sets. In August of 1975, All Platinum (Joe and Sylvia Robinson) bought Chess for $950,000. They attempted only to work with the back catalog, not reactivate the label. Sugar Hill acquired Chess when All Platinum went bust, and MCA from Sugar Hill.
212 YOU ARE NOW ENTERING KLAN COUNTRY: Paul Oscher told me, "I didn't say anything, but fifteen years later I'm sitting in a bar thinking about that shit and I wrote down on a napkin: 'Mississippi / land of darkness / the devil lives there in and around the low lands by the cotton fields / by the white crosses on the side of the highway / Satan lingers / Mississippi, your fertile soil have give rise to the dusty mouths of black folks who through wide gold-toothed grins shout out the blues, oh the blues, those lonesome blues.'"
213 "He immediately agreed to come": Lomax, *Land,* p. 420.
213 "'Hi, Lo,' he said": In his book, among the band members that Lomax names in Muddy's car is Little Walter, then dead half a year.
215 "If you lose just an ordinary sideman": Guralnick interview with Muddy Waters.
215 "Pinetop, he come from the part of the country": Ibid.
215 $3,500 for a one-hour set: As per a contract with the Southwest 1970 Peace Festival in Lubbock, Texas.
216 "I used to be a good liquor drinker": DeMichael, "Father and Son," p. 32.
216 "Champagne for breakfast": Nicholls, "Strangers."

216 "up through Maine": Guralnick interview with Muddy Waters.
217 "I ain't dying": "Car Crash," *Rolling Stone.*

13: EYES ON THE PRIZE *1970–1975*
    Living Blues **Founded:** As the sixties became the seventies, white audiences in South Side clubs became more common, though they were still outsiders. "In the seventies, policemen thought we were criminals," said Dick Shurman, who'd moved to Chicago in the late 1960s. "One time Jim O'Neal and I were leaving and a couple plainclothesmen grabbed us on the way out. They figured we had been picking up protection money. They had me pop the trunk on my foreign car and I had a little compact jack. They said, 'What's this, a machine gun?'"
    It was in this environment that the magazine *Living Blues* was founded, taking the South Side — and other blues scenes — to mailboxes around the world. With seed money from Bob Koester, several of his employees at the Jazz Record Mart and Delmark Records began the magazine to document "the Black American Blues Tradition." Founders included then-husband-and-wife Jim O'Neal and Amy van Singel, Paul Garon, and Bruce Iglauer (who was working as a shipping clerk for Delmark when Koester declined the opportunity to release a Hound Dog Taylor album, giving Iglauer the impetus to found Alligator Records). The first subscriber was Victoria Spivey.
    Living Blues became something of a blues family newsletter. Howlin' Wolf was interviewed in the first issue; Buddy Guy in the second. "I'd go around the country doing interviews with other people," said Jim O'Neal. "I don't know how many would ask, 'Is Muddy Waters still alive?' This was at a time when he had disappeared from black radio and that circuit." The magazine sought to document, not analyze, and so musicians could sound off in a way that the mainstream press would not allow. "I read in *Down Beat* or *Time* magazine while I was in Africa, 'The Rebirth of the Blues,'" said Buddy Guy. He continued:

> You know, they printed that wrong. They should have said it was "The Reprinted of the Blues," because we ain't never give it up. You could come here and Theresa [of Theresa's Lounge] won't allow nothing but a blues band. So don't say "The Rebirth of the Blues." Just say Janis Joplin and the Cream and all of 'em went to playing the blues, because we never left it. If we had left it, they wouldn't have found it out. . . . It seems like to me, all you have to do is be white and just play a guitar — you don't have to have the soul — you gets farther than the black man. (O'Neal and Zorn, "Buddy Guy")

Blues label owners who got their start learning the ropes from Koester as Jazz Record Mart employees included Iglauer; O'Neal and van Singel, who founded Rooster Records; the late Pete Welding of the Testament label; Don Kent of Mamlish; the late Bruce Kaplan of Flying Fish; Pete Crawford of Red Beans; and Michael Frank, whose Earwig label perhaps most closely follows Koester's tradition of recording older, less commercially viable artists. Koester's role as a mentor and pioneer in the independent record business was formally recognized in 1996 when he was elected into the Blues Foundation's Blues Hall of Fame. (Barretta, "The Monarch," p. 28.)

Messinger's Memory of His Parting with Muddy: "I heard from the American promoter Lew Futterman that Muddy was drinking a lot of Piper-Heidsieck and it was costing a lot of money," Messinger told me. "I went to my home on Cape Cod, where I'm from originally. Muddy came back while I was gone, we had made some sort of arrangement about the cars. And I got a panicked message of some sort. 'Where's the money?' I had been sending money to all the designated places. They went back to Chicago. Next thing I know, I got a letter vilifying me and discharging me."

As support, Messinger proffered a letter typed on blank paper — no letterhead — and dated by hand as December 23, 1970. It was to Muddy Waters, from Lyon–Futterman Associates, Ltd., the tour's booking agent. It stated, in part, "This is to confirm the intention of our organization to honor its outstanding financial obligation to you." The letter is signed by Lewis Futterman "for Lyon–Futterman Associates and as a personal guarantee." Messinger continued, "First Futterman was going to be helpful, then he became incommunicado. I never talked to Muddy again. If I had had a road manager like I wanted, none of this would have happened."

Scott Cameron's Developing Relationship with Muddy: Cameron's relationship with Muddy took hold and, with things looking up, Muddy invited his new main man to his South Side home for dinner. Cameron met the family: Charles and Dennis, Dennis's girlfriend Jean, Cookie and her daughter Chandra. Cameron remembered, "I think Big Walter was over there that night, too. Not everyone could fit at the table. There were a lot of scamperings in and out." Muddy served collard greens and smothered steak. Geneva fixed chitlins. "As soon as the sun started going down, Muddy said, 'You gotta go now because they might start shooting.' He'd always send me home before the lights started coming on."

In anticipation of Muddy's higher profile East Coast tour, the *Washington Post* sent a reporter to Chicago. Mr. Hollie I. West found Muddy's "well-kept two-story brownstone stands out among houses that are deserted or crumbling in disrepair." He noted that Geneva maintained a garden and was impressed with the couple's relationship after thirty-three years of marriage; Muddy greeted her with, "How ya doin', baby?" They sat down to eat bacon and eggs. "If I'd known you was a brother, I would've had some pork chops waiting for you. Don't think I can't cook because I can take care of business in the kitchen. Soul food is my specialty — chicken, pork chops, soup. My wife will lay back in a minute and let me burn. Pound cake is my specialty. I use a pound of butter and six eggs. You got to cream that butter until it's almost like ice cream. I cook when the notion hits me. But I'm a pepper man. My family, man, has to watch my hand with the spice." (Hollie I. West, *Washington Post,* September 24, 1971, Sec. B.)

After Scott went from agent to manager, Muddy was booked by William Morris, then Premiere, then Paragon (which handled southern rock bands), and finally Rosebud.

Mr. Kelly's: "We were riding back to Muddy's house from the Kelly's gig in his Cadillac," said Paul Oscher, "and Muddy whispers to me, 'Motherfucker, you're blowing that motherfucker now.' And I knew I was, too. I was playing my ass off. But I really felt good when he said that." Oscher, who was playing through a Guild Thunderbird amp, achieves a deep tone throughout the live recording. His expertise is most exciting in the staccato comp licks he plays during his solo on the Jimmy Reed song "You Don't Have to Go." He shows a profound understanding of when to lay back; where some harp players are compelled to play all the time, he jumps in and out — as in the instrumental "Mudcat," where he lets the band set the shuffling groove, then steps forward for his solo, then is out again. His absence fattens the band dynamic; less is more.

"I got pretty close to Muddy during Mr. Kelly's," said Oscher, "but it's hard to get close to Muddy. Most every night we came back, Muddy would cook fried bologna or something, and we'd sit there and have a few more drinks and talk some shit. So he asked me would I give him twenty percent if he made me a star. We were talking shit at his kitchen table so I said, 'Well, what about ten percent, man?' Then I ran into this girl who was doing public relations for Chess and she told me that Chess had a big interest after the Mr. Kelly's gig to do a record with me. Muddy wasn't going to tell me that Chess wanted to do it because that would be cutting his part out. It was a country thing. Cotton was probably making more money than Muddy at the time. I was in his corner. If he'd told me, I would have said, 'Yeah, of course, I'll give you whatever you want.' But that's how he communicated: indirect ways."

Oscher's departure from the band in 1971 — a beautiful swan dive into a murky swamp — came soon after. He caught a cold that turned to pneumonia and he returned to Brooklyn to heal. But a week after arriving home, he found his harmonica talents mysteriously transformed. "There's a lot of strange things that happened to me," he said, his tone getting hushed. "I don't know if I really want to get into it, but a week after I left Muddy, my skills were stolen from me. I had to go through a relearning how to blow."

Oscher would be replaced by Mojo Buford, the replacement man, who this time stayed with the band nearly three years. His stint would not start, however, until after a West Coast tour that brought George "Harmonica" Smith back into the fold. That tour was documented by a film crew. An edited version of their footage has been released on videotape by Vestapol as *Muddy Waters in Concert 1971*. The audio portion is available through Blind Pig on an enhanced CD titled *The Lost Tapes*. The live footage, shot with several cameras, does a very good job of intimately capturing Muddy and the band. The film crew's documentary footage, shot mostly in the station wagon while driving on the highway, is less professional, with horrific road noises, an interviewer's head disembodied by the car seat before him, and a line of questioning that reveals more about the crew's lack of preparation than about Muddy. By virtue of its proximity, however, it does open a window into Muddy's life on tour. Big Mama Thornton is seated next to him, drunk and interrupting, her frequent demands for a bathroom stop unheeded; she threatens to pee on the floor. Muddy retains his composure, except to shout cautionary warnings to the driver — his accident was recent.

219 "sunup and sundown here in the house": Guralnick interview with Muddy Waters.

220 "I'm up and around": "Back on His Feet," *Rolling Stone*.

220 news about Otis Spann: By 1970, Spann was living a block from Muddy at 4311 S. Greenwood. Boston guitarist Peter Malick stayed there the last couple months of Spann's life:

Spann's home was a two-room apartment, a bedroom with a kitchenette and a living room with a cot. There was one bathroom for all six apartments. There were cockroaches, flies too. No screens on the windows. You lay there at night and cockroaches might crawl over you. There wasn't a whole lot you could do about it. . . . Spann and I played every night in his little apartment. Part of it was that he needed a way to pay the rent. People would come over and leave a couple of bucks. That's how he got by but that's also what he loved to do. (Brisbin, "Malick")

220 "A skeletal-looking man": Guralnick, *Lost Highway,* p. 294.

221 "There are some beautiful white bands": "Rebirth of the Blues," *Newsweek.*
    He told a 1971 documentary crew, "I like to get the Mississippi tone, the down South tone. I like to play an open sound, not playing flats and sharps. I stay with the natural keys like E natural or A natural. I think your instrument and you, when you're singing the type blues that I sing, [it should sound] like some people arguing. I talk to it and it talk to me." (Wyler and Ragsdale interview with Muddy Waters.)

222 "He strolled on stage with a crutch": Random Notes, *Rolling Stone,* July 23, 1970.

223 "As we go to press": Blues News, *Living Blues,* winter 1970–1971.

224 "Lucille got in the wrong crowd": Cookie confirmed Willie's assessment of Lucille: "An older girl that rented upstairs at Lake Park, Doris Priestly, told me then that C. D. had turned Lucille on to drugs."

224 "They're all new people": Guralnick interview with Muddy Waters.

226 According to the papers that Muddy couldn't read: If Muddy had higher literacy skills, a clause such as this may have prompted a question: "The Compositions, including without limitation, the lyrics, music, titles, and characters described therein shall be and are the sole and exclusive property of the Employer, together with all copyright rights therein and all other rights thereunder. . . ." (U.S. District Court, "McKinley Morganfield v. Arc.")

228 "Muddy emotes warmly": Charles Giuliano, "Muddy Waters at Jazz Workshop," *Boston Herald Traveler,* March 19, 1971.
    "The Jazz Workshop was a tough week," said Dick Waterman, who coowned another Boston club. "It was a Monday to Sunday seven-night week with a Sunday matinee. My club, Joe's Place, was working a five- or six-night week, with no matinees. I never asked Muddy to play, and when we were talking, he said, 'Back when not too many people knew my name, Freddy Taylor [at the Jazz Workshop], Freddy wanted me to play.' He said, 'Now I like Freddy. Freddy work you hard. But I got to show the man the consideration.'"

228 "He was in as fine a form": Jon Landau, "A Man of Great Pride, Great Dignity," *Boston Phoenix,* March 23, 1971.
    In New York, Muddy played the Gaslight Theater, a burgeoning blues club — even if it was in the basement. "There was no backstage, it was a kitchen," said Willie Strandberg, fan and friend of Paul Oscher. "Muddy was like a regal king. He was sitting up on the stove, he had a big fur coat on, a Tiparillo sticking out of his pocket, and I said, 'Hey, Muddy, nice to meet you.' He said, 'Oh I love these waitresses, the hippie chicks.'"

230 *The London Muddy Waters Sessions*: Rory Gallagher said:

> I learned a lot watching him tune his guitar and watching the way he sang and performed. . . . The hardest thing was to get the drums and bass in sync with Muddy's type of rhythm guitar. . . . A couple of times Muddy would stop the song if he didn't like the way it was going, but a few suggestions were made by Steve Winwood as well and Georgie Fame, who was playing piano. But with a lot of these types of sessions, there's not all that much verbal communication. A lot of it's just stop and start again: "Can you pick up on that?" or "Can you start in a different key?" (Skelly, "Muddy Waters")

Carey Bell played on and off with Muddy's band over many years. He'd come to Chicago from Mississippi and had gotten his start with pianist Lovie Lee, who later joined Muddy's last band. Bell got guidance from Little Walter, and was strong enough to record with Earl Hooker, subtle enough to record with Honeyboy Edwards.

232 *Can't Get No Grinding*: "'Can't Get No Grinding,'" said Muddy, "I heard that from Memphis Minnie a thousand years ago." Which doesn't stop him, in the blues tradition, from putting his name on the song. (O'Neal and van Singel, "Muddy Waters.")

232 circuit of higher-class cabarets: Some of his higher-class gigs: On the fifth day of 1973, he played the Avery Fisher Philharmonic Hall on a bill with John Lee Hooker and Mose Allison; he returned two months later, playing another "Blues Variations," this time with Lightnin' Hopkins and Bonnie Raitt. Both shows were sold out. He also played the larger Carnegie Hall on June 29.

The New Yorker covered Muddy when he played Mick Jagger's twenty-ninth birthday party on July 26 at the prestigious St. Ritz Hotel in New York. "Andy Warhol had been taking Polaroid pictures. Lee Radizwill began to take Polaroid pictures. Then Muddy Waters came on with his band." He dedicated "Hoochie Coochie Man" to the Rolling Stones and to Marshall Chess and Chess Records. "Muddy Waters, businesslike, packed up his equipment after his set was over. He and his musicians sat at a table near the bandstand. Muddy and his band were geared for rapid appearances, rapid setups, and rapid departures. They were on the road. 'We've been in Chicago, we've been up to Iowa,' he said, 'We're going out to Washington.'" (Trow, "Ahmet Ertegun," pp. 66–67.) The venue was nice, Muddy later told a New Zealand writer, but said he was most impressed by a naked woman who leapt from a cake and made each breast move in opposite directions. (Nicholls, "Strangers.")

232 "For a blues band such as Mr. Waters's": John S. Wilson, "Blues Band," *New York Times*, December 21, 1972.

233 "the essence of the black man in Chi Town": Bims, "Blues City."

233 "if they'd thrown me out the fourth one": Nicholls, "Strangers."

A few days before departing for a European tour behind the *London Sessions*, Sammy Lawhorn dove into double trouble. He told Pee Wee Madison he'd had a skirmish with some furniture movers. "The guys said, 'You got to give us more money.' He said, 'I ain't got no more goddamn money.' They grabbed him, stripped him down, went through his pockets, locked him in the bathroom. They was trying to figure out what to do with him, and when he heard the guy coming at him, Sammy say he had no choice but just dive out the second-floor window, naked. Broke him all up. He was pretty lucky, though. To live."

Sammy told Bob Koester (and also Calvin Jones) that he'd come home and someone was robbing his house. They put him in the bathroom and scared him so bad that he jumped out a third-floor window and broke both his legs. Whatever the cause, whatever wrong Sammy had done, the negotiating was over. He was forced out of his clothes and locked in the bathroom for safe-keeping. His apartment was ransacked, presumably in search of the goods in question. When nothing was found, Lawhorn heard the thugs discussing his fate. And when a decision about terminating his fate was reached, the two or three stories between him and the ground seemed a much shorter distance than the hell that loomed. And so he leapt. He'd recuperated enough to travel to New Zealand, where a reporter noted his difficulty hobbling to a press conference. "Muddy doesn't ask much of the band off the stand, but if he does, they do as they're told." (Nicholls, "Strangers.")

235 Geneva died on March 15, 1973: Mike Kappus of the Rosebud Agency, which later booked Muddy, was handling a club in Milwaukee in 1973, and he recalled Muddy playing there the week of Geneva's death. "Muddy had done a night or two," said Kappus, "then his wife died and he took a night or two off and he finished the week." Scott Cameron independently corroborated Kappus's account. "I said let me call up and cancel it," said Cameron, "and Muddy says, 'No, I need to do this.' I think it probably was better for him emotionally to ride that van to Milwaukee and play that date, release some of this tension, whatever emotional pressure he was under, then ride back home with his band members instead of having to sit in that house all by himself and think about what had just happened."

Willie Smith's memory supports Cookie's claim of Muddy being home. "He called me up that morning," said Willie Smith. "He told me she was dead, so we wasn't out. We might have just come in that night or that morning. She had done got to the point where she would go on off in a trance, wasn't talking, didn't know nobody." Muddy's friend Al Perry came to the funeral. He asked who picked out the plot and was told, "The Old Man had picked that spot out because it was right in the front by the gates so people wouldn't have to look hard to find him."

239 Watertoons: Muddy was not fully disentangled from the Arc and Heavy publishing companies at the time, and so he could not put his own name on the Watertoons songs. Instead, he used Cookie's real name, Amelia Cooper. "I figured," said Terry Abrahamson, who shared songwriting credit with her, "that a little girl wasn't writing any of these songs."

239 "I started to play 'Can't Be Satisfied'": Margolin, "Can't Be Satisfied"; author interview with Bob Margolin.

240 *Unk in Funk:* It is astonishing that, with expectations high and money spent on these sessions, Chess would release a cut as flawed as this seven-minute version of "Rollin' and Tumblin'," which is actually the song played twice. About

three minutes in, as the track is winding up, Ralph Bass bursts in, waving his arms and stomping. Startled, the players stop and the song falls apart. "Everybody," Muddy shouts, "come on in," and the players resume, running through the song again. Afterward, Bass explained he was trying to throw some excitement into the song. There is some life in the moment — the brief moment — when the song falls apart, but it's not any musical magic. The seven minutes would have made an interesting outtake; its inclusion, as reviewers noted, just sounded sloppy.

240 Terry Abrahamson: Abrahamson explains how he met Muddy: "I met Muddy at Alice's in Chicago, a coffeehouse, around 1970. It was a small room, and very narrow. You entered through the front, the stage was at the back, there were seats along the walls, and everybody else sat on the floor. We'd get there early to sit up front. People piled in behind us, so, to use the bathroom, we had to walk across the stage and use the band's bathroom. I go backstage, start talking to the guys. In between nights, I talked to my dad and he said his friend Hy Marzen used to own a bar where all these guys played. It turned out to be the Zanzibar. So I told Muddy that I grew up down the street from Hy Marzen. Muddy misinterpreted this and thinks I'm Hy's son, and introduces me like that. I said, 'No, I'm not Hy Marzen's son.' Muddy said, 'Oh you don't have to lie to me, boy, he didn't rip me off that bad.'"

Abrahamson pitched his song to Muddy before a gig. "I said, 'What do you think of this: 'The men call me Muddy, the women call me Electric Man / When I plug into your socket / I'll charge you like no one else can.' He said, 'That's good shit, boy, you write that down.' I was twenty-two years old and I knew that that would be the artistic peak of my life."

Getting to know Bo proved almost as exciting as getting to know Muddy. "Bo was so entertaining, he was like watching a TV show," Abrahamson said. "He was black as night, his eyes were little red slits. You didn't see any eyeball, just little pockets of red, like blood, above his nose. And when he talked, it was a deep growl, and all mumbles. If you didn't know him, you'd be terrified of this guy. Bo loved to goof on people by getting them scared." (Bob Margolin said of Bo: "This was when that song 'Bad Bad Leroy Brown' came out, and it's like it was about Bo.")

240 Jerry Portnoy: Portnoy got to know Muddy through Paul. "He was living in Muddy's basement and sometimes we'd go upstairs to see Muddy and Muddy would be in his doo rag and watching the Cubs game in the afternoon, drinking champagne. 'Well, boys, you want a little taste?' He was drinking champagne. Piper-Heidsieck. I learned from Muddy Waters, my wine expert."

241 "You don't know how happy I am": Litke, "TV Tribute," p. 15.
241 He played Montreux: The 1974 Montreux set is available on the videotape *Messin' with the Blues*.
241 "It should have been just another show": Margolin, "Can't Be Satisfied."
243 "I got my favorite blues singer": Jones, "Superstar."
243 "I'll have to tell the truth, you're from down in that way": McKee and Chisenhall interview with Muddy Waters.

Muddy charmed Margaret McKee. "Just thank God I'm living. I'm fifty-eight years old, an old man. Cute, too." On the tape, he said "cute, too," in a practiced way; this line has worked before. And he delivers it with a pause, after which, sure enough, she giggles like a little girl.

245 had recently sued Arc Music: Howlin' Wolf's lawsuit in Blues News, *Living Blues,* summer 1974.

Wolf's suit was settled — after his death on January 10, 1976 — for an undisclosed amount. Toward the end of his career, Wolf, despite growing kidney problems — his touring schedule was built around cities with dialysis facilities — was not retiring. "It wasn't unusual to see Wolf take one tune and play it for a half hour, maybe longer, and only remember two or three stanzas of the song," said Bob Koester. "We didn't mind, you know." Reviewing a Wolf gig at the Chicago Amphitheater, Dick Shurman wrote in *Living Blues,* "Wolf summoned all his energy to stalk around, clown with the mike, and sing and play harp forcefully. His was the night's most gutbucket set, and the audience returned the enthusiasm to show that down-home blues still hits hard in '75." (Shurman, "Howlin' Wolf.")

246 *Mandingo:* The internationally known film composer Maurice Jarre, who had scored *Lawrence of Arabia* and *Doctor Zhivago,* requested Muddy's contribution to the scoring of the James Mason film *Mandingo,* directed by Richard Fleischer. The job involved singing their words, accompanied by banjo, ukulele, and washboard, in synchronization with images on the screen. Muddy practiced his reading on his wife's lists at the grocery store; it required all his effort and he could not simultaneously comprehend the words. As much as he tried to familiarize himself with the material, he could not get comfortable in the movie situation — keeping his eyes on the paper, on the screen, and on the other players. "They worked with him a little bit," said Cameron. "It wasn't cut and dry like you'd have to sync to a commercial, there was some space for timing errors or phrasings. I think they probably had a lot more material that they could have used, but it was very hard for him to do things in sync with the film."

247 Bottom Line. Bob Dylan: Al Perry was backstage with Muddy. "Victoria was in heaven, saying, 'It's like old times, Bob's living in my apartment, sleeping on the floor.'" She and Bob got up and played. Oscher was on the gig — playing piano — because Pine had broken his wrist. After the show, Oscher and Jerry Portnoy accompanied Dylan and his entourage to Victoria Spivey's house. "He asked me if I wanted to go on his Rolling Thunder thing," said Oscher, "so I gave him my number. But my phone was disconnected two days later."

248 "tired of being sold to everybody": Murray, *Shots,* p. 191.

All Platinum held a sale at the 320 E. Twenty-first Chess building, though tens of thousands of albums were left afterward. They hired day workers, gave them chainsaws, and the contents of the building and warehouse were destroyed.

14: HARD AGAIN *1976–1983*
Hard Again: Johnny Winter gave his engineer a crash course in blues sounds. "I spent almost twenty-four hours playing him blues records and telling him what I liked. It was real important we got the right sound." Bob Margolin brought a

portable cassette player to the sessions and some homemade tapes of Muddy's original recordings. "They were mostly recorded from bootleg albums because Chess
did not have official releases on the market."

"We didn't practice," said Muddy. "We just got in there and we'd run over a
song and put it down. We caught it." (Obrecht, "Bluesman.") Said Willie Smith,
"Wasn't like it would take a whole year to figure out. Figure out a pattern, work on
it a little, and take it. Once you've been playing with a band long enough to know
what each other are going to do, hell, you just do it. The Chesses, they was slave-
driving in the studio, cussing one another to get you pissed off enough so you could
put all you had into it. With Johnny Winter, it was like day and night."

As the sessions wound down, and the feeling had lasted for so long and trans-
lated so well to magnetic tape, both Bob and Johnny wanted to test the waters of the
way-old school: acoustic guitars. Mud sat between them — three across on
stools — and they knocked out his 1941 songs again: "I Feel Like Going Home"
and "I Can't Be Satisfied." At the start of the 1970s, Muddy said in an interview, "I
try to play straight as I can so the band can follow, but songs like 'I Can't Be Satisfied,' I don't think nobody never been able to half follow that but Spann. That's
why I don't ever try to play it since I got a band." (Guralnick interview with Muddy
Waters.) But he's singing that sucker now, boy, the lead licks on an acoustic National steel guitar, Son Sims rising from his grave to shuck corn, the tractor engine
revving. Johnny and Bob began discussing another take. Muddy was finished. "He
didn't want a bunch of extra songs floating around," said Johnny. "The Chess
people had put out so much of his extra stuff on albums, and he wanted to get paid
for everything he did."

The sessions jolted Johnny Winter, made him reconsider the direction of his
life. "Working with Muddy made me realize that blues was what I wanted to do.
Rock and roll was okay, but blues was my first love. I might not make as much
money as a rock and roll player, but blues made me happier." Johnny brought the
Hard Again band to Westport to back him on his own album, *Nothing but the Blues.*
Muddy stopped by to lay down lead vocals on a bouncing version of "Walking thru
the Park."

Last Waltz: As *The Last Waltz* approached, unbeknownst to Muddy, his role
was jeopardized. "It was mind-blowing," Levon Helm said. "That was just bullshit." In his autobiography, *This Wheel's on Fire,* he expounded:

Two days before the show, our studio manager tried to talk to me. He was
one of the boys on the other side of the desk. I could tell from the awful
look on his face that there was some problem, and he'd been *delegated* to
deal with me. . . . This flunky said, "Um, we've *all* discussed it, and we're
thinking about, ah, maybe, you know, taking Muddy off the show." I just
looked at him. "Anyway, we were hoping maybe you could talk to Muddy
for us."

There was silence for an awful thirty seconds. I was trying to get a grip
before I answered, before I lost control. We were all under tremendous
pressure because of this movie. The whole damn thing had been hijacked
to the *nth* degree. I had to clear my throat before I could speak. "Not only
will I *talk* to Muddy," I managed, as I began to get worked up, "but I will

also take Muddy back to New York, and we will do the goddamn *Last Waltz* in New York. Him and me. That's right." Now I was getting going. "Yes, I'll talk to Muddy, you no-good, low-grade sumbitch! Now get the hell out of my sight, before I have some of these here Arkansas boys stomp you to death!" (Helm with Davis, *This Wheel's on Fire,* p. 261)

The Band rented the Miyako Hotel, near the Winterland venue, for its guests and held a rehearsal there the day before the show. Dr. John noted: "I really wish they had filmed during Muddy Waters's rehearsal, and I just wish somebody had filmed the guitar players in the room watching Muddy, with their jaws hanging open while this guy is playing 'Nine Below Zero.'... There were so many great guitar players there — Robbie Robertson, Eric Clapton, Bob Dylan, Neil Young, Stephen Stills — and the looks on the faces of those guys was worth the price of admission for me!" (Skelly, "Muddy Waters.")

The Last Waltz had, as showbiz events are wont to do, become something larger than itself, including a feature film to be directed by Martin Scorsese. "Joni Mitchell introduced herself to Muddy and he definitely hit on her without knowing she was famous, which made her laugh," said Margolin. "She was heartbreakingly beautiful and attractive. In the dressing room, Pinetop told me, 'I hear one of the Beatles is here,' but didn't realize that he was sitting next to Ringo. Kinky Friedman assured Muddy that 'Jews love the blues.' He was wearing a white satin smoking jacket with blue Jewish stars on it and embroidered scenes of the Crucifixion. Muddy just smiled at another weirdo talking nonsense."

Though it seems intentional, the intensity with which Muddy was filmed was a matter of circumstance. "I noticed that they didn't seem to be shooting Muddy," Helm wrote. "Later we realized that because of some fuck-up, all but one camera had been turned off. We almost missed his entire segment. As he was walking offstage, I stood up to applaud, and Muddy grabbed my head in his big hands and kissed my forehead! What a feeling!" (Helm with Davis, *This Wheel's on Fire,* p. 264.)

The next year, between gigs in Los Angeles, Muddy, Marva, and Scott Cameron left the Hyatt Hotel in a cab to attend a matinee showing of *The Last Waltz* at a theater on Sunset Boulevard. "That was incredible," said Scott. "I was watching Muddy. They flashed him on that big screen up there and his chin just hit his chest. His mouth dropped. I don't think he could have believed how big he looked."

I'm Ready: "You could tell they were old friends," said Johnny Winter about Muddy and Jimmy Rogers, "but they didn't talk too much about the old days. They didn't have time to do much talking in the studio. We worked from one song to the next. Again, nobody ever did any arranging. I asked, 'Do one of y'all want to play the top part and another play the bottom part?' and they laughed and said, 'No, we just play what we feel like.' They thought it was funny to even care."

I'm Ready brought a welcome boost to Jimmy Rogers's career. Since the start of the 1970s, he had resumed gigging, putting out an album on Shelter Records with Leon Russell and Denny Cordell. He was not at all interested in another stint with Mr. Chess, alive or dead. Initially, things had gone well. "Get a gig now, you ask the guy for five thousand dollars and he just smiles. 'Okay, if that's all.' But during that time, if you ask them for five hundred, they'd holler." (O'Neal and Greensmith, "Jimmy Rogers.")

By the latter part of the decade, however, he was gigging less. Following the recording of *I'm Ready,* he and Big Walter stayed together for a while. They played spots from Boston to Austin and around Chicago, including the better-paying gigs on the North Side; streaking was the rage, and dancers often shed their clothes. And when *I'm Ready* was released in early 1978, Jimmy hit the road with the recording band. The higher profile led to a new recording contract, this time with Chicago's Delmark Records.

During a lull in April, Muddy stayed home and Pinetop, Guitar Jr., and Bob hit the road with a Washington, D.C., blues band, the Nighthawks, billing themselves as Jacks and Kings. With Margolin's former band mate and Spann protege Dave Maxwell, they would all guest on the Nighthawks' next album, titled *Jacks and Kings.*

The Legendary Band: Most of the old band regrouped as The Legendary Band and promptly had a recording contract and a tour booked. They hit the road running. Willie Smith still saw Muddy on the South Side; he bought a house a few doors down from Muddy's. "He was living in Westmont but he still used to come over," said Willie. "He'd sit down and talk like we always did. The Legendary Band was traveling pretty heavy ourselves, we didn't never really settle down."

"I lived near Washington, D.C., then," said Margolin, "and had started my own band. Around November, I heard that Muddy was coming to town, so I called the club and tried to arrange to open the show. The booker knew that I had left Muddy and said he'd have to check with Muddy's management to make sure they didn't mind. They didn't, and Muddy later told me that he had been asked personally, and approved. As always, playing in front of Muddy for me was like a kid trying to make Daddy proud. I closed my set with the early Little Walter tune 'I Just Keep Lovin' Her,' and when I came back into the dressing room, Muddy leaped up, put his hands on my shoulders, and said, 'I haven't heard that song in thirty years! You're keeping the old school alive!' It's the most valuable compliment I've ever had."

Jerry Portnoy visited Muddy in Westmont soon after The Legendary Band's first album. When Muddy opened the door, he gave Portnoy a big hug. "Muddy already had the album and he was proud of us. That hug, he made it right between us."

Muddy's Musical Secrets: During Muddy's comeback, educated interviewers formed lines to interview him. This resulted in detailed information about his performing style; the following quotes are culled from Tom Wheeler's "Waters–Winter Interview" in *Guitar Player.* "I play in mostly standard [tuning]," said Muddy, "because it's tough if you're waiting in between songs to tune to G or A. And I'm too lazy to carry two or three guitars around like Johnny Winter." Muddy favored strings made by Gibson. "I got a heavy hand," he said. "A lot of guys want to squeeze and bend their strings up, like B. B., so they have the strings real low. My strings are heavy, like a .012 or a .013 for the first one [the skinniest one, nearest his toes] up to .056 for the last [the one nearest his face]. I don't need to worry about bending, because I can slide so high up there." One of his tricks was to replace the wound third string with a plain .022-gauge. Muddy used a short slide on his pinky finger because he never needed to cover more than three strings — usually just one. Winter explained, "Sometimes I play a whole chord [covering all six strings], so the size of the slide makes a difference."

As crucial as a guitar is to defining a player's sound, Muddy put the emphasis on the amplifier:

"I think on any guitar, if I could make a note on it, you could still know it's Muddy," he said. "But I really can't do nothing with other people's guitars. A lot of the sound is the amp. I'd rather always use my own amplifier. It's the Fender with the four ten-inch speakers, the Super. Even if I forgot my own guitar and had to borrow one, I could make the sound come out of that amplifier. I don't like the Twin — different sound. I like some of Johnny's amps. They're Music Mans and them little guys is tough." (Wheeler, "Waters–Winter")

Margolin said, "Muddy ran his amps with all the knobs set on nine and no reverb or tremolo, controlling his volume from the guitar." (Author interview with Bob Margolin.)

"Muddy loved that real trebly Telecaster sound," said Johnny, "and he got a great sound out of his treble pickup. Sometimes during a verse, maybe just going into the turnaround, [he] will switch the toggle from the bass or middle position to full treble and just let 'em have it. Muddy would tune his guitar to an E chord and put his capo wherever it needed to go.

"You can't exaggerate how distinctive Muddy's playing is," Johnny continued. "In my band, if I stop playing, the main feeling keeps on going, but when Muddy stops, the whole feeling can change." (Wheeler, "Waters–Winter.")

"When I play on the stage with my band," Muddy confirmed, "I have to get in there with my guitar and try to bring the sound down to me. But no sooner than I quit playing, it goes back to another, different sound. My blues looks so simple, so easy to do, but it's not. They say my blues is the hardest blues in the world to play." (Palmer, *Deep Blues*.)

249 "This is a big time for me tonight": Random Notes, *Rolling Stone*, May 20, 1976.

250 "Johnny Winter": Johnny Winter had made a lasting impression with Muddy when they'd met in 1968. "I told him the truth then. 'Man, you got to go places, because ain't many white kids sounding like you at playing music.' He's albino white, he's not *jiving* white, he *all* white!" (Wheeler, "Waters–Winter.")

250 Muddy assembled a band: Muddy's regular bassist, Calvin Jones, was indifferent about being excluded. "It didn't make me no difference. It didn't make me a bit of difference." It also wouldn't have made a drastic difference to his pocketbook, and recognition didn't buy cans of food.

251 "the greatest Saturday-night drummer alive": Author interview with Scott Cameron.

251 "Every country has its own music": Palmer, *Deep Blues*, p. 104.

252 "What I really wanted to do as a producer": von Lehmden, "Muddy Waters' Winter of Content," p. 28.

253 Muddy waltzed across the globe: He opened a string of dates for Bonnie Raitt

in the Pacific Northwest. "By the mid–nineteen seventies, Bonnie wanted opening acts of people whose music she really loved," said Dick Waterman, her longtime manager. "She wanted to come to the gig and sit and listen to Fred McDowell or Sippie Wallace. She was initially uncomfortable with having Muddy Waters open for her. She said, 'This should not be.' We won her over by explaining he was being paid all the money that he was asking, and we were giving him visibility and a bigger crowd. Instead of a club, he's playing for three thousand five hundred and getting better sound and lights. And Bonnie would say on her set, 'I can't tell you how honored I am to have this artist on this show with me.'" The arrangement worked and was repeated several times in different locales.

255 the manager got the rest: Even as Muddy leaned on Scott, he was concerned about the support's strength. On a trip to Mexico City, Muddy had asked Willie Dixon — also signed with Cameron — and Dixon's wife, Marie, to his room. "He said, 'I have some suspicions about Scott,'" Marie Dixon recalled. The discussion was vague. Later, Dixon developed his own suspicions, which led to severing his relationship with the Cameron Organization. "When my husband decided to fight Arc Music," said Marie Dixon, "his intention was to become owner of his songs. He looked at his contract with Scott, and it gave Scott one-third ownership of the songs for the life of the songs. I was standing in my living room when he told Scott Cameron, 'I wrote these songs for myself and my family and not for anyone else and their families.' He didn't mind paying a manager to manage his business, but when it came to giving a third of what was his, it infuriated him."

256 "I got a band and they're on vacation": von Lehmden, "Muddy Waters' Winter of Content," p. 28.

258 "They wanted me and my band": *Sweet Home Chicago,* produced by Nina Rosenstein, directed by Alan Raymond.

258 "Muddy Waters is one of the great performers": Obrecht, "Life and Times."

259 "Eric Clapton": In Minneapolis, on the Clapton tour, arrangements were made for Muddy's former guitarist, Pat Hare, to surprise his old boss with a visit. Hare had kept up his chops in prison. Accompanied by an armed guard, Hare enjoyed Muddy's set from the side of the stage. At the encore, "Got My Mojo Working," Margolin loaned Hare his axe and the pair reunited for a last time. Pat Hare died in St. Paul's Ramsey Hospital on September 26, 1980, a day after learning he was to receive a medical pardon. (Hahn, "Pat Hare.")

260 Muddy married Marva Jean Brooks: Muddy had a favorite produce store on the South Side, Seventy-first and State Streets. "He always thought they had the freshest greens and the nicest cuts of meat," Cameron said. "Then Willie Dixon turned us on to a place at the state line between Illinois and Indiana where a woman grew corn-fed beef and you'd buy a quarter or a half a cow, they'd cut it up the way you wanted and then freeze it, you'd take it home to your freezer."

Johnny stayed around Chicago until Clapton's tour with Muddy played Chicago on the twelfth. Muddy surprised the audience by bringing out Johnny Winter, and then Clapton surprised the audience by bringing out both. The stage was, briefly, a living family tree of blues, Muddy and two of his proteges, each having synthesized their diverse backgrounds — Texas and England — with Muddy's Delta licks and taken the music in different and popular directions.

When Muddy played the Chicagofest, John Belushi and Dan Aykroyd were in town shooting the *Blues Brothers* movie. They sought out Muddy to pay their respects. A few years later, when Mike Kappus visited Muddy in Westmont, they watched Aykroyd and Belushi in *Neighbors*.

261 "contract rider": In addition to money, some of the other stipulations of Muddy's contract were a deli tray for twelve people, beer, soft drinks, Perrier, ice, cups, and sugar-free soft drinks.

262 "The uncomfortable business situation": Author interview with Bob Margolin.

264 new band: Jesse Clay was the first drummer, briefly. Rogers's role was never intended to be more than temporary. "But Scott wanted it to be a permanent thing and he put it in the *Jet* that we were back together again," Rogers said, "and that was wrong. I was just doing Muddy a favor. Muddy meant a lot to me."

Guitarist John Primer had been tutored by Sammy Lawhorn. "Sammy helped me to set the tone on the amp," he explained, "and he was the one that got me into playing slide. Sammy was playing slide in standard tuning and I learned how to play like that from him. I got to the point where I could play in his place when he'd get drunk." (Peabody, "Primer.")

265 "It was hard to believe": Stephen Holden, *New York Times,* April 1, 1981. (Actually sixty-eight years old.)

265 When the Rolling Stones next returned to Chicago: "I was living down the street from [Muddy]," said Cookie, "and he called me to say he was cooking wine chicken. We all thought he could cook it really good, and he said one of the Rolling Stones [Keith Richards] was over and for me to come." Here's his wine chicken recipe, with thanks to the official Muddy Web page, www. muddywaters.com:

- 1 medium chicken, cut up and washed
- tsp salt
- tsp garlic salt
- tsp black pepper
- tsp seasoning (i.e., Accent)
- cup diced onions
- cup white wine

Preheat oven to 350 degrees. Place chicken in baking dish, skin side up. Add the remaining ingredients and bake for one hour, until golden brown. Baste occasionally. The wine should reduce down to a savory sauce.

15: THIS DIRT HAS MEANING *1983 and After*

Funeral, Friends, Tributes: "I hate that Muddy wasn't a storyteller no more than bits and pieces," Cookie said. "If you said to Muddy, 'Where's your mom?' He'd say, 'She died.' And that was it. Muddy never opened up. I know he loved his grandmother, he told me that several times. When I got older, I tried that psychology bit, saying to him one time, 'You must really didn't do well with the death of your mother and then your grandmother,' I said, 'and I know how you felt because my mother died when I was young.' And he's giving me that look like, 'Who the hell do you think *you* are?' And I said, 'You know I always regretted that you never had pictures, you never had anything to say this is who that is,' and he said, 'Well it was just something we couldn't afford, pictures, and it was just something we did.' And we left it like that because I could see it was touchy."

Before the funeral service on Wednesday evening, May 4, Muddy's family and close friends were gathered in the small room where Muddy was laid out. Margolin passed by an old gentleman who was seated in the corner. "He asked me, 'Did you even *know* Muddy?' I ignored his attitude and replied that I had played in his band. He trumped me. 'Well, I knew him in *Mississippi,*' but then he noticed George Thorogood standing nearby and he got very excited and asked, 'Isn't that Mick Jagger?'"

Seven of Muddy's children were mentioned in his funeral program: Joseph, Mercy, Renee, Roslind, Charles (Geneva's son), Deltwaine (Marva's son), and Larry. No one I spoke with, including Muddy's estate, could identify "Larry" (Laurence, Muddy's grandson, was mentioned elsewhere in the program) nor could anyone identify "Poppa." How many children did Muddy have? Here's one answer: he and Geneva raised three — Charles, Dennis, and Amelia. I count six blood children — Azelene, Bill, Mercy, Joseph, Renee, and Roslind.

"The worst thing to happen to my family was when my father died," Joseph said. "We didn't have that backbone no more to put some weight on. Before he died, I signed my basketball scholarship on April 13. Coming back after my first year of college, [Muddy's last wife] Marva decided to move back to Florida, and she's taking Roslind with her, and Renee got married to some guy, she was moving. I didn't see Mercy much. Those first five years, I kind of clung to Cookie, because it was a base. But I've seen everything change. Gangs was in my house and in my neighborhood. If my father wouldn't have moved me out of that house, I would have been a Blackstone Ranger for real. Definitely a Stone. I probably would be dead or in prison. So in a sense he saved my life actually." Being Muddy's heir has not been easy for him. "Some people try to become your friends, but they're not being honest. Even dating girls, I was proud to let everybody know who my father is. Now I don't tell no one, because it's for the wrong reasons. I learned that the hard way."

Junior Wells credited Muddy with his success. "Muddy showed me how to carry myself around people and to remember that didn't nobody owe me nothin' and knowin' not to get the big head or anything like that," Wells told *Living Blues.* (O'Neal and van Singel, "Muddy Waters," pp. 16–17.) "He told me it could take sometime years to get a thing to go for yourself and then sometime you could get it quicker than that and then lose the same thing overnight. He'd say, 'Always remember, whatever you do, do not disrespect the public.'" My own experience with Junior was a bit different. When I saw him on a small stage in the 1980s, he was touring with a sizable band and playing James Brown–styled funk. He was doing two shows that evening. At the first, he fired his trombone player on stage, hitting him in the jaw; then he called the sound man a "fat fuck." I didn't stick around to hear how the second set sounded.

"I have a guitar that Muddy gave me, an old Stella," Jimmy Rogers told me. "It was down in his basement and the neck was broken so I had it fixed. And after the funeral I looked at that guitar and the neck was broken where I had it fixed." When Jimmy died, he was working on an album for Atlantic Records, released after his death with the title *Blues Blues Blues*. On it, Rogers juggles the baton with some old friends — Clapton, members of the Rolling Stones and Led Zeppelin — and passes it to Jeff Healey and other relative newcomers. Perhaps most importantly, before he died, Rogers saw the blues pay off and he was able to enjoy his life. "When I'm goin' after a fish, I don't care how big he is, I'll keep at it. I go to different places around in Illinois, places where I usually have a chance to run out there for three or four hours. I fish for cats, crappies, bass, and stuff like that. . . . And Dorothy [his wife] hangs right there with me."

After Muddy's death, Bob Margolin gave back some of what he'd learned, befriending Muddy's son Big Bill Morganfield and coproducing Bill's first album. They often tour together. "It seems like interest in Muddy is very much alive these days," Margolin said. "Bill and I did lots of interviews and there were as many questions about Muddy as about us. It's a tribute to Muddy's power that people are still trying to get in touch with Muddy through us."

The tributes to Muddy keep on coming. The Blues Foundation, in addition to including Muddy in its inaugural Hall of Fame lineup, has honored many of his recordings. In the Hall of Fame Classics of Blues Recordings Singles, Muddy has five songs: "I'm Your Hoochie Coochie Man," "Got My Mojo Working," "I'm Ready," "Mannish Boy," and "Long Distance Call." In the Albums category, they have included *The Best of Muddy Waters*, *McKinley Morganfield AKA Muddy Waters*, and *Muddy Waters — The Chess Box*. In addition, they have honored several reissues of his recordings.

While Muddy would certainly have been honored by these various accolades, the lasting tribute that may have been nearest his heart is found in a book entitled *365 Ways to Improve Your Sex Life: From the Files of the Playboy Advisor* (James Petersen, ed.). They quote a correspondent, "W. G." from Kansas City, Missouri, who writes about a technique called the "Venus Butterfly."

> Take your penis, hard or soft, in hand and, starting at the south end of the vagina, gently rub the head into the groove of the vagina, lightly sliding it up towards the clitoris. Now reverse the process and slide slowly back down. Repeat. After a few gentle repetitions, the labia should begin to unfold, with the cleft moistening. If it wasn't hard when you began, the penis should now begin to harden. Now you have prepared yourself and your partner for the Venus Butterfly. Gently work the shaft lengthwise into the fold of the vagina. This is when you achieve the likeness of the butterfly, with the shaft of the penis as its head and abdomen and the labia as its wings. What's more, even the smallest penis will adequately stimulate the largest vagina and the smallest vagina will accommodate the largest of penises.

But the Venus Butterfly didn't originate with the mysterious W. G. "For years I have been practicing this technique with great success, tho it is the late great Muddy Waters who should be given credit for inventing it."

274 "I've never been a big shot": McKee and Chisenhall, *Beale,* p. 238.

275 "intensely worldly": Work, *American Negro Songs,* p. 28.

277 Maxwell Street: For information on preservation efforts, see www.openair. org/maxwell/preserve.html and www.maxwellstreet.org.

279 James Cotton's successful solo career: See his Web site, www.jamescotton superharp.com.

279 a successful harmonica instruction booklet: Portnoy's booklet is available through www.harpmaster.com.

280 "When MCA acquired Chess": Patrick Goldstein, "It's Now Money — Not Just Glory — for Bluesmen," *Los Angeles Times,* December 3, 1989.

284 "The blues were around": Fields, *Daily News* article, Library of Congress.

BIBLIOGRAPHY

ARCHIVES, MANUSCRIPTS, PRIVATE PAPERS

Adams, Samuel, Jr. Correspondence. Fisk Archives. Manuscript. Lomax Archives.

Adams, Samuel, Jr., and Ulysses Young. "Report on Preliminary Work in Clarksdale, Mississippi." Library of Congress. October 26, 1941.

Cohan, Lou. Interview with Muddy Waters for *Dark Star*. Estate of McKinley Morganfield.

Dirks, Scott. Union documents. Music Research Department of Chicago's Harold Washington Library.

Fields, Sidney. *Daily News* article. Library of Congress. December 26, 1972.

"Folk Culture Seminar." Course description. Fisk Archives, Special Collections.

Gelms, Robert Frank. WXRT interview with Muddy Waters. Collected by Scott Dirks. Spring 1980.

Jones, Lewis. "Folk Culture Study, Coahoma County, Mississippi." Fisk Library, Special Collections.

———. "The Mississippi Delta." Fisk Archives.

Lomax, Alan. Correspondence. Library of Congress.

———. Field notes and correspondence. Lomax Archives.

McKee, Margaret, and Fred Chisenhall. Interview with Muddy Waters. Memphis–Shelby County Public Library, History Department.

New York Radio interview with Muddy Waters and Otis Spann. Collected by Robert A. Messinger. May 21, 1966.

U.S. District Court. "McKinley Morganfield v. Arc Music Corporation." Exhibit A.

Welding, Pete, and John Jambazian. "Muddy's Harp Players 1952–1955." Library of Congress.

WKCR newsletter. Library of Congress.

Work, John. Correspondence. Library of Congress.

———. Field notes and correspondence. Fisk Archives.

MULTIMEDIA RESOURCES

Alan Lomax Collection. Rounder Records, 1997–present. Compact discs.

Can't You Hear the Wind Howl. Produced and directed by Peter Meyer. Winstar Video, 1998. Videocassette.

Chicago Blues. Produced and directed by Harley Corliss. Rhapsody Films, 1986. Videocassette.

Got My Mojo Working: Rare Performances 1968–1978. Yazoo Video, 2000. Videocassette.

Messin' with the Blues. Produced by Bill Wyman, directed by Jean Bovan. Rhino Video, 1984. Videocassette.

Muddy Waters in Concert 1971. Produced and directed by Link Wyler and Russ Ragsdale. Vestapol Video, 1998. Videocassette.

Sweet Home Chicago. Produced by Nina Rosenstein, directed by Alan Raymond and Susan Raymond. MCA Records, 1993. Laserdisc.

A Tribute to Muddy Waters: King of the Blues. Produced by Toby Byron, directed by Ken Mandel. BMG Video, 1998. Videocassette.

BOOKS

Agee, James, and Walker Evans. *Let Us Now Praise Famous Men.* 1941. Reprint, Houghton Mifflin, 1980.

Berry, Chuck. *The Autobiography.* New York: Harmony, 1987.

Bockris, Victor. *Keith Richards.* New York: Da Capo Press, 1998.

Byron, Toby, and Pete Welding, ed. *Bluesland Portraits of Twelve Major American Blues Masters.* New York: Dutton, 1991.

Calt, Stephen, with Gayle Dean Wardlow. *King of the Delta Blues: The Life and Music of Charlie Patton.* Rock Chapel Press, 1988.

Cantwell, Robert. *When We Were Good: The Folk Revival.* Cambridge: Harvard University Press, 1996.

Charters, Sam. *The Country Blues.* New York: Rinehart, 1959. Reprint, New York: Da Capo Press, 1975.

Cohn, David. *Where I Was Born and Raised.* Notre Dame: University of Notre Dame Press, 1967.

Cohodas, Nadine. *Spinning Blues into Gold: The Chess Brothers and the Legendary Chess Records.* New York: St. Martin's, 2000.

Collis, John. *The Story of Chess Records.* New York: Bloomsbury, 1998.

Corliss, Carlton. *Main Line of Mid-America: The Story of Illinois Central.* New York: Creative Age Press, 1950.

Daniel, Pete. *Lost Revolutions: The South in the 1950s.* Chapel Hill: University of North Carolina Press, 2000.

Dedmon, Emmett. *Fabulous Chicago: A Great City's History and People.* New York: Atheneum, 1981.

Demetre, Jacques, and Marcel Chauvard. *Land of the Blues.* Paris: CLARB, 1995.

Dixon, Willie, with Don Snowden. *I Am the Blues.* New York: Da Capo Press, 1989.

Drake, St. Clair, with Horace R. Cayton. *Black Metropolis: A Study of Negro Life in a Northern City.* 1945. Reprint, with a new preface, introduction, and chapter, New York: Harper Torchbooks, 1962.

Edwards, David "Honeyboy." *The World Don't Owe Me Nothing.* Chicago: Chicago Review Press, 1997.

Evans, Dr. David. *Big Road Blues: Tradition and Creativity in Folk Blues.* Chicago: University of Chicago Press, 1982.

Filene, Benjamin. *Romancing the Folk: Public Memory and American Roots Music.* Chapel Hill: University of North Carolina Press, 2000.

Gart, Galen, ed. *First Pressings: The History of Rhythm and Blues: 1952 Vol. 2.* Big Nickel Publications, 1991.

———. *First Pressings: The History of Rhythm and Blues: 1954 Vol. 4.* Big Nickel Publications, 1990.

———. *First Pressings: The History of Rhythm and Blues: 1955 Vol. 5.* Big Nickel Publications, 1990.

———. *First Pressings: The History of Rhythm and Blues: 1956 Vol. 6.* Big Nickel Publications, 1991.

———. *First Pressings: The History of Rhythm and Blues: 1957 Vol. 7.* Big Nickel Publications, N.d.

———. *First Pressings: The History of Rhythm and Blues: 1958 Vol. 8.* Big Nickel Publications, 1995.

Gelatt, Roland. *The Fabulous Phonograph: 1877–1977.* New York: Collier, 1977.

Gillett, Charlie. *The Sound of the City.* New York: Da Capo Press, 1996.

Guralnick, Peter. *Careless Love.* Boston: Little, Brown, 1999.

———. *Feel Like Going Home: Portraits in Blues and Rock'n'Roll.* Outerbridge and Dienstfrey, 1971. Reprint, Boston: Little, Brown, 1999.

———. *Last Train to Memphis.* Boston: Little, Brown, 1994.

———. *The Listener's Guide to the Blues.* New York: Facts on File, 1982.

———. *Lost Highway: Journeys and Arrivals of American Musicians.* Boston: D. R. Godine, 1979. Reprint, Boston: Little, Brown, 1999.

———. *Searching for Robert Johnson.* New York: Dutton, 1989.

———. *Sweet Soul Music.* Harper and Rowe, 1986. Reprint, Boston: Little, Brown, 1999.

Guy, Buddy, and Donald Wilcock. *Damn Right I've Got the Blues.* San Francisco: Woodford Press, 1993.

Hajdu, David. *Lush Life: A Biography of Billy Strayhorn.* New York: Farrar Strauss Giroux, 1996.

Handy, W. C. *Father of the Blues: An Autobiography.* New York: Macmillan, 1941. Reprint, New York: Da Capo Press, 1991.

Hardy, Phil, and Dave Laing. *The Da Capo Companion to Twentieth-Century Popular Music.* New York: Da Capo Press, 1995.

Helm, Levon, with Stephen Davis. *This Wheel's on Fire.* New York: William Morrow & Co., 1993.

Heylin, Clinton. *Bob Dylan: Behind the Shades.* New York: Summit, 1991.

Jackson, George Pullen. *White and Negro Spirituals.* N.p., 1943.

Jones, Gayl. *Corregidora.* New York: Random House, 1975.

King, B. B., with David Ritz. *Blues All Around Me.* New York: Avon, 1996.

Kurin, Richard. *Smithsonian Folklife Festival, Culture of, by, and for the People.* Washington, D.C.: Smithsonian Institution, 1998.

Leadbitter, Mike, ed. *Nothing but the Blues.* London: Hanover Books, 1971.

Lemann, Nicholas. *The Promised Land: The Great Black Migration and How It Changed America.* New York: Random House, 1991.

Liebling, A. J. *Chicago: The Second City.* Knopf, 1952. Reprint, Westport, CT: Greenwood Press, 1974.

Lipscomb, Mance, and Glen Alyn. *I Say Me for a Parable.* New York: W. W. Norton, 1993.

Lomax, Alan. *The Land Where the Blues Began.* New York: Pantheon, 1993.

Lomax, John Avery. *Cowboy Songs and Other Frontier Ballads.* New York: MacMillan, 1938.

Lydon, Michael. *Rock Folk.* New York: Dial Press, 1971.

McKee, Margaret, and Fred Chisenhall, *Beale Black and Blue: Life and Music on Black America's Main Street.* Baton Rouge: Louisiana State University Press, 1981.

Muddy Waters: Deep Blues. Milwaukee: Hal Leonard Corporation, 1995.

Murray, Charles Shaar. *Boogie Man.* New York: St. Martin's, 2000.

———. *Crosstown Traffic: Jimi Hendrix and the Post-War Rock'n'Roll Revolution.* New York: St. Martin's, 1989.

———. *Shots from the Hip.* London: Penguin, 1991.

O'Neal, Jim. *The Voice of the Blues: Classic Interviews from* Living Blues *Magazine.* Routledge Press, 2002.

Obrecht, Jas, ed. *Rollin' and Tumblin': The Postwar Blues Guitarists.* San Francisco: Miller Freeman, 2000.

Oliver, Paul. *Conversation with the Blues.* New York: Horizon Press, 1965. Reprint, Port Chester, NY: Cambridge University Press, 1997.

Palmer, Robert. *Deep Blues.* New York: Penguin, 1981.

Petersen, James R., ed. *365 Ways to Improve Your Sex Life: From the Files of the Playboy Advisor.* New York: Plume, 1996.

Porterfield, Nolan. *Last Cavalier: The Life and Times of John A. Lomax.* Urbana–Champaign: University of Illinois Press, 1996.

Pruter, Robert. *Chicago Soul.* Urbana–Champaign: University of Illinois Press, 1992.

———. *Doowop: The Chicago Scene.* Urbana–Champaign: University of Illinois Press, 1996.

Romanowski, Patricia, and Holly George-Warren. *The New Rolling Stone Encyclopedia of Rock and Roll.* New York: Fireside, 1995.

Rooney, James. *Bossmen: Bill Monroe and Muddy Waters.* New York: Dial, 1971. Reprint, New York: Da Capo Press, 1986.

Rowe, Bill. *The Half Ain't Been Told.* Amsterdam: Micography, 2000.

Rowe, Mike. *Chicago Blues: The City and the Music.* New York: Da Capo Press, 1975.

Sacre, Robert, ed. *The Voice of the Delta: Charley Patton and the Mississippi Blues Traditions.* University of Liege Press, 1987.

Scott, Frank. *The Down-Home Guide to the Blues.* Chicago: A Cappella, 1991.

Spear, Allan H. *Black Chicago: The Making of a Negro Ghetto, 1890–1920.* Chicago: University of Chicago Press, 1967.

Talley, Thomas Washington. *Negro Folk Rhymes, Wise and Otherwise.* 1922. Reprint, Folcroft: Folcroft Library Editions, 1980.

Tooze, Sandra B. *Muddy Waters: The Mojo Man.* Toronto: ECW Press, 1997.

Tosches, Nick. *The Devil and Sonny Liston.* Boston: Little, Brown, 2000.

Townsend, Henry, and Bill Greensmith. *A Blues Life.* Urbana–Champaign: Chicago: University of Illinois Press, 1999.

Turpin, Edna. *Cotton.* New York: American Book Company, N.d.

Von Schmidt, Eric, and Jim Rooney. *Baby, Let Me Follow You Down: The Illustrated Story of the Cambridge Folk Years.* University of Massachusetts Press, 1994.

Ward, Ed. *Michael Bloomfield: The Rise and Fall of an American Guitar Hero.* New York: Cherry Lane Books, 1983.

Wardlow, Gayle Dean. *Chasin' That Devil Music: Searching for the Blues.* San Francisco: Miller Freeman, 1998.

Welding, Pete. "Muddy Waters: Gone to Main Street." In *Bluesland.* New York: Dutton, 1991.

Welty, Eudora. *Delta Wedding.* New York: Harcourt, Brace, Jovanovich, 1945.

Werner, Craig. *A Change Is Gonna Come: Music, Race, and the Soul of America.* New York: Plume, 1999.

Whitburn, Joel. *Joel Whitburn's Top R&B Singles, 1942–1995.* Menomonee Falls, WI: Record Research, Inc., 1996.

Wilmer, Val. *Mama Said There'd Be Days Like These.* London: Women's Press, 1991.

Work, John, Jr. *Folk Song of the American Negro.* 1915. Reprint, New York: Negro Universities Press, 1969.

Work, John, III. *American Negro Songs and Spirituals.* New York: Bonanza Books/ Crown Publishers, 1940.

Young, Al. *Woke Me Up This Morning.* Jackson: University Press of Mississippi, 1997.

PERIODICALS

Ahlstrand, Clas, Peter Mahlin, and Jan-ake Pettersson. "Muddy Talkin' To." *Jefferson* 14 (1971): 14–21.

Albright, Alex. "The African American Traveling Minstrel Show." *Living Blues* 108 (March/April 1993): 36–41.

Aldin, Mary Katherine. Liner notes to *The Aristocrat of the Blues: The Best of Aristocrat Records.* MCA (1997).

———. Liner notes to *Jimmy Rogers: The Complete Chess Recordings.* MCA (1997).

———. Liner notes to *Muddy Waters: The Complete Plantation Recordings.* MCA (1993).

Balfour, Alan. "Land of the Blues." *Blues and Rhythm* 97 (March 1995).

Barretta, Scott. "The Monarch of Delmark." *Blues Access* (summer 1997): 22–29.

Baysting, Arthur. "Bluesman Muddy Waters." *Thursday Magazine* (New Zealand) (May 24, 1973): 27–29.

Bims, Hamilton. "Blues City." *Ebony* 27 n5 (March 1972): 76–86.

"Blewett Thomas Interview." *Blues Access* 33 (N.d.).

Bloomfield, Mike. "An Interview with Muddy Waters." *Rhythm and Blues* 28 (July 1964): 7.

Blues News. *Living Blues* (winter 1970–1971): 26.

———. *Living Blues* 17 (summer 1974).

———. *Living Blues* 45/46 (spring 1980): 7.

Bozza, Anthony. "John Lee Hooker: Don't Look Back." *Rolling Stone* (June 12, 1997): 40.

Brack, Ray. "No Credibility Gap." *Billboard: World of Soul* (June 24, 1967): 62.

Brack, Ray and Earl Paige. "Chess and the Blues: From the Streets to the Studio." *Billboard: World of Soul* (June 24, 1967): 20–22.

Brisbin, John. "I'm Havin' Fun Right Today." *Living Blues* 135 (September / October 1997): 12–27.

———. "Peter Malick on Otis Spann." *Living Blues* 154 (November / December 2000).

———. "Pinetop's Boogie." *Living Blues* 97 (May / June 1991): 11–16.

———. "Sunnyland Slim." *Living Blues* (May / June 1995): 51–62.

Broven, John. "Paul Gayten: I Knew Leonard at the Macomba." N.p., n.d.

Bruynoghe, Yannick. "In Chicago with Big Bill and Friends." *Living Blues* 55 (winter 1982–1983): 7–24.

"Car Crash Puts Muddy in Hospital." *Rolling Stone* 47 (November 29, 1969): 18.

Corritore, Bob, Bill Ferris, and Jim O'Neal. "Willie Dixon" part 1. *Living Blues* 81 (July / August 1988): 20–25.

———. "Willie Dixon" part 2. *Living Blues* 82 (September / October 1988): 20–31.

Cowley, John. "Really the Walkin' Blues." *Popular Music* 1 (N.d.). Reprint, *Juke Blues* 1 (N.d.).

Crimmins, Jerry. "Lounge Rocks in Tribute to a Blues Great." N.p., n.d.

Cushing, Steve. "Behind the Beat of Blues." *Living Blues* 96 (March / April 1991): 12–23.

Darwen, Norman. "Mojo Buford on Pat Hare." *Juke Blues* 24 (winter 1991): 11.

DeCurtis, Anthony. "Living Legends." *Rolling Stone* (September 21, 1989): 89, 99, 128.

DelGrosso, Maureen. "Otis Spann: From the Delta to Chicago." *Blues Revue* 20 (December / January 1996): 44–46.

DeMichael, Don. "Father and Son: An Interview with Muddy Waters and Paul Butterfield." *Down Beat* 36 n16 (August 7, 1969): 12–13, 32. Reprint, *Down Beat* 56 n9 (September 1989): 58–76.

———. "Muddy Waters Week in Chicago." *Rolling Stone* 34 (May 1969): 12–13.

Dixon, Willie. "I Am the Blues." *Living Blues* (N.d.): 9–10.

"Down Home and Dirty." *Time* 98 (August 9, 1971): 46.

Eagle, Bob. "Big Town Playboy: Johnnie Jones." *Living Blues* 12 (spring 1973): 28–29.

Evans, David. "An Interview with H. C. Speir." *John Edwards Memorial Foundation Quarterly* 8 (1972).

Fancourt, Les. Liner notes to *The Complete Muddy Waters 1947–1967*. Charly Records (1992).

Gershuny, Diane. "Francis Clay: Got the Mojo Working." *Living Blues* 96 (March / April 1991): 47–51.

Gibbs, Vernon. "The Entertainers: Muddy Waters." *Essence* 3 n8 (December 1972): 23, 85.

Gilbert, Jerry. "Muddy Waters: Staying with the Blues." *Sounds* (December 18, 1971).

Golkin, Pete. "Blacks, Whites, and Blues: The Story of Chess Records" part 1. *Living Blues* 88 (September / October 1989): 22–32.

————. "Blacks, Whites, and Blues: The Story of Chess Records" part 2. *Living Blues* 89 (November / December 1989): 25–29.

Gordon, Robert. "Dave Myers." *Oxford American* 21 (1997): 84–86.

Guralnick, Peter. "Muddy Waters: Father of the Chicago Blues." *Grammy Awards Program* (1992): 22.

Hahn, Kevin. "Pat Hare: A Blues Guitarist." *Juke Blues* 23 (summer 1991): 8–15.

Harris, Sheldon. Liner notes to Otis Spann's *Bottom of the Blues.* BluesWay (1968).

Harvey, Hank. "Growing Up with the Blues." *Toledo Sunday Blade* (April 7, 1986). Reprint, *Living Blues* 71 (1986): 25.

Hay, Fred J. "Joe Willie Wilkins." *Living Blues* 42 (N.d.): 8.

Haydon, Tom. "The Case of the Pervasive Percussionist." *Living Blues* 14 (fall 1973): 21–22.

Hentoff, Nat. Liner notes to *Otis Spann Is the Blues.* Jazz Man Records (1980).

Hoffman, Steven J. "A Platinum Mine of Blues." *Living Blues* 30 (November / December 1976): 25–26.

"An Interview with Muddy Waters." *Newsweek* (May 26, 1969). Reprint, *Newsweek* (1971).

Jones, Max. *Melody Maker* (December 10, 1970): 29.

————. "Muddy Waters, Superstar." N.p., n.d.

Juke Blues (summer 1997): 29.

Knopper, Steve. "What's Next for Chicago's Historic Maxwell Street?" *Blues Access* (summer 1997): 102.

Koester, Bob. "Lester Melrose: An Appreciation." *Living Blues* 2 (1971): 58.

Kunstadt, Len. "Birmingham Jones, an Introduction." *Record Research* 90 (May 1968): 8.

————. Liner notes to *The Bluesmen of the Muddy Waters Band Vol. 1.* Spivey LP 1008 (1967).

————. *Record Research* (April 1967).

Lazar, Helen Doob. "James Cotton." *Living Blues* 76 (fall 1976): 22–33.

Leadbitter, Mike. "Chess 1954." *Living Blues* 8 (spring 1972): 24–27.

————. Liner notes to *McKinley Morganfield AKA Muddy Waters.* Chess Records (1971).

————. "Muddy — It's Too Late to Change." *Sounds* (October 9, 1971).

————. "Turning Point for Chess." *Jazz and Blues* 1 n3 (June / July 1971).

Lerner, Guy "Doc." "Muddy Harps." *Living Blues* 99 (September / October 1991): 32–37.

Lindemann, Bill. "Little Walter and Louis Myers." *Living Blues* 7 (winter 1971–1972): 17–25.

Litke, Jim. "TV Tribute: Blues for Muddy Waters." *Rolling Stone* 174 (November 31, 1974): 15.

"Little Walter: Don't Break That Goddamn Drive . . . Don't Slow Down for Shit." *Juke Blues* 5 (summer 1986): 18.

"Luther Tucker." *Juke Blues* 29 (summer 1993): 27.

Malenky, Bob. "A Guitar Lesson from Muddy Waters." *Juke Blues* 30 (spring 1984): 31.

Margolin, Bob. "Can't Be Satisfied." *Blues Revue* 20 (December / January 1996).

————. "Muddy Waters and the Rock Stars." *Blues Revue* 11 (winter 1993–1994).

————. "Paul Oscher and Brian Bisesi." *Blues Revue* 29 (June/July 1997): 66–67.

Marsh, Dave. "Muddy Waters: Let's Say He Was a Gentleman." *Record* (July 1983).

Mazzolini, Tom. "A Conversation with Paul Oliver." *Living Blues* 54 (winter 1982–1983): 24–30.

McCulley, Jerry. "Father and Sons." *BAM* (April 9, 1993): 47–50.

Melish, Ilene. "The Man Who Shaped a Sound." *Melody Maker* (October 6, 1979): 37–38.

Melrose, Lester. "My Life in Recording." *Living Blues* 2 (1970): 59–61.

Moon, D. Thomas. "The Elga Edmonds Story." *Living Blues* 11 (November/December 1997): 36–41.

————. "John Primer: Movin' On with the Blues." *Blues Revue* 24 (August/September 1996): 38–40.

Most-Played Juke Box Race Records. *Billboard* (September 18, 1948): 29.

"Muddy: The Man Who Urbanised the Blues." N.p., n.d.

"Muddy's Back on His Feet Again." *Rolling Stone* 57 (April 30, 1970): 12.

Nemerov, Bruce. "About the Cover Photo." *78 Quarterly* 9 (N.d.): 20.

————. "John Wesley Work III: Field Recordings of Southern Black Folk Music, 1935–1942." *Tennessee Folklore Society Bulletin* LIII n3 (1989): 82–103.

Nerenberg, Michael. Liner notes to *Goin' Way Back*. Justin Time Records (1997).

Nicholls, Dick. "Strangers from a Strange Land: Muddy Waters in New Zealand." *New Zealand Rolling Stone* (June 7, 1973): 34–37.

O'Neal, Amy. "Bill Hill." *Living Blues* 57 (N.d.): 13–14.

O'Neal, Jim. "Blue Smitty" part 1. *Living Blues* 44 (fall 1979): 9–11.

————. "Blue Smitty" part 2. *Living Blues* 45 (winter 1980–1981): 54–57.

————. "Houston Stackhouse." *Living Blues* 17 (N.d.): 20–36.

————. "Joe Willie Wilkins — 1923–1979." *Living Blues* 42 (N.d.): 8–9.

————. "Junior Wells." *Living Blues* 119 (January/February 1995): 9–29.

————. "Muddy's First Chicago Record." *Living Blues* 52 (spring 1982): 4.

————. "Pepper's Lounge." *Living Blues* 5 (summer 1971): 30–35.

————. "Willie Nix." *Living Blues* 43 (summer 1979): 9–13.

————. "Willie Nix." *Living Blues* 101 (January/February 1992): 35–36.

O'Neal, Jim, and Amy van Singel. "Muddy Waters." *Living Blues* 64 (March/April 1985): 15–40.

O'Neal, Jim, and Bill Greensmith. "Jimmy Rogers." *Living Blues* 14 (1973): 11–20.

O'Neal, Jim, David Whiteis, and Bruce Iglauer. "Big Walter Horton 1918–1981." *Living Blues* 52 (spring 1982): 52–53.

O'Neal, Jim, and Tim Zorn. "Buddy Guy." *Living Blues* 2 (1970): 3–8.

O'Neal, Jim, and Wesley Race. "Chicago Blues Club Guide." *Living Blues* (winter 1972–1973): 8–10.

Obrecht, Jas. "The Life and Times of the Hoochie Coochie Man." *Guitar Player* 28 n3 (March 1994): 30–48, 72.

————. "Muddy Waters: Bluesman, 1915–1983." *Guitar Player* (August 1983): 48–57, 67–70.

Obrecht, Jas, and Keith Richards. "Muddy, Wolf, and Me." *Guitar Player* (September 1993): 87–93.

Oliver, Paul. "Remembering Sonny Boy." *American Folk Music Occasional* 2 (1970): 39–44.

Palmer, Robert. "Muddy Waters: 1915–1983." *Rolling Stone* 398 (June 23, 1983): 37–42.

———. "Muddy Waters: The Delta Sun Never Sets." *Rolling Stone* 275 (October 5, 1978): 53–57.

Peabody, Charles. "Notes on Negro Music." *Journal of American Folklore* 16 n62 (1903).

Peabody, Dave. "Primer Life." *Folk Roots* (N.d.): 29, 31, 37.

Piazza, Tom. "Sacred and Profane in Clarksdale: Rev. Willie Morganfield." *Oxford American* 21 (1997): 64–68.

Random Notes. *Rolling Stone* 63 (July 23, 1970): 4.

———. *Rolling Stone* 213 (May 20, 1976): 28, 30.

"Rebirth of the Blues." *Newsweek* (May 26, 1969).

Russell, Tony. "Clarksdale Piccolo Blues." *Jazz and Blues* (November 1971): 30.

Sacre, Robert. "Jazz Life: Dortmund, Germany." *Living Blues* 31 (March / April 1977): 27.

Scala, Rita. "Muddy Waters in Italy." *Living Blues* 31 (March / April 1977): 29–30.

Shaw, Norm. "Charlie Musselwhite." *BlueSpeak* (May 1997): 10–11, 13.

Shurman, Dick. "Howling Wolf Review." *Living Blues* 24 (November / December 1975): 6.

Skelly, Richard. "Muddy Waters: Whom Didn't He Influence?" *Goldmine* (April 6, 2001): 14–18.

Springer, Robert. "They Wanted to Make a Muddy Waters Player Out of Me." *Blues Unlimited* 143 (1982): 25–29.

Standish, Tony. "Muddy Waters in London" part 1. *Jazz Journal* 12 n1 (January 1959): 2–4.

———. "Muddy Waters in London" part 2. *Jazz Journal* 12 n2 (February 1959): 3–6.

Sumlin, Hubert. "My Years with Wolf." *Living Blues* 88 (September / October 1989): 15.

Thompson, Art, and Dan Forte. "Smokestack Lightnin'." *Guitar Player* (August 1992): 101–103.

Tidwell, Emily. "Going Back to Where I Had Been: Calvin Jones and Willie Smith." *Living Blues* 99 (September / October 1991): 18–21.

Townsley, Tom. "Little Walter: The Muddy Waters Years." *Blues Revue* (N.d.): 41–43.

———. "Paul Oscher: Long Overdue." *Blues Connection* 3 n7 (May 1996): 4–9, 13.

Trow, George W. S., Jr. "Ahmet Ertegun." *The New Yorker* 54 (June 5, 1978): 45–81.

Trynka, Paul. "Howlin' Wolf: Deep Blue." *Mojo* 27 (February 1996): 40–50.

———. *Mojo* (April 1998): 77.

Turner, Twist. "Sammy Lawhorn: A Half-Pint and a Pistol." *Blues Access* (winter 1999): 101.

Underwood, Tut. "Bob Margolin: Remembering Muddy Waters." *Living Blues* 99 (September / October 1991): 22–23.

van Singel, Amy. "Theresa's." *Living Blues* 17 (N.d.): 9–12.

van Singel, Amy, Jim O'Neal, and Dave Loebel. "Howlin' Wolf." *Living Blues* 1 (spring 1970): 13–17.

Voce, Frank. "Jimmy Rogers: We Started Hanging Around Together." *Blues Un-limited* 5 (N.d.): 5–7.

———. Article. N.p., n.d.

von Lehmden, Mark. "Muddy Waters' Winter of Content." *Rolling Stone* 239 (May 19, 1977): 27–28.

Walters, David, Laurence Garman, and John Matthews. "Jimmy Rogers." N.p., n.d., 17–18.

Wardlow, Gayle Dean. "Henry Sims." *78 Quarterly* 9 (N.d.): 11–19.

Welding, Pete. "Afro Mud: A Personalized History of the Blues." *Down Beat* 42 (February 27, 1975): 17–18, 34, 36.

———. "Howling Wolf." *Down Beat* (December 14, 1967): 20–23.

———. Interview with Johnny Shines. *Living Blues* 22 (July / August 1975): 24.

———. "An Interview with Muddy Waters." *American Folk Music Occasional* 2 (1970): 2–7.

———. "Last King of the South Side?" *Down Beat* 31 n27 (October 8, 1964): 18–19, 42. Reprint, *Down Beat* 61 n2 (February 1994): 32–35.

———. Liner notes to *Chicago Blues: The Beginning*. USA: Testament T-2207 (N.d.).

———. "Muddy Waters." *Rolling Stone* (November 9, 1968): 10–11, 22.

———. "Muddy Waters: An American Original." *Guitar World* (March 1982): 81–82.

———. "Muddy Waters — Folk Singer." *Down Beat* (May 9, 1964).

———. "Muddy Waters, the Troubador, Los Angeles." *Down Beat* 34 (1967): 24–25.

———. "The Real Folk Blues." *Down Beat* (October 22, 1964).

Wenner, Jann. "A Letter from the Editor." *Rolling Stone* 1 (November 9, 1967): 2.

Wheeler, Tom. "Waters–Winter Interview." *Guitar Player* 17 n8 (August 1983): 58–62.

Whiteis, David. "Sammy Lawhorn." *Living Blues* 95 (January / February 1991): 47–49.

Wilmer, Val. *Jazz Beat* (October 1964): 14–15.

———. "The First Time I Met the Blues." *Mojo* (N.d.): 84–94.

Wisner, Steve. "Mojo Buford." *Living Blues* 42 (January / February 1979): 22–27.

———. "Sunnyland Charles and the Globetrotters." *Living Blues* 38 (May / June 1978): 27–30.

Wolfe, Charles. "Where the Blues Is At." *Popular Music and Society* 1 (1971–1972).

"Year of Jubilee." *Time* (May 12, 1941): 92.

NEWSPAPERS

Boston Herald Traveler, March 19, 1971.

Boston Phoenix, March 23, 1971; May 10, 1983.

Chicago Daily News, June 1967.

Chicago Defender, March 26, 1955.

Clarion-Ledger, May 4, 1983.

Des Moines Tribune, September 23, 1981.

Illinois Entertainer, May 1981.

Los Angeles Times, May 1983; December 3, 1989.

Memphis Commercial Appeal, September 21, 1981; June 9, 1997.

New York Times, December 21, 1972; April 1, 1981; May 1, 1983; April 23, 1988.

Philadelphia Inquirer, May 5, 1983.

San Francisco Examiner, May 2, 1972.

Tri-State Defender, 1961.

Village Voice, December 8, 1966.

Washington Post, September 24, 1971.

ACKNOWLEDGMENTS

A band mate of Muddy's, in an early interview for this book, shared this advice from Muddy: "If you don't want someone to know what you're thinking, keep it in your pocket." Muddy was dead nearly fifteen years when I began this book, and I am indebted to those who, in his lifetime, rattled Muddy's pocket. I thank those writers who published their information, Muddy's friends and family for opening themselves to me in interviews, and Muddy's band mates, who allowed me to repeatedly interrupt their lives, were frank and forthcoming, and shared their photographs and memorabilia with me.

Researching this book was a race against time. Nearly all the intimate friends from Muddy's early days in Mississippi and Chicago had passed away before I began my quest. Jimmy Rogers was still alive and, through the good reputation of Dick Shurman, Jimmy welcomed me into his South Side home. As daylight slipped away for evening, I drifted with Jimmy's casual and detailed recollection. The shock of his death six months later, followed shortly by the passing of Junior Wells, fueled my desire to find Muddy's family and friends.

Much of the research that supports this book comes from *Living Blues* magazine, which, since 1970, has run long and unexpurgated interviews with members of the blues community. I'd like to acknowledge the magazine's foresight and contribution by listing the founding editors, as noted in their first issue: Jim O'Neal, Amy van Singel, Diane Allmen, Paul Garon, Bruce Iglauer, Andre Souffront, and Tim Zorn.

Even before I began this book, I enjoyed the warmth of Peter Guralnick's friendship. He has given me advice and good counsel, helping me through not just this book but also the writer's wending path. Mentor, yes, but more importantly, friend.

From the time I began this book, I received encouragement from Dick Shurman, Jim O'Neal, and Mary Katherine Aldin. Their support was unflagging and essential to whatever I may have accomplished. Additionally, Dick Shurman helped me navigate Chicago, and his introductions around town always yielded a warm welcome and a new friend.

Over the course of this book, I benefitted from the research and efforts of several assistants and friends: Lisa Roy, Brad Cawn, Torrie Arnold (who saw a bear), Abe Gaustad, Vanessa Roberson, Melissa Dunn, Scott Bomar, and Andria Lisle.

Many times, writers working on related topics get competitive, creating an atmosphere where everyone suffers, especially the reader. I encountered generous collaborators, however, among them Nadine Cohodas, author of *Spinning Blues into Gold: The Chess Brothers and the Legendary Chess Records,* and Tony Glover, Scott Dirks, and Ward Gaines, authors of the forthcoming *Blues with a Feeling: The Little Walter Story.* We all benefitted from sharing information.

My sense of Muddy's story was sharpened by my collaboration with filmmaker Morgan Neville. Check out our Muddy Waters documentary, *Muddy Waters Can't Be Satisfied,* available on home video through Wellspring (www.wellspringvideo.com).

My manuscript had traveled many miles by the time it found its way to Geoff Shandler, my editor. Geoff intuitively grasped the essential story and deftly foregrounded it. He made my writing better. I only got to him because of Michael Pietsch, who enlisted me in this expedition and then let me proceed at my own pace. Liz Nagle alerted me to the twists and turns of Little, Brown's process, guiding me with grace even when I resisted. Karen Landry, copyeditor, sharpened my work and remained good-natured through a difficult process. Thanks to all at Little, Brown. Hosannas to my agent, Dick McDonough, for taking care of business.

This book was improved by the suggestions of its readers through its various incarnations: Joy Allen, Robert Duffy, Jim and Mary Lindsay Dickinson, Alex Greene, Chip Rossetti, Adam Miller, Ross Johnson, Jeff Talman, Zachary Lazar, Elaine Gordon, Dick Shurman, Peter Wolf, and my wife, Tara McAdams.

The loan of tapes and transcripts sharpened and intensified my vision of Muddy's world. Several people shared their personal interview tapes with me: Peter Guralnick, John Brisbin, Paul Trynka, Jas Obrecht, Robert A. Messinger and Andy Allu, Larry Lasker, and Howard Stovall.

In Memphis and Mississippi, I'd like to thank Robert Morganfield, drummer / librarian Ross "Baron of Love" Johnson, Lauren Johnson, Lula O'Neal, Bruce and Sylvia Feldbaum, Meredith Carter, Rick Ireland and Mary Heffernan, Knox Phillips, Shelly Ritter, Scott Barretta, Tom Freeland and the T-list, Panny Mayfield, Monsieur Jeffrey Evans, Ed Porter, the Waltons and the staff of Computerlab, and Harry's Kwik Check on Madison. At Stovall: Howard and Gil Stovall, Nancy Stovall, Norma Weiland, Pete Hunter, Linda Donnelly, Manuel Jackson Jr., Magnolia Hunter, and Mary Emerson. At the Memphis / Shelby County Public Library: Libby Carroll, Nathan Tipton and everyone else at the Arts Department, and Jimmy Johnson, Patricia LaPointe, and the History Department staff.

In Chicago: Angela Rogers, Bobby Stovall, Dave Waldman, Steve Cushing (Does your public radio carry his "Blues Before Sunrise" show?), Tom Heimdal, Heather West, Jimmie Lee Robinson, Michael Frank, D. Thomas Moon, David Whiteis, Sho, Billy Flynn, Buddy Guy's Legends Club, and the hospitality and friendship of Belinda and Tim Gordon, and Ian and Nadine Schneller.

In London: Val Wilmer, Paul Trynka, Cilla and Mick Huggins at *Juke Blues,* Sylvia Pitcher, Chris Barber, Mike Evans and the Chelsea Arts Club, Tim Tooher, Tasha Lee, Mike and Ski and Bob in Ray's Blues Basement, Jim Irvin, Mat Snow, Keith Briggs and Tony Burke at *Blues and Rhythm,* Joe Boyd, Bruce Bastin, Paul Oliver, Paul Jones, Charles Shaar Murray, Neil Slaven, Tony Russell, Harold and Barbara Pendleton, and the ever-resourceful Alan Balfour.

Guitar consultation: Doug Easley, Stefan Grossman, Trey Harrison, and Jas

Obrecht. The discographers: Phil Wight, Fred Rothwell, Les Fancourt, Chris Smith, Howard Rye, and Bill Rowe.

Continued inspiration: James Luther Dickinson.

In memoriam: Townes Van Zandt, Jeff Buckley, Randall Lyon.

I could not have created this book without the following people and organizations, to whom I express great thanks: The Corporation of Yaddo; Judith Gray, Joe Hickerson, and Sam Brylauski at the Library of Congress; Jeff Place at the Smithsonian Institution; Beth Howse at the Fisk Archives; Matt Barton and Anna Lomax Chairetakis at the Lomax Archives; Bruce Nemerov and Mayo Taylor at the Center for the Study of Popular Music, Middle Tennessee State University; Jeff Rosen; Jane Rose; Steve Berkowitz; John Work IV; Sebastian Danchin; Guido van Rijn; John Bredar and family; Bob Margolin; Scott Cameron and Nancy Meyer at the estate of McKinley Morganfield; Levon Helm; Butch Dener; Andy McKaie at Chess / MCA / Universal; Ryan Null at Universal; Joy Graeme; Kip Lornell; Nolan Porterfield; Axel Kustner; Davia Nelson; Mike Kappus; Willie Strandberg; and Chris Bourke at the New Zealand desk.

This project took a long time. My wife, Tara McAdams, came through the mud with me, writing with me, advising me, caring for me, covering for me. Thank you, with love.

INDEX